CONTEMPORARY ITALY

CONTEMPORARY ITALY

*ITS INTELLECTUAL AND
MORAL ORIGINS*

By

COUNT CARLO SFORZA

Translated by
DRAKE AND DENISE DE KAY

1944
New York
E. P. DUTTON & CO., INC.

DG
555
S44

5/2/44 · 00000 - 2.52

24805

BOOKS ARE WEAPONS IN THE WAR OF IDEAS

A WARTIME BOOK

AMERICAN BOOK—STRATFORD PRESS, INC., NEW YORK

FOREWORD

A Foreword is almost always an Afterword: one bends over and surveys the book one has written—one explains it, one excuses it.

To explain it I have only to tell you how it was born: of a long series of lectures and discussions at the University of California in 1942–43 on contemporary Italy and its origins. However, lectures not being convertible into a book, this one was written only after I had forgotten, if not my courses, at least the form I had given them. Nevertheless it was through a long personal experience that I glimpsed which were the bonds between the past and the present that had to be clarified further for the better comprehension of the Italy of the twentieth century: the Reformation was as necessary as the Counter-Reformation; the smiling Settecento as the French Revolution and its Italian forerunners. And then, and above all, the men: if it be true, as I believe, that the Italians are the most individualistic of peoples, and if Alfieri, a man of great judgment, could write: "Nowhere does the plant, man, thrive as vigorously as in Italy," one cannot bring Italy to life with ideas alone. One must show, just as they were, the men who most powerfully influenced Italian thought—from Machiavelli, who, first on the threshold of the modern world, dared put away like an old suit the phantom of the Roman Empire to substitute for it just Italy; down to Mazzini and Cavour, the two supreme artisans of the Risorgimento *; down to D'Annunzio, who alone can explain the birth of Fascism, since he was its inventor, Mussolini being no more than its skillful plagiarist.

I foresee the critics: "Why Machiavelli and no other political historian? Why Manzoni and not Leopardi? Why not a single one of the statesmen between Cavour and Giolitti? . . ."

Because I have wanted to write my ideas, my impressions, and not an encyclopedia. Nothing is vainer or more unnatural

---

* *Risorgimento.* Literally *resurrection.* The accepted word used for the gradual awakening of and the recovery of nationhood by Italy during the revolutionary epoch of 1847–71, often including the preceding Napoleonic and post-Napoleonic periods.

than to write a book with other books. Such as it is, even with its omissions, especially with its omissions, it is a testimony. I say especially with its omissions, because it is the gaps and disproportions that constitute a book's autobiographical element. It is not difficult to learn to write a well-constructed and well-balanced book; but that belongs to literary cookery. It is precisely what I have not wanted to do. Machiavelli declared that he wrote only about what he had *"imparato per une lunga pratica e continua lezione delle cose del mondo"* (learned by long practice and a continual lesson in the things of the world). With him it was a point of pride; let us say that for me it is only modesty.

Even admitting that modesty and pride are at times in the human heart but two faces of an identical complex, it was surely only modesty that impelled me in the chapters on Fascism often to use the first person. I was more often the actor than the spectator during the horrible and mad adventure: how could I have divided myself in two? Absolute impartiality never exists in books of contemporary history; and those who write them become the more suspect when they cry up their objectivity. That is the reason that whenever I speak in the first person it is to make it very clear that I write as a witness. The only thing I wish for this book—nothing else matters to me—is that my readers will feel that my evidence has been weighed with one sole desire—to tell the truth, the whole truth, and nothing but the truth.

SFORZA

CONTENTS

Contents

PART SEVEN: ITALY AFTER VERSAILLES

PART NINE: PERMANENT ITALIAN AND EUROPEAN PROBLEMS

NOTE

This book being a study of the relationship of ideas and civil life in Italy, and not a literary history, nor just a history, men and books are often quoted without chronological precision.

But for the convenience of readers a table of dates will be found at the end of the volume.

PUBLISHER'S NOTE

The translators have asked us to call attention to the fact that Count Sforza, who is equally at home in Italian and French, presented the original manuscript to our editors in French.

CONTEMPORARY ITALY

PART ONE: THE ORIGINS

I

FROM THE RENAISSANCE TO THE RISORGIMENTO

THE HISTORY OF THE ORIGINS OF THE ITALIAN NATION IS AT the same time modest and august; but the shadow of Rome prevented the historians from transcribing in their dead *storie* —almost all of them destined to be no more than *testi di lingua* (oral legends)—the profound realities of the incessant and anonymous struggles that made Italy what she is. The historians and the poets desired only the resurrection of the Empire; the birth of modern Italy eluded them. It is only with difficulty that one may reconstitute from the naive writings of unknown chroniclers and the articles of old statutes the unceasing conflict that went on in all the countrysides and around the old castles between Lombard lords and Italian townsmen; between Italians become feudal by grace of some Otho and men of the glebe; between *missi dominici* (administrative officials) and villages or leagues of villages which succeeded in imposing the first written accords. Yet it was during that obscure strife, unique in world history, that a miracle happened: an Italy, no longer Roman, but Italian, which gave birth after only a few years of the Italian language's existence to our most perfect and universal poet, Dante. With him came Petrarch and Boccaccio, while all the other literatures were to wait centuries before producing their Racines, their Cervantes and their Shakespeares. The silent travail of our masses not only created the atmosphere from which our artistic geniuses emerged, but forged the real unity of Italy, because the strug-

gles and the births were identical everywhere, along the Mediterranean as along the Atlantic, in the North as in the South—
with the single difference, of which we shall further on see the
consequences, that the struggle, and consequently the history,
tended to be communal in the North, whereas in the South it
was more subordinated to the monarchy.

Two great events contributed to Italian life an intellectual
complexity and a moral disquiet which it had lacked in earlier
centuries: the Renaissance in the fourteenth century and, more
than has been realized, the Reformation and Counter-Reformation in the sixteenth. But of these movements the first,
though born in Italy, had nothing specifically Italian about it;
just as the second, though born in Germany, was not essentially German. Both expressed tendencies of the human soul:
the Renaissance expressed the joy of life and love and beauty;
while the Reformation was one of those shocks experienced
from time to time as a revolt against the monotony of mun-
dane pleasures in a flight toward ultra-human ideals. It is vain
to try to raise national flags over two episodes of the eternal
alternation of human aspirations. The Renaissance was not
essentially Italian, and in fact it soon propagated and re-
affirmed itself, minus a few artists of genius, among other
peoples, just as the Reformation was by no means in its best
essence a German movement.

The artistic enrichment which the Renaissance produced in
Italy was especially observable among the grandees like
Lorenzo de' Medici at Florence, the Sforzas at Milan and
the lesser lords and their courts of poets and savants. Among
the masses of the people it helped especially to propagate a
religious skepticism which—interrupted from time to time by
emotional flights like that of St. Francis of Assisi and his disciples—seems to have very deep roots in the Italian mind,
from the distant days when the laborious and courageous
Italic peoples of pre-Roman times, such as the Samnites, borrowed with an indifferent nonchalance from the Etruscans
their temples, their auguries, their religious ritual. In fact, the
relics of the old Italic communities—which imperial Rome
wished perhaps too much to make uniform—still seem to say
to us: "These cool, reasoning, indefatigable builders, these
fine-speaking Etruscans, if we don't copy some of their temples

and rites, will continue to insinuate that we are savages. . . ."

Having admitted that the Renaissance was only occasionally an Italian event makes it easier not to agree with those who show off their German patriotism by defining the Reformation as a German contribution to the world's progress, worthy to be put on the same footing as the Renaissance. In reality, the German Protestant Reformation, at least as it appeared in the sixteenth century, was nothing more than one theology opposed to another theology, with as many angels and police agents as on the opposing side—one might even add with a popery of their own, as it was said in Germany: *"Quod illis est Papa, nobis est scrittura"* (The Scriptures are to us what the Pope is to them). Furthermore, a century later Pascal's reproach to the Jesuits might with equal force be used as a reproach to the Protestantism of Luther which initiated the most immoral servility toward the German princes, long before the peccadillos of Jesuit confessors of kings.

One might even wonder why Rome was struck with such terror over the German monk's revolt. After all, the theology of Catholics was simpler and their theory of grace was not bettered by Calvin's. Their historic culture, moral and even Biblical, was infinitely superior to that of the German revolutionary. Even the immediate results of the Reformation were totally deprived of those moral exaltations which generally embellish the first phases of a religious movement. It was Giordano Bruno—considered by the Church of Rome as one of its most dangerous enemies—who defined the German peoples become Protestants as: *"più barbari e scellerati che non eran prima, dispreggiatori del ben fare"* (More barbarous and villainous than they were before; scornful of good principles).

Probably the Roman Church was more fearful of increasing Italian skepticism than it was of the German revolution itself. The latter served only to make Rome comprehend that the indifference of the Italians, who had smiled as at an archaistic phenomenon on the accession to the papal throne of a holy, simple and fervent Fleming, Adrian VI, might become in the long run still more dangerous. For this reason the Counter-Reformation was essentially an Italian phenomenon: Italian in its good effects—reestablishment of moral life and order; and Italian in its bad effects—since it lacked (being a negative and not a positive movement) those secret forces of imagination and poetry which had brought the miraculous into the Franciscan movement in the eighteenth century—forces of imagination and poetry which, at least among the elite, were manifest three centuries later with the Risorgimento.

The balance sheet of the Counter-Reformation from a strictly Italian political and moral point of view can be summarized thus:

Politically, an enormous advantage, since the Catholic reaction, harsh as it was, extirpated the Protestant centers which had formed in the North; the names of the streets and palaces of Geneva—Calvin's city—still tell us how many noble and sturdy spirits we lost, Italians who abandoned all rather than renounce the new faith they had embraced. One cannot but recognize that at least the formal religious unity of the Italians was not broken, and that the disaster of a Protestant North and a Catholic South was averted—a disaster which would certainly have diminished the Italian artistic and intellectual contribution to the world's moral wealth.

Even morally the influence of the Counter-Reformation doubtless had fortunate aspects, especially in the northern and central zones of Italy, which later were to prove the strength of their religious feelings in giving so many adepts to the Jansenist movement which identified itself with the struggle against the Jesuits. Yet, viewed as a whole, it was with the Counter-Reformation (but who would dare assert that the Counter-Reformation caused it, or was the sole cause?) that a period of decadence began from which Italy did not recover until the generations of the Risorgimento. The *distinguo* of a morality which sought transactions with life in the tribunal of the confessional was multiplied in convenient political deals, in the substitution of tacit secret struggles for the open struggles for liberty; in bitter inner scorn for sovereigns and popes who were honored and served in public. This created a national atmosphere which was cold, despite the inflated verses of false poets, wary of all generous action, sensible, fundamentally, but as the Chinese civilization is sensible. This comparison with China has a deep meaning, for me at least, for never have I felt so clearly as during my long years in China how precise was the similarity between the prosaic Confucian pragmatism and Tridentine Catholicism in the Italian manner which tells the very people who gave us St. Francis: "Beware, beware, the ideal can not be found in this world; we must be content with any obtainable good, even a second-class good, and not let it escape our grasp when it comes within reach. . . ."

People became so sensible, so reasonable, that not only the springs of true poetry dried up, but the religious spirit itself seemed positive only when it became formal, cold and more fearful of Hell than aspiring to Heaven. The famous pass-word of the epoch is revealing: "*Parum de Principe, nihil de Deo*" (Not too much about rulers, nothing at all about God).

To be sure, the line of the great Italian spirits continued, even in the penumbra of decadence, but at the price of what sacrifices! Giordano Bruno burned alive; Galileo persecuted; Vanini, Campanella, and later Giannone, imprisoned, exiled; and with so many others, Vico himself—of whom we shall write separately—keeping to himself the sensational results of his meditations which foreshadowed the nineteenth century.

But the masses, which are nowhere heroic, submitted. From the beginning of this epoch intellectual Europe, which had for centuries admired so much whatever was Italian, which had until within a few decades learned by heart the last universal Italian masterpiece, *Gerusalemme liberata,* began to assert (happy at their delivery from a too long Italian suzerainty): "These Italians compose exquisite verses, but verses that are not true poetry; they paint charming decorative canvases, but they are no longer true painters. . . ."

They were not wrong, since Marino, the most admired Italian poet of the seventeenth century, in his *Adone* had thus defined the poetic art of his time:

> *È del poeta il fin la maraviglia;*
> *Chi non sa far stupir vada alla striglia.*

(The aim of the poet is to amaze; let him who knows not how to astonish get employment as a groom.)

The prose was no more heroic than the poetry: Italian biographies and autobiographies had always been worthy of the tongue that gave us Cellini's *Vita;* but there was nothing comparable to it in the seventeenth century, when people seemed afraid to be themselves. Even the adventurers wrote only dull chronicles of their services in the courts of Italy and elsewhere, with never a personal accent.

From the beginning of this epoch an increasing number of Italians began to leave Italy, not feeling at home in a lifeless atmosphere. It is true that this has always been an Italian trait, so much so, in fact, that even before this time there had been a saying current in Europe: "The Lombards are the world's fifth element." But it was not until the beginning of the seventeenth century that these expatriates became famous: Mazarin and Alberoni in political life; Luca Giordano and Tiepolo in painting; Lulli, Cherubini, Spontini, Paisiello in music; Piccolomini, Caprara, Montecuccoli, Eugene of Savoy in arms; and in architecture in Poland and Russia many men of note, among them Cicerini, whose descendant was the well-known Soviet Commissar of Foreign Affairs, Chicherin.*

It is true that outside Italy other peoples were not much more advanced. In fact, through habits of long subjection in France, Holland and Spain, they continued to translate and print Italian books, some of which achieved continued success; but they were works more brilliant than profound, or works more encyclopedic than original, like Boccalini's *Ragguagli di Parnaso* (Advice from Parnassus) that even Edgar Allan Poe read and quoted; while the *Scienza nuova* of Vico, the book that with its intuitions anticipated the development of human culture by two centuries, had no better reception beyond the Alps than on the Italian side.

Not until the end of the seventeenth century did the reaction begin, first in artistic literature in which the pompous and artificial baroque was dethroned by the quaint but almost natural Arcadia movement, the course of which we shall examine later; and afterward in the sphere of historical and political thought which manifested a sudden deep interest for reforms putting an end to the passivity of a dormant world.

It is only fair to add that already everything was contained in a world which was beginning to become small. Italy, which had given so much to Europe, commenced to feel the beneficent

---

* He said so himself during the Genoa Conference to the King of Italy, who repeated it to me.

influence of the development of thought in England and France, even in the workaday world, through a revolution without shock, yet profound, and became conscious of it from Milan to Naples. The study and influence of Spanish literature ended. The infatuation for the French language and literature began, despite the sarcasm—at times witty—of numerous publicists who, accustomed to the Spanish bombast as to something indigenous, felt the new French infiltration as an invasion. But it had become the fashion, and nothing can resist the fashion when, as happened then, the gentlemen and ladies of Turin and Venice, of Rome and Palermo, suddenly stopped dressing *"alla spagnuola"* and began everywhere to dress *"alla francese,"* wearing lighter wigs and less somber velvets.

The Risorgimento which gave the world once again a proof of the unsuppressible vitality of the Italian nation was not a miracle that all of a sudden became manifest in 1821 and 1831 with the revolutions against the Bourbons and Savoys and pope-kings. The Arcadia movement, with its return to nature, is already a *risorgimento* from the heavy, cold and artificial atmosphere of the seventeenth century; Vico with his intellectual temerities is already a *risorgimento;* the Italian forerunners of the French Revolution were already a *risorgimento,* since their thought had ripened, Italian style, in the discreet *Annali* of Muratori and in the ardent pages of Mario Pagani without any direct influence from the great French Encyclopedists.

II

THE NEW NATIONAL CONSCIENCE: MACHIAVELLI

MACHIAVELLI'S TOMB IN THE CHURCH OF SANTA CROCE IN Florence bears a cold and academic inscription: *"Tanto nomini nullum per elogium."* (For such a great name no praise is necessary.) What ought to have been engraved on it is: "To the first political and historical thinker of modern times."

Machiavelli was the first to batter down the moral and political scaffolding of the Middle Ages; it is in Machiavelli's pages that for the first time one sees active virtue installed in place of monastic contemplation, experimental science in place of theology. Of this revolution of the mind, Descartes, Galileo, Bacon and others have been cited as authors, but too seldom Machiavelli, who was the real initiator. Why?

Because Machiavelli is still so much an Italian of our own day, a European of today, that we have not yet succeeded in reaching in his case the cool judgment that emanates from old tombs.

Machiavelli is still hated with the same hatred that the feudal French of the twentieth century retain for the Revolution of 1789, but aggravated by a moralistic prudery or pseudo-prudery.

Each century has its characteristic vices—vices that the moralists of the epoch bothered little about castigating. But each century changes the moral sanctions of the preceding one, just as women's fashions and literary styles change. And then people are scandalized over the depravity of the former generations and, as always, feel the need to give concrete form to the vices of a vanished generation by personifying them in this or that individual. Such was the case with Machiavelli.

Why was, and still is, Machiavelli pilloried to such a degree by those who know nothing about him except as the author of *The Prince,* and are not familiar with his complete works?

For three reasons: first, because his most celebrated book,

The Prince, is still read and discussed four centuries after its
first publication, having remained as sensational as a modern
adventure novel; second, because it is read by a public that
sees the work out of its proper frame, the Europe of the
fifteenth and sixteenth centuries, and detached from the rest
of its author's works; and third, because—and this is a unique
case in history—both the Catholic Church and the Protestant
churches are in accord in their excommunication of Machiavelli, although regarding him from opposite points of view.
The Jesuits and other polemical Catholics of the Counter-
Reformation abominated the Italian patriot whose ideal of
national unity menaced the Pontifical States. The Protestant
writers were glad to discover in the author of *The Prince* the
personification of papist perfidy. Both sides succeeded, and
what had previously been baptized "Machiavellianism"
changed its name in the eighteenth century and was called
"Jesuitism"—in reality almost as incorrect a designation.

But here we must limit ourselves to studying Machiavelli's
influence on Italian thought and political life.

To understand it—and him—we need only imagine the
young Machiavelli in 1497 at the age of twenty-eight listening
to the inflammatory sermons of Fra Girolamo Savonarola in
the Churches of Santa Reparata and San Marco in Florence.
As happens occasionally in skeptical Tuscany, all the Floren-
tines became lit with burning enthusiasm for the tyrannical
moralist who did not become a Calvin—first, because he
wanted to remain a Catholic; but also, and especially, because
Florence in the long run was not Geneva.

The Italy of Savonarola and the young Machiavelli was
in this tragic situation—that, rich, powerful, refined, she had
produced a civilization and an art that were the marvel of a
still half-savage Europe; but she no longer believed in the
ideas that had brought about her grandeur in the Middle
Ages, nor in Europe as the unitary symbol of the world, nor
in the Church as rival or successor of Europe. When the ideas
which have given life to a people are extinguished, regimes
may continue to live for a time but they are moribund. It was
not Ludovico Sforza who destroyed the Italian liberties when
he called the French into Italy; it was the fact that the Sforzas
in Milan and the Medici in Florence had suppressed the liber-

ties but had not succeeded in founding real dynasties like those of Aragon and Castille in Spain and the Capets in France.

Savonarola saw the danger and wanted to avert it—with his preachings. In the solitude of his cell he had imagined that the social edifice could and must be saved by a return of the Church to its primitive purity; by a return of the communes to their ancient liberties. But the people abandoned him, and the Church burned him alive. Savonarola failed because, after having accurately described the evils from which Italy was suffering, he proposed only convent remedies.

The young Machiavelli emerged cold and ironic from the churches where Savonarola preached. On March 9, 1497, he wrote his impressions to a friend: *"Il nostro frate* (our monk) divides all men into two groups: those dear to God, including himself and his partisans; and the rest, his adversaries, adepts of the Devil." *

Before the arrival of Machiavelli all the Italians kept seeking among the phantoms of the Middle Ages solutions for the country's crisis. He was the first who, awakening Italy from a long immobility of the political spirit, said quite simply:

Of the Church: "If one wants to explain its decadence it must be admitted that the least religious people are those nearest to the Church of Rome, the center of our religion."

Of the Communes: that only those states, great or small, in which *"tutto è al servizio di tutti"* (all things are for the service of all) are truly free and deserve to live.

And of the Nobles: *"Gentiluomini* are called those who live fatly and lazily from the revenues of their land, without even giving themselves the trouble of improving them. In every republic or *provincia* they are harmful; but especially where they have castles and vassals who obey them because there . . . they are enemies of all civilization. . . ."

Of the Empire he says not a word; he despises it too much. He is the first of the Italians who derided it. For him the Ghibellines were like the heroes whom later Berni held up to ridicule: *"Andavan combattando ed eran morti"* (They kept on fighting and yet they were dead).

Machiavelli's political conception derives from his experi-

* *The Living Thoughts of Machiavelli,* presented by Count Carlo Sforza. New York, Longmans, 1940. Pages 108-13.

mental way of viewing history—which is his, and only his, at a time when all the others were still entangled in syllogisms, scholasticism, citations. Nothing of that sort is found in Machiavelli. He thinks, and he says: The Middle Ages have given us anarchy; we must, therefore, establish a new power, a real and living one, the State. The State, having in itself its ends and its means, has no need of any theological investiture; it *is*. Its instruments will be the science of the State and the art of the State.

For the science of the State, Machiavelli declares that interests and passions can vary in intensity but never in substance, men's faculties never losing their productive force; a nation can eclipse itself, but the work of each individual survives in humanity. Here we have already a Vico a century in advance of his times—a Hegel three centuries before his day.

For the art of the State—for every science has its art—Machiavelli's definition is in synthesis: the calculation of the social forces.

But there you are: by the art of the State does he mean *The Prince?* That is the eternal problem Machiavelli raises with his terrible little book. To attempt to solve it one has to study *The Prince* in relation to its times and to its author.

One of the worst scandals of modern times is not the "Machiavellianism" of *The Prince* and of Machiavelli, but the facility with which people have gained an unctuous renown as moralists by attacking *The Prince*. However, it should suffice to recall that Frederick II, the preeminent Prussian perjurer, the Satanic assassin of Poland, the inevitable predecessor of Bismarck and Hitler, is the author of a mawkish and virtuous anti-Machiavelli.

Before Machiavelli, Philippe de Commines, the most trusted councillor of Louis XI, the king who recoiled from no crime or treason to unify France under the monarchy, wrote maxims and stated programs absolutely identical with those that the little book of Machiavelli seems to have "discovered" afterward. The difference is that the Flemish politician was a prolix and dull writer; all is in that, or nearly all. After Machiavelli, Louis XIV, the "very Christian" king, wrote in his *Maximes pour le dauphin:* "In each treaty insert a clause which can be easily violated; thus the entire instrument can be renounced in a case where the State's interests suggest the necessity." And a century later not a king but a philosopher, one of the most honest precursors of the French Revolution, Montesquieu, wrote in *L'Esprit des lois* *: "The right of legitimate defense sometimes implies the necessity of attacking, if one nation perceives that a longer peace would be useful to a second nation in preparing to attack and destroy the first; and if attack is the only means to avert that destruction."

French Machiavellianism? No, only the realism of the times, from the sixteenth century down to the eighteenth and even the twentieth, to judge by the Munich accords of 1938 by which Czechoslovakia was betrayed and abandoned by her ally, France.

Let us examine the incriminating passages of *The Prince*. All told, there are three.

In his third chapter Machiavelli counsels whoever usurps a realm to exterminate the preceding dynasty. Atrocious counsel? But who would have been scandalized if a less frank and direct and slyer Machiavelli had written: "No throne is safe while pretenders, issues of a former dynasty, are alive." In England, Queen Elizabeth showed that she was aware of it, just as Lenin knew it three centuries later in Russia, and neither the "Virgin" nor the Bolshevik had read *The Prince*.

In the seventh chapter we have the apologia for treason and murder in the person of Cesare Borgia. The passage shocks us, but we are not so sure that it shocked quite as much those who were reigning in Spain, France and England, or the Sforzas and Medicis of the day. It was the custom in Europe—just read Shakespeare. Let us not forget, furthermore, that in his next chapter, the eighth, Machiavelli condemns the crime of Agathocles, the tyrant of Syracuse, and concludes that genius does not suffice to make a great man of that sanguinary despot. Contradiction? Perhaps not; we shall see later the mocking definition Machiavelli gives of his book.

The third incriminating passage is in the eighteenth chapter: "A prudent lord should not keep his word if it be harmful to him and if the reasons that dictate his promise have disappeared. If men were all fools, this precept would not be good; but since they are bad and would break their word to you, you

* Book X, Chapter 2.

ought to do likewise. . . . But a promise should be violated by simulating and dissimulating: for men are so simple and so obedient to present necessities that he who deceives will always find people who will let themselves be deceived."

Just what is his theory? It is not only the same as that of Louis XIV, the king who loved to be honest and thought he was, but that of all the jurists in the world with their clause *de rebus sic stantibus*. The English Protestant moralists who have so often condemned the cynicism of the Italians—culpable only in being too frank—have never uttered a word to deplore the fact that Lord William Cavendish Bentinck in 1814 promised the Sicilians in England's name their liberty and independence, and the promise was violated; that in 1882 England promised to evacuate Egypt as soon as possible, and is still there; that Sir John Simon, when China was attacked by Japan, violated the engagements of the Covenant . . . and the list could so easily be continued for all countries.

But I have said that in the author of *The Prince* we must study the man as well, a method I shall often make use of in this book; since the history of Italy is above all a history of men.

In a letter written on December 10, 1513, to Francesco Vettori, Machiavelli tells how it came into his mind to write *The Prince*. It was, said he, just a *ghiribizzo* (a word one might translate as "whim," "something really not important") to distract him while writing his *magnum opus, Discorsi sopra la prima deca di Tito Livio* (Discourses on the First Decade of Titus Livius), which he commenced in 1512 and finished in 1522; *The Prince* was started in 1513 and completed in 1516, after numerous interruptions. This was the most unhappy period of his life; the Medici had driven him out of Florence, where they had destroyed the republic. Relegated to a little family estate, the Albergaccio, in the valley of Pesa, he was barely able, by cutting and selling the timber on his estate, to realize sufficient income to bring up his four children. Obliged to vegetate far from Florence, seeing Italy go to ruin, living in a world of liars and cowards, Machiavelli wrote *The Prince*. He dedicated it to a Medici, one of the new masters, hoping for employment and some florins; it was a humiliation rather than a sin. Condemning *The Prince* would be blaming Machiavelli for having tried to reenter political life, and for having endeavored to serve and save Italy at the moment of the greatest national crisis of her history. For my part, though I have said no to worse tyrants than the Medici, I do not dare pass judgment on Machiavelli.

One might say of *The Prince* what Machiavelli wrote of *La Mandragola* (The Mandrake), that dramatic masterpiece which, for the first time in Europe, dethroned the marvelous and chance in literature by inaugurating the study of characters:

> *Scusatelo con questo, che s'ingegna*
> *Con questi van pensieri*
> *Fare el suo tristo tempo più soave*
> *Perchè altrove non have*
> *Dove voltare el viso*
> *Che gli è stato interciso*
> *Monstrar con altre imprese altra virtù.*

(You should excuse him—for with these frivolous thoughts he tries to make these gloomy days less sad. He has no other place to look, since he is forbidden to show his virtue * by other deeds.)

The lines are bad, but pathetic. Machiavelli laughed in order not to weep. Charles VIII had invaded Italy, whose chiefs were not united; and the Florentine, exiled by the master of his Tuscany, warned in vain.

This man whom posterity has accused of corruption lived and died poor. The very day of his death, June 22, 1527, his son Piero sent word of his father's death to distant relatives. He informed them first that he *"lasciossi confessare le sue peccate da frate Matteo"* (consented to confess his sins to Brother Matthew) the word *"lasciossi"* giving them to understand that he did it to please his family; and he concluded: "My father left us in the most extreme poverty" (*in somma povertà*).

What did he leave to Italy? The modern conception of the nation. Before his time Italy was still the *"giardin dell' Impero"* (the garden of the Empire) of the Dantesque Utopia.

---

* *Virtù* in this sense is not virtue as we use that word today; the Italian word had not in the sixteenth century the moral connotation we give it; it signified the force of character of a man.

He made of it a homeland, a nation autonomous and independent.

It goes without saying that Machiavelli's homeland is not yet quite the Italian nation:

> *Una d'arme, di lingua, d'altare,*
> *Di memorie, di sangue, di cor*

(One in arms, in language, in religion, in memories, in blood, in heart)

as the Italians of the Risorgimento conceived it. The nation of Manzoni's couplet is an idea post-dating the French Revolution. But Machiavelli remains the first Italian who affirmed the necessity of an Italy, an ethnic unity, merely equal to France and Spain, which were then becoming unified, an Italy without illusions and dreams of imperial hegemony. As I said at the beginning, he is the first political thinker of modern times.

Had Machiavelli known a George Washington, a Mazzini, a Cavour, a Garibaldi, he probably would have written a different *Prince*. He would have understood that to make a great nation it does not suffice to have one individual will dominating, or giving the illusion of dominating, a people (the two Bonapartes, with all the disasters they inflicted on France, a Mussolini, a Hitler, would have been the counterpart of his Borgia); he would have understood that what matters above all else—even though it be the most difficult thing—is the free play of individual wills united in a common ideal. But that could not have been seen in his century—which had only princes.

III

THE NEW SCIENCE: VICO

THE FREE AND DISPASSIONATE THOUGHT OF MACHIAVELLI IS no longer found in the succeeding epoch. Guicciardini, though only a few years younger, is made of other stuff. In his *Ricordi* he writes: "Three things I want to see before dying, but I fear I shall never see them: a well-ordered republic, Italy delivered from the barbarians, and the world rid of these rascally priests." But he was the Count Guicciardini; he was rich; he had too much to lose. That is why he never published his *Ricordi,* and why he served the popes, if not the foreigners. Already the atmosphere of the Council of Trent pervaded, whence issued the consecration of absolute monarchy, with the end of feudal privileges but also with the death of communal liberties. The throne and the altar became equally undiscussible. There was no longer a place for a Machiavelli. In fact, the titles of the most admired works of the entire seventeenth century were of this sort: *De re aulica* (Concerning Court Matters), *Del servive nelle corti* (How to Serve in Courts) and so on. In such an atmosphere only courtiers could speak of political problems, with the unique exception of Paolo Paruta, who, honest but mediocre, is not worthy to be counted a pupil of Machiavelli.

But this was not the case in the sphere of science and philosophical speculation. And to think of the Italians baptizing the seventeenth century as an epoch of general decadence! It can only be explained by the spirit of false modesty of our literati. How could they forget that the generations of this "decadence" produced Giordano Bruno, Vannini, Telessio, Campanella, Ludovico Antonio Muratori and—greater than Galileo himself, though ignored by his own century and the next—Giambattista Vico who, with his *Scienza nuova,* is at the root of all the discoveries and all the sciences of the nineteenth century.

Giordano Bruno is a troubled and captivating genius, his

spirit entirely projected toward the future, but having visible bonds with the past, bonds which, nevertheless, did not prevent him from becoming a "miscreant"; and, what is more, those bonds have nothing to do with his subsequent return toward a sense of the divine which took shape only in his mind, unswayed by the religious influences of his time. He died proudly, still young, in the Campo di Fiori at Rome, burned alive, after having cast these immortal words at the judges of the Inquisition: "You are more terrified by your sentence than I who must suffer it." Bruno was the first saint and martyr of the new science in Italy. But he represented only himself, so singular was his life, so strange his genius, so unequal his books.

If the papal judges burned Bruno alive, Vannini was burned in France, at Toulouse. The two "atheists" were perhaps more deeply conscious of God than all the theologians and false poets of their time.

More representative of a certain aspect of the Italian character—generous, turbulent, extreme in its conclusions and its dreams—was Campanella, a native, like Bruno, of southern Italy. To the friends who, to induce greater prudence, reminded him of Bruno's fate, Campanella responded with the epigraph he had read on a church belltower: *"Non tacebo."* (I shall not be silent.)

In putting aside the syllogisms of medieval science, Machiavelli had initiated the experimental method with his *"cosa effettuale"* (causatives). Bruno had continued it with his *"lume naturale"* (natural knowledge). Galileo, so measured in his words but so absolute in his thoughts, had written: "Only the blind need a guide." Campanella repeated it in verse:

> *"Il mondo è un libro, dove il senno eterno*
> *Scrisse i propri concetti."*

(The world is a book in which the eternal Wisdom has written its concepts.)

If Galileo was necessary, with his constant principle that one must first study the facts, Bruno and Campanella were equally necessary, because they emerged from the laboratory where Galileo had secluded himself and, linking their innovating researches with the intuitions of the ancient Greek philosophers, gave to the new scientific movement its metaphysical conscience.

Campanella is an almost unique type in the numerous Pleiades of great Italians. He has more divinatory genius than Galileo, though he lacks the good sense with which the Tuscan philosopher was so richly endowed. Desiring complete and perfect solutions, he falls from contradiction to contradiction. Sometimes he departs from the naturalism of Telesio and ends in the Aristotelianism of Thomas Aquinas; expecting from Galileo astronomic verity, he falls into astrology. Not for nothing have spiritists saluted him as their forerunner; and the Communists (if only communism will some day declare itself) will proclaim him the boldest precursor of Lenin. For in his program of universal monarchy he seems to create a monarchy ruled by the Emperor and the Pope; but these are only words that signify, for him, human society. In Campanella's society man has no longer any rights, neither to choose a wife nor to acquire property, nor to bring up his children, nor to discuss, nor even to say yes or no. His *Città del Sole* (City of the Sun) is the apotheosis of communism, of the enslavement of the individual to an automatic society.

Dreams—but dreams inspired by a profound love of humanity. And to that love he remained faithful to the point of martyrdom, having passed half his life in prison, his body seven times submitted in vain to torture. "They tore my veins and arteries; they broke my bones; the earth drank ten pounds of my blood; then, buried in a ditch, without light or air, perpetually cold. . . ." He never yielded.

Quite opposite in its outward aspect—calm, colorless, humble, undramatic—was the life of another Southerner, Giambattista Vico; he was, it appears, in the latter part of the seventeenth and first part of the eighteenth century the accomplished type of the Italian scholar, like Muratori at Modena; but his books, his ideas, contained the germ of all of the newest and most daring that the nineteenth century has given the world.

In Vico's Italy scholarship and scholars were as good as the best in all Europe; but intellectual speculation slumbered. Bayle and Locke were suspect; Italy wanted to be happy, without any disturbances; Bruno and Campanella were forgotten.

Had they been remembered, they would have been even more than "heretics"—they would have been specters of remorse. No more tragedy for the Italians. The Arcadia, with its powdered shepherds, had started, representing the little that Italy could realize as a return to simplicity, to nature, after the Spanish bombast.

Vico had studied everything, learned everything; but he remained a scholar. What made him the greatest philosophic precursor of modern times was the sudden strange vogue that broke the Italian slumber: the infatuation for Descartes, of whom everyone in Italy was speaking, even the ladies with their *"cavalieri serventi"* (admirers), even the abbés in their sonnets, all of them, and without having the least idea of what it was all about. Vico also read Descartes. "That beautiful novelty," he exclaimed; "why, you'll find it in Epicurus and Lucretius." On the other hand, what struck Vico as a new message was Francis Bacon, of whom he declared: "Neither the Greeks nor the Romans had a Bacon."

While the Jesuits were attacking Descartes as a dangerous innovator, Vico denied him by a vaster affirmation which sketches the new doctrine; he wrote the *Scienza nuova,* which proclaims that the truth is not in its immobility but in its *"farsi"* (becoming), and that as there is a logic for the movement of ideas, there is also a logic for the succession of facts. The *Scienza nuova* is psychology applied to history; it is the philosophy of history. Here Vico frees himself from the theological conception. "The human spirit," he says in it, "is the God of man, as God is the spirit of the All." But at the same time he frees himself from pragmatic history, which considers only the personal aspect of events. If, as Croce says, history is the activity of the mind, and the activity of the mind is reality—*all* reality—Vico would be the philosopher of the mind, and philosopher only.

It was perhaps natural that Vico should be ignored by his century; on the one hand, he lacked the feverish passion of a Giordano Bruno and a Campanella; on the other, he could not please the "beaux esprits" who had begun to read the French Encyclopedia as a new Bible. The mania of the eighteenth century—prideful in the case of Rousseau and infantile by dint of "clarity" in the case of Voltaire—was to condemn the entire past in the name of abstract principles. For the French "philosophers" religions were all snares invented to deceive people; kings were all tyrants. Had Vico been able to live in France during the Revolution—which occurred nearly a quarter of a century after his death—and if he had deigned to speak in the midst of so much violence, he would have said:

"Even admitting that everything of the past is bad, do you think you can destroy by force, with a blow, the work of centuries? You quote your principles to me; but there is an authority to which we all must bow: the authority of the human race to which, if you are men, you cannot deny your submission. . . ."

Revolutionaries in the midst of their struggles—at the Bastille, in the Paris Commune, at the Kremlin—revolutionaries whose souls are, as it were, burned by the injustices they have suffered or against which they have fought, can feel only impatience for conceptions which, understanding everything, seem to admit everything. And yet Vico's promised land was the idea of progress. It was Vico, much more than the facile talents of the Encyclopedists, who opened the way to the nineteenth century. It is from Vico that Morgan derived his views on pre-history, and Muller his interpretation of myths; Wolf, the Homeric theory, and Mommsen Roman history, and Savigny the greater importance of the common law than of the laws; Fustel de Coulanges the conception of feudalism, and De Sanctis literary criticism, and Karl Marx the idea of class conflict, and Croce the origin of several of his philosophical ideas. It is unnecessary to say that almost all forgot to quote him, except De Sanctis and, after De Sanctis, Croce, who helped materially to explain Vico to the new generation.

During his lifetime he was ignored. He lived walled in the eighteenth century, like Bruno and Campanella in their dungeons. In Naples, where he taught at the University, it was vaguely known that Vico had exceptional gifts, but they knew him in the way of that Neapolitan improvisor, Marino, who exclaimed on the day of the philosopher's death: "What a pity! He would have had genius if he had not been mad."

In truth, in Italy Vico was almost alone with Machiavelli (who was himself a profound psychologist, but not a metaphysician) in seeing clearly into the future, without sentimental bonds with the past. Aside from these two, almost all the

Italian geniuses of the past believed that they were restoring an old world whenever they invented or created with power. The politicians believed they were restoring the Empire; Dante believed that he was following Virgil; Christopher Columbus believed that he would rediscover Solomon's Ophir and Alexander's Indies.

De Sanctis did not exaggerate when he wrote that the *Scienza nuova* is the Divine Comedy of science, the vast synthesis that sums up the entire past and opens all futures.

For a century Vico's thought lay buried in the libraries. The nineteenth century first rendered him justice.

IV

THE CENTURY OF THE OPERA: METASTASIO

IF THE SIXTEENTH CENTURY GAVE ITALY IN MACHIAVELLI the first political thinker of modern times, if the seventeenth century gave the world in Vico the most profound and original predecessor of all the sciences and researches that made the glory of the nineteenth century, it is to the eighteenth century that we owe the return of joy, of the gaiety of life, as well as of simplicity, that the world seemed to have forgotten during the pompous and inflated Spanish influence period of the seventeenth century.

In the seventeenth century nothing in Italy's social life had remained traditionally Italian. Everything had come from Spain; the ceremonies of the courts and of the aristocracy, the exaggerated politeness in the cities where, in the South, every man and woman had themselves called *don* and *donna;* the low bows at meetings in the streets, the hand-kissing, the salutations that terminated letters—where "I kiss your hand" and even "I kiss your feet" had replaced our former and simple *"state sano"* (keep well), and where everyone declared himself in the last line, written after a large blank space, *"umilissimo e devotissimo servo"* (your most humble and devoted servant). Here is how even a mind that remained as fresh and simple as the poet Francesco Redi addresses his niece, a very young person: *"all' Illma mia Signora, Padrona Colendissima* (to my most illustrious lady, most worshipful mistress)—*La Signora Maria Cecilia Redi."* The use of the third person, the *lei* and the *ella,* instead of the old Italian *voi,* (second person plural) became general. Only the peasants continued to address each other with the unaffected frankness of Dante's time.

An English writer, Thomas Coryat, complains of this Italian *lei,* since, he wrote, "we must speak to a man as if he were someone else and, in any case, in an abstract form, as if we

22

were addressing the idea of a man, not the man himself." The same Coryat remarks that even when Latin is spoken one must not say *placetne tibi* (does it please you), but *placetne dominationi tuae* (does it please your lordship), the translation of *Vostra Signoria*.

An unknown but interesting writer, Lelio Pascali, about the same period describes in a book on the duties of a pedagogue how one should pay a call. First a servant is sent to inquire whether your visit would be irksome that day. The reply is always: "Far from it, enchanted"; that gives time to change clothes, tidy up a salon, place footmen along the stairway. When the visitor arrives he is received at the top of the staircase and led with bows to the dusted salon. If the visit is paid to a sick person the place of honor is a chair beside the bed, the visitor's retinue, if there are any, being seated at ten paces distance. The details varied from city to city: at Rome the place of honor in a carriage was at the master's right, at Naples, opposite the master with back to the coachman; at the opera it was the corner of the box facing the stage, but one must stay there only a few minutes, to leave it free for other visitors; as to what was happening on the stage no one cared.

As a contrast or corollary to so much formalism, violence to the point of bloodshed and death was not rare; but always with characteristics which were pure seventeenth-century style. A case in point was an incident which occurred at Modena and which caused no astonishment—it was merely thought that "everything went off very well." A *cavaliere* started to beat his servant and ended by firing a pistol at him; the servant, who was armed, although wounded, fired in his turn at his master, both fell in agony. A passing Capuchin heard their confessions; absolved, they both rose, embraced, and fell dead in each other's arms.

The inevitable reaction took place with a new vogue which lasted a century: the Arcadia.

De Sanctis in his *Storia della letteratura italiana*—a model and monument of art and criticism unequaled in all literature— is unjust to the Arcadia. Coming to the end of the eighteenth century, he asks: "What was Italy doing? The Arcadia; it was the true product of her individual and moral existence, its poets representing the golden age, and in the nullity of the present life fabricating abstract themes and insipid loves between shepherds and young shepherdesses."

Modest as was its art, artificial as it was in parts, the Arcadia represents for the Italians a return to nature, to the natural. (De Sanctis was a man of the Risorgimento. He had fought for Italy, accepted prison and exile; and in common with other heroes of the Risorgimento he had a proud intolerance for the gentle and indifferent Italy of the past.)

With all its faults, all its mincing ways, the long vogue of pastoral art which was the Arcadia represented first a clear break with the Spanish turgidity; then it permitted Italy to accept certain French literary and artistic influences which were precious. If the Italians became Italian again, if in the nineteenth century the Risorgimento became possible, the Arcadia was a necessary and happy moment of that evolution.

A unique case in our literary history, the movement had its origin and greatest success in Rome—whereas ordinarily Italy's capital did not give, but received, as did the priests.

It was on a fine spring morning of 1692 that the Arcadia was born by chance. About fifteen men of letters had gathered together to read their poems reciprocally, as was the custom; most often this took place in the salon or the gardens of Queen Christine of Sweden, a happy exile in Rome. But this time they had gathered in the Prato di Castello, which was then only pasture and orchard. The pastoral scene made an impression even on the men of letters, and one of them exclaimed: "One feels as if Arcadia were about to come to life among us again." Perhaps the need of it was in the air; and so Arcadia was born. It was natural that, since this was Italy, it should become an academy. But the president merely called himself the *Custode* (guardian), and all the prelates, jurists, poets and poetasters who were members assumed the names of Greek shepherds; under these names they published their verses.

This lasted a century, down to the French Revolution. On the eve of the terrible 1789 this might have appeared a game; but it was in somnolent Rome governed by a gerontocracy of priests who created one pope after another, none of them being either a Carafa or a Peretti. It was the era of nepotism—each pope enriched members of his family and made them princes; but in their turn these Altieri, these Rospigliosi, these Corsini, these Borghese built palaces and villas and played at being Maecenas. The Arcadia created a sort of democracy among these people; everyone in Arcadia was equal; only talent counted. At first it was only talent at versifying; but without Arcadia we should not have had Goldoni, the Gozzi, the Verri.

The mode invaded all Italy; each town had its Arcadia. At Milan they were the *Transformati,* at Siena the *Intronati* (Crazed ones), at Bologna the *Gelidi* (Frozen ones), at Bologna the Erithean Shepherds, at Naples the Drunkards, elsewhere the Rozzi (Rough ones), the *Fervidi,* the *Flemmatici* (Phlegmatic ones).

Their negative work was not negligible, since they destroyed the artificiality of the seventeenth century; but their output, with rare exceptions, consisted exclusively of myriads of madrigals, sonnets, odes—*per monaca* (for a nun, when they celebrated the entombment of a young girl in a nunnery), *per nozze* (for nuptials), *per elevazione alla sagra porpora* (for the nomination of a cardinal), *per laurea* (when a young man of the nobility received a degree at a university).*

The Arcadia originated a by-product which disappeared with it, and with the hard problems of the nineteenth century: the *improvvisatori,* extempore poets who invented and recited impromptu their verses on a theme given them at a *ricevimento* (reception) or a dinner. One of them, Bernardino Perfetti, seemed so marvelous that they crowned him at the Capitol as they had crowned Petrarch in the fourteenth century. These much admired poets were accompanied on the harpsichord; toward the end of their recitations, as they became tired, no one grudged them if some of their verses limped. One day an acrid cardinal remarked aloud: *"Troppe sillabe, qui"* (Too many syllables here). Interrupting his improvisation for an instant and turning to the Cardinal, the *improvvisatore* remarked:

---

* When my great-great-grandfather presented his doctorate thesis at Parma on the propositions of Galileo (science was in fashion), a collection of fifty sonnets was published, praising the genius of the young student who never did another thing in his life.

"Chi ferra inchioda; e chi cammina inciampa;
S'improvisa, Eminenza, e non stampa."

(Bind yourself with iron and you're nailed down; walk and
you'll stumble; one improvises, Eminence, and one doesn't
print.)

It was from the Arcadia, and from the humblest of the im-
provisers that the eighteenth century's most famous poet
stemmed—the man who more than any other represented the
sensibility of his epoch, Pietro Metastasio.

On a hot Roman evening of 1709 a grave citizen dressed
in the heavy black habit of priests and legislators, Gian Vincenzo Gravina, famous Hellenist and jurist, one of the fourteen who seventeen years before had founded the Arcadia,
stopped in the Piazza dei Cesarini to listen to a child who,
standing on a stool, was improvising verses surrounded by a
crowd of small children. The verses were correct, the voice
agreeable, the child handsome; when the boy noticed the sage
listening to him he improvised several verses expressing excuses and respect. When he stopped and the group dispersed,
Gravina asked him his name.

"I am Pietro Trapassi, son of Felice who sells spices in the
via dei Cappellari quite near here. I am eleven, I have a
brother and sister. Yes, my father sends me to school—I know
how to read and write."

Gravina told Pietro: "Come to my house tomorrow morning in the via Giulia. I am the Abbé Gravina."

Gravina was rich and famous; his title of Abbé was only
honorary, as for so many of the Roman bourgeois. That evening at the Trapassis' house they must have been happy at
the gift of books that the boy received. Gravina, who lived
alone, without pleasures, offered to take the little Pietro into
his home and educate him. The Trapassis accepted, and the
transformation began by the translation of his name into
Greek, from the vulgar Trapassi to the sonorous Metastasio.

The life of the young Metastasio is typical of the middle-
class Italian of those times—a mixture of imagination and cool
good sense. The boy had long studies of the classics and law
under Gravina, until his protector's sudden death. Still a very
young man, he found himself heir to a part of the latter's for-

tune. He dissipated it in a Rome that admired him. On the brink of disaster he halted, fled to Naples to complete his law studies with the famous lawyer Castagnola, who stipulated: "No poems." But Metastasio fell in love with a daughter of Vico and wrote little songs for her. Castagnola dismissed him, but the famous singer, Mariana Bulgarelli, called la Romanina, divined his genius and received him at her home, loved him both as a lover and as a son, just as across the Alps Madame de Warens loved Rousseau. La Romanina was a woman of genius and revealed his way to Metastasio. His first famous drama, *Didone abbandonata* (Dido Abandoned), was written under her inspiration and with her advice.

Singers, both male and female, in the Italy of the eighteenth century were far more important personages than before or after that period. They were not only the wheels of the musical vehicle; they were the king-pin; and music was written by composers who had in mind the *divo* and *diva* who would sing it. The singer was not a music box; music was the synthesis of the written note and the individual who sang it. Fanny Burney (the future Madame d'Arblay, author of novels famous in her day) wrote apropos of a great singer of the eighteenth century, Gaspare Pacchierotti, that if he had not been a singer he would have been a poet. It was Pacchierotti who showed his respect for his art when, as an old man, he said to the tenor Rubinia, then quite young: "Our art is too difficult and too long for the life of one man. When we are young we have the voice, but don't know how to sing; when we are old and begin to learn we no longer have the voice."

It was in this atmosphere of deep respect for musical art that la Bulgarelli and Metastasio lived.

The *Didone abbandonata* gave Metastasio immediate fame throughout Europe: afterward came *Catone in Utica, Adriano* and a hundred others. Metastasio called them tragedies; actually they were melodramas—poetry transformed and penetrated by music; Rousseau, Voltaire, the whole world learned them by heart. When Metastasio, Caesarian Poet at Vienna, died at eighty-six, a medal with the inscription, *Sophocli Italo,* was struck in his honor. Adulation never spoiled his cool good sense. Writing from Vienna to a friend some years earlier, at the summit of his glory, he sent him a mock biography which

began: "In the eighteenth century lived a certain Abbé Metastasio—a tolerable poet among bad versifiers."

He is less popular nowadays, though several of his verses
have become a part of the current speech of several generations of Italians, and today they still quote:

> *Passato è il tempo, Enea,*
> *Che Dido a te pensò*
> (The time is past, Æneas, when Dido thought of you)

when they laugh at an unhappy lover; or

> *Ne' giorni tuoi felici*
> *Ricordati di me*
> (Think of me in your happy hours)

and so many others. Perhaps that is the best way to survive:
in Italy Metastasio shares this immortality with Dante and
Manzoni.

It was with Metastasio and under his sway that the Italian
opera reached its peak. Opera could germinate only in the
Italian language, influenced by Italy's literary culture and
popular instinct, which, on the other hand, was always a sterile
soil for tragedy. To be sure, the Italians wrote and presented
innumerable tragedies in the course of centuries—from Al-
bertino Mussato and his *Ezzelino* to Scipione Maffei and his
Merope, to Alfieri and his *Saul.* But these tragedies did not
spring from their souls, save perhaps in the case of Alfieri.
They were the result of the eternal mania of the Italian
letterati to find inspiration in the forms of the past. Tragedies
did not interest the people, any more than our literature in
general did; they remained in the academic hothouses. Scholars and critics could get warmed up over some of them; the
ordinary townsman liked only the *commedia dell' arte,* and
the peasants their *maggi* (May songs), sung from improvised
platforms near the church, as I have myself seen them—
probably the last survival in Italy—in the Alpine villages of
my Lunigiana, where they would say respectfully about some
old man: "He has *el libron del Maggio,*" which was an old
copybook manuscript of the eighteenth century containing in

condensed form, according to the rules of the *commedia dell' arte,* the lives of saints or paladins.

Opera was the point of juncture (which tragedy had never been) between nobles and upper class townsmen, on the one hand, and the common people who had instinctively invented it. As it was perfected under Metastasio, opera is a pre-romantic product in the category of the dramas of Shakespeare and Calderon, with three essential elements: music, action, scenic effect. Since the action must be rapid and violent, it follows that the tirades of the old tragedies are no longer admissible; that the French tragedy heroes—Auguste who perorates like Bossuet, and Athalie like Bourdaloue—are no longer popular in Italy; and that (so rare a case in Italian literature) Metastasio uses a language which, because it is true, does not grow old. As a writer of opera texts, Metastasio never had any of the vexations of all libretto authors (except, after him, Arrigo Boito). A musician himself, he loved to write for music. Goldoni, Gaspare Gozzi and Parini bitterly ridiculed singers; the former friend of la Bulgarelli never did. Sometimes in his dramas he described a hero like the singer for whom he destined the part. And thereby he characterized more truly than poets possessing a more fiery genius.

Metastasio is neither pseudo-classical like Voltaire, nor artificial like Alfieri; his is the spontaneous form that the entire nation desired, and his heroes and heroines are neither pseudo-Greeks and pseudo-Romans nor are they reminiscences of the powdered set he frequented in the salons; they come from the music of Pergolesi and Jommelli; they are Italian music made flesh.

Metastasio died on April 14, 1782, at Vienna, where he had always pined for Italy but thought too much of his post of Poeta Cesareo to abandon a city which was becoming less and less Italian and had begun to remember that it was German.

Soon after came the Revolution and young Alfieri with his fierce republican tragedies which supplanted Metastasio's dramas on all the Italian stages. If Metastasio seemed to have been forgotten, it was because what in his art seemed unworthy of the nineteenth century was then disdained. When the eighteenth century is studied as a phenomenon analogous —though on a smaller scale, if you wish—to the Renaissance, it will be realized that the quaint Arcadia and the rich and serene Metastasio were precious and necessary links in the formation of contemporary Italians. Alfieri was an instrument of conflict; Metastasio was a long state of the soul. Not for nothing do the peasants of Italy, those authentic Italians, still read him.

V

THE ITALIAN FORERUNNERS OF THE FRENCH REVOLUTION: FROM THE JANSENISTS TO PARINI AND ALFIERI

ONLY IN THE LATTER PART OF THE EIGHTEENTH CENTURY, after the peace of Aix-la-Chapelle (1748), does one see in Italy, practically everywhere, new ideas born and new aspirations asserting themselves, of which the two generations of the Arcadia and Metastasio knew nothing. In Lombardy the signs of the dawn of political liberalism—which triumphed in the nineteenth century—became doubly manifest with a synchronous movement of innovatory ideas and practical reforms. Lombardy was finally detached from the Spanish corpse and reunited with living Europe.

It is true that in Milan there were no august precursors such as the South had given with Giordano Bruno, Campanella and Vico. But there was a live protagonist absent elsewhere, from the drowsy Piedmont of the Savoys as from the realm of Naples: the bourgeoisie. Matured and strengthened by the Jansenists, the bourgeoisie sallied out to war against ecclesiastical privileges; it was they who, supplying the functionaries of a state organization in process of forming, undermined the influence of the aristocracy. The "philosophers," a small separate army raised from the ranks of the bourgeoisie but including also several "enlightened" aristocrats, comprised the rest. Literature began to court the new sovereign. Goldoni, for instance, ridiculed the vanity of the nobles in ten of his comedies; and in Milan itself there was Albergati, who in his comedy, *I Pregiudizi del falso onore* (The Prejudices of False Honor), represents the bourgeois, the self-made man without other coat-of-arms than work and probity, who without boasting imposes himself on nobles forced to treat him as an equal.

At the same time all Italy stops talking of her "primacy" and her "woes," as she had done continuously since the Cinquecento (when there was no talk about primacy, as they still

31

had it). Despite the rhetoricians and the Jesuits, Italy went to the school of the rest of Europe and borrowed from it the instruments of average daily culture. In a thirty-year span she gave herself three translations of the first English encyclopaedia : the *Cyclopaedia* of Ephraim Chambers, of which the Italian editions—Venetian (1748), Neapolitan (1754), and Genoan (1775)—were all three placed on the Index; and the French *Encyclopédie* with two editions—the first at Lucca * in 1758 and the second at Leghorn in 1770–79.

I have cited these publications because they reveal the intellectual atmosphere of the epoch; a collective, honest seeking of the truth, a growing disgust with the crotchets of the past, but no great individual geniuses.

There was one genius, as we have seen : Vico. But it is not among exceptional geniuses that the moral physiognomy of an epoch should be sought. The precursors of the nineteenth-century ideas of liberty who appear in the eighteenth are more like lightning flashes that were beginning to streak the skies of an Italy till then so peaceful in its serenity and its Metastasian pleasures.

Significant of this essential trait of Italian political thought of that day—an aspiration toward reforms and liberty, but without the universalist and rationalist dreams of the French —is an essay by the Triestan Antonio de Giuliani † on the *Vicissitudini inevitabili delle società civili,* a veritable manifesto against all despotisms, even the enlightened despotism of the Emperor Joseph II whom Giuliani had served and judged dangerous, as an Utopianist in the French manner.

Others, equally forgotten writers, preached reforms and ideas of liberty which, to be sure, had been inspired in them in great part by the French innovators but which bore a thoroughly Italian stamp : for example, the Piedmontese Radicati, who calls for a purified Christianity; the Trentinoan Pilati, who invokes a reform of the clergy and suppression of the monks; a Count Vasco, who died in prison in Turin for having

---

* Its editor was the patrician Luccan, Ottaviano Diodati, of the same family as Giovanni Diodati who, having become Protestant, published at Geneva in 1603 a celebrated translation of the Bible in Italian.

† Born and died at Trieste, 1755–1835. Croce republished in 1934 (Bari, Laterza) the little book which everyone had forgotten and which had become unobtainable.

written, about the year 1780, a book called *La Monarchia moderata*.

More profound was the moral influence of the Italian Jansenists. The most zealous converts among them were grouped at Piacenza—to such a point that *Piacentino* currently became synonymous with Jansenist. Their emphasis on points of doctrine was at variance with that of the French "philosophers"; the priest Tamburini, for instance, while extolling the boldest reforms, criticizes the disciples of Rousseau who build the concept of citizen on "the natural man, who has never existed."

The French Jansenists had said, and their Italian disciples had repeated: "Everything comes from God, and nothing from men; above me is only God who alone operates in me, and is able to do everything." But Italian Jansenism was not merely a theological controversy on grace; it became a democratic movement, inasmuch as it wanted to be a return to the primitive purity of the Church, in antithesis to the wealth and abuses of the Church of Rome—which the most ardent Italian Catholics, as Dante and Manzoni were, never hesitated to deplore. A little later Ugo Foscolo, defining the Italian Jansenists as "implacable against all convent doctrine, against all Jesuit practice and against all sacerdotal interference in the affairs of the realm," compared their action against religious abuses to nothing less than that of Dante's four centuries before. What is certain is that the Italian Jansenists were the most lofty moral characters of the second half of the eighteenth century in Italy. Historians have spoken of them as of a current that vanished after a celebrated event: the conversion of Manzoni to Catholicism in 1810, the work of a Jansenist, the Abbé Degola. But what I saw about me as a child and adolescent toward the close of the nineteenth century—in the old duchies of Parma and Piacenza where the Jansenists had been so influential—makes me think of certain streams that disappear under the earth to reappear quite as pure and clear in other distant valleys.

How, grown to manhood, could I otherwise explain my mother, profoundly Christian, gathering about her knees her four children every Sunday to read them and comment on the New Testament, imposing on herself an extreme simplicity of life, giving all to works of charity, full of love and benevolence, but firmly pushing away from her family circle all the priests who wanted to domineer outside the Church. She would not have admitted belonging to the condemned group, but she was of it; when she died in 1906 she was still young.

No analogous spiritual current existed in France on the eve of the Revolution.

A picture of Italy on the eve of the French Revolution would not be complete without an allusion to the adventurers. With Gorani, with Casanova, with Cagliostro, they were an element of the European fever of the epoch; some of them honest—the term adventurer acquired a derogatory sense only in the nineteenth century *—others debauched, they were all, in all the European capitals, premonitory signs of the awakening of Italian vitality.

They are all so well known—about Casanova, the most licentious of them, there is a vast literature—that I will limit myself to recalling but one among them, a character unique in this group of profligates, all the more because he is completely forgotten; an adventurer who in the midst of the strangest incidents retained a deep sense of the religious in life. This was the Dominican missionary Boetti who, sent to the Levant to convert the Turks and Kurds, ended by attempting to found a new religion conciliating Christianity and Mohammedanism. He succeeded in imbuing crowds with fanaticism, became a political leader at the head of 80,000 partisans, took possession of Armenia and Kurdistan and governed them for six years, flouting the authority of the Sultan of Constantinople. Captured by the Russians in 1791, he ended his life in an Orthodox convent on the shores of the White Sea. Boetti acted in the French manner in believing that he could constitute a society on the basis of theoretical concepts; but he was Italian in retaining, in those Voltairian times, the intuition of the importance of the religious sentiment.

Two Italians, Parini and Alfieri—these ones famous—show in the most precise way the importance of the French Encyclopedists in their intellectual development, and, at the same time,

---

* *L'Avventuriere onorato* (The Honored Adventurer) is the title of one of Goldoni's comedies.

how much the direct interference of republican France in the affairs of Italy repelled them.

Parini, more of a moral than an intellectual character, at the end of his century—which was Metastasio's—gives us this new spectacle: the poet who looks for his art in a religious, moral and social world. His *Giorno* discloses an irony that is no longer Ariosto's, deriding everything; the irony of the moral sense is awakening. He speaks like Rousseau when he says:

> *Forse vero non è, ma un giorno è fama*
> *Che fur gli uomini eguali, e ignoti nomi*
> *Fur plebe e nobilità.*

(Perhaps it isn't true, but it is said that one day men were equal; and that plebeians and nobles were unknown distinctions.)

When the Revolution triumphed, Parini served in the public offices of the Cisalpine republic; but when the French removed the statue of Christ from the reception room of the Commune he retired from public life, declaring: "Why should I remain where the citizen Christ cannot enter?"

Alfieri is, as a poet, the antithesis of the musical Metastasio. He writes:

> *Me trovan duro?*
> *Anch'io lo so:*
> *Pensar li fo.*
> *Taccia ho d'oscuro?*
> *Mi schiarirà*
> *Poi libertà.*

(Do they find me harsh? I know they do: I force them to think. They call me obscure? Some day liberty will make me clear.)

Young, rich, noble, he traveled about all Europe to escape the suffocating regime of the old Savoys in his Turin. He returned from London enthusiastic about the English, who had decapitated Charles I; at Paris he acclaimed the capture of the Bastille. Twelve years before he had written a treatise in which he declared:

"The laws, solemn and reciprocal social contracts, should be the expression of the will of the majority, expressed by the voice of the people's freely elected representatives." Any other legislation and any other mode of government are tyrannical, he said. And not to be misunderstood, he added: "I was born and brought up under the tyranny of one man; it is the most common species in Europe: the term monarchy is only the meticulous name that ignorance, flattery and fear have given to tyranny." "Tyranny can be hereditary or even elective *; the latter is the most harmful of all; under that form of government the people attain the last degree of political stupidity."

Alfieri fulminated against the clergy and nobility, against the doctrines and institutions of the Christian religion as he knew them, with a vehemence nothing approaches in French literature before the Revolution of 1789.

Next—being perhaps more Italian than revolutionary—he abominated the Jacobins; his *Misogallo* (published after the French troops entered Florence) remains a witness of his hatred. The French, who were irritated by it, might have replied: "Poet, 'tis also from thee who glorified Brutus that we learned our methods."

* Allusion to the Papacy.

VI

THE FRENCH REVOLUTION: NAPOLEON
AS AN ITALIAN

ONE OF THE MOST POPULAR SONGS IN FRANCE WHEN THE
revolutionary armies invaded Italy said in two of its tiercets:

> *Enfin de Paris au Japon,*
> *De l'Africain au Lapon,*
> *L'Egalité se fonde.*

> *Tyrans, le sort en est jeté*
> *Le bonnet de la Liberté*
> *Fera le tour du monde!*

(At last from Paris to Japan, from African to Laplander,
equality is founded. Tyrants, the die is cast. Liberty's cap
will circle the earth.)

The French people, believing they had become, as André
Chénier said, "the example of the world," * thought also that
their conquests were acts of "philanthropy" toward oppressed
peoples.

But the Italians sang other songs. I quote two strophes of
one that remains in my memory among the songs that old servants sang to us evenings in that Lunigiana, so distant then
from the modern world:

> *Selle, stoffe, morsi, briglie,*
> *Copertine, sproni, striglie,*
> *I lenzuoli, i materaggi,*
> *Le fettuce pei sellaggi,*
> *Panno blu, panno scarlatto;*
> *Poverini, ch'hanno fatto?*

> *Le coperte per i letti*
> *Gli stivali, i fazzoletti,*

* *Avis aux Français,* 1790.

37

Le camicie, le calzette,
I calzoni, le berrette,
La marmitta, il tondo, il piatto;
Poverini, ch'hanno fatto?

Saddles, silk stuffs, bits, bridles,
Horse blankets, spurs, curry combs,
Sheets, mattresses,
Saddle girths,
Blue cloth, scarlet cloth:
Poor things, what have they done?

Counterpanes,
Boots, handkerchiefs,
Shirts, stockings,
Breeches, caps,
The kettle, the plate, the dish:
Poor things, what have they done?

The complaint continued with the hundreds of objects that the French stole from the hamlets as from the towns and sent to France. And with these *"poverini,"* poor things that had done nothing—*"ch'hanno fatto?"*—but which they carried away, they also carried off from all the museums and palaces of Italy the most famous masterpieces of painting and sculpture, and in France it was thought the natural thing to do. For if an Italian chronicler, G. A. Sala, could write that an invasion of Goths and Huns would have damaged us less than the sojourn of these heroes, liberators of humanity, in Paris they explained: "Would not the most beautiful works of Greece and Rome be best placed and preserved in the land that has the best laws and the greatest enlightenment; in the only nation that has a school; among the most powerful and industrious of peoples?" *

The folk and the peasants of Italy saw innumerable wagons passing on the roads of Tuscany and Liguria bearing to Paris the treasures of Florence, Rome and Naples. But probably what irritated them still more was that for these thefts the French gave them a "philosophical reason."

Of the three terms of the republican formula, "Liberty,

* *La Décade,* 30 Messidor, year IV.

Equality, Fraternity," the Italians long had known fraternity and equality, and though they were not always practiced, they did not constitute an impossible ideal, since in Italy the relations between the classes, even in the eighteenth century, had always been flexible and harmonious. North of Rome feudalism and its titles were hardly more than vain words; and everywhere the Arcadia had created a sort of democratic society in which ranks had disappeared under the pastoral names its members adopted. But the love of liberty, of political liberty, became more and more animate—on account of the French, and despite the French. This strange fact became manifest: that the French, who had never thought except as Frenchmen (even in the times of the *Encyclopédie,* despite their affirmations), were using in their conquests—and, unconsciously, for their conquests—a cosmopolitan language; and the Italians, who, aside from Machiavelli, had always been universalists, began to translate in the most exclusive of Italian senses the formulas the French brought them. Liberty? Yes, they said or thought; but liberty for ourselves, among ourselves, without foreigners.

The Italians hated the French invasion, but were not so sure about their hatred for Napoleon: they felt in him the crowned Italian, the Emperor of the Ghibelline tradition. In his hatred of the Revolution Taine was wrong when he declared that the Italian *condottiere* of the fifteenth century could be recognized in Napoleon. No, indeed! Napoleon was Italian because he was possessed by Dante's fixed idea: the *Monarchia del mondo* (universal monarchy).

The cosmopolitan union of all nations under one scepter, the scepter of a feudal Caesar, is not in the spirit of the French Revolution. Napoleon imbibed it in the long dream of his Italian ancestors. Though doubtless unconsciously, nevertheless Napoleon put the power of France at the service of the perennial dream of old Italy.

One need only realize Dante's ideal of Emperor—the master of a State "who daily extends his frontiers and will not let himself be limited even by the ocean"; this is Napoleon at Boulogne, at Wagram, at Friedland.

Emperor, in the Italian style, Napoleon rendered a great service to Italy. He destroyed the Holy Roman Empire, the most dangerous of the Italian illusions of the past. Here was the elimination of every Ghibelline dream, of every Guelph dream. Italy finally became the Italy that Machiavelli wanted her to be; the old shadow of the crown of the Caesars disappeared for all time—that shadow which had stunned the Italians into a stupor and silenced them at the very moment they had beaten the Germans. As on that Holy Saturday night of 1175 when, the Italians having encircled the Germans, the Emperor Frederick Barbarossa saved the day for himself by ordering his heralds:

> *Tu intima, o Araldo: passa l'imperator romano,*
> *Del divo Giulio erede, successor di Trajano.**

(Declare, herald: "The Roman Emperor passes, heir to divine Caesar, successor to Trajan.)

And Carducci, who depicted the scene in his famous poem, concludes:

> *Deh come allegri e rapidi si sparsero gli squilli*
> *De la trombe Teutoniche fra il Tanaro e il Po,*
> *Quando in cospetto a l'aquila gli animi e i vessilli*
> *D'Italia s'inchinarono e Cesare passo.*

(How joyous and rapid sound the fanfares of the Teuton trumpets between the Tanaro and the Po, when, at sight of the Eagle, the arms and standards of Italy bowed, and Caesar passed.)

In destroying the old worm-eaten throne of the German kaisers, title-bearers of the Holy Roman Empire, Napoleon unknowingly aided the rapid political unification of the German people under the domination of Prussia, thus rendering the most atrocious disservice to those French whom he loved as instruments of his glory, while not recognizing himself as one of them. It is strange that this should be contested; since Napoleon wrote (without being aware of it, and therefore honestly) in the last of his writings, his testament dictated at St. Helena, expressing the desire to be buried "on the banks of the Seine among that French people which I have loved so

---

* *Sui campi di Marengo la notte del sabato santo 1175,* one of the most famous poems in the *Rime nuove* of Carducci.

much" (*"ce peuple Français que j'ai tant aimé"*). One speaks
in that manner only of a people which is not one's own.

When Napoleon was at the same time sovereign and prisoner on the island of Elba, a deputation of Lombards, almost
all of whom were nobles, went to see him. They confided to
him that they wanted to prepare a revolt against Austria, using his name as standard bearer but—and here they hesitated
—would he consent to aspire only to the Italian throne and
never again to a French throne? Napoleon was a marvelous
liar; he did not want to go so far, but at the same time he
did not want to discourage them. *"Non son io Italiano?"* he
replied (Am I not Italian?). The fact is enshrined in an
anonymous and extremely rare brochure that appeared in
Italy in 1815 *; diplomatically, it states the above in indirect
terms, but a clearer oral tradition which passed down the generations of my family must have told the truth since, when I
asked Prince Victor Napoleon, whom I, as a young diplomat,
often saw in London and Constantinople and who knew in
detail the entire history of his uncle, what he thought of
Napoleon's answer, he confined himself to replying: "He was
in a cage; he wanted to get out of it."

The Italians willingly pardoned Napoleon his exactions, the
excess of orders from Paris when they were ready to give their
confidence to the Viceroy Eugene de Beauharnais, the sterile
death of so many Italian soldiers in Spain and especially in
Russia, where they often saved the retreat. Had not Napoleon
restored the realm of Italy, had he not placed on his head
the iron crown, had he not exclaimed in Italian: *"Guai a chi la
tocca!"* (Woe betide him who dares touch it!)

---

* My principal regret over the burning by the Fascists of one of my properties
on the seaside the night of October 26, 1926, is in the destruction of a collection
of brochures of the Risorgimento, with contemporary marginal notes of my ancestors. The report on the visit of the Lombard nobles to Elba contained notes of
my great-great-grandfather, who had been in contact with the visitors.

PART TWO: THE RISORGIMENTO

VII

ROMANTICISM: MANZONI

ITALIAN CRITICS OFTEN SPEAK OF VITTORIO ALFIERI AS THE poet who gave modern Italy a genre she lacked: tragedy.

The role of Alfieri in Italian political thought is infinitely more important than that of the creation of a genre. Alfieri is the initiator of that fierce aspiration for liberty which was common to the poets who succeeded him, from Foscolo and Leopardi to Carducci. But more individualistic than any of them, almost an anarchist before the invention of nineteenth-century anarchy, he never hesitated to define, for what they were, the liberties of the last two great Italian republics of his day: Venice and her *"oscena libertà posticcia"* (obscene unnatural liberty); Genoa and her *"sessanta parruche d'idioti"* (sixty idiot periwigs). Later he felt the same horror for the "liberty" of the Convention in France which he flagellated in his *Misogallo*. This libertarian did not even continue to be enthusiastic for the American Revolution; as soon as he became aware that in the minds of the Americans of the thirteen colonies economic elements were mixed with their moral motives he became disinterested in it, irritated.

Alfieri, that aristocratic descendant of a long feudal line, hated kings with a hatred and scorn, without exception. Perhaps with one exception: Frederick II, king of Prussia; at Frederick's death he wrote a sonnet with this last line:

Ma di non nascer re forse era degno.
(But perhaps he was worthy of not being born a king.)

43

He would probably have been surprised had he known how many great ministers of kings had slight esteem but not the least hatred for their "august masters": for example, Cavour, Bismarck, Gladstone. They had to deal with poor mediocrities not worth hating.

The tragedies of Alfieri—a rare case in Italy's literary history—really made history: they forged the soul of at least two generations. His *Timoleone* was played in Naples for a long period during the Republic of 1789, "to elevate the people."

The proof of the potential unity of Europe, even at the threshold of the nineteenth century, is found in the almost perfect analogy of sentiment and passions in Alfieri and in the *sturmer und dranger* of Germany, the German romantics and this proto-romantic Italian being in agreement in finding lifeless and soulless the tepid intellectualism of Voltaire and the optimism of the French Illuminati who, he said, prostituted *"la viril nostr' arte"* (our virile art).

From a political point of view the poets who followed in the steps of Alfieri were as different as possible from him: Pellico, a pious Christian; Niccolini, who drew his pathos from the evocation of medieval heroes of liberty like Arnoldo de Brescia. Neither they nor any other patriotic poets have had in common with Alfieri the Dantesque disdain which in Italian literature is a sign of moral grandeur.

One other poet, and only one, Vincenzo Monti, had, after Alfieri, the Dantesque traits. But if I cite the fact it is to mark the difference between the two types. Alfieri was Dantesque because his soul was as proud as Dante's; Monti seemed Dantesque because, endowed with almost miraculous gifts of external poetic form, he accomplished a Dantesque style, perfect in its form but external and decorative. At the beginning of the nineteenth century, so rich in the profound verity of Manzoni and the true emotion of Alfieri, Monti reproduces the type of the Italian *letterato* of the Cinquecento—which D'Annunzio resuscitated in the twentieth—for whom everything can equally become the theme of fine poems: an Austrian emperor and a Napoleon, a popular revolution and the election of a pope. Leopardi was a good judge when he wrote that Monti "was truly a poet of the ear and the imagination, but never of the heart." Can one blame Monti? No; for him the serious thing in the world was the beauty and purity of literary form, and the rest—including politics, the nation, liberty— were merely passions of human beings who had not understood that formal beauty is everything.

If I stop at Monti it is because at the threshold of the nineteenth century he represents one of the most brilliant relics of the centuries of the most sickening Spanishism—but added to it, a perfect form. When the French of the Revolution arrived in Rome, a political agent of the Republic, Basseville, was killed. Monti was by nature the court poet of all that happened. Consequently he wrote the *Bassevilliana,* a raging invective against the French Revolution. When Napoleon and his French became masters of Italy, Monti excused himself in a letter to a friend, Falfi: "Compelled," he wrote, "to sacrifice my opinions, I attempted at least to save my writer's reputation." As Croce has written somewhere, Monti never wrote or spoke against his conscience; diverse events and contrasting doctrines by turns roused in him the fire of imagination, and he always remained faithful to a single party, that of fine literature.

Monti was a poet. For other reasons, more humane even if more prosaic, quite a few of the men born before the French Revolution and before the innovating breeze that was romanticism thought as he did. Contemporaneous with Monti, but known only in Lunigiana and Tuscany, an old Minister of State, Nicolao Giorgini, allied to my family, had been successively in power under an aristocratic republic, under the Jacobins imposed by France, under Napoleon, under the Bourbons of Parma. In his memoirs, written in the evening of his long life, which as an adolescent I read in manuscript at home, I found this final remark: "One had to do one's best for the people. It is true that it was sometimes annoying to have so many successive regimes; and yet, the more of them I saw, the more it seemed to me they differed very slightly from each other."

There we have, on two different planes of intelligence, the pre-Risorgimento Italian character, as it was created by Roman law, by its application in the struggle of our Communes, by the development of the shrewd force of inertia with which defense was possible against the Spaniards, Germans, the temporal power of the Popes. Here was a series of generations, cold, skeptical, distrustful of all exaltation which was not poetic in the Monti manner, resigned to transactions exactly as the confessional authorizes them—within the limits of personal honesty, without any duty of risking martyrdom.

If the political renaissance of the nineteenth-century Italians is due to the French Revolution, their personal renaissance coincides with romanticism. But here it must be understood that Italian romanticism was not an iconoclastic adventure against the entire past as it was with the Germans, the English and even the French—so devoted to precision.

When one says 1815, one's thoughts turn only as far as Napoleon's fall and the Congress of Vienna. For the intellectual and moral life of Italy, 1815 is the year in which was published in Milan a little book of very short poems, the *Inni sacri* (Sacred Hymns). No one paid any attention to the verses of the young Manzoni who, five years previously, in 1810, thanks to the influence of Jansenist priests, had become, or had again become, a Christian and a Catholic after a long rationalist youth spent in Paris. With his *Inni sacri,* one of which, the *"Pentecoste,"* is an immortal canticle, and some years later with his *I Promessi sposi* (The Betrothed), Manzoni showed a new way to Italy after the *Secentismo,* the Arcadia, the pseudo-classicism of the Napoleonic epoch. It was Manzoni who gave Italy, not romanticism, but an Italian romanticism.

In a certain sense, Italy had started on the road of romanticism even before Manzoni. The romantics wanted to forget the ancient classic themes; but Italy had gone mad over Ossian. The romantics wanted literature to present simple, sober human beings; but Goldoni in his hundred comedies had created the simplest and freshest types of Italian life. The romantics did not want empty forms; but Parini, Foscolo and Alfieri were already on the scene.

Manzoni impressed the mark of his genius on the new ideas. His *Inni sacri* are religious lyrics, but based on the love of humankind. *I Promessi sposi* is the first famous novel whose protagonists are just ordinary anonymous people. For us Italians, it is an unrivaled masterpiece. Why is it that the foreign

literatures do not appreciate it to the same degree? Because, as
an Italian critic, Giovita Scaldini, wrote in 1829, after the
novel's publication, one does not find oneself in it "freely
wandering through the great variety of the moral world";
one does not find himself "under the great canopy of heaven
which covers all sorts of existences, but under the roof of the
temple which covers the congregation and the altar." In which
judgment Scaldini was partly right; but his remarks would lead
one to believe in a limitation of Manzoni's art. No, it was
Manzoni himself who forced his art, as by a stern moral duty,
to preserve always a serenity and an Olympian elevation; an
art so much loftier than Goethe's, because with the German
poet it had a savor of sensuality and egotism, while in Manzoni, become Christian, it is resignation and love. Never was
a poetic genius more heroic, daring to suppress part of his
work the moment it seemed to him that it would not serve his
ideal of beauty and kindness.* Such restraint and such a sacrifice are probably unique in the history of poets and literature.

But there was perhaps a lesser reason for the lack of universal appreciation of *I Promessi sposi,* and, as it is a vulgar
reason, it is more valid. People giving too much importance to
external literary forms, it was thought that *I Promessi sposi,*
whose subtitle was *Storia milanese del XVII° secolo,* was an
historical romance like those of Sir Walter Scott, so cold, so
formal, all written with the same receipt, as a cook with his
dishes. They did not perceive that *I Promessi sposi* is a world,
like Shakespeare's tragedies, but a world disciplined by the
moral law, by the Christian doctrine that the author has imposed.

Manzoni was the first of the Italians of the eighteenth
century to synthesize in himself what was necessary for his
country: a profound knowledge of foreign thought, with which
he had been imbued during his ten-year residence in Paris, and,
at the same time, the keeping of his Italian originality. Shortly
afterward we have the same double cultural inspiration in
Cavour.

The most mysterious problem of the poet's long life, a life

* In 1900 my father published in a volume of *Scritti postumi* of A. Manzoni
some of the great chapters eliminated at the last minute by Manzoni from his
novel, whose title, before its publication as *I Promessi sposi* in 1825, had been
Gli Sposi promessi.

without the least Byronesque or Lamartinian adventures, is his conversion to Catholicism. He made of his entire life a testimony of his religion; but he covered with a veil of modesty the successive stages of his conversion; in his book on *La Morale Cattolica* there is nothing personal. At first the Jesuit faction distrusted him; they did not care to have laymen touching religious things. Those were the times of *parum de Deo,* understood in the sense that all autonomous reflection on religious problems might become dangerous for orthodoxy; furthermore, certain guardians of the Church felt that Manzoni's moral world, whence came his poetic emotion, and his vision of divine grace were inexplicable without the Jansenist origin of the poet's religion.

Later, perhaps because the last remains of Jansenism had disappeared forever, these secret resistances dissipated and Manzoni was acclaimed as the greatest Catholic poet of the nineteenth century. Not even the *"zelanti"* (zealots) of the temporal power of the popes dared object that Manzoni, as senator, eagerly voted for the law presented by Cavour to Parliament in 1861 proclaiming Rome the capital of Italy. Milanese bigots busied themselves about him, hinting that he should abstain from voting for the law: it would be so painful to the heart of Pius IX. Manzoni would invariably answer with his firm gentleness: "I am old; how would I dare present myself to God if I had avoided helping to render the Church the service of delivering it from a temporal power which had weakened it?"

I have the anecdote from Giambattista Giorgini,* who in 1846 married Vittoria, a daughter of Manzoni. Giorgini was for long years one of the dearest and most intimate friends of the poet; allied to my family—our two properties adjoined—I saw him daily during my adolescence. He was then very old, but endowed with a miraculous memory. It was about him that an Italian critic, Bonghi, wrote: "Giorgini alone could describe Manzoni's soul; but his talent is equaled only by his laziness." Giorgini died in 1906, at the age of eighty-seven. In contrast to his father-in-law, he never returned to the religion of his infancy; but at the moment of death he said slowly in Latin:

* Grandson of the Minister of State Nicolao Giorgini, quoted previously.

"Domine, commendo tibi animam meam." (Lord, to thee I commend my soul.)

A hundred times I asked Giorgini questions on the conversion of Manzoni. He always replied: "I can only answer you with the single word Manzoni used: 'Grace.'" So it remains a mystery. But at times Giorgini gave one to understand that it was a psychological mystery such as can be found in love dramas.

VIII

THE NEO-GUELPHS AND THE CATHOLIC TRADITION

MANZONI, THE ARDENT CATHOLIC, VOTED FOR THE SUPPRESsion of the temporal power of the popes, a suppression which had been one of the supreme aspirations of Dante, greatest of Catholic poets, but a Ghibelline. Was Manzoni therefore a Ghibelline or a Guelph, or, as they began to call it then, a neo-Guelph? Manzoni ignored all these divisions. His politics were simple: he wanted the independence and unity of Italy; he believed ardently in the necessity of a moral law in politics; but there is not a verse nor a phrase of his that can be cited to support such theses as Gioberti's, who at one moment saw the solution of the Italian problem in a federation under the presidency of the Pope.

Gioberti apart, even the other neo-Guelphs did not really want political solutions favorable to the Roman Curia. They were noble spirits and they wanted to show that fidelity to the Church could be in harmony with love for the independence of Italy. They pointed out in books that had a momentary celebrity that *The Divine Comedy* had been wrong; that Dante's ideal Ghibelline was contrary to the reality of Italian history exactly as it had developed in the Communes—therefore contrary to the entire course of the people and civilization of Italy. Dante's Holy Roman Empire would probably have reduced Florence to the rank of a city without commerce, and perhaps even without beauty. Carducci, whose anticlericalism would have made a Ghibelline of him, thought so, two generations after Gioberti, when he sang in his sonnet on Dante:

> *Odio il tuo santo Impero e la corona*
> *Divelta con la spada avrei di testa*
> *Al tuo buon Federico in val d'Olona.*

(I hate your Holy Empire, and the crown I would have forced with sword point from the head of your good Frederick in the vale of Olona.)

The neo-Guelphs of Manzoni's time were in reality nothing more than liberal Catholics; they were of a stamp essentially different from that of analogous groups in France, in Belgium and elsewhere. It is enough to cite the names of the leaders. Outside Italy were de Maistre (though he was half Italian), de Bonald, Gunther, Gorre—all reactionaries who had not an atom of the sincere love of liberty which inspired a Balbo, a Gioberti and even a Rosmini. I say even a Rosmini, for his writings show him to have been full of distrust of the progress of the humble, which cannot be found in the others. Almost all of the liberal Catholics of Italy had been influenced, if unwittingly, by Jansenism, like Manzoni himself. Not a few of them did not hesitate to say, or at least to think, that the temporal power diminished the moral authority of the Pope. Rosmini later knew what it had cost him to have written his famous brochure on *Le cinque piage della Chiesa* (The five plagues of the Church).

The little group of neo-Guelphs which was near becoming very powerful on the advent of Pius IX to the pontificate rendered a great service to Italy's moral unity precisely because it was a group of thinkers and not of politicians. To evaluate them, one most recall the reactionary violence in Europe after 1815 and the imprudence with which so many Catholics had identified themselves with it. In France, the reaction had been violent. It was natural, since the Revolution had begun there in 1789. It was Louis XVIII who, as a man of the eighteenth century, prided himself on being a wit, who gave the Ultras the name of "White Jacobins." The consequence was inevitable: soon nothing was more hated in France than the "priest party," so-called even among those who considered themselves true Catholics.

But the violence in Italy was still more uncompromising, more fierce, less hypocritical. It was only natural that all-powerful Austria should suppress by force the constitutional liberties at Naples, should help in the suppression of attempts at revolution in Piedmont, should cruelly strike at the Carbonari who plotted at Milan and Venice, and should urge the Pope and the Dukes of Modena and Parma to deal rigorously with the liberals. At that moment the most ardent spirits began to leave for exile and initiated the powerful centers of

Italian action at Paris, London, in Brussels, in Switzerland, in Corsica, at Corfu. Nevertheless, after they had gone the flame continued to smolder under the ashes. The Italian reaction was different from the French. In France, 1830 and the fall of Charles X were also anti-clerical movements. In Italy they fought inside the Catholic citadel. That is why Italy had a liberal Catholicism, aspiring with all its soul to independence and national liberty and taking its title of nobility from the memory of the deeds of the pontiffs who in the distant Middle Ages had protected latinity against the invading Longobards and blessed the leagues of Italian cities against the German emperors.

This movement was enormously important, since it made acceptable to millions of Christian souls the concept of Italian liberty and independence; ideas, unquestionably, natural for all Italians, but which, after more than two centuries of slumber, had been extolled by the armies of the Revolution, which pious souls considered as armies of miscreants.

The miracle of a complete and ardent acceptance, even on the part of many millions of Catholics, of the struggle for the liberty and unity of Italy is in great part due to this brilliant and honest meteor of neo-Guelph literature, despite the fact that among the champions of that struggle were anti-Catholic deists like Mazzini and ferocious anti-clericals like Garibaldi.

IX

THE THREE MAKERS OF UNITED FREE ITALY: MAZZINI, CAVOUR, GARIBALDI

THE UNITY OF ITALY ALREADY EXISTED, AFTER ITS FASHION, in the fifteenth century, as is proved by the unanimous reprobation which struck Ludovico Sforza, guilty of having invited the French to invade the peninsula—a route they learned only too well—a misfortune for us, but also a misfortune for them.

Throughout centuries of serfdom and division, unity and independence remained the dream of all minds. But why did the miracle of Italy's unification become a reality about the middle of the nineteenth century?

Mazzini and Cavour are not the least important reasons. Each in his sphere of action knew how to canalize to the service of the Italian cause the two sovereign principles of the century: the principle of liberty and the principle of nationality.

Before their time Metternich had been a much greater politician than the official books on the Risorgimento have accustomed the Italians to admit. The six or eight volumes of his memoirs, if read with attention and without prejudices, show him to be not only an exceptional diplomat but a statesman with an acute vision of his duty and even, at times, a certain prescience of Europe's future. Strong, without Bismarck's brutality, Metternich was the master of the Europe created by the Treaty of Vienna. What was it, then, that was lacking in the Rhinelander who became an Austrian? Why did he deceive himself in the most essential of his problems, that of the Austrian Empire's hegemony in Italy?

Metternich did not comprehend that the century of liberty and national independences would prove to be also the century of the middle classes; and that the middle classes were economically badly pinched behind the old customs barriers of the little states. It is undeniable that the Italian movement for union was above all spiritual, since—a rare event in Italy—

Turin at first, and Florence afterward, joyfully accepted their fate of no longer being the capital of Italy, once Rome had come under consideration.

Metternich should have been able to observe that it was not only the dangerous Mazzini who talked about Italy, but that the economic congresses that had been in the habit of holding their conferences every few years in different cities of Italy were, before 1848, demonstrating in a prudent but unequivocal way that the economic life of the entire country felt the need of a sweeping wave of unity. Imperial Austria, for her part, needed Italy to uphold the Austrian power in the Mediterranean, where Napoleon had given Venice to Austria by the Treaty of Campoformio. And Austria also needed Italy for the prestige of her Italian possessions, which made all the German peoples so respectful of the Hapsburg crown. The Emperor at Vienna not only possessed Lombardy, Venetia and the Trentino, but he was the real ruler of the duchies of Modena and Parma and the Grand-duchy of Tuscany, through dynasties which recognized him as their head. He was the master in the Pontifical States, as Pius IX learned without delay, to his cost, when he decided in 1848 to act as an Italian and as an Italian prince.

From all this one may deduce the very great courage of a Mazzini and a Cavour when they undertook the struggle. They succeeded because they knew how to identify the two concepts of liberty and independence.

Let us begin by studying Mazzini the man, inasmuch as his life was a sublime example of absolute devotion to a single idea: the resurrection of Italy. In studying the man we ought particularly to study the *esule* (exile), that constant and tragic figure of Italy's political history.

Each of us retains some memory of our childhood or of our adolescence which later becomes either a warning or a ray of light.

So it happened to Mazzini when he was sixteen. Born in Genoa in 1805, frail and delicate in the early years of his childhood, but with a precocious and lively intelligence, the young dreamer was walking one Sunday afternoon in the year 1821 in a narrow street of old Genoa with his mother, Maria Mazzini, who remained all her life his most intimate friend. At the street corner they encountered a group of men, evidently strangers in Genoa, all showing in their tired faces an expression at once fierce and sad. Suddenly one of them approached Maria Mazzini and her son; with an inborn dignity he held out a white handkerchief and said: "I pray you, for the Italian outlaws." The mother understood, and silently, gave all her money; other passers-by gave after her. The gentlemen beggars were the vanquished combatants of the Piedmontese insurrection of 1821, those men who had believed that Charles Albert of Savoy was ready to lead the revolt in Italy against the Austrians. At the last minute Charles Albert had changed his mind, and the unfortunate insurgents had reassembled in Genoa with hopes of being able to embark for Spain—which had become liberal—and escape the prosecutions in which so many of them were later condemned to death.

"That day," Mazzini wrote years later, when he began his short autobiographical preface for each of the succeeding volumes of his *Scritti*, "that day was the first when, confusedly, came to my mind, I shall not say an idea of the nation and liberty, but the thought that one might, and by that fact, one should fight for one's own country. . . . The idea that there existed in my country an evil that was consuming it and that must be fought, the idea that in this combat I should perhaps have to take a part, that day struck my mind, never to leave it. The sight of these outlaw patriots, of whom several later became my friends, haunted me night and day. I would have given anything in the world to have been able to follow them. I did my best to study the history of their generous undertaking and the causes of their defeat. I tried to collect names and facts. They had been betrayed, abandoned by those who had themselves sworn to concentrate all their strength for the attempted revolt. The Italian king himself, Charles Felix of Savoy, had summoned the Austrians. . . . The sum of all these details that I assembled led me to think: Would it have been possible to conquer them, if everyone had done his duty? Why not start all over again? That idea possessed me constantly and the impossibility of perceiving in what manner I could transpose it into action weighed heavily on my soul."

A romantic style, the style of the generation, but a sincere style; Mazzini never lied. These thoughts—his parents later confirmed them—continued to haunt the young university student who went into mourning for his country.

Later Mazzini wrote, referring to those days: "My mind was full of visions of drama and of romances that I felt I could write; but the shame of our national humiliation turned me away from them. . . ." From his ultimate formula, *Pensiero e Azione* (Thought and Action), he chose action and joined the Carbonari in 1829. Initiated with the dramatic ritual of secret societies, he obeyed, he worked; but his soul was not satisfied. Apropos of this epoch, he wrote: "Our leaders splashed about without having any definite aim, hoping to get liberty even from a Louis Philippe. We young fellows found our only pleasure buying rifles and making cartridges, waiting a conflict which was inevitable."

The government had its spies among the Carbonari; one of them, a Frenchman, betrayed Mazzini, who was arrested. The police had long suspected him. "What the devil," the governor of Genoa demanded of Mazzini's father, a worthy professor of anatomy at the University, "what the devil is your son thinking about when he walks alone at night? We don't like people who think, if we don't know their thoughts; we don't like young men who walk about alone at night."

Mazzini was taken away to the fortress of Savona, where he consoled himself by reading Dante, the Bible, Tacitus and Byron and by taming the sparrows that came through the bars into his cell. His case came up before the Senate of Turin; he was found guilty, but as the public prosecutor had only one witness and two were required, the court had to acquit him. This single minor decision—based on respect for forms— proves how unjust it has been to complain of Fascism by comparing it to former tyrants. At Turin the Savoy monarchs, at Naples the Bourbons, in the duchies the Hapsburg-Estes were intolerably cruel, but cruel in accordance with their laws; they violated them, so to speak, never. Naturally the Bourbons, like the Savoys, violated their constitutions, as princes always do; they had confessors to absolve them.

Mazzini acquitted, Charles Albert and his police committed their greatest error, they allowed the young conspirator to go into exile; in their eyes he was a little cracked and they were satisfied to be rid of him. In fact, the greater part of the future history of Italy derived from the long exile of Mazzini. It was in Switzerland and France, and chiefly in England, that the Genoan dreamer became the greatest master of civic dignity that Italians have ever known.

Shortly before Mazzini's acquittal an insurrection organized by the Carbonari had broken out in the duchies of Modena and Parma and in the *Legazioni,* the provinces near the Po belonging to the States of the Church. After three weeks of the revolt the Pope and the Dukes began to tremble for their thrones. But the revolution was at the mercy of an Austrian attack; naively, the liberal leaders had counted upon the promise of France to avert such an invasion since non-intervention was the essential principle of Louis Philippe's foreign policy. The French cabinet had promised the Italian Carbonari that if the Austrian Empire violated this principle France would declare war against it. But at the last moment Louis Philippe, with typical Bourbon disloyalty, intimated to Metternich that his "non-intervention" was nothing but words, and some weeks later, despite the courageous resistance of Italian recruits, the Austrians who had entered the valley of the Po suppressed the insurrection.

The main fault of the Carbonari leaders was to count on the support of France rather than on the Italian masses, the people. They were honest patriots, but most of them still cherished an admiration for Napoleon, who during his "reign" on the island of Elba let it be understood, as we have seen, that he regretted not having been more "Italian." They believed in princes, in diplomacy, foreign aid—was not Lafayette in France an ardent Carbonaro? What they lacked was a religious inspiration. Mazzini replaced the Carbonari, which was a political system, by the *Giovine Italia*—young Italy—which he created as a moral and religious system.

The entire Mazzinian school never deviated from this concept. In order to act swiftly for Italy's good, Mazzini preached: What finer propaganda than insurrection crowned by martyrdom? What more noble fate than to give one's life for Italy and humanity?

On the practical side he added: Everything for the people and with the people; for the unity of Italy, for the Italian republic, without compromise and without hope of foreign assistance.

During the years preceding the great explosion of 1848, aided by his *Giovine Italia* and from his hiding places in France and England, Mazzini was the inspirational source of all the events and the noblest thought of Italy.

Mazzini's moral generosity, so rare in political leaders, had taught him that the only way to get men to risk their lives and die was to appeal to their disinterested motives. Mazzini offered the Italians a "religion, a faith and an apostleship"; he told them that victory, permanent victory, comes only with respect for principles, respect for justice and truth, by sacrifice and constancy in sacrifice. And in addition he gave his perpetual recommendation: "As individuals and as a nation you have a mission given you by God."

Contrary to the Carbonari, he saw and proclaimed the social aspect of the Italian problem. "Revolutions," he wrote, "ought to be made by the people and for the people; as long as revolutions continue to be as they now are, the heritage and monopoly of a single class, undertaken uniquely to substitute one aristocracy for another, we shall never find salvation." The cry of the poor was always with him. "I see," wrote Mazzini, "the people pass before my eyes in their livery of misery and moral subjection, in rags and famished, picking up the crumbs that wealth has insolently cast them, or lost to reason in a riot and the intoxication of a wild and brutal joy suffused with anger; and I recall that these brutalized faces also bear the mark of God, the imprint of a mission equal to our own. I raise my vision to the future and I foresee the people arising in their majesty, brothers in the same faith, with a sole bond of equality and love, and an ideal of civic virtue which daily increases in beauty and power. I foresee the people of the future who have not been spoiled by luxury, who have not been driven by misery, conscious of their rights and duties. And before these visions my heart beats with anguish for the present even as it glorifies the future."

It is impossible not to feel that these lines are inspired by a love that Karl Marx never felt through his somber prophesies, often dictated solely by hate. But it is almost equally impossible to maintain that Mazzini's social (or socialist) idea is marked by any profound original thought. Truth obliges one to admit that most of Mazzini's formulas of political philosophy stem from earlier sources. The idea of republican unity had been known before him by Italian Jacobins disgusted by the egoistic and shabby diplomacy of the Directory and the frauds of Bonaparte. The concept of nationality had already been formulated by German historians, and, in a certain sense, for Italy herself, by the first of our modern thinkers, Machiavelli. That formula of an "Italian primacy" which Mazzini often proclaimed was one in which he did not himself believe. In his eyes—if not in those of the naive and emphatic Gioberti —the *"primato"* was chiefly a myth necessary to encourage a nation that needed to recover from a long and somber period of servitude; and it was at the same time a means of dispelling the hopes, then existing not only among the Carbonari but among the neo-Guelphs as well, of a French "initiative," which would mean a French hegemony. His socialist views, quite natural for a spirit as generous as his, he took from Saint-Simon.

But he was greater than all these thinkers or apostles whose works he had studied, by reason of his moral greatness—his was the grandeur of the man who believes, writes and acts. From his poor lodgings in London's Tottenham Court Road he rose to a position of intellectual, moral and political influence unique in Europe. Metternich was the most powerful man in Europe when he said of Mazzini, and of Mazzini alone: "I had armies which fought heroically, though composed of different races, I succeeded in uniting kings and emperors, tsars and sultans—and the Pope. Many a time it was difficult. But no one gave me more trouble than a brigand of an Italian, emaciated, pale, poor, but eloquent as a tempest, inspired as an apostle, sly as a thief, and as tireless as a lover—his name is Giuseppe Mazzini."

Mazzini's great period of Italian activity stopped with the events of 1848–49; after 1848–49 the Italian renown of Mazzini increased no further. Not only was Cavour in power in Turin, having created there a new prestige for the Savoys, but Louis Napoleon, the man Mazzini most despised, was now Emperor of the French, and there were some people in Italy who began to think that the old Carbonaro of the Romagna revolution of 1831 would one day think of his oath to work for Italy. However, in 1849 an event occurred that revealed Mazzini's personality in a novel and unexpected light; the conspirator, the dreamer, the idealist became transformed into a practical statesman, into a far-seeing chief of government, into a first triumvir of the Roman Republic.

Mazzini had left Milan at war—where his presence had not been fortunate—for a Tuscany where he found it hard to achieve an understanding with a demagogic dictator, Guerrazzi. Meanwhile Rome had proclaimed the Republic, inscribing at the head of its records the *Dio e Popolo* (God and the People) of Mazzini, who quitted Florence for Rome, where he arrived March 5, 1849, slipping into the city by the Porta del Popolo without being seen. "Filled with emotion and like a worshiper, but feeling," he writes, "a breath of new life" after the disillusion of Milan and Tuscany.

How right he was! Without seeking the post, he was immediately elected one of the triumvirs and shortly became the chief and the master. He formed a government which should be worthy of his life ideal: "Here," he warned the Assembly, "we cannot be moral mediocrities. He suppressed intolerance, class conflict, attacks against property and against the churches and priests. His attitude toward the Catholic Church gives the lie to the legends depicting him as an anti-clerical fanatic. Was it the necessity of suppressing all pretexts for intervention on the part of a foreign Catholic power, or his innate respect for Christianity? The fact is that he soon succeeded in converting to the Republic's cause several priests and monks. With the money realized from the nationalization of Church properties, he bettered the salaries of the poor clergy; under his government religious services and processions continued without interruption.

Confronted before long by the most contemptible of the political crimes of the nineteenth century—the expedition against the Roman Republic that the fanatical Catholics in France imposed on Louis Napoleon—Mazzini was able to combat the French while suppressing the slightest anti-Catholic manifestations. One day during the siege, fearing an imminent French advance on the city, the Romans near the San Pancrazio gate had taken some confessional boxes from the churches to make barricades. Mazzini, who was passing by, said: "Remember that in these confessionals your mothers and mothers' mothers have for generations heard words of comfort," and the confessionals were immediately returned to their places. To a nun who wrote him, fearing the suppression of the convents, he replied: "Fear nothing; pray God for our country and for men of good will."

With the Pope himself, who had fled to Gaeta, Mazzini showed how ready he was for any reasonable compromise; anticipating Visconti Venosta in 1870–71, he tried to persuade the Assembly to define the guarantees to be offered to the Supreme Pontiff, and declared himself willing to take into consideration any suggestion that the Catholic powers desired to make in their own behalf. "Our duty," said he, "is to make a distinction between the Pope and the Prince, and to maintain our rights as Italians without using violence against the Catholic faith."

With regard to his diplomatic notes to foreign governments, and even to General Oudinot, the treacherous commander of the French expedition, Lord Palmerston said that they were "masterpieces of reasoning and dignity." The French expeditionary force was double the strength of the Roman army and was armed with the most modern artillery of the period; Mazzini soon realized that a long resistance was impossible, but he decided to leave a great example—and he and his volunteers nobly succeeded in that attempt. Whoever studies all the acts of the Roman Republic may possibly criticize Garibaldi's tactics, or the demagogism of some leaders like Sterbini; but there is not a decision, not a speech of Mazzini which does not excite admiration for a man who had had no experience in practical politics. When the end of the Republic seemed imminent, after a siege in which several thousand heroes resisted and often repulsed the attacks of a well-organized modern army, Mazzini succeeded in his last miracle: all, patricians as well as plebeians, saints like Father Ugo Bassi and sinners like Ciceruacchio, fought and died side by side, moved by a common love for Italy and for Rome.

In the last days, when the private houses of Rome were bombarded by the French, six thousand women offered their services to succor the wounded; and when the populous Trastevere was in part destroyed by the besiegers' bombs, Mazzini ordered that the poor families of the Trasteverini should be lodged in the sumptuous palaces of the Roman princes, on the simple promise that there would be no thefts or vandalism; the promise was given in the name of *Dio e Popolo* and was scrupulously observed.

When the French entered Rome, Garibaldi began his famous retreat toward the Adriatic with 3,000 men who had refused to surrender. Mazzini remained hidden in Rome for several days; he hoped to be killed by the French, but finally his friends persuaded him to leave the city. Giving the slip to the French police, he escaped again to England.

Mazzini's second exile lasted, so to speak, uninterruptedly until his death on March 10, 1872.

To understand Mazzini, to understand the significance of his operations in Italy and his operations during his exile, we should never forget that there are two Mazzinis: the first, who worked for the Italy of his day; the second, who worked for posterity and the world.

As I have said, Mazzini ceased in 1849 to be an important political factor as regards Italy. He was not even satisfied with the unity and independence of Italy attained a decade later; he feared that the monarchy would spoil the good that had been obtained. "It matters little to me," he wrote to Daniel Stern, "that Italy, a territory of so many square kilometers, consumes its wheat or cabbages, paying less for them; Rome matters little to me unless a great European initiative should come out of it. What does matter to me is that Italy should be great and good, moral and virtuous, that she should succeed in fulfilling a mission in the world."

Italy had disappointed him in the field of practical politics in following Cavour who, viewing Europe as she was, was in the habit of saying (and this was an indirect response to Mazzini) : "I am resigned; there are in this continent three powers interested in undoing the *status quo*, France, Russia and Prussia, and two which are interested in preserving it, Austria and England. I regret that the former are not more liberal, but what can one do about it? I cannot side with the other two."

The rest of Europe ended by disillusioning Mazzini quite as much as Italy had done.

In Hungary, a country which had had a great significance for him and his friends, his friend Kossuth was forgotten in his Italian exile; and the relative independence of the Magyar nation was achieved in 1867 by Deak, Kossuth's enemy, with the consent and support of the Austrian Emperor.

In Germany, not the old liberals of Frankfort, but the King of Prussia and the cruel genius of Bismarck made an iron unity, and the old liberals bowed to their new masters like satisfied courtiers.

The Poles were, as always, slaves.

And slaves, too, were the Czechs.

The Yugoslavs, regarding whom Mazzini had written a series of eloquent *Letters,* were still divided under different flags.

Mazzini's ideal Socialism was increasingly waved aside by masses and leaders who sought nothing but material advantages. It was the cause of their defeat when the Fascist storm broke, for men die for ideas, not for a salary. If Mazzini had only tried to win to his cause the Italian peasant, as Bakunin once suggested to him in London! But Mazzini had replied: "For the moment nothing can be done in rural Italy." This was his worst tactical mistake, and it will—if we are guilty of it—be the worst mistake of those who will succeed Fascism in Italy. Vague promises to our peasants, instead of deeds, can only mean a disaster for Italy, for Italy's liberty, for social progress.

A literal narration of Mazzini's career might lead one to believe that it was a complete failure. He admitted it himself, implicitly, in a moving letter addressed on April 5, 1853, to one of his disciples, Emilio Visconti Venosta, who had let him know, after the vain revolt of March, 1853, at Milan, that he no longer believed in the Mazzini tactics. A reading of the letter is tragic, even to this day. Visconti was probably right; but I recall very well the old Marquis Visconti Venosta, an honor to European diplomacy, telling me in 1906 at Algeciras, where I was his young secretary at the Moroccan Conference: "That letter and its four pages I can still recall it by heart; and I often think of the sorrow I felt in having had to separate myself from Mazzini."

Yes, Mazzini's abortive risings, after 1849, perhaps did

more harm than good; but even the old Visconti, then a great historic figure of official European diplomacy, admitted in our discussions: Who can measure the evil and the good? Who can tell how great was the regenerating influence of Mazzini in the hearts of millions of Italians, even when his efforts resulted not only in defeat, but in complete futility?

The French Revolution had exalted the Rights of Man; Mazzini preached the Duties of Man. He purged patriotism of all the egoistic ideas that the French, despite many fine words, had introduced in it. He was the first to include moral considerations in the nascent conflict between capital and labor.

When Mazzini's action became less essential to an Italy which had found Cavour, exile was an aid to the Genoan in his work. He formed a democratic European central committee which, after 1850, launched appeals to the "peoples of Europe," inasmuch as they were "individuals of humanity," exhorting them to elect democratic assemblies which could father the "representative congress of free nations." That seemed then a Utopia; but today, after World War II, these are the very ideas that practical statesmen must try to spread through the world. Mazzini, after all, was no more of a Utopian than Lord Clarendon when that British statesman tried in vain at the Congress of Paris to impose on Europe the principle of mediation before recourse to war.

Even the stupid attempts that were made by irresponsible persons in the United States in 1942 and 1943 to revive the possibilities of a Hapsburg empire in central Europe prove that most of Mazzini's pages could still be profitably meditated by leaders of currents of opinion in the world; for example, his pamphlet *Italy, Austria and the Pope,* in which, in 1844, he replied to the English Secretary of State who had opened his letters in order to inform Vienna of the plans of *Giovine Italia.* In this passionate pamphlet Mazzini defined imperial Austria as "the Chinese principle of immobility," and to describe to the free English the power of the Hapsburgs exactly as it was, he simply reproduced a part of the Austrian catechism for the children of Italian schools:

"Q.—How should subjects behave toward their sovereigns?

"A.—Subjects should behave toward their sovereigns exactly as faithful slaves toward their masters.

"Q.—Why should they behave like slaves?

"A.—Because the sovereign is their master and his power extends over their property as over their persons.

"Q.—Is it a blessing that God grants us in giving us good and Christian superiors and kings?

"A.—Yes, it is one of the greatest blessings that God can grant when he gives us good and Christian kings."

Mazzini's private life, the sacrifices of his forty years of exile, were the noblest witnesses in support of his precepts. Born for love, art, happiness, he renounced his home, his family, marriage, to dedicate his life to the apostolic task to which he had consecrated himself. During his exile in London he evoked the admiration of England's noblest spirits and the filial love of the little Italian organ grinders who were still victims of the white-slave trade. He learned to love England profoundly, and to feel at home in London.

But when he felt that a new and irrevocable death sentence had been passed against him, replacing the old sentences of Charles Albert's tribunals, he returned to Italy to die. After some weeks the end came on the morning of March 10, 1878, at Pisa, where, in a room with whitewashed walls, he was surrounded by a few faithful friends. His rambling words were hard to understand, but in his final moments his voice again became clear; he suddenly sat up and, looking fixedly at his friends cried: "Si, si, credo in Dio." (Yes, yes, I believe in God.) He fell back and expired.

Historians often emphasize the antithesis between Mazzini, the idealist, and Cavour, the empiric; some of them describe a Cavour who did not rally to the idea of Italian unity until 1860.

Here is what the young Count de Cavour, an officer relegated to a lonely Alpine garrison, wrote a kinsman in 1831: "The Italians must regenerate themselves; their moral nature has been corrupted by an ignoble Spanish and Austrian domination. . . . But the young aspire to become a nation. Great sacrifices, great efforts will be required. A future war will again make us a nation." That was in 1831; the Italians were already fighting at Bologna and in the Romagna against the Austrians and Papal mercenaries.

It is the same with social questions, of which one finds no trace in Cavour's works; yet in 1858 he wrote a friend: "If it were not that I feel that Italy's national problem is in my hands, I would perhaps have preferred to devote myself to bettering the condition of field and factory workers; there can be no liberty without social justice." What other statesman of the middle of the nineteenth century had such ideas? Twenty-five years before, the young Cavour had written in his journal:

"We, who have no religious faith, must expend our tenderness to the profit of humanity."

But here we must limit ourselves to studying in Cavour the antithesis of Mazzini: Cavour the victorious negotiator.

The daily action of diplomacy—in the negotiation of a treaty, or in an international conference—is indefinable; it is a matter of instinct. Only instinct will tell one if on a particular day it is prudent to be audacious, almost insolent, and whether on some other day it is not better to keep silent, while knowing that one could show that one is right.

The most perfect masterpiece of diplomatic action that I know of is that of Cavour during two months of the Congress of Paris in 1856, after the Crimean War. He had against him the fact that he was invited to the Congress solely because he had succeeded in sending an Italian contingent to fight against the Russians; and he did not sit at the Congress on an equal footing with the plenipotentiaries of the great powers. He could only speak when the others were willing to admit that the representative of little Piedmont had something to say. Yet it was he, Count Cavour, who was the victor at the Congress.

Before and after, Cavour made some mistakes, but they were small ones. At Paris he was constantly inspired by his genius. To study Cavour's work in Paris is to describe him.

He himself created his whole position; luck served him at only one point. Perceiving quickly that Count Walewski and the other ministers of Napoleon III all detested Italy, he found at once two men who kept secret contacts open for him with Napoleon III, one of them being Prince Jerome Napoleon and the other Dr. Conneau, still more of an intimate of the sovereign than his anti-clerical cousin. Conneau in particular was a constant intermediary between Cavour and the weak and changeable sovereign. Count Arese had the good sense to suggest Conneau to Cavour; Arese, the great Lombard landed proprietor and disinterested friend of Queen Hortense who had refused an offer of the Emperor to demand of the Emperor Francis Joseph that his—Arese's—properties be spared from seizure. Arese had replied: "Ask it for all or for none." And this pride obliged even the Empress who hated liberal Italy to respect the old friend of her mother-in-law.

At the first meetings of the Congress, Cavour showed himself very modest, keeping in the background. On the few occasions when he had to speak, he did it as briefly as possible. True, Count Buol, the Austrian plenipotentiary, perhaps because he had known Cavour at Turin, soon confided to his colleagues: "No, no, I know him; he will give us threads to untangle." Cavour behaved courteously toward the pompous Austrian, but one day he tossed out this phrase that killed his imperial colleague: "Count Buol talks as if it were Austria that had captured Sevastopol."

Cavour's problem was formidable. How could he some day rise and speak freely about the rights of nationalities, foreign dominations, the rights of people, in an assembly composed of old diplomats, conservative by the very nature of their profession, trained to respect treaties and fearing to wound one of the most powerful of their colleagues, Austria?

Cavour waited until the last moment. When the signing of the treaty of peace seemed imminent he decided to address, not the Congress directly, but the plenipotentiaries of France and Great Britain exclusively, with an identical note on the situation in Italy. The principal argument of his note was the occupation of the Legations in the Papal States. This point allowed him to take his stand on legality rather than on nationality; he offended less. But the fact remained that for the first time his note put in question the very existence of the temporal power.

This Cavour did on the Italian plane. At the same time he was equally directing a policy that could be defined as Piedmontese, endeavoring to obtain the annexation to Piedmont of the duchies of Parma and Modena. In this he failed, and it was perhaps for the best that he did.

The matter of Austria's seizure of the property of Lombard

patriots was at the same time Italian and Piedmontese. When Count Buol spoke of an "amnesty including almost all the cases," Cavour instantly replied: "No, not agreed, if there is a single exception." The next day he went to Napoleon and gave him to understand that he was not terrified by the idea of a war with Austria, even without allies. Lord Clarendon, after a series of conversations, gave him this answer: "You are perfectly right about Italy; only it must not be talked about." Cavour replied that he had decided upon a war "to the knife" (he used the English phrase) with Austria, and declared that England would be obliged to aid Italy. To which Lord Clarendon replied: "Certainly, with all our hearts."

When Cavour returned to Turin, d'Azeglio observed that he had come back "without the least little duchy in his pocket." That was true, and that was the defeat of the Piedmontese part of Cavour's policy at the Congress, but he had triumphed as an Italian. Italy's feelings were expressed by the Tuscan patriots who sent his bust to him with the famous words of Dante engraved beneath it:

"Colui che la difese a viso aperto" (He who defended her boldly).

Paris gave the measure of Cavour's diplomatic genius. Then came the war; but wars are poor times for statesmen, contrary to the general opinion. During wars the course of events is forced. It was in 1860 that Cavour showed his moral grandeur.

Garibaldi had conquered Sicily and the Kingdom of Naples with his Thousand. Now was the time to consummate unity— the statesmen of the Right wanted to do it with more prestige for the King than for Garibaldi. Baron Ricasoli (who certainly had nothing of the timidity of the reactionary in his noble character) telegraphed Cavour: "The ideal solution would be to proclaim the dictatorship of the King." And what was more imprudent, he said to the King himself: "It is humiliating for you to accept half of Italy as a gift, even though it be the gift of a hero." Ricasoli thought that Garibaldi himself would bow to the dictatorship of the King, proclaimed with the aim of pursuing an Italian policy to the limit; and he was right, for Garibaldi was the most disinterested of men and, being a romantic, he believed in the legend of the king. But Cavour objected. "What would the liberal world say of a *coup d'état?* Haven't we always wanted to achieve Italian unity without going through a Cromwell? Italy must win her independence without sacrificing her liberty; monarchic absolutism must be abolished without falling into a revolutionary despotism. Only from Parliament must we draw the power to govern above factions." This was his reply to Ricasoli and—in a more elementary form—to the King.

Friends and admirers close to Cavour kept insisting: more power to you! (The King was forgotten.)

Cavour replied that they counted too much on him and too little on the power of liberty; that he had no confidence in dictatorships, and still less in civil dictatorships; that more things could be done with a good parliament than with absolute power, and that thirteen years of power had taught him that a ministry with nothing to fear from the revelations of a deputy, and one not afraid of extreme parties, gained more than it lost with a parliament in session. "I never feel so weak as when the Chamber is closed."

About this time Cavour wrote Madame de Circourt: "If the Italians had to choose a dictator they would choose Garibaldi, not me. . . . What is more, I cannot betray my origin, nor deny the principles of my entire life. I am the son of Liberty; what I am I owe to Liberty. If the statue of Liberty must be veiled, let others do it, not me."

Garibaldi, meanwhile, asked the King to deprive Cavour of power. (Garibaldi actually thought the King could do such a thing, and honest as he was, perhaps believed it because of some twaddle the King must have uttered to him in his bragging manner.) Cavour did not reply directly; he appealed to Parliament. "A man," he stated, "that the entire nation loves declares that he has no confidence in us; it is for Parliament to declare whether or not we should retire."

Parliament by an immense majority voted for Cavour, at the same time passing a law authorizing the Government to accept the immediate annexation of provinces of central and southern Italy which might express by a plebiscite their will to unite under Victor Emmanuel's scepter. Many deputies feared that Garibaldi, dictator at Naples, would not yield, but Cavour thought better of him. On October 13, 1860, two days after the law was passed, Garibaldi assembled all his counselors, the moderates and the republicans; the discussion continued interminably. At length the dictator arose and serenely declared: *"Si faccia l'Italia!* (Let Italy come into being) and let the electors for a plebiscite be convoked." He did more than that; he dictated his last decree:

"The two Sicilies form an integral part of Italy, one and indivisible, under the constitutional King Victor Emmanuel and his successors." The plebiscite sanctioned the decree.

Republicans of the Puritan type, like Mazzini, were bitterly disappointed; a unique occasion to found the Republic had been lost.

Of the triad who made Italy, Garibaldi was the man of the people. He was republican by natural feeling, not on account of theoretical reasons, yet he helped to create a monarchy which alone in Europe, and especially thanks to him, could exist only as a democratic magistracy—to such a degree that it signed its death warrant when it became an accomplice of the adventurer who strangled liberty. Garibaldi was likewise a man of the people in his faith in progress and justice; he was as Christian as St. Francis of Assisi, his rage against priestly governments being merely an expression of primitive Christianity.

Like Mazzini, Garibaldi was a great lover and a great hater. Cavour, who always had the power of complete understanding, never hated; at most he despised, as when, passing judgment on the honest but mentally destitute demagogue in great part responsible for the defeat of 1849, he wrote: "A democracy without intelligence and without energy imagined it could defend liberty with phrases and proclamations."

Mazzini alone could elevate men's minds. Garibaldi alone could temper their hearts for the battlefield. But only Cavour could direct all efforts, including those—at times divergent—of the apostle and the hero.

Cavour remains the greatest statesman Italy has ever produced, for in him is combined the practical genius of a Mazarin with the tenacious patience of a Washington.

X

THE PRINCES

WITH THE ONE EXCEPTION OF CHARLES ALBERT OF SAVOY, who awaited his "star," the other sovereigns of Italy had everything to lose by the country's independence; it was, therefore, natural that they should combat the Risorgimento. From the most powerful, like the King of Naples, to the weakest, like the Duke of Modena, all were equally ferocious opponents of the liberal movement. Their persecutions were often frightful, their breaches of promise always ignoble; but they thought they were defending the truth when as a matter of fact they were defending their positions if not their persons; Italian historians have exaggerated in depicting them as monsters.

In Oriani's book, *La Lotte politica in Italia,* which Fascism pretended to have discovered, one reads, for example, that Ferdinand II, the King of Naples, was only "an Austrian viceroy, protected by the Austrians and confiding only in them." * The truth is that Ferdinand II especially distrusted Piedmont, and that he always tried to maintain his complete independence against Austria, France and England, indeed against all nations challenging it. As for the Duke of Modena, Francis IV, it is true that he abominated everything that had any suggestion of liberalism and that he exiled or decapitated his noblest subjects; but in private life his word was sacred. My great-grandfather, suspected by the Duke because of his liberal ideas and entreated by his friends to leave the duchy and go south into tolerant Tuscany, instead went up to Modena, the capital, and asked the Duke whether he might remain on his estates, keeping his opinions to himself. The Duke replied: "If I have your word that you will no longer speak publicly of politics, nothing will happen to you." Characteristically of those times, before returning to Lunigiana my great-grandfather thought it best to have the promise confirmed by the Duke's confessor. This incident also confirms

* Chapter V.

that there was more than one solid base on which one could rely; whereas, under Fascism, with which these former despotic regimes have been compared, to their discredit, all was quicksand, uncertainty and treason.

As the earlier regimes were merely a negative element in Italy's history, at Naples as at Modena, at Parma as at Lucca, the Savoys, at Turin, alone must be studied, even in their reactionary epoch, since from this state emerged the kings of united Italy.

On the fall of Napoleon, King Victor Emmanuel returned to his capital Turin from Sardinia, where he had found cover during the storm and where he did nothing toward improving the island's condition. The very day he returned to his Madama Palace he reestablished all the dignities and dignitaries existing at the time of his flight in 1798. A courtier hesitated: "Where can they be found?" The King replied: "Look them up in the Palmaverde of 1798." (The Palmaverde was the court calendar.)

In the Piedmont of the post-Napoleonic period we find a condition contrary to that of France: of the two Piedmontese kings of the Holy Alliance, the first was as insensate and intolerant as France's Charles X; while the second, Charles Felix, had the benevolent tolerance of Charles X's predecessor, Louis XVIII. Charles Felix was the last king of the elder branch of the Savoys. In the Senate at Rome, where an aulic and unrealistic royalist lyricism was the fashion, it always amused me to observe that no one stopped to read the inscription that Charles Felix had had inscribed on a medallion of himself: *"Postremus styrpis suae"* (The last of his race), though this medal with others of Piedmont was visible in a medal case in one of the Senate halls. Without possessing Louis XVIII's culture, Charles Felix governed like him; for he too had lost the assurance of the eighteenth-century kings in the revolutionary storm of the Napoleonic period. His successor was Charles Albert of Carignan, of a younger branch, no member of which had for centuries succeeded to the throne. Compromises of Charles Albert with the Carbonari in 1821 had made him so suspect to the elder branch that Charles Felix —whose inscription on his medal shows how much he loved his very distant cousin—agreed to authorize for him the title of

Royal Highness only three months before his own death, in January, 1831. Things of this sort are very grave matters between princes. Three years before, Châteaubriand, coming to Italy, declared that the country was everywhere "enchained, and ripe for a revolution." It was natural that Charles Albert, suspected by Austria on account of his momentary liberalism in 1831, suspected by the liberals for having abandoned them, should maneuver without much dignity. One can only judge the man by what he did in 1848, that year which is richer in historic Italian potentialities than the two or three centuries preceding it.

The epoch of 1848 had its poets and its panegyrists. And even discounting a few of their enthusiasms, they bring to us, almost intact, the beauty and the force of that famous year.

It cannot be denied that the war that Charles Albert conducted in 1848 against the *Tedeschi* (Germans) was badly conceived and ill-conducted. The fault lay not so much in military deficiencies, which were serious, as in the fact that Charles Albert, a hesitating or limited intelligence, never could understand that it was vain to speak of Italian independence without also speaking of Italian liberty. One had either to accept both ideas or else be satisfied to act like the Duke of Modena. In the nineteenth century one could no longer attempt to eat the Italian artichoke, even leaf by leaf, save with the sauce of liberty. The worst fault of Charles Albert, who vacillated so before giving a constitution to his people in 1848, was not to have understood this fact.

The war of 1848 rendered the Italians the great service of transforming the Italian question into an European question, and of proving that regional states, from the duchies to the Kingdom of Naples, and especially the temporal power of the popes, had become incompatible with the Italian national conscience. It was in 1848 that the Italians saw clearly. Vanished were the neo-Guelph illusions of an Italian role for the Papacy; but also vanished were the old Savoyan tactics of aggrandizement at the expense of Lombardy.

As regards Charles Albert, it is henceforth proved that the Piedmontese army had not been prepared either militarily or morally for a national war; that the Piedmontese intervention was tardy and slow, to such a point that Cavour exclaimed in his *Risorgimento:* "Each day we lose is a disaster"; that Charles Albert's anti-liberal generals sabotaged the efforts of the Lombard volunteers, and that the King did not intervene to impress upon his military men their new duties; that the constant determination of Charles Albert to separate the cause of liberty from that of independence paralyzed all enthusiasm and all wills. At Milan the antithesis between a dynastic policy of annexation and a large policy of national union seemed obvious to everyone; and at a distance one cannot but admire the patience and abnegation of the Lombards. Not only the bitter criticisms of Cattaneo, but even the malignant ones of Brofferio seem today justified. One wonders—since Charles Albert was not destitute of intelligence—why it was that he failed to grasp that it was mad to believe in the possibility of an easy annexation of Lombardy, when the memory, still so very vivid, of the French betrayal of Campoformio and the new national idea would have made a straight-out Lombard annexation seem like a crime of dynastic egoism.

When Charles Albert was defeated at Novara on March 23, 1849, the Austrian conditions for an armistice were so hard that he preferred to abdicate the same evening. His oldest son, Victor Emmanuel II, succeeded him.

A myth is more quickly formed in the case of kings than in that of other actors of historic roles, for they are symbols that synthesize currents of ideas or interests. Thus it is that, although Victor Emmanuel's son, Humbert I, exercised very little political and still less intellectual and moral influence on his times, the term "Humbertian Italy" has come into common usage. Naturally then, myths developed inevitably about an adventurous life like that of Victor Emmanuel, who began his career as king of a small, defeated country, and died twenty-seven years later in the Quirinal at Rome, king of a great nation. He was a devout Catholic, yet he dispossessed the Pope of his estates; he was, as Duke of Savoy, the inheritor of the anti-liberal policy of his father, still it did not prevent him at the end of his life from selecting for his cabinets men of the Left. Furthermore, the myths had in Victor Emmanuel himself a clever, even if sometimes slightly vulgar propagandist; in that he was a unique exception in his family. His father, Charles Albert, was the most hesitant and secretive of men, while it did not even cross the minds of Victor Emmanuel's son Humbert and his grandson Victor Emmanuel III that there was such a thing as shrewd publicity.

Victor Emmanuel II was the typical bragging type of Provençal village hunter who reduces everything to its relation to himself. The honest arch-royalist Lamarmore put even his physical courage in doubt after the campaign of 1866, and the Tuscan statesmen of 1860 were shocked by his utter ignorance of Italian history. Having to choose between loyal servitors like d'Azeglio and crafty flatterers like Rattazzi, he invariably chose the flatterers. In later years, when he became more and more addicted to the chase and to ancillary loves, a prime minister having suggested that he attach to his retinue an embassy secretary to bring official matters to his attention, and having submitted the names of two or three men qualified for the post—among them a young Viscount Tornielli, who in 1896 became ambassador in Paris—the King immediately replied: "No Counts! I want fellows who will pull off my boots when I come in from the hunt, if I happen to be alone with them." Although he was, and loyally remained, a constitutional king, whenever he could he embarked on secret diplomatic intrigues from which, later, his ministers had to extricate him. Even worse than these transactions were such incidents as when, ignoring the fact that accepting money creates obligations—specially so when one has decided not to repay it—he accepted huge sums from almost unmentionable people like Ismail, the Viceroy of Egypt.

But it is none the less true that, despite all these defects, he was in a way a great king. First, because he submitted to the chief duty of a king—to accept a great minister, though having no love for him. King William of Germany, though a nullity, was a great sovereign, since he submitted to Bismarck. Victor Emmanuel was a great king because, jealous of Cavour and detesting him, he nevertheless kept him continually in power.* It must be admitted as well that if documents have a great importance, so has tradition, and even legend, when it does not

* On his solemn entry into Milan after the victories of 1859, Victor Emmanuel had Cavour seated at his left in the royal coach. The crowd kept shouting: "Viva Cavour!" Turning to his Prime Minister the irritated monarch grumbled: "I seem to be like nothing more than an impresario exhibiting his prima donna."

run completely counter to the truth, as it did for the first act of Victor Emmanuel's reign: his meeting with Marshal Radetzky the day after the defeat of Novara and Charles Albert's abdication.

In millions of modest Italian homes there is an old colored lithograph hanging on the wall of the principal room. It shows Victor Emmanuel standing with Radetzky in the courtyard of a farm at Vignale, and with a haughty gesture dismissing the offers of the victor who, with sly gentleness, asks only two little things: the suppression of the *Statuto* and the abolition of the tricolor flag. From unquestionably authentic documents, discovered and published in 1935 * by the American historian Howard McCaw Smyth, it is proved that this colloquy with the Austrian marshal resulted in a quick agreement on the basis of a common interest in safeguarding the monarchic principle. Victor Emmanuel had already helped to create the amicable atmosphere by his previous conversation with Marshal d'Aspre in which he vaunted his opposition to the "Italian" policy of his father as a reason for obtaining more favorable conditions. Radetzky granted them, and then in a report to Vienna gave his reasons for doing so: the necessity of not bankrupting the new king and of not making demands that would favor a republican movement in Piedmont; the desire not to hurt Piedmont's peasant population with heavy war taxation; the advantage to be gained by flattering the vanity of the new king, who might thus prove amenable to an Austrian policy. Radetzky added that it was a matter of "exalting the king as savior and pacifier of the nation which had been ruined by Charles Albert and democracy." Nothing was said about the *Statuto,* nothing about the tricolor flag.

The legend of the Austrian impositions at Novara and of the King's proud refusal had its origin in a letter that Carlo Cardona, who had been minister at General Headquarters in 1849, wrote in 1866. Later Cardona had spoken to the King about the dangers of the armistice—and it was from this point that the huntsman who was also a king began to embellish the tale. And indeed there was a kernel of truth in the falsehood: Charles Albert, as we already know, had not understood that it was impossible to fight for the independence of Italy

* In *The Journal of Modern History,* June, 1935.

and not at the same time fight for liberty. His son did understand this fact, and since it was only in Italy that he had
opportunities for territorial aggrandizement—the secret
mania of all kings—he accepted the necessary instrument,
liberty. Shrewd, active, adventurous, he believed that even
with the *Statuto* applied more and more to Parliament's advantage, he would still have a personal influence. The reason
he abominated Cavour was that the great minister never left
him anything to do. And to Cavour, the King was nothing
more than a bungler.

But if the colored lithograph of Vignale is a pious fraud,
a curious triptych which I greatly admired as a child when
walking past popular taprooms is not. From the front view,
one saw Victor Emmanuel; on inspection from the left side,
vertical bars showed Garibaldi's face; while from a right-
hand view the same bars showed Mazzini. Popular sentiment
had united the three men in an equality of recognition and,
from a strictly political point of view, the Italians were right.

It was in the moral sphere that Victor Emmanuel's influence
was unimportant or, at least, completely negative. He it was
who in April, 1865, declared that he had "confidence in the
star of Italy." Famous phrases are almost always those of a
minister or of a literary man on a salary, but this one is almost
certainly authentic, reminiscent of the "star" of the old Savoy
saying that his father in his youth had dug up.* The phrase
was natural to the gambler temperament of Victor Emmanuel;
and Italian statesmen were too strongly imbued with a religious sentiment for their mission to have suggested to him a
metaphor harmful to Italians, those inveterate pessimists always inclined to attribute to chance what was meritorious in
their leaders and the people as a whole.

* Charles Albert used note paper inscribed with the heading, *J'atans mon astre*
(I reach my star).

XI

THE POPES

WATERLOO, THE FALL OF NAPOLEON, THE END OF THE GREAT
fear, the Treaty of Vienna unchained on Europe a reaction
that was even more stupid than it was cruel. The old court
calendars represented the tables of the law. As previously
noted, Victor Emmanuel I, having returned to Turin, referred
for all court procedure to the Palmaverde of 1798. In the
south of France the *Terreur blanche* (White terror) in a few
months killed more Frenchmen than were killed in the entire
period of the Red terror.

This is what always happens in countries that have kind
customs and pleasing manners when they break loose. It was
in peaceful Tuscany at the beginning of the Napoleonic wars
that they killed more *Francesi* than in all the rest of Italy. In
1815 in Rome the Pope sent the Jews back into the ghetto and
issued a Draconian law against Freemasons. In the duchies of
Parma and Modena, where my ancestors lived, nothing could
be claimed, not even the most obvious rights, unless one first
presented the *biglietto pasquale,* a certificate from one's priest,
declaring that the petitioner had taken communion on Easter
Sunday. In aristocratic households there was always among
the servants a spy who reported to His Royal Highness everything that had been said at table.* His Highness had time to
read everything, just as the Emperor of Austria, Francis I,
himself read all the reports of the jailers of the Steilberg regarding the tortures inflicted on Pellico, Confelonieri, Marcon-
celli and Oroboni.

The King of Spain not only reestablished the Inquisition,

---

* Prince Louis Napoleon Bonaparte, at the time a Carbonaro vagabond in Italy
—a quarter of a century before becoming Napoleon III—spent a week-end with
my great-grandfather in the country. For dessert a *croccante* in the form of a
royal crown was served; my grandfather said: "Cut it, Prince; it is for the Bonapartes to destroy the crowns in Italy." Three days later the remark reached the
ears of Duke Francis IV and my great-grandfather escaped prosecution only with
considerable difficulty.

but forcibly took back all the convent properties from Spaniards who, during the French regime, had legitimately pur-
chased them.

In France, where the change in the people's minds had been
still more radical, and where the king, Louis XVIII, was free
from any religious fury—and was probably, in his heart of
hearts, a skeptic even concerning the fate of the Bourbon
restoration—a projected Constitution of the Kingdom had
been prepared by his order. In Article XXII it guaranteed
"liberty of religion and conscience." Pope Pius VII protested
against this Article in a letter that he addressed on April
29, 1814, to a French bishop. "By nothing more than the
fact," he declared, "that the liberty of all religions is established without any distinction is truth placed on the same level
as error, and the holy and immaculate Bride of Christ, the
Church, without which there is no salvation, is placed on the
same footing as the heretic sects and even as the perfidy of
the Jews. . . . Our astonishment and our sorrow were no less
profound when we read Article XXVIII of the Constitution
which maintains and promises liberty of the press, a liberty
which menaces faith and morality with the greatest dangers
and certain ruin."

Fearing still more the hysteria of his Ultras than the repre-
sentations of the Pope, Louis XVIII ended by adopting a
different Article, which guaranteed the liberty of religion but
declared, at the same time, that the Catholic religion was the
religion of the State.

In Italy, no Louis XVIII was to be found; and everywhere
the Church—especially through the instrumentality of the
Jesuits, whom Pius VII had immediately revived—constituted
itself, from Piedmont to Sicily, the inspirational force of the
blindest repressions. It was then that there originated the
myth of the mysterious power of freemasonry which had
formerly never seemed important to the Church, though a
long and prudent tradition of the Curia had always viewed
with distrust all cryptic and ritualistic mysticism. In all the
States of the Church, but particularly in the North, the Freemasons and the Carbonari were pursued and often killed at
street corners without the police ever looking for the assassins.
The latter belonged to the sect or band of the *Sanfedisti*, fanat-

ical Catholics, their name being a contraction of *Santa Fede*— Holy Faith.

The Vatican was so blind that its rulers did not even realize that the Powers which had destroyed Napoleon were beginning to think that things were going too far in Rome. At Vienna, as in Paris and Munich, the Powers wanted, of course, to use the Church against nascent or renascent liberalism, but they also wanted to keep the Church in subjection. Metternich was neither a St. Louis nor a Philip II. Himself probably agnostic in point of religious faith, this over-zealous Roman Church annoyed him; he felt that an unexpected break between politics and religion had come and that the formula fashionable after 1814, "Union of throne and altar," did not in itself suffice to destroy this new liberalism which was still more dangerous than the illuminism of the eighteenth century and the revolutionary fever of 1789.

The word "liberal" had been invented at that time in Spain, where they wanted to reestablish the constitution of 1812; they called the reactionary party *servil* and the constitutional party *liberal*. From 1814 to 1860 the word "liberal" roused among reactionaries the same fears as did "Bolshevik" after 1917. Parenthetically, it is curious to observe that after the Revolution France never again supplied new words to the political dictionary, whereas Spain and Italy have furnished a good many; for example, and again from Spain, *Quinta collona*—Fifth Column—a savory phrase emanating from the Franco sympathizers concealed in Republican Madrid at the time of the Civil War.

The more the popes played politics, the more they lost moral prestige; but Rome was unaware of it. It was thought possible to stem the tide—and the phenomenon lasted throughout the entire nineteenth century—by attempting to elevate still higher the position of the Pope. In the Middle Ages the popes had at times had to endure biting reproaches from ardent Catholics like St. Bernard, Dante and Catherine of Siena; and yet how much more profound was their political and psychological influence! We must believe that the fear of being discussed and condemned by the conscience of the faithful—a fear that does not exist today—even the risk of rebellion and schism— which also no longer exists—carried with it a larger possibility of human action. Today popes no longer risk having to go into exile for their ideal of justice, as happened in the case of Gregory VII, but on the other hand they now run the risk of remaining congealed in the stellar atmosphere to which they have been hoisted, and consequently of being forgotten while the great problems of humanity are being discussed.

One prelate alone perceived that the Church had taken the wrong road—Cardinal Consalvi, the Secretary of State, whom Pius VII had sent as his plenipotentiary to the Congress of Vienna.

It was a misfortune for the Church not to have had at her service after 1870 a Cardinal Consalvi to negotiate with Italy in lieu of Cardinal Antonelli with his peasant deceits. (Antonelli was not even a priest.)

The dispatches that Cardinal Consalvi sent to the Pope from Vienna, where he had represented him at the Congress in 1814 and 1815, have a clarity of vision rare in diplomatic correspondence. While he duels with Metternich and Talleyrand for the restitution of the Marches and the Legateships to the Holy See, in almost every one of his dispatches he tries to make the Pope realize that the times when the temporal power was possible have ended. On December 17, 1814, he writes: "The man [Bonaparte] has been overthrown, but the revolution remains, and the ideas have not been corrected." He dares caution the Pope that "certain measures taken so hurriedly at Rome" have made a bad impression even in the court atmosphere of the Congress. He enumerates the measures: "the great edicts against the Freemasons, the too rapid reestablishment of the Jesuits, the demonstrations relative to the national properties, the reconstitution of *all, all* the convents. It is unbelievable what a bad impression this last thing has made."

Repeating his warnings in another dispatch of February 4, 1815, he concludes: "If an earthquake destroys a house, where is it written that it is always advantageous or a duty to rebuild it exactly as it was?"

This was the essence of good sense; but it was not—not even with Consalvi—the sort of sentiment of religious renovation which would have been necessary to the Church. During the Congress, Lord Castlereagh approached the Cardinal on a question of high moral character which touched the practical Consalvi very lightly, as one can see from the following passage in one of his dispatches: "He [Lord Castlereagh] went so far as to tell me that England desired the cooperation of the Holy Father in an affair that he had much at heart and about which he spoke with an earnestness (*premura*) that your Eminence could scarcely imagine. And what was it all about? Your Eminence will be as surprised as I was when I learned that he had in mind to speak about the suppression of the Negro slave trade." Consalvi was very intelligent, but too exclusively a politician; in a subsequent dispatch he gives a long explanation of his hesitations.

"I had to bear in mind that a too curt response would not have been pleasing in view of the tremendous interest that the English government takes in this affair, as is proved by the text itself of Lord Castlereagh's note. I got a clear idea of the necessity of adding something which would satisfy the English government without, however, compromising us. Other reflections presented themselves to my mind which seemed to me very serious, such as the fact that in order to recognize a certain usage as contrary to humanity and charity, the head of our religion should have had to undergo pressure from a non-Catholic power, and that the Holy See has remained so long silent on a subject of such serious interest. I reflected also on the fact that we might offend the Catholic powers which hold to the preservation of this usage which is very useful to their pecuniary interests."

These few lines should be enough to explain why the Catholic Church for a long period during the nineteenth century lost its prestige. Catholic papers—*La Civiltà Cattolica* leading the way—accused the sects. The sects would have counted for little if great popes had sent out from the Vatican stirring and creative thoughts, instead of being in all matters and everywhere on a narrow and fearful defensive. During the pontificates of Pius VII, who died in 1823, of Leo XII, dead in 1846, one got the impression—it matters little whether wrongly—that the Church distrusted even her most faithful subjects if they did too well in their studies. Who can prevent the superior man, they seemed to say, from going over to the other side, as Sièyes and Grégoire and Talleyrand did? Manzoni himself, the great Catholic poet, was long considered as suspect.

That the sects counted for nothing in the abatement of the Church's prestige is proved by the flame of enthusiasm and faith that fired all the Italians when Pius IX succeeded Gregory XVI and uttered phrases of love in place of the old formulas of hate. One must go far back to past centuries to find in Italy as intense a communion of hope and confidence as that of the Italians for Pius IX in 1846–48. When Prince Metternich, still all-powerful in Vienna, saw this, he exclaimed: "I had foreseen everything but a pope whom the Italian liberals would acclaim." Pius IX had read, when he was still bishop of Mastai, at Imola, the *Primato morale e civile degli Italiani,* in which Gioberti offered the Papacy a generous role as Italy's guide, with new glories for the Church. It is Gioberti's book, which moved almost all the pre-1843 Italians, that explains Pius IX. Unless, perhaps, a *stornello* then sung in skeptical Tuscany explains it better:

> Pius IX is the child of our soul
> An idol of our hearts
> A banner, a song. . . .

In a word, not a man, but a symbol created by men.

As Pope, once the 1848 fever had passed, Pius only repeated the formulas of his four predecessors; but the man— the man the Italians had so loved—often vacillated in his feelings. He cursed Victor Emmanuel, and admired him; and of greater import is it that, as Pope, he often fulminated against Italy while continuing to love her.

Some of his intimates told how a high-ranking German having, one day after 1870, addressed to him an allocution charged with hate of liberal Italy, the Pope turned to a pontifical dignitary near him and murmured: "This stupid German cannot comprehend the grandeur and beauty of the Italian national idea."

Perhaps because he remained so Italian, despite himself, Pius detested Napoleon III much more than he did Cavour or Garibaldi; Napoleon guaranteed the Pope his pontifical estates with a year of occupation. Such are the things one probably never forgives. When Louis Napoleon, a year after the *coup d'état*, proclaimed himself Emperor, the Pope, referring to the French expedition against the Roman Republic in 1849, exclaimed: "So much the better. Heaven has paid our debt to Bonaparte." When Pius died in 1878, several weeks after Victor Emmanuel, almost all Italians mourned him deeply. In their hearts they had not forgotten the Pope of 1848.

His successor, Leo XIII, won Europe's respect but was less pleasing to the Italians. A diplomat, a nuncio in other lands, he had never had contact with the Italian soul; he was a man of the Restoration even in his culture, which was only classical (his Latin verses were exquisite); to the finest act of his pontificate, the encyclical *Rerum Novarum* he gave only his name—which, however, is a great deal. Even his sarcasm, his wit, was still rooted in the eighteenth century. When he was nuncio at Brussels, at a reception in the royal palace in the "blue room" the old Count de ——, a Voltairean of the Prince de Ligne school, thought to embarrass him by offering him snuff from a snuff box whose cover bore the miniature figure of a woman in a position of Pompeian obscenity. The nuncio examined it curiously and then remarked: "Very pretty. Madame la Comtesse, I take it." *

Leo XIII was so far from the world of reality that in an epoch of nationalism—"irredentism" had just had its birth—he dreamed of the destruction of Italian unity which, he thought, should be dissolved into a federation of little Italian republics under the presidency of the Pope. He dreamed of a departure from Rome followed by a triumphal return after a victorious war waged by Austria-Hungary against Italy—an idea that Francis Joseph had the good sense to reject. In fact, he proved to Leo XIII that it was not only impractical, but above all dangerous to the Papacy.

Italy and the world remained long in ignorance of these intrigues; in fact, they became known only after 1919 when, through an initiative that I myself undertook,† republican Austria consented to open to us the archives of the Empire

---

* This unpublished anecdote was told me at Brussels by the grandson of Count de ——; but he, having become very devout, made me promise not to identify his grandfather.

† I was then Undersecretary of State for Foreign Affairs.

for all sorts of historical researches. Our discoveries obliged us to recognize that Francis Joseph and his ministers had manifested, with regard to the temporal-power maneuvers of Leo XIII, more political and historical wisdom than Bismarck, the French Republic and the Pope himself combined.

The Emperor had sent Baron Hubner to the Vatican to console and tranquillize the pontiff, who had talked of quitting Rome and establishing himself in his *"cara Salisburgo"*—his dear Salzburg—awaiting the crusade of the Catholic powers against Italy. Here is the text of the imperial instructions that Hubner was to deliver in an affectionate and reverential manner: "In the event of the flight of the pontiff to Austria, his personal claustration would cease; but we doubt that the liberty and independence of the supreme head of the Church would be less constrained by the laws of our country as well as by the regard that the Pope should have for the sovereign who gave him asylum, than they would be in Rome where the Law of the Guarantees, even though bad in itself, gives him a juridical position, and where, notwithstanding everything else, he is master in his own palace." Leo XIII had not thought that the "apostolic" sovereign could, the moment it became a matter of national interest, become as cold toward the Church as Joseph II had been.

Francis Joseph was an attentive reader of his ambassadors' dispatches from Italy. We discovered after 1919 that Count Paar, who represented him at the Vatican, wrote, three years after Leo's election: "It is true that they talk a great deal at the Vatican about the impossibility of remaining here; but in all this we must perceive a special desire to keep the Roman question the order of the day." The dispatches of his successor, Count Revertera, are still more merciless; he often mocks the diplomatic strokes of the Pope of whom he said in 1889: "His Holiness exhibits satisfaction at having drawn the world's attention, and above all over having agitated the Italian Government."

Leo XIII considered as an offense the King of Württemberg's visit to Rome; and was in despair over the second renewal of the Triple Alliance through which Italy—thanks to the wisdom and dignity of Count Robilant—was assured of important advantages in comparison with the first treaty.

Francis Joseph had to send Baron Hubner again to the Vatican to calm the old pontiff. But the Pope ended by turning to France, whose diplomats lacked in their dealing with the Vatican the skeptical wisdom of their Austrian colleagues. Perhaps they feared to be mistaken for "laics"—a crime in France against "good society."

Leo did not succeed there either. And the day after his death, which occurred on July 20, 1903, the President of the French Republic officially visited the King of Italy at Rome.

Pius X, Leo's successor, was a good and simple country priest, but he judged the situation with the good sense his famous predecessor lacked; and, after a short period of bad blood, it came about that the Italian statesmen and the new Pope were tacitly in accord on the understanding that the old Roman question was dead.

The following year, in 1904, Giolitti declared to Prince von Bülow that Italy asked no guarantee for the "Roman question." "It is dead," he declared. The German fully agreed.

It required the narrow-mindedness of Sonnino, with his Treaty of London; it required the necessity Mussolini was under of buying at any price a partner who would guarantee him as honorable, to make possible in 1915 a hostile movement, and in 1929 a rapprochement between the Papacy and the Italian Government, concluded in dangerous conditions.

Later we shall see that the risks of a reconciliation with Fascism were honestly and clearly recognized by Pius XI, the Pope who in a moment of optimistic illusion had ratified the treaties of the Lateran between the Holy See and the Fascist State.

PART THREE: THE POLITICAL LIFE OF NEW ITALY

XII

THE PARLIAMENT AND THE PARTIES

UNTIL THE FORMATION OF AN ITALIAN SOCIALIST PARTY and, much later, in 1919, of a Christian Democrat Party, the Italian Parliament had this unique characteristic: it was composed exclusively of liberals, divided into two parties more by passions and interests than by doctrinal differences.

Italian liberalism was not exactly the same thing as British, Belgian or French liberalism. The term implied a little of all these types, but Italian liberalism was above all the watchword common to all the elite of Italy, from Turin to Palermo, which would bring to fruition the cause of Italian liberty and independence.

The result was that when the first Italian parliament met at Turin in 1861 all Europe had to recognize that it was untrue that Italy's union was the result of a happy coincidence of circumstances—as certain Italian writers had maintained. It is a strange trait of the *genus literatorum* in Italy that they defame the nation through an excess of love, always finding that it has not done enough; an old malady that springs from nostalgia for the Roman Empire. The Italian deputies, the Right as well as the Left, showed a complete agreement in their fundamental feelings, such as had not even existed in the sub-Alpine parliament where a Solaro della Margherita, a good Piedmontese and a good administrator, had maintained that it was mad to drown wise old Piedmont in a dubious Italian adventure. Solaro della Margherita represented the little embittered clerical group who for a decade had fought Cavour's reforms, principally those suppressing the privileges of the clergy. In the great Italian mass the Piedmontese clerical group had disappeared. The *clericali* Italians (thus they must be designated, for they represented only a slim minority of Catholic electors) sulked at the new Italian political life. Even before the War of 1859 they had shouted as their rallying cry: *"Ne eletti, ne elettori"* (No elected, no electors). The slogan made a great hit with the rulers of conservative Europe, who had no love for the birth of liberal Italy. Actually the thing had small significance for Italy, since most of the deputies and senators were Catholics—and *praticanti* (practicing) Catholics.

In 1867 a Roman ecclesiastical congregation gave an official character to the formula *"Ne eletti, ne elettori,"* in declaring *Non expedit* (It is not expedient) that Catholics should take part in political life. But even the *Non expedit* was obeyed only by the clergy and the organized Catholic societies, to such a point that in 1895 the Vatican had to emphasize its position and declare that the *Non expedit* signified prohibition. This, however, did not change the attitude of the mass of Catholics, who continued to vote everywhere in the South and almost everywhere in the North. Only nine years later, in 1904, the successor of Leo XIII, Pius X, retreated, and admitted that in certain cases it was not only permissible not to abstain, but that it was necessary to vote. The elections of 1903 and 1909 enlarged the breach, and the *Non expedit* remains in Catholic minds exclusively as a memory of a mistake and an illusion— the most inexplicable in the long pontificate of Leo XIII— namely, that the unity and liberty of Italy had been an invention of the "sects" and that it sufficed to close one's eyes and wait to see the good old times of the Hapsburgs and the Bourbons return.

Quite differently serious was the cause of the organic gap that prevented the Italian Parliament—honest and well-intentioned as it always was in the mass—from representing, interpreting and developing certain historical and social tendencies which in Italy long remained in obscurity. Why was French liberalism stronger and more determined in France than Italian liberalism in Italy during the nineteenth and twentieth centuries? The reason is that it had on its side the tacit favor of the French peasant. French liberalism—and it would be perhaps more exact to call it French democracy—signified for the French peasant that they would never again fall under the domination of the *château*. Likewise, the vague mistrust that the French peasant always had for the *curé* as too friendly with the *château* stems from the instinctive memory that his fields and farms dated from the suppression and sale at auction of the properties of the clergy achieved by the Revolution. The peasant had his children baptized and their first communions were family celebrations, but he himself rarely went to church.

There was nothing like this in Italy. The Risorgimento constituted one of the purest and most honest of revolutions; but this revolution had for its gospel the "duties of man" of Mazzini and the speeches of Cavour and d'Azeglio, the tragedies of Manzoni and the lyrics of Berchet—all preaching the reconstitution of Italy and of Italian independence as a supreme religious duty of all Italians. The echo penetrated deeply throughout all the cultivated classes of the Italian nation, the classes with which the love of our literature and of our nation had been identified for centuries. But the anonymous masses who worked and suffered in silence in the fields of Italy for centuries were not galvanized by these appeals. They said to themselves that despite the beautiful phrases of the newcomers they would remain,

> *"Un volgo dispargo che nome non ha,"* * (a scattered people that has no name).

as when the Franks followed the Longobards on the Lombard plains. Only the appeal and sacrifice of Pisacane, killed by the Bourbonians at Sapri in 1857, were aimed at the same time at Italians and peasants; but he lived and died unnoted. I have said in Chapter IX that the principal mistake of Mazzini was to ignore the Italian peasantry. In Italy no voice was heard uttering the message that Saint Just shouted to the French in the midst of the Terror: "The era of happiness has arrived—a new thing in the world's history." Robes-

* Manzoni: chorus of the *Adelchi*.

pierre's young friend brought death to thousands of Frenchmen on the guillotine, where he ended by perishing himself
with Robespierre.

But were the Italian liberals less cruel? One may doubt it
when one thinks that the French Revolution with its horrors
transformed the French peasants into one of the most contented
social groups of Europe; while under Louis XIV, a few
generations earlier, La Bruyère describes them as "certain
sullen animals . . . scattered about the countryside, livid and
deeply burned by the sun, attached to the earth that they dig
and move about with an unconquerable stubbornness. . . . At
night they retire into lairs where they live on black bread,
water and roots. . . ."

The only forceful idea of the political class that governed
Italy from 1860 to 1876, the year it yielded the power to the
Left, was Liberalism. Since independence and unity could not
be hoped for without liberty, all became liberals, even those
who philosophically were least so, like the friends of Rosmini.
In united Italy in the parliaments that sat first at Turin, then
on the Roman road at Florence and finally at Rome itself,
the division into Right and Left originated much more from
the traditions and memories of the heroic effort than from
doctrines: on the Right sat those who, as young men, had believed more—or if not they, then their parents—in the sufficient efficacy of prudent reforms; on the Left those who, having fought with Mazzini and Garibaldi in the secret societies
and popular revolts, believed more in the action of the masses
and, above all, were not afraid of them.

How did this Parliament operate and what did it do—this
Parliament composed of honest and practical but not overly
generous men on the one side, and of inexperienced talkers on
the other?

In judging the work of the Italian Parliament we must not
forget in what state they found the Italy of the Hapsburgs,
the Popes and the Bourbons: no railroads binding the country,
no primary schools in the South, three-quarters of the Italians
unable to read or write, no great industry. And yet, what
progress even in the early years! In the North, Turin, which
in 1849 spent 50,000 lire for its schools, increased that ex-

penditure to 700,000 in 1869—a low figure in comparison with 1919. In the South, Naples spent for her schools in 1861 only 50,000 lire, but passed the million mark in 1871; the most modest rural Communes of Italy all possessed their schools after fifteen years of unity.

What is difficult to explain is that Italian thought, which expressed itself so forcefully under despotism, seems to have been struck with inertia for a rather long period after the union. Granted that, even then, there were remarkable men in the sciences and letters, yet there were very few with a European reputation. It would be difficult to cite more than De Sanctis for literary criticism, Sacchi for astronomy, De Rossi for archaeology, the acid and discontented Cantu for history, the young Lombroso for social hygiene.

The Parliament reflected this general mediocrity. There were few in it who one felt might some day replace the Sellas, the Lanzas, the Ricasolis, the Visconti Venostas. But on the other hand, the anonymous work of national union continued constantly: a single group, the *permanente,* represented for a moment Piedmontese nostalgia. If there was no great political experience, moral rectitude remained sovereign, in contrast to France where finance caused corruption equally under the Second Empire and under the Republic. "Political power has never enriched anyone in Italy," declared a deputy one day. And this was absolutely true until the appearance of Fascism.

No parliament in Europe was faced by such complex problems as that of the Italians, with its four centuries of arrears to settle—and yet it managed. It might have quoted the answer of a French aristocrat to a friend encountered after Thermidor who enquired: "What did you do?"—"I survived."

Liberty at home; a foreign policy more correct and idealistic than that of any other great power; great public works; discipline and honesty the rule in the administration; laicism without offense to religious sentiments—these were Parliament's assets.

Its principal fault, in my opinion, was that, composed of nobles, of northern upper bourgeois and southern small bourgeois, it did not have a clear idea that Italy would not be thoroughly unified even in political ideals until the day that the peasants felt that this free nation, about which they had been told in the primary schools, signified for them as well as for all other Italians a worthier and happier life.

Parliament had a unique opportunity when, in its early years, the clerical properties were sold. It was then that they could have raised a great part of the peasantry to the dignity of small proprietors, especially in the South. But nothing of the sort was done. Parliament did not even consider this side of the problem. Twice only were the peasants considered. The first time was in 1867, with the Rattazzi law concerning Church properties, which declared that the convent lands should be sold in small parcels and that the purchase price could be paid by peasants over a long term by installments. But, alas, this was never repeated, even when the Socialists, after 1900, had become a party that had to be reckoned with. Later, in 1919 and 1920, the Christian Democrats prepared a project of agrarian reform of which we shall speak later— a project that Fascism later torpedoed.

This indifference as regards the most essential problem of southern Italy is the most serious fault of Parliament in all its history. All parties are culpable, but the southern deputies, who too often represented coalitions of the old privileged coteries and not the masses, were at the same time culpable and victims. The liberation of the South, in 1860, from the long asphyxiating tyranny of the Bourbons found the majority of the Neapolitan provinces with an aristocracy, some of whose members were generous—Pisacane had been one of them—and with a populace rich in millenary wisdom but unprepared to play a role in the mechanism of modern life. The parliamentary regime in that region invented a bourgeois class without historical roots, save at Naples and some few other centers. The deputies of the South—even when they thought themselves progressive—were so in the most infantile and dangerous sense of the parliamentary slogan: "Less taxation but greater expenditures." Never, save for a very few individuals like Fortunato, and later Salvemini, did they rise to the level of studying the fundamental reasons for the southern discontent and the means of curing it.

It is true that the northern deputies, Sonnino and Franchetti among others, zealously studied the conditions of the South. An investigation that they undertook is famous, but too many of their southern colleagues lived from hand to mouth: they were not bad fellows, not corrupt, but fearful of the great quasi-feudal electors, from whom they received their instructions rather than from the people.

The problem of the South still remains one of Italy's primary problems.

XIII

THE PROBLEM OF THE SOUTH

UNTIL THE LEFT VICTORY OF 1876, THE MINISTERS WHO governed Italy were chiefly northerners who regarded the southerners as amusing or touching individuals, but always as minors requiring direction. Cavour alone had felt the gravity of the problem. During the long fever which was his death agony he often repeated: "Venice is easy, Rome is easy, but the South. . . ." As a matter of fact, Venice was delivered in 1866, five years after Cavour's death, Rome in 1870; but nothing radical and constructive ever happened to the South.

After 1876 several of the most prominent ministers were southerners, but they were members of "advanced" parties, among whom, even more than among the intelligent conservatives, there was a reverential respect for high functionaries, those "experts" who were of the same sort as before 1876. They were a group of people imbued with the honest but narrow mentality of the old Piedmontese bureaucracy, and for them to go south as prefects and administrators was a faraway exile.

It had always been so in our history; only one of our great classical writers knew and loved the South—Boccaccio. One of the pleasures of the Italians in reading Dante is that so often in a parenthetical line or two he describes with a vividness that has never been equaled the aspects and landscapes of the peninsula, from "l'Arzana de' Viniziani"—the arsenal of Venice —to Carrara, or Florence, or Rome. But never a line on the South; he had never been there, and Dante described only what he had seen. Petrarch, Ariosto and Machiavelli never traveled south either. Manzoni's longest trip southward ended at Rome. Leopardi was in Naples only as a sick man; Mazzini spent but a brief time in the South, and most of it in prison.

Why this regional detachment and remoteness?

The difference between the North and the South is not more marked in Italy than in France or Germany or the United

States of America—though in Italy the cleavage is perhaps a little sharper. This explains the refrain of the French song in the times of Charles VIII's expedition into Italy: "We will conquer the Italies. . . ."

Indeed, in Italy the cleavage unquestionably is sharper, and yet I have a thousand times heard northern Frenchmen, for instance, traveling by rail to the French Riviera, arriving at Valence, an hour south of Lyons, exclaim with a disdainful grimace: "Here's where France ends." But if the Italian fissure is more clearly defined, it has nothing to do with pretended differences of "race," such as Greek influences among the southerners, and Germanic and Celtic among the northerners. The reason is exclusively historical and occasional. For centuries the States of the Church created in the middle of the peninsula a zone having nothing in common with the rest of the country, a zone which was neither northern nor southern and which prevented all contact between the two main parts of the country.

For centuries it was as if they had been separated by an impossible distance.

The actual substitution of the one Italy for the "two Italies" was the work of the railroads. One day Bonaparte imagined— in one of his Rousseauesque reveries—that Calabria, Sicily and Sardinia ought to converge toward the coast of Tuscany and Latium, thus rounding out an Italy which was too long for his taste as a recruiter of cannon-fodder. One of the principal meritorious contributions of the Italian liberal governments between 1860 and 1890 is that, despite financial difficulties that were often frightful, they created a vast network of rapid communications down to the extremity of the boot, and this they did with mountains to pierce and torrents and abysses to bridge, making the engineering problem more difficult than anywhere else in Europe. As a matter of fact, the railways of southern Italy are works of engineering art and tunnels in a proportion double that of any other European system.

It was probably the long period of distant detachment from the rest of Europe that made of the Italian South an isle for philosophers and thinkers. Giordano Bruno, Campanella and Vico are three aspects of the speculative audacity of yesterday's southern Italy, as Benedetto Croce is today the living flower. In the philosophers of the Italian North in the first half of the nineteenth century, men like Rosmini and Gioberti, foreign influences are apparent. With Croce, these influences, even that of Hegel, have only been material that aided him in the original elaboration of a new thought.

Those who in Italy and elsewhere resent the self-complacency that every North evinces toward its South must be pleased to know that it was a Neapolitan thinker, Croce, who gave the whole of Italy the example of an untiring struggle conducted with austere serenity for the ideal of human liberty.

If Italy's North has given the world some of the greatest artists not only in the domains of poetry, painting and sculpture, but even in that of music—Verdi was born on the plain of the Po—it is the South that has given Italy her greatest intellectual heroes, audacious in thought, sober in expression, beginning with the sages of the school of Salerno who, first in the Middle Ages, risking the furies of the Salernians, robbed the tombs of the *campo santo* (cemetery) of corpses to study the mysteries of life.

As for the middle-class southern Italian, he is to the ordinary Italian (just Italian) precisely what the latter is to the northern European; there is the same accentuation of qualities and faults. There is also an analogy in the fatality of legends and ready-made formulas with which people try to explain this accentuation.

The truth of the matter is that those who in the North of Italy have continued to give currency to the old portrait of the gay, gossiping and lazy southerner speak an outmoded language. One has only to make contact at Milan and Genoa—and why not also in New York and Buenos Aires?—with merchants or technicians from Puglia or Basilicata to find them reserved and obstinate, the exact opposite of the old cliché. There are, of course, specific southern failures; and one meets a good many of them, because the small bourgeois of the South aspires to become an office clerk at Milan, whereas a Piedmontese or a Lombard never seeks employment at Naples. Miserable poverty pushes the children of the southern small bourgeoisie—of relatively recent formation—to dream of nothing but becoming petty employees. It is these white-collar slaves who produce that strange paradox: that while Fascism had more sincere partisans in the North than in the South, the majority of the Fascist agents, officers and police spies was composed of southern small bourgeois, content even to wear the Fascist uniform, provided it meant a salary paid by the taxpayer.

The Lombards' struggle with the marshes of the vast plain of the Po lasted four or five centuries; but in the end they triumphed and by the sweat of their brows made their land one of the richest regions of Europe. In the South the work is more heroic, for it must constantly be renewed, save in two or three cases (as in the Campagna) almost everywhere conditions are somewhat like those on the slopes of Vesuvius where, tirelessly, new vines are planted after every eruption of the volcano. The contest of the southern Italian with his land affords one of the rarest examples of human resistance; and it is a silent contest, devoid of all grand gestures. That is why one likes to call attention to the obvious clichés that the North of every country is fond of using when describing its South.

The Normans debarked in the Neapolitan provinces; they were one of the peoples richest in the vigor of their epoch, as they proved in England. But in southern Italy they disappeared, quickly swallowed up. Later the French and Spaniards suffered approximately the same fate.

If one studies the reality of history nothing is left of the trenchant theories of an Italian South fatally different from a North sprinkled with Germanism. At the very most, the races —if in this case one can even speak of races—are like those rivers that suddenly disappear in the course of their valleys and, after a long subterranean passage, reappear on the surface in the form of small lakes or springs.

The only true difference between North and South in Italy is of the economic order; the land south of Rome is infinitely poorer than that of the North. As the civilization of *Magna Graecia* was ephemeral there, and probably less brilliant than has been thought, so, too, Rome was only a stepmother for this little-known South from which came vague mutterings of agrarian revolts, this South from which, before Rome's day, rich Carthage recruited her mercenaries.

The Italian southerners sometimes complain of the egotism of the industrial North. They should also and specially com-

plain of the poets, their own and others. Seven centuries before
Christ a Greek lyric sang of Calabria as "the happiest land
in the world"—poor tragic Calabria, which always will be
one of the most sterile lands of Europe. And so it was for a
thousand years, from Virgil to Goethe. Literature was the in-
voluntary artisan of the legend of the happy southerner,
scarcely deigning to rise to garner the fruits of the earth
which grew in wild profusion about him.

What is stranger still is that for a long time the southerners
themselves believed in the legend. It is sad and comic at the
same time to reread today, in the solemn addresses that Naples
sent in 1860 to Victor Emmanuel, the description of the treasures that the ancient realm of the Two Sicilies declared itself
proud to put at the disposition of free and united Italy. This
was the result of self-deception, stemming from the South's
economic segregation under the Bourbons and especially from
the pleasant legend of its being a land of entrancing scenery
"where the orange tree flourishes." It was forgotten that
behind the paradises of the shore the desert reigns, since the
sun is only a lure where there is no water. For in the South
where, contrary to the rest of Italy, rain falls only in winter,
instead of a Po, an Arno and a Tiber, there are only torrents
which are dry in summer and which in winter destroy the fields
with their floods. When one speaks of the Italian South one
must never forget that drought destroys three out of ten
harvests with mathematical precision. The Puglia aqueduct, a
gigantic construction projected and executed by the liberal
governments of democratic Italy, has solved nothing but the
hygienic problem. May I, in parenthesis, recall here an ironic
example of Fascist publicity? The construction of the Puglia
aqueduct required twenty years, but its inauguration took place
a month after Mussolini's accession to power. Thanks to a
clever publicity, that inaugural ceremony sufficed to persuade
foreign writers and journalists—most of whom asked nothing
better—that the aqueduct was a miraculous proof of Fascist
realization.

One historical fatality is still more responsible than men for
the failure of liberal Italy as regards the South.

The history of the North (and in a certain sense even of
Rome, often enough, despite the opposition of the popes) is

based on the autonomy of the Communes. The South, on the contrary, crystallized entirely from the Abruzzi to Calabria around a single center. First it was Benevente, then Naples. And this center could give it only a feudal organization, which tended to remain even when the fief commenced to disappear, first politically, then juridically. It was the same in Sicily, in Sardinia, in Corsica, and there was just one reason: lack of industry and commerce, sole creators of that *popolo minuto* or *grasso* (small business men and big business men) who in Florence, as in all the cities of the Lombard League, were able to organize against the *grandi,* the feudal nobles of the castles, obliging them to come to the towns and live as townsmen. It might be said that at Naples the bourgeoisie was not born until the great fever of 1799.

As I have said, these poor lands which, because of a literary illusion, believed themselves rich, were always bowed under the burden of taxes and, still more, under the uncertainty of harvests infinitely less rich than in the North, on account of lack of water which made the year's fate depend on a little rain.

The resurrection of the Italian South is a problem of public works, of creating artificial lakes, of regulating flood waters, of reforestation—for without forests there is no certainty of rainfall. This was the great duty of united Italy; but the only man who realized it, Count Cavour, died at the moment when his genius and will-power were most necessary.

In a sense Italy has in the South greater possibilities than any other country, for she possesses at home her colonial empire to develop, not peopled with foreign natives but with one of the most intelligent and awakened populations of Europe.

In contrast to Cavour, the statesmen who succeeded him feared excessive expenditures; for them a balanced budget constituted a supreme dogma.

But after the folly of the Fascist regime one cannot help but think that with the hundredth part of what Fascism spent on wars in Spain, in Ethiopia, in Europe, the solution could have become a reality, thus doubling the moral and economic power of the nation.

XIV

STATE AND CHURCH: PIUS X

WE HAVE SEEN IN CHAPTER XII HOW LONG AND TENACIOUS
were Leo XIII's illusions regarding the lack of vitality of
Italian unity. The entire political activity of his pontificate was
but a long series of efforts which created difficulties for Italian
foreign policy, first in Vienna, then, with more apparent success, at Paris. At his death in 1878 Leo XIII left for his successor, as regards what was sometimes still called "the Roman
Question," a disastrous situation. Abroad, even the politicians
and diplomatic writers of ultra-conservative tendencies had become accustomed to consider the law of the Guarantee as a
masterpiece of wisdom and suppleness—even if they did not
say so. The absolute liberty of the Cardinals during the Conclave at Rome where Leo's successor was elected was, for the
world, the test by fire of the law of the Guarantees.

Giuseppe Sarto, the new Pope, who took the name of Pius
X, was no diplomat: he was only a good and prudent country
priest. Patriarch of Venice at the moment when the Conclave
chose him, he had pleased all Italians by his apostolic simplicity. At the moment of leaving for the Conclave, from
which he was to emerge as Pope, a frank and jovial Milanese
priest, one of my friends, Don Ernesto Vercesi, remarked to
him: "Your Eminence will be the new pontiff." Cardinal Sarto
answered: "How dare you believe the Holy Spirit capable of
such stupidity?" At the beginning of the Conclave Cardinal
Sarto was seated next to Cardinal Lecot at one of the *Con-
gregazioni generali*. The latter enquired in French whether he
was archbishop of some Italian diocese. "I do not speak
French," answered Sarto in Latin. The Frenchman replied:
"Alors, non es papabilis, quia Papa gallice loqui debet." (You
cannot be Pope because a Pope must speak French.) *"Deo
gratias, Deo gratias"* (Thank God, thank God), Sarto agreed
gaily.

Become Pope, he showed his detestation for the political

struggles and adventures in which his predecessor had delighted. He even found that Leo XIII had not appreciated at
its proper value the unlimited liberty which the pontiff enjoyed
in Italy without having to administer populations that would
have been hostile to any pontifical government. This explains
why Pius X put a great deal of water into Leo XIII's diplomatic wine, while maintaining the ritualistic protestations on
the "imprescriptible rights" of the Church—protestations
which, indeed, were a part of the wise and tacit equilibrium
which had slowly established itself between Italy and the Vatican since the entry of Cadorna's soldiers into Rome, on September 20, 1870. The next day, while the Catholics of Ireland
and Belgium wept over the misfortunes of the Papacy, a young
Italian diplomat who had been attached to Cadorna as diplomatic adviser, Alberto Blanc,* asked to be received by the
Secretary of State, Cardinal Antonelli. Entering the study of
His Eminence, he bowed and began: "How shall we get out
of it, Eminence?" The witty Cardinal replied: "You are the
ones who entered; it is for you to get out." And they laughed
together at the quip, after which the Cardinal formulated the
first of the infinite number of demands—and all were reasonable—that the popes presented to the Italian Government during the "rupture." This first was that, for pity's sake, even the
Trastevere should be occupied by Italian troops and not left
to the pontiff!

That was the real Rome, Rome as it actually was in a workaday world, despite the Vatican's official protestations.

Naturally, when in the second year of the pontificate of
Pius X the President of the French Republic, Emile Loubet,
came to Rome to pay a solemn official visit to the King of Italy,
the Pope protested. This was in April, 1904; but in September
of the same year at the time of the general elections, ques-
tioned on the attitude that Catholics should observe, not only
did he not confirm the *Non expedit,* but he declared to the
bishops that they should *"regolassero"* (arrange things) as
they thought best. Catholics were elected deputies, as *Catholic*
deputies—that being the only novelty—and they at once swore
allegiance to the King whom Leo XIII had always stigmatized

---

* Twenty-five years later, Baron Blanc, Minister of Foreign Affairs under
Crispi.

as a "despoiler," and to the *Statuto* which he had described as
the work of the "sects." In the successive elections of 1919,
sixteen deputies were elected specifically as Catholic candidates. One of them, soon afterward, at a sitting of the Chamber, being asked by an anti-clerical colleague to declare
whether he would accept Rome as the capital of Italy, immediately rose and answered: "Yes, of course," and the entire
Chamber applauded.

The whole world was looking on in admiration. In 1911,
when I was Minister in China at the time of the Revolution,
Yuan Shi-kai, then omnipotent dictator, asked my advice on
his double plan: to set aside the Ching dynasty, but to retain
for it a sort of religious prestige. "What is that famous Italian law," he asked me, "of which I have heard people speak
as a masterpiece of sagacity, by which Italy proclaimed the
Pope sovereign, at the moment she dispossessed him, and
thanks to which two sovereigns have been able to live tranquilly for long years in the same capital? And what did Europe
say of that solution?"

I explained to him, *à la Chinoise,* the subtleties of the law of
the Guarantees. Some weeks later he proclaimed a decree
which eliminated the Chings and at the same time raised them
to divinity; the next day he sent me an *iju* (a jade scepter)
with a scroll expressing his thanks.

In 1911 an English Catholic congress gathered at New-
castle-on-Tyne. Cardinal Bourne addressed it, declaring that
he expressed "the thought of all Catholics," a formula indicating an understanding with the Pope. He declared: "The
Italian Government has the duty of discovering and giving the
Pope those guarantees of independence which compensate him
for the loss of the temporal power." The era of negotiation on
the basis of the renunciation of the temporal power began on
that day.

The same year, four months later, on the occasion of the
festivities for the inauguration of the too gigantic monument
to Victor Emmanuel II at the base of the Capitol, Pius X
thought he ought to publish one of his ritualistic protests, but
he no longer spoke of the lost territorial sovereignty; he only
demanded *"libertà e indipendenza"* (liberty and independence).

We shall show later that conciliation was ripe under Pius X's successor, Benedict XIII, a conciliation which, had he lived —would have assumed a more worthy form for the State and have been less dangerous to the Church than that which was realized under Fascism.

If Pius X's pontificate powerfully aided the political conciliation of Church and State, it was less happy for the moral and intellectual influence of the Church in the Italian nation. Born in the humblest class of the people, possessing like all Venetians a witty gaiety, and of a simple and kind bearing, Pius X won all hearts. His name became synonymous with apostolic simplicity; but for the priests who would have liked to explore new ways in the interest of the Church this simplicity did not exclude a cold violence of reaction against what some called modernism, and others, Christian democracy. This aspect of the papal career of Pius X proves once again that perhaps we sin from demagogism when we admire peasants whom fate has raised to the summit of the social scale, and whom we admire on account of their origin. If they have not exceptional gifts, like Alberoni, they risk remaining, more than others do, prisoners of formulas and traditions.

The prejudices of the aristocrat sometimes have a counterweight in his skepticism. Those of the peasant have no counterweight.

Under his Venetian simplicity Sarto was a dangerous spirit, for he was narrow-minded. He proved it at the precise moment when, proclaimed Pope, he had to choose his pontifical name. Probably never was a cardinal more sincere than he when he declared that he did not want to become Pope. He proved it by his answer when he was asked the traditional question:

"Well, since I am called to suffering, I shall take the name of the Pope who has suffered most, Pius."

Like Sarto, Pius IX had been charming, pleasant, simple in his private life, but on the development of the liberalism that characterized the nineteenth century he knew of nothing else to do than to oppose it with maledictions of the Syllabus. When Pius IX died in 1878 the Roman Church was isolated in the world, morally and intellectually. The eleven years of the pontificate of the new Pius, from 1903 to 1914, reestablished approximately Pius IX's situation from which Leo XIII had turned aside, notably with his encyclical *Rerum Novarum*. Pius X's policy was of pitiless rancor against all priests who thought that the Church ought to be reconciled with modern democracy; of violent persecutions against all those who, as followers of de Loisy and Tyrrell, sought from within the Church to make an "appeal to the Gospel as interpreted by them, in favor of religious democracy," to quote the precise words Pius X used in his encyclical *Pascendi* of September 8, 1907, and in his letter of August 5, 1910. All that was called Loisyism, Tyrrellism, Americanism, was annihilated by the papal condemnations. But if some priests like Tyrrell and Murri left the Church, the great majority, while submitting, preserved in secret their doubts and sufferings. Pius X never understood, in his simplicity, the tragedy of those souls. To a priest, a friend of mine, whom he wished to put on guard against their influence, he said:

"Those are arrogant men; no good can come from the haughty."

Such spirits, merciless in opposition to the noblest characters whose doubts and sufferings they are unable to comprehend, often end by giving all their trust to the fanatics who please them by their absolute certainty. From the beginning of his pontificate Pius X was dominated by Cardinal Vives y Tuto, Spaniard, Capuchin and Inquisitor. In the anterooms of the Vatican—anterooms are often disrespectful—the sobriquet of Vives y Tuto quickly became *Vives fa Tutto* (Vives does all). Poor Vives came to a tragically Spanish end—I am thinking of the Spain that killed infidels for the good of their souls. In 1912, after ten years of mad persecutions—thanks to which the denunciation of a modernist became for every intriguing priest the surest means of promotion—Vives ended by revealing himself as exactly what he was, without anyone who saw him having the least doubt of it: mad, mad in the clinical sense of the word. To stifle the scandal he was immured in a convent of Spanish nuns at Monte Porzio Catone, near Rome, and there he died, under the night-and-day surveillance of his nurses who heard him groan: "The Church must be saved from the modernists. . . ."

On the death of the unfortunate Vives, two other cardinals dominated the mind of Pius X: De Lai, Prefect of the Consistory which nominates bishops, and Merry del Val, the Cardinal Secretary of State.

The knowledge of diplomatic language that the polyglot Cardinal possessed seemed like a hermetical science to a Pope who was unable to understand even the Latin of the French bishops and who, in order to talk with the French clergy, was obliged to impose on them the Italian pronunciation of Latin.

Merry del Val's masterpiece was the separation of the Church and State in France which—from the point of view of the Roman Church that has little love for the healthy liberty of regimes of separation—signified the economic ruin of the Church in France and of its missions in the Orient. From the point of view of Pius X, incapable of comprehending the tactical mistake made in his name, France was responsible for all the checks sustained in Paris, the France that he called familiarly among his intimates "the diabolic trinity of free-masonry, Christian democracy and modernism."

He went so far as to define modernism as "the Church's French evil," language which uttered by a simple priest would have seemed blasphemous.

It is not strange that the Protestant armies of Germany seemed to Pius X the instrument chosen by God to punish France. When death surprised him on August 20, 1914, he was absolutely certain that nothing in the world could prevent the complete defeat of the French; and in his naïveté he said:

"Thus they will understand that they must become obedient sons of the Church."

XV

FOREIGN POLICY

ITALY BEING ENGAGED IN A WAR WITH TURKEY IN 1911, Conrad, the Austro-Hungarian Chief of Staff, put all his influence in Vienna to work in order to gain the old Emperor's consent for a "preventive war" against Italy. Aerenthal did not hesitate to define Conrad's projects "a policy of brigandage," and Francis Joseph sided with his Minister of Foreign Affairs. Conrad resigned, but continued to preach his great plan among his close friends.

In the course of his recriminations, Conrad added that Austria should have seized a former opportunity that chance had offered her against Italy, that is, the tragic days of the Messina earthquake. Conrad's intimates and his protector, Archduke Francis Ferdinand, have on several occasions admitted it.

Conrad's ideas must have appeared to the initiated not far from realization, since the German Ambassador at Rome at that time dared send the Consulta this communication: that it was well understood that in the event of an Austro-Hungarian war with Italy, Germany would remain neutral, the treaty of the Triple Alliance being mute on that hypothesis!

Proof of the hardiness of myths agreeable to a nation's vanity, these facts, historically certain, have not prevented and will not prevent sentimental German writers from continuing to cast doubts on Italy's loyalty during the period of the Triple Alliance. The truth is that the meticulous study of the diplomatic documents of the period will only demonstrate that if—in that *mariage de raison* which was the Triple Alliance—there were thoughts and acts of dubious fidelity, they were chiefly on the side of Germany and Austria-Hungary. The fact is explicable when one recalls that, as regards Italy, the treaty had no positive aims but was entered into for negative reasons. Italy understood that she could not live under the constant menace of a neighbor who detested her by tradition and necessity. (Did we not represent that principle of nationality so hated in Vienna?) Italy felt in her very flesh the spear point of the Trentino, the menace of that powerful and malevolent neighbor; she knew she could expect no protection of law in the anarchic Europe of the post-1878 period; she could only accept an alliance. At least she gained by it the neutralization of any eventual temporal plot of the Vatican which might become dangerous in case of a return to power of the French Right parties.

But from the start Bismarck wanted for himself a liberty he denied his allies. The most natural Italian endeavors to bring about trustful relations with France he defined to the Italian Ambassador as proofs of disloyalty; and that at the moment when he himself was trying his best to flirt with Paris.

When Italy occupied Massawa in 1885, the first staked-out area of what was later to be the colony of Eritrea, Bismarck protested in the name of the integrity of the Ottoman Empire; and this happened at the time when, in his intimate conversations with European statesmen, he was launching the idea of a final partition of Turkey. As a matter of fact, Bismarck had been vexed only because the occupation of Massawa had come about as the result of an understanding between London and Rome; and he wanted Rome to be on bad terms with London, especially when he himself was having bitter-sweet discussions with the British Government over colonial questions.

It is proper to say here that the first idea of an Italian occupation of Massawa was born of conversations at Cairo between the Italian agent De Marcino and Sir E. Baring (later Lord Cromer). The English agent encouraged his Italian colleague to suggest to the Consulta the occupation of Massawa; he feared that France might take it first, and at that time they still had far to go to achieve the *entente cordiale*.

This did not prevent Lord Cromer when he wrote his *Modern Egypt* from expressing the pious regret that Italy had not reserved her strength for improving the condition of Sicily and Calabria. Whether Lord Cromer's remark had any truth in it or not, he was the last man who had any right to utter it.

At the time of the Congress of Berlin in 1878, Bismarck explicitly offered Tunisia to Count Corti for Italy. Except that the offer was not formulated until after it had been made to

France, in agreement with Lord Salisbury, and after having ascertained that the Quai d'Orsay would have taken action. To have embroiled Italy with France and profit by their embroilment—what could have been more "Machiavellian"?

As for Austria, the serious point of friction was at first Albania and Macedonia. Count Nigra, the Italian Ambassador at Vienna, had succeeded in establishing an accord with the Ballplatz on the basis of the most complete reciprocal disinterestedness, an accord later confirmed between Tittoni and Goluchowski. But what did actually happen? My personal recollections as a very young diplomat at Constantinople will tell: From the very day following the accord, continuing from 1901 to 1904, at each audience after the Friday *Selamlik* the Austro-Hungarian Ambassador, Baron Calice, succeeded in extracting from the Sultan half-promises in favor of the Albanian Catholics—in favor of Albanians, simply Albanians—against the Epirote Greeks. All this was immediately made known to the Italian Embassy, it being greatly to the Porte's interest to create opposition to the Austrian invasive proceedings. The Embassy never failed to remonstrate and to report to the Consulta, which, in its turn, reminded Vienna of the Nigra accord. As it was impossible to cite analogous Italian intrigues, these incidents were invariably the cause, in Vienna, of endless arguments against the spirit of mistrust of the Italians, who couldn't understand, in their anti-clerical liberalism, that the Emperor had the duty of protecting Catholicism in the Orient.

Not only for the German historians, but even for the Americans and English—who should know better how to judge—the legend is still current that, on the day of its test in 1914, Italy broke an alliance which had lasted since 1882. Let me recall that after the renewal of the Triple Alliance on June 20, 1902, but before its ratification which took place July 8—and only the ratification counts—Prinetti, the Italian Minister of Foreign Affairs, declared at Paris and London that the treaty contained "no engagement obliging Italy to participate in an aggression." Prinetti authorized his two colleagues, Delcassé and Lord Lansdowne, to communicate his assurances to their respective Parliaments—which was done at the Palais Bourbon and the House of Commons on July 3. The declaration that Delcassé read and whose every word was fraught with meaning was as follows:

"The declarations which have been made to us by the Italian Government have permitted us to acquire the certainty that the policy of Italy, as a result of her Alliance, is directed neither directly nor indirectly against France; that it could not in any case admit of a menace for us, and that in any case and under any form Italy could not become either the instrument or the auxiliary of an aggression against our country."

The German Ambassador at Paris transmitted to Berlin the impression of intense relief these words, listened to in a religious silence, had produced.

At Rome Prinetti plainly confirmed them to the German representative.

The ratification of the treaty took place just a few days later, on July 8. Consequently the spirit in which Italy had adhered to the renewal of the Triple Alliance was recognized in Berlin and Vienna.

As for the relations between Italy and France, they were often difficult for the very reasons which might have strengthened them: it is never easy to speak in measured terms of "historical bonds," of "fraternity of race," of "identity of culture" —just as it is not prudent to cite Lafayette too often among Americans and Frenchmen. French statesmen and diplomats who knew how much I had at heart an *entente cordiale* between my country and France have more than once ill concealed their surprise at seeing the tepid reception I often gave, while minister in Rome or ambassador in Paris, to suggestions of festivities, anniversary celebrations and Franco-Italian love feasts. It is possible that they eventually understood that I was thus serving the cause which they most assuredly did not have more at heart than I.

The dissimilarities of temperament and psychology of the French and the Italians would not be of great importance if they were revealed exclusively in our two literatures, in which Corneille and Racine are closed books for Italians, as Leopardi and Manzoni are for the French. But, alas, the psychological differences constantly manifest themselves in ways of reasoning, of envisioning events and the future. The potent Cartesian clarity of French rationalism is to Italian minds like a beacon light in the night: an excess of light that ignores the value of shade.

It is not immaterial to reflect that the golden age of Italo-French understanding was not the community of faith shared during the war, but the form assumed by the Triple Alliance after 1902.

French historians have not always rendered justice to the loyalty that inspired the Italian policy in the period of the Triple Alliance; their excuse has one name: Crispi. But, after all, the real fault of the Sicilian patriot was in being endowed with an intensely emotional temperament. An intellectual maturity, which he always lacked, could alone have persuaded his ardent patriotism that Italy could not emerge armed and complete, like Pallas Athene, from four centuries of foreign and Papal domination; his temperament should explain his feverish agitation, his constant quest for immediate success, his naive satisfaction at the first flattering phrase Bismarck addressed to him.

Crispi had always reproached men like Minghetti and Visconti Venosta, whose proud moral dignity he could not even comprehend, for having been too "French." Just as he never understood that his predecessor in the Ministry of Foreign Affairs, Count de Robilant, had better safeguarded the national dignity by his silent action than he himself had by his exaltations. Robilant had signed the Triple Alliance; yet Bismarck said of him: "What an unmanageable man!" As for Crispi, the Sicilian, the occupation of Tunisia in 1881 had cut him to the quick, as had the conclusion of our unfortunate war with Austria in 1866. From that time he kept ever alert.

More than once, in the manner of old men, Giolitti has narrated to me in his patriarchal home, which had once been Cavour's, how astonished he was when, as a young man and Minister of the Treasury with Crispi, the latter summoned him urgently one fine morning to inform him that France was preparing a surprise attack on Spezia, that he had "proofs" of it. All the reasonings of Giolitti to demonstrate to him that the thing was impossible, were in vain. The well-meaning Crispi who, notwithstanding Giolitti's advice, had managed to get an English naval squadron to come to Genoa on his urgent appeal, thought he had saved his country from a terrible danger.

To make clear the emotional immaturity of the old conspirator that Crispi always continued to be, I need only recount what Giolitti told me, in the evening of his life, regarding this incident. Giolitti, having in his turn become President of the Council, had wanted to know how Crispi had been able to deceive himself on the alleged French plot. He found that the incredible story had originated in a secret report that people in the Vatican, paid by Crispi as informers, had sent him.

However, it would be very unjust to believe that Crispi's policy was a precedent for the Fascist period. The old Garibaldian never wanted to do anything but serve Italy, his ideal. To make use of Italy, filling his mouth with her name in order to deafen a gagged nation, would have seemed to him the worst of blasphemies. Respectful to Parliament, he believed in liberty. There is nothing in common between him and the Mussolinian phenomenon. Or perhaps we ought to say that at the most and because of his typical intellectual limitations there was a similarity between him and the honest naive small bourgeois of the classic "Roman" type, former combatants, and the like, who at the beginning of Fascism were engulfed in its turbulent torrent where so many kinds of desire mixed without blending.

But, aside from the Crispi period, the Triple Alliance was regarded by Italian statesmen solely as a guarantee of peace, notably with respect to Austria, with whom we had to be either allies or enemies, and as a guarantee of our territorial integrity which (we have made mention of this in speaking of Leo XIII) for a time appeared to be threatened by the Pope's dream of a "crusade of Christian princes" against Italy.

Generally diplomatic documents soon lose their savor, based as they are on hypotheses. But instructions sent by Visconti Venosta from Rome, some years before the conclusion of the Triple Alliance, to Count de Robilant, then representing Italy at Vienna, are still so living, especially after Mussolini's "stab in the back" against France, in June, 1940, that the essential passage deserves quoting:

"If a war should be provoked by a folly or imprudence of France, or if it should break out over the clerical question, our position would be clear; and we should have a direct and common interest with Germany. But if a war should result from the deliberate will of Germany to attack France, Italy could not take part in the war on Germany's side; she would not seem an ally but rather a hired assassin whom one pays his price. Furthermore, the result of a war between France and Germany would always be harmful and dangerous to Italy. If Germany should again crush France, she would want to dismember her in a way that she would wrongly judge to be definitive; one of those contrivances that are excessive, artificial and ephemeral, like those that served Napoleon to make and break his peaces. And Italy would have neither strength nor a future in a Europe that had lost its equilibrium."

Apart from the allusion to the importance which French affairs held in Italian eyes, this page of Visconti Venosta describes not only his own thought, but that of all statesmen worthy of the name who succeeded him.

In his day Bülow spoke disdainfully of the Italian understandings with France and Great Britain during the Triple Alliance as of "waltz turns." In like manner, the war having supervened, from Berlin and Vienna came an avalanche of "deutsche Treue" (Germanic fidelity) on her former Latin ally. In truth, even and especially in the extreme form that Italy's measures of pacific prudence took in 1902, our conduct might have been an example of loyalty for everyone, beginning with the Germany of the Hohenzollerns. Italy guaranteed her neutrality to France and Great Britain and informed her allies of it; while Bismarck had concluded his famous treaty of counter-assurance with Russia at a moment when an Austro-Russian war seemed possible (which augmented the gravity of the act) and kept his treaty secret, although he was formally obliged by one of the articles of the Triple Alliance to communicate conventions of this kind to Rome and Vienna. But it is understood that Italy alone is "Machiavellian"; and I wonder—this again explains not a few misunderstandings between French and Italians—how many French political writers have thought that, and wished to underline the fact.

Four years after the renewal of the Triple Alliance of 1902, the Conference of Algeciras over the Morocco question showed the perfect loyalty of democratic Italy even in the delicate situation in which she found herself there, between the Triple Alliance on the one side and the Mediterranean understandings on the other.

Those of my generation who saw the Italo-Turk war of 1911 did not believe in the possibility of a world war. Nor did those believe in it either who, immediately after the Italo-Turk war, saw the Balkan wars. But the very few who, like myself, were present behind the scenes at the Algeciras Conference sensed that the World War was possible.

It is not, therefore, profitless to describe what this Conference was, since I am one of the very few still alive who took part in it.

On the threshold of what became the long-drawn-out Moroccan affair we find the accord of France with Italy and England. By two accords signed in December, 1900, and on November 1, 1902, Italy and France promised each other their mutual disinterestedness in Morocco and Libya. By the Anglo-French declaration of April, 1904, crowning negotiations started in July, 1903, by Delcassé and Lord Lansdowne, the two countries promised each other a reciprocal diplomatic support in Egypt and Morocco; and in what touched Morocco, England recognized that it appertained to France, as "limitrophe" power in Algeria, to assist the Cherifian empire in all the reforms it required, France engaging herself not to change the political status of that empire.

On October 3, 1904, a Franco-Spanish treaty registered "the extent of the rights and the guarantee of the interests" resulting from their special situation.

On March 23, 1904, two weeks before the signature of the Franco-English accord, Prince von Radolin, German Ambassador at Paris, said to Delcassé:

"I am going to ask you an indiscreet question. Is it true that an accord is going to be signed between you and England?"

Delcassé answered that France wished to maintain in Morocco "the actual political status," but to ameliorate it, and he added: "Under whatever form France may be led to lend assistance to the Sultan, commercial liberty will be rigorously and entirely respected."

Radolin found these declarations—so Delcassé noted— "very natural and perfectly justified."

Italy found herself in a more delicate situation than England. By the protocol of disinterestedness signed in December, 1900, apropos of Libya and Morocco, Italy was morally bound to favor the French solutions in Morocco. While remaining a member of the Triple Alliance, Italy had acted fully within her rights in concluding a Mediterranean accord with France, a right that Germany herself had recognized. In fact, when in 1882 Mancini had negotiated the Triple Alliance, he had not been able, despite his efforts, to obtain from Bismarck, in addition to the guarantee of Italian territories, that of "primordial common interests." In other words, Germany had refused Italy aid to assure her the maintenance, if necessary for her, of the Mediterranean equilibrium. If, therefore, some years later Italy sought first from England, then from France the protection of her interests in the Mediterranean, it was because Germany, refusing her that protection, had implicitly recognized that her ally could, without her, in complete independence, settle that order of problems. This is so true that when the Franco-Italian settlement happened the Chancellor, who in 1898 had said, "Germany has no interest in the Mediterranean questions," * repeated in the plainest terms that "the Franco-Italian accords relative to these questions did not, in the main, bear upon the spheres of influence of the Triple Alliance." † Under these conditions how could they be astonished in Berlin that Italy should hesitate to sacrifice, for the sake of an alliance which had always ignored the Mediterranean, treaties signed outside that alliance for the settlement of Mediterranean problems? It was Germany who had not wanted, when Italy entreated her, to take any cognizance of those problems. How could Germany, therefore, in their regard invoke the general obligations of an alliance that she had refused to extend to the Mediterranean? Nevertheless, that was the ground of Prince von Bülow's objection, since he sought to assign to Italy the role of "second," and no more.

This is why at Berlin they were uneasy and offended when, on the eve of the Conference, Marquis de San Giuliano, having succeeded Tittoni at the Ministry of Foreign Affairs, proposed to Marquis Visconti Venosta that he go as First Dele-

* Reichstag, February 8, 1898.
† Reichstag, January 8, 1902.

gate to the Conference, in place of Silvestrelli, the Ambassador at Madrid, who was thought to be very Germanophile. Visconti Venosta accepted on condition that he be given no instructions; he would act in accordance with our alliances and our *ententes,* which were in no way contradictory. He asked also, old-fashioned man that he was, to have but a single political secretary. At that time I thought that I had had enough of a diplomatic career. I had resigned; the post was offered me and I accepted. The next day I left for Algeciras with the old Marquis, his son Enrico—who was his private secretary *—and two chancellery clerks.

At Algeciras we lodged with almost all the other representatives at the Hotel Reina Cristina, which became for three months the harbor of European diplomacy. With its pointed bow-windows, central turret, its massive and squat belvederes, the hotel recalled an illustration from the works of Sir Walter Scott. The building is low and extended, like the houses of that land. Galleries face the bay; little columns ornament them as well as the octagonal bow-windows. In the center a patio adds an Andalusian note. The entire ground floor opens on the patio—billiards and ping-pong rooms, reading rooms, smoking rooms furnished English style. The garden has the luxuriant vegetation of the far south; gardenias, magnolias, eucalyptus, myrtles, palms, lemon and orange trees blended their violet shadows and heavy perfumes. The very long dining room had, at one of its extremities, two round belvederes which gave a semi-privacy. One of them had been reserved by the Spanish diplomats who had come on the staff of the Duke of Almodovar. But the other belvedere was, for them, a cruel problem: Should they favor Germany or the friends of France? It had been decided to close it when the news arrived that Visconti Venosta had been chosen in place of Silvestrelli. The Spanish master of ceremonies felt relieved and reserved the belvedere for him.

The French plenipotentiary was Paul Revoil, a lawyer who was pleading a case; the German was the Ambassador Radowitz, more of an old-style diplomat than a German, but flanked by Tattenbach, more German than diplomat. Sir Arthur Nicolson represented Great Britain; it would be difficult to be more

---

* His younger brother Giovanni later replaced him.

hesitant, or harsher than he, according to the occasion. The American was Henry White, an accomplished man of the world, and conciliator by definition; his secretary, Louis Einstein, made up for the ignorance of his chief in the matter of Mediterranean problems. The president of the Conference was the Spanish Secretary of State, the Duke of Almodovar, much more Arab than the octogenarian Mohammed Torres, disgusted at having to spend the last days of his life as First Delegate of Morocco in the daily intimacy of so many *giaours.*

The conference had two periods: the first, from January 16 to March 3, 1906; the second, from March 3 to the signing of the Act on April 2. The first was dominated by the maneuvers of Holstein, who was then still the Grey Eminence of German policy at Berlin; the second, by the decision of Bülow to liquidate the adventure and retire with honor.

Men of great designs are often dangerous; by that I mean those men who, being only literary imitations of the truly rare statesmen, exaggerate in their own minds their great designs.

Mazarin, Richelieu, Frederick II, Cavour, probably had plans in less complete form than the school history books teach the children of France, Germany and Italy. Unquestionably Cavour wanted the liberty and independence of Italy; but he would have been at a loss to say, when Garibaldi debarked at Marsala, whether it was by a centralizing unity as it developed several months later, or by federal union. Indeed, this improvisation of political genius is verified practically everywhere, even outside the direction of government; Marx wrote the *Manifesto of the Communists* quite a few years before having discovered his reasons for it in *Das Kapital.*

There are those who, wishing to raise their stature, set themselves grandiose goals where the fantastic surpasses the real; such was the case with Holstein.

In the autumn of 1904 the Chief of the German General Staff, von Schlieffen, had declared in a secret gathering presided over by Bülow:

"The only solution from the military point of view I see is an immediate war with France; England is still weakened by her war with the Boers; Russia has the war with Japan on her hands; France is isolated. . . ."

It was only known later that the provider of political ideas to von Schlieffen was Holstein. He and von Schlieffen saw each other at least once a week, but always in secret. Holstein was among those who love the shade. It was Holstein who wanted —behind a hesitant Bülow—the Kaiser's voyage to Tangiers in 1905, "to break the encirclement," he said. At Algeciras Holstein's instructions proceeded from these premises. He had not yet discovered—as he later complained—that William II was "a big noise who can't make up his mind."

Those who lived through the first weeks of the Algeciras Conference must have got the impression that the famous German discipline was a myth. The French often attributed the difference of language of the two German delegates, Radowitz and Tattenbach, to a perfidious Machiavellianism. Nothing was less true. Radowitz was executing formal instructions, and knew no others; while Tattenbach represented the style and ideas of Holstein. Not realizing that, by his very outbursts, he passed and missed the mark, Tattenbach, whose rough manner first gained him some sympathy in this suave conclave of diplomats, continually confided to neutrals that Germany certainly did not want war, but that, if they compelled her to it, she would crush the French "like bedbugs." He was extremely fond of this comparison.

One day he came to complain to the Marquis Visconti Venosta about the cold attitude of the Italian delegation. The First Italian Delegate reminded him that this attitude was only the result of the circumspection dictated by the bonds of the Triple Alliance on the one hand and the Italo-French accords on Morocco, well known in Berlin, on the other.

Tattenbach, blind to the fact that the grand old man to whom he was speaking was the living symbol of European political thought, in the most honorable connotation of the term, proceeded to sermonize him on the true interests of Italy, as if Visconti, former disciple of Mazzini and old friend of Cavour, did not know what they were.

Visconti listened to him with long and patient courtesy, but finally remarked:

"Would you tell me, my dear Count, if you are doing me the honor of speaking according to the instructions of your Government?" Tattenbach admitted that he was not. Whereupon Visconti ended the conversation with:

"I could be your father, my dear Count, so you will allow me to make one remark. The idea you have of diplomatic negotiations is that one ought to jump at the throat of one's adversary, throw him to the ground, kick him and then say: 'Let's have an accord.' That method, if it gets to be general among you, will bring you misfortune."

I had been the silent witness of the conversation. Tattenbach having departed, the Marquis looked at me; I was smiling. He merely said:

"You are right. Let's go for a walk. If we sent a telegram about this we'd risk having the thing taken seriously."

The policy *à la Holstein* had both in Algeciras and London the opposite result of what Berlin had expected of it. The British delegate, Sir Arthur Nicolson, emphasized his support of his French colleague Revoil—and God knows he had little love for the man, Nicolson being so much the reserved and laconic old Englishman, while Revoil was a voluble and florid lawyer.

No need to recall here the interminable controversies of the Conference; destined at the time to conceal the fear of war or the instigation to conflict, they were in themselves senseless, and for a long time now have been covered by a fog of forgetfulness and indifference. The meeting of March 3 alone remains vivid in my memory, as it was the turning point of the adventure; and also because it showed an aspect of the sudden dangers that can surge up, in the midst of a gathering of diplomats.

Bülow had finally understood that the policy of Holstein had brought Germany to an impasse: it was either war or a diplomatic defeat. He now wanted only one thing: to liquidate the whole matter, but on condition that Germany should not appear to be isolated in Europe. The meeting of March 3 proved to the world, on the contrary, that the Reich was isolated; but—and this is the fact that the historians often ignore—the proof came much more by chance than by any firm desire of Germany's adversaries. Historians often see many deep laid plans where few exist.

It was only a point of procedure that brought to light Germany's isolation. Should they adjourn the Conference, in view of the fact that the reports on the Bank were not yet ready and that the Germans did not want a discussion on the Police so long as the question of the Bank had not been settled?

Sir Arthur Nicolson saw there the occasion he had been looking for. "Since we cannot profitably examine for some time the project of the Bank, and since we have, up to now, had too many vacations, I propose that tomorrow afternoon's meeting should be devoted to the organization of the Police."

Count Cassini, who immediately understood what was up, approved. Revoil did the same. The Entente Cordiale was mobilized. Discomfited and agitated—and everyone was aware of it—Radowitz rose to declare that the Bank matter should be settled before considering the Police, and that, consequently, it would be best to adjourn once more. The Duke of Almodovar, who was presiding, concluded that in the presence of two contradictory opinions he would consult the Conference; as President he could not do otherwise, but it is certain that he did not, at the moment, realize the symbolic importance of the matter. The voting was in alphabetic order, according to French spelling of national names. Radowitz renewed his objections. The Austro-Hungarian delegates, with some hesitation, stated a similar opinion. The Belgian Baron Joostens said that he would agree with the majority. White was more definite: "I see no inconvenience," he said, "in beginning at the Committee's meeting the examination of the Police question. I think, moreover, that if our President absents himself on the occasion of a visit to Madrid of the King of Portugal it would be expedient that, at the time of his departure, the study of all the articles of the program should be as far advanced as possible." Revoil, who had already given his opinion, insisted: "The question of the Bank cannot be taken up. It is conformable to precedent to pass on to that of the Police." Sir Arthur Nicolson stated that as he had taken the initiative of the proposition he did not have to repeat himself; he approved.

Then came Marquis Visconti Venosta's turn. Radowitz recovered hope, for if he should vote with Germany—it was certain that The Netherlands and Sweden would follow him—there would be six votes against the English proposition, and six for it, the Belgians having to abstain for lack of the majority to which they had promised their vote. This would check the proposition. But the Italian delegate had begun to speak, and in an impressive silence declared: "I propose, in the interim, to devote a meeting of the Committee to a first exchange of views on the question of the Police."

France had won. The Netherlands delegate took the side of the last speaker, and the Portuguese delegate did the same. Count Cassini reiterated his adherence to the views of Revoil. The Swedish plenipotentiary declared he would abstain from voting, and put himself at the Conference's disposal, that is, of the majority which from that moment was formed, since eight delegates, to which the Belgian delegate would be added, had voted for the proposal. The Moroccan delegation voted no. But the Spanish delegation added a yes to the nine preceding. That made ten for and three against. Here was the proof that Germany was isolated, since only Austria and Morocco voted for her.

After that meeting the Conference lost all political interest. Bülow rallied whole-heartedly to the idea of its liquidation. On the last day Visconti Venosta loyally defined Italy's role by the following which he dictated to the French journalists:

"In my quality of representative of a country profoundly attached to the cause of peace my mission consisted in playing a role of loyal mediator. Furthermore, I have refused to believe that the Conference's failure would have necessarily provoked a war. But it might have created disquiet and uncertainty about the morrow, prejudicial to all economic and financial interests. This is what my Government has desired to avoid.

"Italy could not, moreover, forget either its alliance with one of the Powers in the case, nor the happily reestablished cordiality of her relations with the other, nor, finally, the identity of her views with those of this latter on the Mediterranean questions. Thus placed in a situation which was, in certain regards, delicate and difficult, I could not do otherwise than pledge myself to a loyally conciliatory action.

"As for the relations between France and Italy, which are, I believe, the aspect of the matter which interests you most particularly, you can say that they are as good after the Conference as they were before. Nothing has weakened the understanding that reciprocal interests had suggested with regard to the Mediterranean."

All through the Conference Tattenbach, wanting to belittle Visconti Venosta, kept remarking to every listener: "He is a Francophile," and some of the French, thinking to praise him, were saying the same thing. Both were wrong, with aggravation of the error for the French in that, without being conscious of it, they cheapened the meaning of Visconti Venosta's position, even in respect to France. Visconti had expressed the whole of his conception, which was also that of all Italian statesmen (almost including Crispi), in a speech he delivered in the Italian Senate on February 10, 1899, six years before Algeciras, where he declared that "Italy's interests are intimately associated with the great general interests of European peace," that the Italian people desired "to live in good harmony and friendly relations" with France, and that "to cultivate, to entertain the germs of antagonism and hostility between the two peoples is not to work in conformity with the great cause of civilization and human progress."

Three days after the end of the Conference, Visconti Venosta read with me in Paris, where we had stopped for the night on our way back to Rome, the famous telegram that William II sent to the Austro-Hungarian Minister of Foreign Affairs, Count Goluchowski:

"At the moment when I am sending, with the consent of your very gracious sovereign, the Grand Cross of the Order of the Red Eagle to the Count von Welsersheimb in gratitude for the very successful action he exercised at Algeciras, I want to express to you, with all my heart, my sincere thanks for the unshakable support you gave my representatives.

"You have accomplished a fine action as a faithful ally. You were a brilliant second in the field and, in a similar case, you can count on a like service on my part." *

* A great part of the Austrian press commented irritably on this imperial appreciation which, according to them, diminished Austria's role. Count Goluchowski, likewise, was far from gratified. Some weeks later William II, being in Vienna, aggravated this dissatisfaction.

One evening, after dinner, as the German Emperor was talking with his Ambassador in a salon, Francis Joseph being absent, he turned suddenly to Count Goluchowski and calling to him familiarly, "Golu! Golu!" he cried, "come here, now, and sit beside *your* Emperor!"

It was, of course, only a manner of speaking. But "Golu" thought it a little too cavalier. He came and sat down beside "his" Emperor and listened with resignation to the compliments reserved for him.

We read it in the *Temps* which was brought to us at dinner. Indifferent and prophetic, Visconti merely said: "He is a fool; he'll lead Austria to her ruin."

More irritated than my chief by the semi-romantic and semi-theatrical language of William II, and convinced that his *Gothische wahn* (Gothic delirium) which Heine had already made ridiculous, had become a grave danger for peace, I wrote in silence, then and there, on the menu a project for an autograph letter of the King to the Kaiser. Briefly, the letter affirmed our loyalty to the alliance, guarantee of peace, but added that a firm alliance could exist only between equals, not between duelists and "seconds," and that Italy being a country of public opinion, such manifestations as the telegram to Goluchowski did not strengthen the alliance. Visconti read it and said: "Yes, this is good; I'll give it to Sonnino [then Prime Minister] for him to have copied by the King."

At Rome Sonnino at first approved, but next day declared to Visconti that it would be better to keep silent, that it was *"acqua passata"* (water under the bridge). So little, however, was it *"acqua passata"* that in 1914 Berlin did exactly what the telegram promised: It rendered "a like service" to the Austro-Hungarian aristocratic and military caste which had plotted the destruction of Serbia.

As we shall see, it was the Austria of the Hapsburgs that provoked war in 1914; while Germany certainly wished the war, or, at least, all the advantages of the war; yet, without the pressure of the dominant Austro-Hungarian caste, she would not have decided at that time to unchain the conflict. Everything was going too well with her, even without war.

XVI

RELIGION, CLERICALISM, ANTI-CLERICALISM

A RATHER WIDESPREAD OPINION HELD OUTSIDE ITALY DE-
scribes the Italians as lacking religious ardor or, at least, any
mystical tendency, when the truth is that few European peoples
have had as passionate outbursts of religious feeling as they.

A generation before St. Francis of Assisi, Joachim de Flora
exalted the soul of half of Italy.

Dante places him in his Paradise:

> *Il calavrese Abate Giovacchino,*
> *Di spirito profetico dotado.*

(The Calabrian Abbé Joachim, endowed with prophetic
spirit.)

Even today his cult lives on in the Calabrian churches where,
on his feast day, they sing this anthem of which it is hard to
say whether it inspired Dante or echoes him: *"Beatus Joachim,
spiritu dotatus prophetico, decoratus intelligentia . . ."* (Blessed
Joachim, endowed with prophetic spirit, adorned with intelligence . . .)

Joachim, like Francis of Assisi, the son of rich parents, aban-
dons all, as did the *poverello;* he makes the pilgrimage to
Jerusalem on foot. Having returned to Calabria, he finds
refuge as a simple lay brother with the Cistercians of Sam-
bucia. But there, in contrast with what Francis was to do, he
devotes long years to studying the Bible, he composes works
that harbinger Savonarola's wrath in which the Church's sal-

vation can be seen as attainable only by the transfer of the pastoral functions to the monks and contemplatives. The condemnation of the Holy See in its temporal power seems implicit in Joachim's doctrine. But Joachim was not a haughty man; he bowed before the verdict of the bishops and the Pope, and that saved him. The Church at first protected, and then adopted the pure ascetic whose doctrines had been condemned in 1212 by the Council of the Lateran.

Europe was then torn by heretical sects imbued with deep mutual hatreds. In Italy they found a less propitious field than elsewhere. Joachim's message had sufficed the Italians, thanks to the Christianity he preached: it sought to separate itself from the coldly literal interpretation and rise to the purity of the Gospel age; but all this without revolt, without heresy.

If the heretical movements seemed at times to continue on into the thirteenth century, it was mainly because they were instigated and encouraged by Emperor Frederick II, fighting against the popes.

Joachim de Flora had been dead only a short time when his heritage was recovered in Umbria, but relieved of all apocalyptic vision, by Francis of Assisi who enunciated the first human message of which one dares to say that it approximates that of Christ: Christianity's salvation is confided by Francis to the inner man; the Church will be saved by the work of souls, by the unanimous aspiration of the faithful.

All of Francis of Assisi is in his *Cantico di sole* (Canticle of the Sun) whose original title in the thirteenth century was *Laudes creaturarum* (The Praise of Creatures).

This fragment of Christian poetry, as inspired as the *Te Deum*, praises and thanks God for "Brother Sun which lights up the day," for "Sister Moon and the stars," for "our sister Mother Earth which sustains and keeps us"; and finally, in the last of his immortal strophes, Francis praises and thanks God "for our sister, the bodily death—from which no living man can flee."

The entire canticle makes us feel that, contrary to so many Christians of his time, Francis had more confidence in a God of love and compassion than fear of a punitive God. Even without his gift of lyrical flight of the spirit, his disciples continued to think that this lower world is not solely a *lacrimarum vallis* (valley of tears); had not Francis dictated in his rule for them: "Let the Brothers be *gaudentes in Domino, hilares*"? (happy in the Lord, joyful)

But these simple folk, these *hilares,* often had the souls of martyrs, especially in the stormy generation following that of St. Francis.

After the Council of Trent religious fervor in Italy assumed a different form. St. Philip Neri is perhaps the last of the great Italian saints who relived the joyous intoxication of St. Francis of Assisi. After Philip Neri a new series began, that of the ascetics, like St. Louis of Gonzaga.

From the political point of view, one of the abiding traits of the Italian spirit through the centuries had been the quest of a balance between the two powers: the State—which from the time of the Guelphs and the Ghibellines was called the Emperor—and the Church. In that quest appeared the first and most delicate exercise of the spirit, so essentially Italian, of *combinazione,* of which I shall speak further on.

Even the most ardent Ghibellines never freed themselves from a kind of attachment to that Roman Church which everyone regarded as a masterpiece of Italian organization. The Roman Commune never missed an occasion to undermine the temporal power of the popes, at least down to the dawn of the sixteenth century. Italian narrators often describe with keen relish the outrages inflicted on popes too avid of temporal successes. But the Italians never took the side of the antipopes. For them the antipopes were only puppets of the German Emperors. Not only were they of foreign make, but even for Italians not of the Catholic faith the equilibrium would have been lost and Italy would have risked becoming *Tedesca* (German).

The Church herself often compromised in Italy. She never tried to oppose the dissemination of Italian masterpieces in which she was sometimes maltreated—in the *Divine Comedy,* for example, or Petrarch's *Canzoniere.* And if she prohibited a single work of Dante, the *De Monarchia,* the reason was that it had been written in Latin and, what is more, no one was reading it.

The same tolerance was observable two centuries later with respect to Ariosto, whose satires and comedies were anything but respectful to the clergy and the traffic in indulgences, an evil of the first part of the sixteenth century.

This tradition of tolerance did not end with the Counter-Reformation. In 1617, and a second time in 1667, the Inquisition of Spain solemnly inscribed Dante and Petrarch in its Expurgatory Index. At Madrid they wanted to incite Rome to act; but the popes turned a deaf ear, and they even derided these Spanish fanatics. The popes were Italians; they knew these poets by heart; how could they proscribe Dante and Petrarch whose poems formed an essential part of their own mental lives?

If the heresies of the Middle Ages had so little hold on the Italians, and if the same could be said for the Reformation of the sixteenth century, it was primarily, at least in the first period, due to the atmosphere of moral liberty that was breathed more widely in Italy than in any other country of Europe. The *pataria* of the Lombard and the *catari,* from the east, were merely social revolts: Italy's peasant revolts.

Foreigners, especially those of Catholic countries, have had in the past some difficulty in understanding the complexity and subtlety of the political relations between the Italian people and the Church; to attempt to understand them one should never forget that Dante, the greatest Catholic poet of the entire world, did not hesitate to put several popes in the third *bolgia* of his hell—that of those guilty of simony. It is there that the poet, encountering Pope Nicholas III, addresses the bad Popes in an apostrophe that all the Italians have known by heart for five hundred years. Despite his *"riverenza per le somme chiavi"* (reverence for the pontifical keys) he cries to them:

> *"Fatto v'avete dio d'or et argento:*
> *E che altro è da voi all'idolatre,*
> *Se non ch'egli uno, e voi n'orate cento?*
> *Ahi, Constantin, di quanto mal fu matre.*
> *Non la tua conversion, ma quella dote*
> *Che da te prese il primo ricco patre!"*

(Gold and silver you made your god: in what do you differ from the idolator, that he to one and you to hundred bow? Ah, Constantine, of how much evil wast mother—not thy conversion, but that dower which on the first rich pope thou didst bestow.)

What appeared during the Risorgimento and the second part of the nineteenth century to too many Catholics as an Italian "anti-clericalism" was in reality just anti-temporalism, a tradition going back to the greatest poet of Christianity, to Dante himself.

Six centuries after Dante, Manzoni, the purest and most inspired Catholic poet of the nineteenth century, resumed Dante's thought, not in his *Inni sacri,* devoted solely to the mysteries of religion, but in his life. Very old, living in Milan and going rarely to Turin for sessions of the Italian Senate of which he had been a member since the establishment of the Kingdom in 1860, his close friends urged him to take care of his health and not go to the provisional capital to vote for, as he said he wished to do, the law proclaiming Rome the capital of Italy. The gentle old man replied:

"How shall I dare present myself soon to God having neglected to render the Church the greatest of services, the suppression of the temporal power?"

In his numerous addresses to Italian pilgrims Pius XI often quoted poems of Manzoni or episodes from his *Promessi sposi.* Pius XI had a boundless admiration for Manzoni. In the first months of his pontificate he received my father at the Vatican. They had been intimate friends when as plain Monsignor Ratti he was director of the Ambrosian Library at Milan. In those days they had often talked of Manzoni, whose unpublished writings my father owned and was then publishing. At the Vatican the conversation fell anew on the poet, and the Pope exclaimed:

"How happy I should be, dear friend, if from this place I could persuade all Catholic Italians to read, read, and read again all of Manzoni. . . ."

It was the same Pope who in 1931 published his encyclical *Non abbiamo bisogno* (We do not need) against the pagan theories of Italian Fascism, while so many foreign Catholics, victims of a hypocritical propaganda, believed, or still wished to believe, that the Fascist regime had reestablished religious values at the summit of Italian life.

XVII

REGIONS AND DIALECTS

DISREGARDING THE MYSTERIES OF THE STONE AND BRONZE ages, it must be conceded that in the Greek civilization of southern Italy some of the traits of the Italian of today can be discovered. The civilization of the Etruscans between the Arno and the Tiber was flourishing as early as four or five centuries before Christ; likewise, in southern Italy, that of the Siciliotes and the Italiotes. The civilization of the Siciliotes and Italiotes, descendants of the Greeks established in Sicily and the southern part of the peninsula, was the exclusive base of all their political and social organization. The same can be said for Etruria where, until its conquest by the Romans, there was only a federation of twelve cities, a federation closely bound by religious ties, but which enjoyed the greatest administrative autonomy for each of the twelve cities.

When Rome's domination had extended throughout all Italy, the *civitas* (the city) remained the base and key of the social life of all Italians.

In no other nation have traditions, fables and popular poems necessarily originated in the cities. During the Middle Ages when, in France, they sang the epic *Chanson de Roland,* Italian rhymes taught that Rome had derived from Alba Longa, Alba Longa from Lavinium, and Lavinium from Troy through Aeneas. Virgil's long-popular glory for Italians has consisted in this: that he sang the origin of their nation in the only form pleasing to Italians, that of an affiliation of cities.

Even today the names of the Italian regions that we think of as so alive—Piedmont, Lombardy, Liguria—are not in common usage. The inhabitants of a town of the long Ligurian region which extends from the French frontier along the sea down to Genoa, thence continuing southward to the mouth of the Magra River, will never say that his region is Liguria; he calls himself a Genoan or, at least, says that he is from the Genoan district. It was always so, in contradiction to Gaul where most often the name of the city disappeared and that of its environing region was adopted by the city: thus Lutece, chief town of the Parisii, became Paris; Avaricum, chief town of the Biturges, became Bourges; similarly with Amiens, Rheims, Rennes and so many other cities of France.

This voluntary union of the peasants with the town, which existed almost everywhere in Italy, constitutes one of the most enduring wefts of the Italian social fabric. In no other country is patriotism in its sanest, most normal and fecund form—not in its miserable racial or national deformations—bound, as it is in Italy, first to the city, to the *municipio*. De Sanctis, the Italian critic, to whom, as we shall see later,* the world owes the finest of the many histories of Italian literature, said in his speech to the Neapolitans in 1874: "Italy, gentlemen, is not an abstraction; she is the home, the family, the commune, the province, the region. Those who feel themselves bound to these interests are the best Italians. . . . I repeat, if you want to be good Italians, start by being good Neapolitans. Woe to him who sees only the Italy of the academy and the school." Thus, fifty years before the Fascist adventure, De Sanctis condemned one of the most blustering and spurious Fascist enterprises: the fight against the old traditions of local patriotism. By that alone Fascism showed how foreign all its action was to Italian character.

The secular bond of Italian generations has been created by the city, by the *municipio*. The history of Italian cities is so long and tenacious that it goes back often not only to the heritage of Rome but even to pre-Roman Italy. The little jealousies surviving even today between Parma and Piacenza, between the Lunigiana and its southern neighbor, the Tuscan Versilia, between Lucca and Pisa, probably go back to traditions anterior to Rome, like the notable differences in their dialects.

Republican Rome, furthermore, made of Italy an immense federation of cities, each free to administer itself in its own territory and in its own way. This is reminiscent of the British world in its most recent form, since the democratic word

* Chapter XVIII.

"Commonwealth" has been substituted for the proud "Empire."

The vital force of the Italian cities was seldom destroyed. If the German dominations in Italy were of very short duration and—save for the Longobards—left no imprint, it was due to the fact that they ignored the strength of municipal life in Italy. The Germans had a kind of inferiority complex which kept them away from the Italian cities where they still felt, on the one hand, the splendor of the Italian regime, and on the other, the marvelous and, for them, mysterious germs of the new Italian life. Thus it was that the Germans, while ignoring the towns, naively applied their tribal and rural conceptions to a country where the city was everything. This explains why they left no more traces of occupancy than the German armies have left after years of occupation in Poland, France, the Low Countries and Czechoslovakia.

A king of Hungary once affirmed that any nation that speaks but one language *"imbecillis est."* If that be true—and within certain limits it is very true—the Italians are better off than other European peoples. An Italian is the richer for being an Italian and a Piedmontese, an Italian and a Sicilian, and so on, than a Briton in being both English and Scotch, or English and Welsh. The region enriches the Italian with an interior heritage more varied and ancient than the simple contribution of a poetic Welsh sentiment or realistic Scotch mysticism.

Every Italian is profoundly Italian through his common heritage of thought and language; but in his heart of hearts he is still more of a Venetian, Lombard or Neapolitan without, for all that, ceasing to belong to the common homeland. There is sound reason for the fact that Italians feel a sort of unpleasant embarrassment whenever they meet a compatriot whose accent fails to reveal his native soil; he seems to them either a comedian or a speaker for the radio. We even prefer the accent of the Levantine Italian, being at least able to tell if he comes from Pera or Galata or Alexandria or Cairo. The little liking Italians have for comedy, unless it be in patois, is explainable chiefly on this account.

If the Italians separated themselves from their literature after the Cinquecento, it was owing to the Spanish influence, with its pompous and bombastic style. There were no longer any poems other than those vaunting the victories of the Catholic powers at grips with the Crescent, even those rather puny victories of the Knights of the Order of Santo Stefano over the tartans of Mussulman pirates; and with them poems about the Virgin, about Mary Magdalen and her tresses; patriotic poems without a *patria* to inspire them, religious songs without a true religious sentiment; love songs devoid of tenderness and passion—in short, a repertoire of admirable technical skill, and yet absolutely barren with respect to love, as it was of the Christian faith and feeling for the native land.

Take for example, what was intended to be patriotic, a sonnet of Filicaia's that our fathers all learned by heart with its too famous line,

> *Deh, fossi tu men bella o almen più forte*
> (Ah, wert thou less beautiful or at least more strong)

addressed to an Italy which was, one feels, only a literary tradition, just as in another sonnet we read about the *"candido seno"* (pure white breast) of beauties that never existed. The more Filicaia pompously reproaches Italy for no longer exerting her might, the more he speaks of foreigners as of enemies who were all our serfs, and the more one is convinced that these are only literary exercises. Good Filicaia is inspired by identical furies when he chants the glories of the King of Poland or the King of Spain.

The language itself, formerly so plain and clear, became alienated from the common people; even in the forms of daily life it did not escape turgidity. How could the soul of a people reveal itself through a language which had been overstuffed by their literary mandarins? The Italian people no longer sang or loved, save in the dialects, as when in periods of political oppression a cipher language is adopted by conspirators.

So long as the Italian tongue had retained all its vigor there was no dialectal literature except at the two extremities, Venice and Sicily. When Italian literature had fallen to the level of the Filicaias and the Chiabreras the patois found wings—almost their revenge. In all the cities a multitude of poets with thirty different accents sprouted up as if by magic; popular poetry and popular comedy boldly took possession of the entire

life of Italy—customs, traditions, hates, loves—that the orthodox man of letters had disdained.

Here is one of the paradoxes of Italian life: throughout
Europe dialectal literatures are only rough drafts, preliminary
essays, suppressed by a national literature when it asserts itself,
as in France with the luster of a Bossuet and the genius of a
Racine. Only in Italy the dialects follow a literary epoch of
incomparable brilliancy, almost avenging themselves for its
tyranny after it has sunk into slumber. Then the dialects burst-
ing forth revealed the hearts of the old Italian *gentes*. Pulcinella (Punch), who takes possession of the Neapolitan
theater and ousts the Italian authors, become too stilted, is
probably that old Maccus who appears in so many Roman
bas-reliefs. In Pulcinella one feels the people through whom
the Greeks have passed, as well as the Romans and the Byzan-
tines, the Normans and the Spaniards. Were they always
serfs? Perhaps. But, as in the *commedia dell' arte,* of which
Pulcinella is one of the heroes, *servo di due padroni* (servant
of two masters), and between the two seeking his liberty.

Italian men of letters have too often spoken of the *commedia dell' arte* as of a vulgar episode of our artistic life. On
the contrary, Pulcinella at Naples, Harlequin at Venice and,
with them, Brighella, Pantalone, Captain Fracassa, yield us
the secret of the life and popular customs far more than do the
classic exercises of the seventeenth and eighteenth centuries. In
the latter we find nothing but fine sentiments which are rarely
from the heart. In the *commedia dell' arte,* as in a good part
of the dialectal poetic literature, only the vulgar side of life
is shown, because it is laughable. But not so the dreams,
pudicities, inner loyalties; and yet, sometimes we sense them
in secret depth of hearts.

Voltaire, who often judged lightly, replied in Italian to
Goldoni, who had sent him from Venice one of his comedies
(not in the Venetian patois): *"Oh che purità! Avete riscattato
la vostra patria dalle mani degli Arlecchini."* (Oh, what
purity! You have redeemed your country from the hands of
the Harlequins.) Voltaire was always a little flattering when
he was greatly flattered. Goldoni knew what he owed to the
Arlecchini. Would he not continue throughout his life to pro-

duce comedies in Italian, together with comedies in the Venetian dialect with Arlecchino, Pantalone, Brighella?

If Italy's greatest geniuses appeared almost at the beginning of her literature, it was, on the other hand, only at the end of their vogue that the dialects gave us their two greatest poets: Carlo Porta at Milan and Gioachino Belli at Rome.

Porta appeared and established himself in Milan at the same time as Bonaparte's French soldiers, whose arrival seemed an earthquake to the Milanese. He was a petty employee whom nobody knew. One fine day all Lombardy knew his verses by heart. Even today the types that Porta invented are the heritage of all Italy, almost like some characters in the *Divine Comedy* or Don Abbondio of *Promessi Sposi*. When one meets an old titled dame, forgotten by time, who thanks the good Lord for the blue blood that courses through her veins, one labels her the Marchioness Travasa. Italians have the same feeling for Porta's popular hero Giovannin Bongee that the Spaniards have for Don Quixote's squire.

If Porta came to Milan with the French Revolution, Belli arrived at Rome with the restoration that followed Waterloo.

The Romanesco dialect is very close to Italian; as a matter of fact, a current saying in Italy to indicate the perfect pronunciation of our language is: *Lingua toscana in bocca romana* (Tuscan tongue in a Roman mouth).

Belli is a great poet, of a seemingly impassive serenity, while Porta ill conceals his passionate indignation toward the French invaders, the nobles, the gallant abbés, the too flaccid common people like Giovannin Bongee and Marchionn di Gambavert. Without the least apparent indignation, Belli nails to the pillory the politicians of the pontifical courts, the abbés who are nothing more than courtiers of cardinals or Roman princes. Each of Belli's sonnets is a pure masterpiece. If it must be admitted that Porta is untranslatable, one yet wonders why Belli should not have been translated into French, German, English and Spanish.

Like the Europe of today, Belli's Rome did not even suspect the power of his sonnets. It was only the Italy of the post-1870 era that discovered and recognized Belli. The Rome of his day asked him, indifferently, the same question that Cardinal Hippolito d'Este had posed to Ariosto: "Eh, Messer Lodovico, where have you found so many cock-and-bull stories?"

The "cock-and-bull stories" of Belli, like those of Porta, were the Italian genius itself, which so often has found in the dialects expressions giving additional riches to the language. For example, as to rhyme: the French language—and still more the English—possesses thousands of very short words, and very light, almost veiled rhymes. The Italian language is harder and more crystalline; admirable for thought, it is less so for musicality, despite the legend to the contrary. The dialects offset this, having all the short words of the French and English; whence the greater lightness of their lines.

There are foreign writers, among those who know so much about the details of Italian life and so little about its ardent and passionate soul, who have drawn hasty generalizations from the fact of the vitality of the dialects. In their judgment the Italian unitary sentiment is more artificial than actual.

The fact is that when the history of our dialects is rightly understood it proves the contrary. The dialects produced poets when the language congealed into the artificial and stilted style, when the country was in need of intellectual and political liberty. With the Risorgimento and the great writers it produced, the dialects began to fall silent. They were no longer felt to be necessary.

Only after decades of liberty and unity the dialects showed anew how vital and useful they were. Testoni at Bologna, Pascarella and Trilussa at Rome, Di Giacomo at Naples have, at times, given us works of perfect art. A novel trait in Italian literary life appeared in the Italian writers who had the greatest vogue in the twentieth century and who were wealthier in inner richness and began to incorporate in their novels dialogues in dialect and to enrich their language, despite their consummate mastery of it, with words taken from the dialects. Fogazzaro had several of his characters in *Piccolo Mondo antico* (Small Ancient World) speak in Venetian; Verga, likewise, had his peasant characters that Mascagni's *Cavalleria rusticana* popularized throughout the world speak in Sicilian; Matilde Serao often had her pretty employees and Maupassantian puppets talking in the Neapolitan dialect.

And yet the Italian language had never been so copious and

so rich; the old quarrel over the nature and laws of the language was extinct; what Manzoni had been unable to impose as a precept, the usage of free Italy had instinctively adopted: no more *puristi,* nor classical purists, nor purists of the *uso toscano;* the Italian language with or without "Tuscan usage" had conquered all the Italians.

In this new atmosphere there was no longer any fear of dialects; it was as if they had decided to meet, no longer playing hide-and-seek, making each other's acquaintance, giving for the common use their most secret wealth.

The Italians who, in a completely unified Italy, wrote their comedies and poems in patois showed—and show—that they were more poets than scholars, and that they were willing to sacrifice material advantages to their need to express their art in the form dearest to their souls. In fact, writing in dialect signifies consent that the most intimate and subtle meanings should no longer be comprehended beyond a narrow regional circle; the Italian dialectal poet submits himself to the law that governs actors who enjoy an incomparable influence when they happen to be, for example, Eleonora Duse, but whose genius vanishes the moment they fall silent.

The dialects, furthermore, enriched not only literature but the language of everyday conversation. Thanks to them, thanks to the sap they keep in us, the real Italian never has any set phrases; his words circulate freely, with a constant freshness of expression that begins to be lacking in the French middle-class man of medium culture whose vocabulary is full of crystallized and obligatory phrases. But what foreigner, even among those who know Italy well, is capable of seizing this charming individuality of daily life in which one senses the palpitation of the Italian soul?

In Italy the patois themselves repeat the country's secular law: unity of essential things at Rome; extensive variety of sentiments in each region, each province, almost in each little commune.

CULTURE: DE SANCTIS, CARDUCCI, CROCE

THE THREE GENERATIONS OF THE RISORGIMENTO—I IN-
clude in it the Napoleonic—with their wars and conspiracies
had lived more feverishly than all the Italians of the three
preceding centuries. The intellectual and artistic labor had also
been infinitely more intense. Whence the diminution of vitality
that we have noticed in Parliament from the time it ceased to
be sub-Alpine and became Italian; whence the fact that, from
the time that Italy became unified, no poet even distantly approaching Leopardi or Manzoni, nor a thinker equaling Rosmini, or even Gioberti, issued from her womb. The country for
a while seemed like a thoroughbred that wins the race, but falls
exhausted even while the onlookers' plaudits are greeting his
arrival at the post.

It was more than a crisis of fatigue. There was, on the one
side, the dejection of having to say good-by to old dreams and
illusions rooted in the heart, and on the other, the double labor
of readjusting the traditional forces of the regions in a more
national synthesis, and of putting the regions themselves in
closer contact with the intellectual life of Germany, France
and England, of which most Italians had become the slightly
suspicious admirers, while others—a rare few—wondered
whether, fundamentally, there was so much to admire.

The Italians of the Risorgimento and even of the preceding
generations had been both ahead of and behind the nations
that the seventeenth and eighteenth centuries regarded as being
in the advance guard of the European awakening—England
and France. They had been in advance because their historic
heritage—Rome, the Christian idea, the Renaissance itself—
had given them a universalist feeling which instinctively was
stronger than elsewhere. Even during the political fevers of
the Risorgimento one of the most popular refrains of our
national songs was the celebrated verse,

"Rippasin l'Alpe e tornerem fratelli."
(Let them [the Germans] return across the Alps and we shall again be brothers.)

In the juridical sciences, in the newly-born law of nations we had always remained ahead of other peoples; we had never for an instant denied the universalist spirit which inspired Dante's policy and which permitted Thomas Aquinas to define and desire a *"Societas Nationum"* six centuries before Woodrow Wilson. But, offsetting this—as we have seen in the early chapters of this book—how much time and talent have been lost on an artificial literature, on verses lacking true poetic feeling, on the play of intellect without a sound basis in life, on hot house flowers that the great wind of liberty instantly withered, leaving a sense of emptiness among the mediocre, who are always in the majority. Other elements, some of them external, others internal and sickly, helped to create a wave of sterile discontent.

For example, the entire Mediterranean, the entire Red Sea, the entire Black Sea and all the great cities bathed by these three seas had had Italian as their *lingua franca* of culture and commerce down to the middle of the eighteen-hundreds. What stupefied and alarmed people in Italy was that immediately after the political unification which ought to have afforded additional strength to Italian influence, the Italian language began to lose ground in Turkey, Greece, Rumania, Egypt—where French superseded it, despite France's defeat in 1870. It is true that there were reasons for this fact: the construction of oriental railway lines that connected the Levant with Vienna and Paris, and thereby made the water route via Brindisi or Naples a longer distance to travel; the Austrian Empire's sudden distrust of the language of a great new independent nation, whereas formerly Italian had been the official language of the Austrian bureaucracy throughout the Levant, even in the documents of the Imperial and Royal Embassy at Constantinople; the pacific invasion of the Levant by French Catholic monastic orders which had begun to flee from the lay atmosphere of the Republic. But nevertheless, the fact remained.

Above all, the thing that increased the discouragement and,

consequently, the sterility, was the pitiful showing that Italy made compared with the sudden brilliant fortunes of Germany, which was unified at approximately the same time as Italy. The world seemed to admire everything about Germany: her armies, universities, discoveries and industrial applications; her rapid enrichment, her progress—real or imaginary—in social policy. "Aren't we too old?" Italians began to murmur, especially some of those literati who formerly had been so sure of an Italian *primato* (primacy), who seemed to think: "Perhaps it is true that the Latin people are not made for liberty, while the open, honest, proud children of the pure forests of Germany. . . ." It goes without saying that the German professors accepted and encouraged this homage; they never omitted to send back their acknowledgments in the form of scholarly volumes proving how scientifically true it all was.

With a little more serenity and a little less of that self-criticism which has been a constant characteristic of the Italians, Italy would have discovered a very simple truth: that as regards Germany's fortunes, the potential differences of the two peoples in an industrial period were all in favor of the Germans; and that their progress in unification had been similar only in appearance; for Italy had been made by uniting a swarm of tiny States, while the German unity had been nothing but a progressive aggrandizement of a single State, Prussia, which previously had already been one of Europe's strongest powers.

But there was more to it than that, and no one thought of it in Europe. What to Italians seemed their sudden exhaustion was in reality a general and contemporaneous impoverishment of all the great European nations. There was a widespread European crisis which was especially noticeable in Italy for the eternal reason that the "newcomer," whether man or nation, is judged more severely than those who are already solidly established in a tradition of prestige.

England, citadel of political liberty, rich in her heritage of poets and thinkers, had, it is true, infused a new spirit in the natural sciences with Darwin, but she herself had fallen back, and had contributed to the sterilization of European thought with the sudden wave of facile generalizations on sociology, of which Herbert Spencer was the pontiff and propagandist, which came after Darwin.

France was no longer the France of the Encyclopedists or of the Revolution; when the great voice of Hugo was about to become silent, France could only bring forth the realistic novel in which art entered the service of biological and social whims, themselves an echo of Spencer's preachings.

In Germany they lived with the pomp and insolence of *nouveaux riches,* on the prestige of philosophers and historians of the two last generations—a prestige which had increased especially in southern Italy, where an Hegelian school had long existed. But the German scholars, like Faust, had by that time sold their souls to the Devil for material power. The most mediocre of them, incapable of achieving the level of a Ranke or a Mommsen, had succeeded only in inventing a gigantic new German toy, a mean and narrow philology, which, under the name of "the historical method," substituted itself for the humanist thought that had remained so large and generous in Italy, with Vico, with Muratori and the best scholars of the Risorgimento. The German "historical method" and the excessive respect with which Italians surrounded it created in Italy a cloudy atmosphere in which only "specialization" was respected, an atmosphere in which no one spoke any longer except of the "literature of evidence," whether it was historic or scientific evidence, in which every author suspected of having any originality or imagination whatever was distrusted.

It was natural that in so dull an epoch something still worse should happen: the sudden apotheosis of Positivism. Insufficient, but intellectually honest in England, dangerous in America, with its excess of pragmatism, Positivism became in Italy one of the humiliating phenomena in the intellectual life of a nation. For years they took seriously economists like Achille Loria and criminologists like Enrico Ferri, who generalized certain intuitions of Lombroso (who had genius), and repeated them as pretentious dogma in books which give proof of the mental baseness to which one can descend when one accepts historical materialism and evolutionism as revealed religion. Whoever, like myself, attended as a student Ferri's lectures at the University of Pisa without doubt observed

Italian intellectual life in the vulgarest form to which it attained between 1860 and 1900.

Not at the University of Rome seat of the law school, but at the *Scuola Normale* near the Tower where for Dante's Ugolino *"più che el dolor pote il digiuno"* (fasting was more effective than grief) another representative of the Italian science of that epoch, Alessandro D'Ancona, pontificated. He was deserving of some respect, for he was incomparably more erudite than Ferri, but he was a master limited by this "historical method" about which I have already spoken. A great expert in popular poetry and folklore, he reduced all his studies to extrinsic questions of chronology and text, without ever approaching their poetical or ethical bases.

Nevertheless, even then, in an Italy stupefied by Positivism and cramped by the "historical method" with which the excellent D'Ancona for thirty years atrophied thousands of young Italian scholars, there were two men who might have been the intellectual glory of that generation: Francesco De Sanctis in criticism and aesthetics, and Giosuè Carducci in poetry.

Both of them were passionately Italian; and one of them, De Sanctis, had suffered prison and long exile for Italian liberty. They were—genius apart—infinitely richer in mind than the most gifted of their contemporaries, imbued as they were with the thought and art of all Italy; nevertheless each remained definitely of his own region. De Sanctis was profoundly a Neapolitan, not only in his speculative aptitudes, but even in his southern gay and colloquial simplicity, while Carducci was the first to convey alive the humanism of Florence and Tuscany to the national conscience, vivifying by his poetic spirit what was too cold and transparent in all that came out of Tuscany.

De Sanctis was not in the strict sense of the word a philosopher, but he is the only nineteenth-century European critic whose works are inspired by a unique aesthetic thought. His education had been philosophic; like so many Neapolitans of his generation he had meditated on Hegel, whose works he had even translated while, in 1848, the Bourbon King kept him imprisoned in a dirty and somber cell of the Castel dell'Ovo in Naples for thirty-two months. Afterward there was exile in Malta, Turin and Zurich. It was during these years of teaching and meditation, until his return to Naples with Garibaldi, twelve years later, that De Sanctis, guided by a prodigious instinct leading him always to discern the essential element in poetry, arrived at his conception that the abstract content has no importance in itself, that what counts is the life it acquires—when it does acquire it—in the fantasy of the poet. Fantasy, which is the creative faculty, had not concept and ideas, but *fantasmi*. It is by bathing himself in *fantasmi*, forgetting himself in them, that the poet communicates life to them; and the critic, for his part, forgetting himself in the work of the poet, reconstitutes it, makes it live again. The *Saggi critici* and especially the *Storia della Letteratura italiana*—the result of thirty years of studies and meditations—are the masterpieces left by De Sanctis. It can be said of his *Storia* that it is not only a most perfect example of literary criticism but that it is, in fact, a most complete spiritual history of a people. To those rare individuals worthy of it, encountered during my peregrinations about the world during Fascism, who asked me what book on Italian thought and history to read, I always answered: "De Sanctis—but take care; you won't find in him a single date. It's for you to know the facts; De Sanctis will illuminate them for you with a new and brilliant light."

A strange book, his history of Italian literature—if one judges it by customary standards! When did Dante die? When was Petrarch born? One must search in the chapter where by chance the year of Boccaccio's birth is mentioned, and then calculate on one's fingers: nine years after the birth of Petrarch and eight before the death of Dante!

Such as it is, this book reads like a poem—the poem of intellectual Italy. And today when one exhumes from the library one of the numerous erudite volumes in which Italian and foreign critics imbued with the "historical method" spoke with self-sufficiency and disdain of the omissions and the errors of De Sanctis * one can but smile. They were the kind of people who, had they been capable of reading Shakespeare, would have written memoirs denouncing the fact that, for instance, Shakespeare brings the sea right up to Milan.

* Ferdinand Brunetière, the sovereign critic of the French toward the close of the nineteenth century, was an exception. He often deplored in his writing that De Sanctis had not been translated into French.

Carducci himself, despite his genius as a poet, did not understand De Sanctis, or, more exactly, De Sanctis offended one of Carducci's two personalities: the scholar who was not much warmer or more human than the honest D'Ancona. For in Carducci the scholar and the poet lived separated by an airtight partition, through which the poet received from the scholar merely the images of medieval history which he transformed into poems.

Being both poet and historian of literature, Carducci imitated and continued a long succession of Italian poets, from Petrarch to Parini, Alfieri, Foscolo, Leopardi, born in an Italy often under foreign domination, for whom literature and its study were the means of exercising a moral and political function in the life of the nation. Carducci imitated them; true poet he was, yet his poetry was preeminently patriotic. Leopardi, indeed, had sung of Italy, but his most perfect poems have universal motives; but for Carducci there was no other world than Italy—which explains his small fame beyond the Alps. Italy for him was not just a nation like the others, but the inheritor of Greece and Rome, the cradle of Western civilization. For this reason his early verses are only invectives and satires against the rulers of Italy unified after 1860, who to him seemed too compliant and too meek administrators.

Son of a conspirator, himself a witness of the reawakening and the disillusions of 1848, he may have given the impression of changing in the course of his long life, which he began as an ardent republican and ended with a poem to Queen Margherita: actually he never changed, for he loved only Italy and desired only Italy's grandeur. Foreigners stupidly had traduced the military valor of the Italians; so he sang and loved all Italians who were fighting with the name of Italy on their lips, whether they were republican and Socialist students going to die in Greece, fighting the Turks under the command of Ricciocci Garibaldi, one of the sons of the hero, or whether they were soldiers of the royal army fighting against the Ethiopians. But Carducci was a son of the Risorgimento. His warrior ideal never included the bestial brutality of imperialism and militarism, or, at the most, he accepted of militarism what he thought useful for the moral discipline of the Italians;

and, even when he seems to sing of war as such, he aspires to the day when the war "against tyrants" will no longer be necessary and the *"giustizia pia del lavoro"* (the pious justice of labor) would reign over the world.

Italian as he was, and perhaps too much so, he never fulminated against the Germans or the French; he reserved his wrath for their masters; in his sonnets, *Ça ira,* he described with an almost filial love the France of the Revolution. Of the two poets of the generation preceding his, Petölfi and Mamelli, he loved only Mamelli, because he was human, chaste and kind, without an atom of the Hungarian violence of the other. We shall see later how D'Annunzio falsified the truth when he proclaimed himself *"figlio"* (son) of Carducci. All the pagan sensualism, the exclusive and ferocious nationalism which swept over Italy with D'Annunzio—mud that later fertilized the growth of Fascism—had nothing in common with the sincere poetry of Carducci. In fact, when Fascism appeared with its pseudo-patriotism, it ignored Carducci. This it did through an instinct of self-preservation, and from its point of view Fascism was right.

Carducci was less read after the coming of D'Annunzio and Fascism, though his poetry places him among poets who excel in their own epoch. The reason for his decline in popularity was that D'Annunzio and Fascism represent two long periods of intellectual and moral depression. Croce, so sparing of literary praise, has defined Carducci as the "last authentic Homerid poet."

Carducci's place was not filled by anyone in Italy, least of all by D'Annunzio. Of Carducci might be quoted the fine line that he himself wrote describing Torquato Tasso's arrival at lyrical Ferrara, so rich in poetry:

> *D'Italia grande, antica, l'ultimo vateor viene!*
> (Comes now the last poet of great ancient Italy!)

Carducci's influence on Benedetto Croce's generation can not be exaggerated, though it was less profound and less essential than that of De Sanctis. Croce himself has called his generation *Carducciana.*

But Carducci is only a poet; his work as thinker and critic

is modest. Croce is a philosopher, whose influence on the mode of thought of all Italians, and of foreigners as well, has been tremendous. Even those who reject Croce or who do not like him, and those who would find it offensive to be called *Croci-ani*—a current literary adjective in Italy—have been much influenced by his doctrines; as—if I dare say it—we are all Christians, even those among us who deny that they are.

Universal spirit as he is, Croce is preeminently Italian even in the love of the history of the region of his birth. The first years of his intellectual life he spent in studying Spanish influence on the Italian South, on the comedians and prima donnas of the old Neapolitan theaters, on the patriots of the Neapolitan Revolution of 1799, on the history of Pulcinella, on the commedia dell' arte.

In his autobiography—a slim book, dramatic by dint of not containing a single fact—Croce explains why he gave up his studies and became a philosopher, and what his thoughts had been before this decision about professional philosophers:

"I had a profound respect for professors of philosophy; for I further supposed that they, as specialists, must be in actual possession of this abstruse science from whose table I had with such pains collected a few crumbs. I did not know that I should find within a few years, to my astonishment and annoyance, that most of them possessed nothing of it whatever, not even the little that I, by mere will to understand, had succeeded in making my own.

"But in general, apart from this secret effervescence from which a bubble came now and then to the surface, I was for six years, from 1886 to 1892, wholly turned toward the outer world, I mean toward antiquarian studies; and during that period, among other things, I composed many of the essays afterward collected in my volume on the Neapolitan Revolution of 1799; my annals of the Neapolitan theater of the Renaissance to the end of the eighteenth century; fragments of a book on the eighteenth century in Naples, which now figures as 'Eighteenth-Century Portraits and Anecdotes' in my volume of papers on seventeenth-century literature, and other essays making up a series of 'Historical Curiosities.' I also set on foot, at my own expense, the publication of a library of Neapolitan literature, and started, with a few friends, a review called *Napoli Nobilissima,* dealing with topographical questions and the history of art, in which some of my Neapolitan histories and legends first appeared.

"Apart from any service they may have rendered to the increase of knowledge in the narrow field with which they dealt, and considered only in their relation to myself and my spiritual life, I can now see in these works a certain positive value: first, the delight with which I called up these pictures of the past in a flight of youthful imagination, insatiable in its quest of dreams and of exercise for its literary powers; second, the persistent and conscientious research by which, as a formal discipline, I schooled myself to labor in the service of knowledge." *

Before this period of Neapolitan historical erudition Croce had, while still an adolescent, left Naples for Rome, where he lived with his uncle, Silvio Spaventa, one of the leaders of the Right. It was there that he first attained a clear perception of his own nature. While a student at the University he listened with passionate absorption to the lectures of Antonio Labriola who, having become a Socialist, had introduced and explained the theories of Marx in Italy. "These lessons," Croce later declared, "came unexpectedly to meet my harrowing need of rebuilding for myself in some rational form a faith in life and in the aims and duties of life; I had lost the guidance of a religious doctrine, and at the same time I was feeling the obscure danger of materialistic theories, whether sensistic or associationistic, about which I had no illusions at all, as I clearly perceived in them the substantial negation of morality itself, resolved into more or less disguised egotism. Herbart's ethics taught by Labriola restored in my mind the majesty of the ideal, of *that which has to be* as opposed to *that which is,* and mysterious in its opposition but, because of this same mysteriousness, absolute and uncompromising."

Labriola was the living masterpiece of Neapolitan talent. He had infinitely more ideas than he set down in his rare writings; he was the most amazing conversationalist that Italy possessed at the end of the eighteen-hundreds. I was a law student, twenty years old, when I was presented to him one evening at the Café Aragno at Rome; the conversation hap-

* *An Autobiography.* Oxford, Clarendon Press, 1928. Pages 47-48.

pened to be on the difficulty of reading all the books that had been written on this or that theme. Labriola, shrugging his shoulders, remarked: "Books, books . . . they are only other men's speeches. Who can busy himself with everything that has been said in the world?" Labriola's wide knowledge and his hatred of pedantry, the profound study of Vico's *Scienza nuova* and the works of De Sanctis—these are the things which helped Croce to become Croce.

Most philosophers evidence the genealogical tree of their thoughts. Croce's originality consists in the fact that his intellectual roots are in the entire history of human thought. Croce's philosophy is what happens to him, about him, in his life, in his work, in his study, with no problems set from outside, like puzzles or themes. With regard to the great masters of the past, Croce's attitude always has been, not one of blind respect, but of critical collaboration. "I am," Croce wrote in his *Hegel,* "and I believe one has to be, Hegelian; but in the same sense in which any man who today has a philosophic mind and culture is and feels himself at the same time Eleatic, Heraclitean, Socratic, Platonic, Aristotelian, Stoic, Skeptic, Neo-Platonic, Christian, Buddhist, Cartesian, Spinozian, Leibnitzian, Vichian, Kantian, and so on. That is, in the sense that no thinker, and no historical movement of thought, can have passed away without fruit, without leaving behind it an element of truth, which is either a conscious or an unconscious part of living and modern thought. An Hegelian, in the sense of a servile and bigoted follower, professing to accept every word of the master, or of a religious sectarian who considers dissension as a sin, no sane person wants to be, and no more do I. Hegel has discovered, as others have done, one phase of the truth; and this phase one has to recognize and defend; this is all. If this does not take place now, it matters little. 'The idea is in no hurry,' as Hegel was wont to say. To the same content of truth we shall come, some day, through a different road, and, though we may not have availed ourselves of his direct help, looking back on the history of thought we shall have to proclaim him, with many an expression of wonder, a forerunner."

This page alone reveals the elasticity and eternal youth of Croce's thought and the impossibility of reducing it to a few pages, as can easily be done for so many cold philosophic systems. Those who wish to comprehend Croce's thought need only read his *Estetica,* his *Logica,* and his *Filosofia della pratica;* * whoever tries to make a résumé of a system like Croce's would be undertaking a work as vain as the attempt to give an impression of the elegance of Palladio's villas and Michelangelo's domes by describing in detail merely their measurements; one would have nothing but a sense of emptiness and vacuum. Renewing and continuing De Sanctis' thought, Croce, with his *Estetica,* revolutionized all current ideas on art, down to his time; with his *Logica* and his *Filosofia della pratica* he has shown, humbly and proudly, that no philosophic formulation can be the last word of the All, that it can be nothing more than the last survey mark of the problems set forth; and at the same time the first survey mark of future philosophic formulations which, in their turn, will resolve other problems.

It has been stated that Croce is the poet of philosophy. That is very true, but it would be only a part of the truth if one did not add that Croce's spirit is profoundly religious, since his thought is constantly imbued with the duty of knowing and serving the True, nothing but the True. In conceiving the unity of the spirit as the eternal ideal rhythm of art and logic, identifying art and philosophy, in declaring that all history is contemporaneous, Croce has laid the basis of a new mentality in Italy and in the entire world. It has also been stated that Croce will not leave a philosophic school. What high praise for Croce! If his ideas and tolerant comprehension have not created a school it is because they have infiltrated, consciously or unconsciously, the minds of those who think, of those who will not despair of life, of those who—even if the positive religions dry up in them—wish to keep the religious sense of life and history.

Few men have done a more lasting service to the moral elevation of Italian thought than Croce. And Croce the man has always been worthy of Croce the thinker. When Fascism affirmed itself triumphant in Italy, in the very early years of its power, pressure and flatteries were exerted from a hundred sides to induce him to consent to "explain" the Fascist phenom-

* All translated into English.

enon, and thereby justify it. Croce never hesitated: he felt immediately, instinctively, that Fascism was carrying Italy to her ruin, and he did not yield. If, in 1924, he gave his vote in the Senate to those who, after the discussion on Matteotti's assassination, wanted to believe in the promises of "normalization" of a baffled Mussolini, it was because he feared a still more dangerous wave of Fascist violence if the Cabinet was overturned. I had said to him: "You know that every word of my speech is true, where I posed Mussolini with the dilemma, 'either incapable or a liar'; you know that your name belongs to Italy and the world even more than to yourself. . . ." Moved as I have never seen him, he answered: "I am too fearful, not for myself, but for Italy—of the violences that Mussolini would unchain, for he will not draw back, and the King will do nothing."

In 1927 I had ceased to take part in the meetings of the Senate, which was no longer anything but a parade in the service of the Fascist propaganda, and from which our speeches no longer reached the Italian people. Croce ceased his attendance in 1929. His last act as senator was a service rendered to Italian political thought: a short speech, each line of it a formidable argument to explain his vote against the treaties of the Lateran between Mussolini and Pius XI.

PART FIVE: SOCIAL MOVEMENTS

XIX

ORIGINS AND EARLY SUCCESSES OF SOCIALISM: BISSOLATI

THE FIRST WORKMEN'S SOCIETIES FOUNDED IN ITALY, UNITing social preoccupations with practical ends, sprang up between 1848 and 1859. Most of them had been created by disciples of Mazzini. In 1863 there were 453, with some 150,000 members; in 1873 they had risen to 1000, with 200,000 members.

Besides this movement there was the anarchic organization headed by Michael Bakunin, a Russian prince in whom mediocrity of intelligence was compensated by an ardent dynamism and, perhaps, by a profound love of the poor—Russian style. He had established himself at Naples, and later at Locarno, where enthusiastic Italian friends had made him the gift of a villa. The titles of the little Italian newspapers of Bakunin's partisans indicated that he had recruited his adepts in that substratum of Italian revolutionary violence which created so many difficulties for the later organizers of a Socialist party with deputies in Parliament. At Fano there was the *Communardo*, started shortly after the Paris Commune; at Leghorn there were the *Satana*, the *Ateo*, the *Ladro* (Thief); at Ancona the *Lucifero*, at Ferrara the *Petrolio*, at Milan the *Anticristo*. These names and these hatreds in the manner of Vanni Fucci, that Italian so typically Italian in Dante's *Inferno*,* horrified Mazzini, who saw no social progress that did

---

* *Le mani alzò con ambedue le fiche,*
  Gridando: "Togli, Dio, chè a te le squadro."
                                        Inferno, XXV.
(Lifted his hands aloft with both the figs,
Shouting: "Take them, God, for at thee I aim them!")

not include a religious sentiment elevating all classes. Mazzini had been perhaps too severe with regard to the Paris Commune which he had judged only on the malignant testimony of the French press. Garibaldi, endowed with his man-of-the-people common sense, saw more clearly when, in 1873, he wrote: "The defeat of the Paris Commune is a misfortune for humanity. . . . I say it with pride: I am an internationalist."

What Mazzini did not understand, what Garibaldi did not try to understand, what the intellectuals of the Bakunin type disdained to see—being otherwise occupied gossiping in the crowded cafés of the cities—was that a great movement of Italian social renovation—Italian style—is only possible in Italy on the day when the peasants, especially those in the South, threaten revolts demanding a redistribution of the land. All the rest is only politics for Marxist or pseudo-Marxist writers.

The Italian Socialists—even when they become powerful and influential, like Turati—have always ignored the first distant symptoms of a rural Socialism. This has been their great mistake.

At the end of the winter of 1877 some dozen persons under the influence of Cafiero, a disciple of Bakunin (but more active and more generous than the Russian), were in the habit of gathering in the evening in a village called San Lupo, near Benevento, in southern Italy. The opportunity to do *qualche cosa* (something), but something practical (as their decision had been), came to them on the night of April 6 when the rural police approached the house where Cafiero's friends had foregathered. They fired on the police and wounded two. Then the band, carrying a red and black flag, left in the night for the neighboring village, Letino, where they occupied the municipal building. The syndic and the *giunta* requested a written statement discharging them from all responsibility. The invaders, having written it out on the syndic's own table, gave it to them to read: "We the undersigned declare that we have occupied by force of arms the municipality of Letino, in the name of the Social Revolution." Their signatures were affixed to it. The syndic, satisfied, pocketed it and left.

Second act: The band then took the cadastral and civil government registers, made a pile of them near a great cross in the center of the commune's square and set them afire. The whole village had turned out, moved but not displeased. The women cried: "We want partition of the estates"; and that cry was the only one that counted. The insurgents replied: "We are here for that. You have arms; partition the estates among yourselves." The village priest Fortini mounted on the pedestal of the cross and, inspired, said: "These men are true apostles of the Lord; the Gospel wills it!" He joined the band, which marched on another neighboring village, Gallo, with cries of *"Long live the Social Revolution!"* Tamburini, the priest of Gallo, felt safe on seeing his colleague of Letino at the head of the rebels and said philosophically to his flock: *"è buona gente"* (they are good fellows); "they are only changing the government and burning the registers." Nothing could have been more pleasing to the whole village. There was a new consignment of cadastral registers to the flames. Next they went to the mill, where they destroyed the flour meter that determined the tax, then so detested, on the charge for grinding. Joy was unconfined.

But the city—where lived the *Signori*—sent troops. The rebel band retreated into the forest of Matesa where intense cold, snow and hunger subdued the rebels. Arrested, they were judged at the Capua assizes. The jury acquitted them. Among them were the son of a family with an ancient title of Count, a lawyer and a chemist.

Two years later a similar episode occurred at Calacabiano in Sicily. And later still another in Puglia.

For a long period there was silence, resignation. Then risings of the same kind broke out afresh in Sicily, but this time on a larger scale, at the close of 1893. At Catania, three years earlier, they had formed a *fascio dei lavoratori* (organization of workingmen). The word propagated itself; very soon there were *fasci* throughout the island. Disorders were sporadic, more in the villages than the cities. Once more they burned the communal registers. They also burned the local tax offices. Crispi, firm believer in conspiracies, proclaimed a state of siege. The few men who had placed themselves at the head of the *fasci,* Dr. Barbato, de Felice, Verro, Bosco and others, were condemned to severe penalties of imprisonment. The whole of Italy was shocked. There were repercussions in dis-

tant Lunigiana in the North, where disorders broke out, but
these were typically political, not peasant revolts as in Sicily;
for, if in Lunigiana misery was far from being as grim as in
Sicily, there always had been in compensation two traditions
lacking in the South: one was Mazzinian, the other anarchist;
Socialism had not yet made its appearance. It was only subsequent to the mad repressions of Sicily and Lunigiana that
Socialism asserted itself, and Barbato, de Felice and Bosco
were elected deputies.

In 1896 the Socialist daily, *Avanti,* began to appear under
the editorship of Bissolati, and as long as it remained in his
hands the seriousness and competence of its discussions were
truly remarkable. Antonio Labriola, as we know, had popularized the Marxist doctrine in Italy. In the void that Positivism
had left, and before the influence of Croce was felt, Socialism
seemed to the majority of Italian youth the most generous and
comprehensive path open to them. This hatching of Socialism,
and even the simple method of Socialism, were precious for the
development of the Italian middle classes. It was an exclusively
Italian phenomenon, nothing like it having appeared in Germany, and still less in France, where the dividing line between
the possessors and the innovators remained fixed and impassable. It was a great advance for Italy to be no longer able to
organize political conflict based on magnificent but often un-
real names, like Liberty or Republic. The codes and the juridic
forms were no longer considered as the expression of a natural
immutable law; the parties of the Right and Left very soon
appeared to those aware of the concept of social classes struggling among themselves for their interests, to be extremely
trivial divisions.

Even the moral life gained an advantage from the increasing strength of Socialism: not only did De Amicis, then a
famous writer, become a Socialist for reasons of sentiment, but
the books of Giacosa, Renato, Fucini, Verga, Matilde Serao
were impregnated with a deep sympathy for the sufferings of
the humble. An ultra-conservative French writer who had
come recently to Italy could write, almost despite himself,
struck by the widespread humanitarian sentiment then existing: "Among the Italians there is a tender and just feeling
for the sufferings of the populace, due to the intimacy, almost

a mixture of the classes, in a society which has remained fundamentally less proud and more Christian than ours."

The men, the leaders, counted for a great deal: Prampolini,
who was a sort of primitive Christian, converted all the peasants of Reggio in Emilia into Socialists by the purity of his
love alone; Turati at Milan was the quintessence of humanism;
De Amicis, great heart if not great artist, put all his heart at
the service of the movement; De Felice gave it his flaming
soul. Of all these men I knew intimately only one, Bissolati.
Evoking his memory, I shall show why Socialism so suddenly
gained a formidable domination over the Italian soul—and
why that domination vanished when to men of an angelic purity
like Prampolini, of moral nobility like Bissolati, of fineness
of spirit like Bonomi, succeeded the scientific charlatanism of
Enrico Ferri and the political charlatanism of Mussolini.

Bissolati was among the little group of bourgeois intellectuals who, having introduced Socialism into Italy between
1880 and 1890, became toward 1900 the leaders of the new
party. Others, like Antonio Labriola, may have had a deeper
knowledge of the economic thesis of Socialism, but Bissolati
had this power: one had only to be near him, and it seemed
entirely natural to be a Socialist or to aspire to be one. He
was to the Socialist organization what a saint is to the organization of the Church: he makes converts, and directly one has
been converted one is surprised to find so few saints.

The elite of Italian youth influenced by Bissolati, Turati,
Labriola and Bonomi was carried toward Socialism. The ideals
of the Risorgimento which had enflamed three generations of
Italians could no longer be a live force, since Italy had been
unified and was free. The Church herself was not absolutely
against the new current: the famous encyclical *Rerum Novarum* which Leo XIII published in 1901 had even given some
Catholics the idea of founding a workers' party under the
aegis of the Vatican.

But from Marxism flowed two fatal ideas. If one of them
carried spirits like Bissolati to a religious will-to-action for
the progressive alleviation of the proletariat, the other, by its
concepts of force and dictatorship that Marx imagined in the
service of a social and moral renewal, was bound to establish
among troubled spirits as objects-in-themselves, the dangerous

instruments that Marx, despite his Jewish apocalyptic spirit, had nevertheless conceived exclusively as a means for fraternity and peace. From 1850 Mazzini had dimly glimpsed this somber and dangerous side of the new evangel of Marx. Bissolati, who in so many ways recalls Mazzini, experienced it personally in 1912 when he was expelled from the Socialist party as a result of an attack by a young journalist, Mussolini, who, at the party's Congress at Reggio, provoked and obtained the expulsion of the moderate members.

This is how it happened. Bissolati had never, either in spirit or act, separated the struggle against the social injustices from the most loyal love for the Italian homeland. In 1908, at the time of the Austrian *coup* for the annexation of Bosnia-Herzegovina, he was one of the first in Italy to point out what hidden dangers the new policy of force inaugurated by the Hapsburg monarchy might hold for peace. In 1911 he had approved the Italian conquest of Tripolitania and Cyrenaica, declaring that a colonial policy was not incompatible with a regime of democracy.

But at the Socialist Congress of Reggio—one of those Congresses which had become more and more like the old Byzantine Councils where for months they discussed the theological question of the *filioque* clause—the expulsion of Bissolati and his moderate comrades would have been long and difficult if they had indulged in the discussion of ideas. Luckily for the demagogue there was a fact—one of those tangible facts which they, and only they, knew how to travesty into treason. A little while before, a madman having fired a pistol at the King without wounding him, the deputies had proposed that the Chamber should go *en masse* to the Quirinal to felicitate Victor Emmanuel; and Bissolati, who had always rejected every act of violence, had thought it fitting and proper to go with the others to felicitate a sovereign who had proclaimed when he mounted the throne that he would consecrate himself "to the guardianship of liberty."

The aforesaid Mussolini, who had acquired a certain notoriety the year before by organizing violent demonstrations against the departure of troops for Libya, declared to the Congress that "attempted assassinations are for kings only trade hazards, like a mason's fall from a scaffold"; that the act of

Bissolati constituted a recognition of the monarchy, and that consequently it was contrary to Socialist thought.

An intoxicated mob ejected Bissolati from the party, and Mussolini's period began. The choice between the two men was one of two opposing worlds of ideas and sentiments. Mussolini showed himself, then and there, as a demagogue who could terrify the bourgeoisie, and would lead the proletariat to victory through terror. The masses believed in Mussolini; henceforth there would be no place among them for a man of the moral and intellectual purity of Bissolati.

My friendship with Bissolati became intimate during the first World War. From the first moment he had favored Italy's intervention at the side of the Allies "in order that our country should help to be a valid instrument to bring to birth from this international crisis the new world whose dawn we foresee," as he wrote on August 2, 1914, to our common friend, Bonomi.

On Italy's entrance into the war he volunteered; he was then fifty-eight years old. He fought with our Alpine troops in the trenches in the Alps and, twice wounded, remained at his post.

Respected by all Italians, he was invited to enter a coalition Cabinet during the war and accepted.

Deeply faithful to the conceptions of which Woodrow Wilson had become the apostle, he wanted an understanding— both during the war and afterward—with the Slav nations struggling to escape the Germano-Magyar hegemony. Not having been able to convince the Minister of Foreign Affairs, Sonnino, he resigned from the Cabinet, in which he had accepted office against his will, for he would have preferred to stay with his Alpine troops. In the letter of resignation he sent to Prime Minister Orlando on December 28, 1918, he declared: "It seems to me that a superior interest of Italy—superior even to the difficult question of what is due to the Yugoslavs—ought to counsel concessions on what the Treaty of London assigns to us, concessions which could find elsewhere compensations desired by the Italian soul. But our last discussions prove to me that I am not in accord with the actual directive of our foreign policy. Therefore, I beg you to accept my resignation as a Minister."

A few days later he thought it his duty to explain to the

Italian people his conception of a just peace. And on January 11, 1919, he decided to speak to the people of Milan at the Scala Theater.

Contrary to my advice (he had asked for it, writing me at Constantinople, where I was High Commissioner) he wished to reaffirm in his Milan speech not only the necessity of an *entente* with the peoples which had submitted to the Hapsburgs up to that time, but also his lack of enthusiasm for the annexation of the Alto Adige as far as the Brenner Pass. It seemed to him that north of the purely Italian populations of the Trentino one could trace a good geographic frontier and accept it without going so far as the Brenner. Consequently, he wrote in his speech: "If Italy demonstrates that she has no scruples about offending three national sentiments at once—the German, the Slav and the Hellenic—she will lose the authority and the strength which would be necessary to curb the egoism and the instinct toward violence which will emerge at the Peace Conference." *

His speech, which he wrote entirely himself, began by establishing that the League of Nations, destined to "close the era of international anarchy and to initiate the era of human law," would be falsified from the outset if the nations did not conclude just peaces.

After having given a lengthy description of the bases on which Italy ought to make peace with the Yugoslavs, a peace of justice and, at the same time, one useful to our country, he declared that, acting in this manner, "the Italian homeland would become in Europe the advance-guard nation of the Wilsonian movement."

The speech, which was subsequently read, could not be delivered at the Scala. A tumult as violent as it was artificial prevented Bissolati from being heard, and he had to withdraw after a few words. The demonstration had been organized by Mussolini. Bissolati had conceived his speech as the continua-

---

* I replied to Bissolati: "I don't say you are absolutely wrong regarding the Upper Adige, though my conscience accepts the frontier at the Brenner since the Germans have several times tried to invade us, while we have never wanted to invade their country. I am incomparably more in agreement with you as to the Dodecanese. But the only problem of the hour is that of the Entente between the peoples who had to suffer the domination of the Hapsburgs. That's the problem of the hour; it's the only one that counts today."

tion of all he had said to the soldiers in the trenches when he encouraged them to resist and die for an ideal of peace, "in order that our sons shall not see this." But the men who had understood and shared his thoughts were either dead on the field of battle or dispersed in the cities and countrysides of Italy. In their place there was only the new wave of adolescents who had hardly glimpsed the war, who could not comprehend, had they wanted to—and they did not—the dream of human liberation which Bissolati had shared with so many of their elders. The newcomers saw in the war only this: some of them, adventure and military glory, whence, later, came the will to seek them at Fiume with D'Annunzio; while others saw in it an opportunity they had missed to make their way in life, to taste the pleasures of life—and they, too, voyaged to Fiume. Young men, eager to follow D'Annunzio, were incapable of understanding Bissolati.

At Milan, at the head of this mixture of immature spirits and adventurers was this same Mussolini who had already succeeded in vanquishing Bissolati in 1912—but then, with entirely different reasons or pretexts.

The Italian Socialist Party, which had never abandoned its distrust of the war, saw the defeat of its former comrade not without a certain satisfaction. In the ignominious way in which Bissolati had been treated after the war, Italian Socialism could see only a demonstration of its wisdom and foresight when it had confined itself to seeing in the war exclusively a "conflict of capitalist interests." There, they said, is the end of Bissolati who had thought otherwise.

As a matter of fact, in remaining deaf to the current of ideas on a just peace, on the liberty of nations that Bissolati had proclaimed, the Italian Socialist Party merely separated itself further from the deepest feelings of the nation. Unfortunately the vulgarization of Marx's formulas had had on the militant Socialists and their leaders the effect of diminishing the individual ascendency of conscience. The party, become an organization, had lost its romantic force, as happened later in Germany. When Fascist appetites, parading under a defunct idealism, hurled themselves to the assault against all the Socialist positions, it was perceived that—with a few admirable exceptions—the party organization which had nearly dominated

Italy was only the framework of an administrative organization; the only life that counts, the moral life, no longer existed. It was then understood why there had no longer been room for the Bissolatis.

Bissolati died on May 6, 1920. Six months later I finally achieved, with the Treaty of Rapallo, that just peace with the Yugoslavs which I had so often discussed with my friend, who was already very ill; the shadow of death hung over him, and he knew it. Nevertheless, he continued to interest himself in what was our mutual desire, that the first peace freely consented to by both contracting parties since the World War should be an Italian peace.

Former skeptics, the former comrades of Bissolati, the Socialists, rejoiced over this peace when it became a fact. In the parliamentary discussion preceding the vote their orator, Treves, declared: "It is the first treaty after the war which, in a sense, denies the war, since it proves by the facts that very serious territorial questions are solvable and can be settled by free accords."

But at the vote, prisoners of their formula, prisoners of their former attitude toward Bissolati, they lacked the courage to vote in favor of it, and took refuge in refusing to vote.

The Socialist Party, well supplied though it was with morally respectable leaders, some of them of fine intellect, like Treves and Turati, was no longer equal to its task. Enmeshed in theories, it gave the impression of ignoring the values of human idealism that Bissolati had tried to keep alive in its heart. Actually it was not so; but appearances are also a reality. Without realizing it, they were preparing the party's death on that day when they, even the best of them, accepted or submitted to Bissolati's expulsion by Comrade Mussolini.

XX

THE CRISIS OF SOCIALISM

WITH THE PRAMPOLINIS, THE TREVES, THE TURATIS, THE Bissolatis, Socialism had become a powerful party in Parliament, as it had previously become in the country at large. But it was already easy to see that its strength was sapped by two mistakes. The first was the almost exclusive importance given to the problem of the workmen of the North—since the army of electors was in that region. Even a lofty and noble spirit like Bissolati, from the moment he had a presentiment of the distant Fascist crisis, could think of nothing better than the creation of a mass of workers in the framework of the General Federation of Labor, in the unions, in the cooperatives, in the workmen's syndicates, leaving out—without disavowing them but without becoming identified with them—the sections of the party. He did not think about, or did not dare to look for, a new force in the silent and unorganized mass of the peasants of the South. Others certainly thought about them, the most ardent being Gaetano Salvemini, who felt deeply the misery of the rural common people of his native Apulia; but Salvemini was an independent, as he always remained.

The other psychological or tactical error committed by the Socialist Party was an ostentation, more apparent than actual, of ignoring the universal national fact—patriotic sentiment.

When Giolitti, taking account of the Mediterranean modifications resulting from France's establishment in Morocco, decided in 1911 on the occupation of Tripolitania and Cyrenaica, the Socialist leaders looked behind them instead of about them. When, twenty years earlier, Crispi commenced his policy of conquests in Ethiopia, the Italian nation did not view the enterprise with pleasure. Many of those who had fought for Italy's liberty and for whom the word "invader" remained the symbol of all injustices were still alive. The great Lombard industrial bourgeoisie—then still more influential than under Giolitti—was against it, primarily because they opposed additional taxation. Mortally and instinctively opposed were the people, women as well as men. The women threw themselves on the rails in front of trains transporting soldiers to Naples; heroic legends were related about them.

The atmosphere of the time was charged with hatred, not only because salaries were too low, but because Crispi had thought to ward off the discontent of the masses by a policy of seizing the Socialist newspapers and imprisoning the Socialist leaders. He had not understood that a colonial policy could be initiated only in a country where national concord is complete. Yet his hero, Bismarck, had given him the example: though Germany was so much richer than Italy, Bismarck dared not undertake a single international initiative while he was fighting either the Catholics, during the *Kulturkampf,* or, later, the Socialists. But poor Crispi, full of good intentions as he was, always lived in a world peopled by his dreams, like Don Quixote.

Giolitti, infinitely more balanced than Crispi, embarked on the Tripolitan war only after having assured himself of the benevolent neutrality of quite a few Socialists, one of whom was the most serious interpreter of the pure Marxist thought, Antonio Labriola. He had written from 1902 that some day Libya would become "the ideal colony of the Italian proletariat, receiving for centuries the nation's demographic surplus." Dreams, illusions—but the life of a people is made of them also, and in writing as he did Labriola indicated that he felt like the living Italians.

A new fact came to light with the Libyan war. In the countries where, as Garibaldi avowed, not a single peasant had inscribed himself among his volunteers between 1849 and 1870, hundreds and hundreds of them volunteered for the war; they wanted to see with their own eyes what this new Promised Land was like. Giustino Fortunato, one of the noblest spirits of the Italian South, whose interests he passionately defended, and who had always fought Crispi's imperialist policy, regarding it as infantile, wrote at the time of the Libyan war: "Who could be more convinced than I that Tripoli will be a sterile and costly enterprise? But it is fated, and I have come to the point when even I can shout 'Hurrah for the war' if it proves to me that fifty years of national life have not passed in vain, and that something fine and promising springs from our Italy."

It was of slight import if, during this national outburst of enthusiasm—whether natural or manufactured, it matters little—the Socialists and especially the Syndicalists organized anti-war meetings here and there, and if in Parma and the Romagna they conducted some successful strikes. It was not a Socialist phenomenon; it was merely the eternal fruit of an old Italian revolutionary restlessness which impelled the youth to refuse army service, leaving them free to go and die joyfully as volunteers in the wars for the Boers and the Greeks.

What really was a serious matter for Socialism was that most of its leaders sulked at the great adventure. They would have had perhaps a good argument had they said and preached that it would have been better to spend those billions to give a new economic life to the South and the Islands—lands which might have become our best colonies. Instead they sulked, because these idealist movements, not foreseen in the tables of the Marxist law, did not appeal to them.

The Socialist Party, which till then had been a precious instrument for the elevation of the working classes, gave the impression that it did not know sufficiently how to renew itself. The idealistic and moral ferments which were so vividly active in a Prampolini seemed to have drained away. Turati and Treves continued to say things that were often useful, often courageous, but Socialism seemed no longer the intoxicating message it once had been; enrollments continued to increase, but passion for the Cause diminished. Crispi's persecutions had given martyrs to Socialism; whereas Giolitti offered the country universal suffrage and social laws, such as State insurance. Persecutions had helped Socialism more than its successes.

XXI

A PRACTICAL SOCIAL REFORMER:
GIOLITTI

GIOLITTI TOLD ME ONE DAY THAT HE WAS NOT A LITTLE SUR-
prised when Sonnino, chatting with him one afternoon in the
Chamber, after the failure of his second and very brief experiment of "conservative" government, admitted that he had
become convinced that Italy could be ruled only by the liberal
method (which henceforth signified the democratic and parliamentary method). This was the same Sonnino who some years
previously had published in the *Nuova Antologia* an article
whose title, *"Torniamo allo Statuto"* (Let us return to the
Statuto) told everything, considering that all the liberal and
parliamentary evolution of Italy since 1848 had been only an
interpretation, more and more extended, of a *Statuto* stingily
conceded by Charles Albert to his "subjects."

The most important leaders of Socialism had arrived at
analogous conclusions, but they could not say so. Their silence
was long held against them as indicating a lack of political
courage. But it was often the contrary. From a personal point
of view they had everything to gain, since Giolitti desired above
all to have them participate in power, as he proved by offering
a portfolio to Turati in 1904 and to Bissolati in 1911.

If these honest and generous men refused the posts offered
them, and if they continued to use from time to time the old
Marxist vocabulary, it was on account of a settlement of duty
—even from the patriotic point of view. They did not want to
let the masses fall into the hands of irresponsible demagogues
like a young and already turbulent Mussolini and like the editors of an *Avanguardia Socialista,* who in Milan pretended to
combat the bourgeoisie, while the actual object of their hate
were men infinitely superior to them, like Treves and Turati.

The man who transformed the social policy of Italy was not
a Socialist; he was Giolitti, sprung from the small bourgeoisie,
the functionary class—the magistracy. A legend has come into

being about Giolitti suggesting subtle cleverness, skepticism, lack of generosity. When later I speak of Giolitti, the man, it will be seen that the legend, which has spread outside Italy, even to the United States, is without any basis of fact.

In his speech at Cuneo in 1880 Giolitti had declared: "In a democratic country like Italy the future is in the hands of the most numerous classes."

Becoming Prime Minister in 1891, and holding that office five times, and for a great many years, one of the points on which he never varied was that the State had a supreme interest in favoring the economic elevation of the working classes and their association with the country's administration.

By the full liberty he gave to strikes he rendered to Italy an economic and moral service of immense scope. During a long agrarian strike in the province of Mantua and other regions of the plain of the Po, a rich landed proprietor, Count Arrivabene, telegraphed him:

"I wish you to know that to prevent the loss of harvests I, Count Arrivabene, am obliged to labor in the fields, day and night, with the members of my family and friends."

Giolitti replied: "I am happy, *Signor Conte,* that you have undertaken labor which can only improve your physical health and which will help you to understand how hard and bitter are the days of your peasants. Distinguished compliments."

The episode was slight, but very Giolittian. The upper classes were divided on it, some saying that Arrivabene had deserved the lesson, while others refrained for only one reason from saying that Giolitti was a Bolshevik—the name had not yet been invented. It might be added here that Silvio Arrivabene was one of the pillars of Queen Margherita's salon.

It was from this period of the strikes, which were so advantageous to the economic development of Italy, that the mistrust of King Humbert and the Queen for their Piedmontese Prime Minister dated. Giolitti confided to me that the Queen nourished for him a real hatred, and that sometimes she was even discourteous to that proud and intelligent woman who was Giolitti's wife. In his memoirs Giolitti confined himself to writing of King Humbert with a reserve that veiled a secret pity: "During the reactionary period he submitted to the influence of the conservative parties and followed their advice; but it must be realized that the fear of Socialism and popular agitations was then common in all governing classes. . . . However, when I saw him, after the failure of the reactionary policy, at Savigliano, at the time of the inauguration of a monument to General Arimondi, who died in Africa, he was very cordial to me, ending by saying: 'Remember that you have a friend in me.' Translated into the vulgar tongue this meant: The King avoided me for a long time, but the day when, having entered my district he was obliged to meet me, he told me that if I again became strong he would again become my friend."

In the speeches delivered by Giolitti as Prime Minister there are phrases that express with great simplicity his social theories. In 1901, for example:

"The principal reason for the hostility toward the unions is that their action tends to increase salaries. I understand that the interest of the industrialists is to hold down salaries; but what interest in the matter has the State? It is an error, a veritable prejudice, to believe that low salaries serve the progress of industry. The badly nourished workman is always weaker, physically and intellectually; the countries with high salaries are at the head of industrial production.

"We praise as a fine thing the excessive frugality of our peasants, but whoever does not consume does not produce."

After having demonstrated what a mistake the State had committed in preventing strikes in the past, he continued:

"The Italian people have no revolutionary tendencies; a period in which real social justice was dispensed by the Government and the governing classes would lead all our people to love our institutions. . . . We are at the dawn of a new historic period; blind is he who does not see it."

For twenty years, in all his speeches, he continually repeated these ideas. And the facts, the realization, always followed as he had prophesied. With this sole reservation that he made in his speech on April 8, 1911: "Great reforms should be proposed when the times are ripe, when the country is tranquil. Men of the Government should not be pioneers; they should be men who understand the times in which they live, who feel the conditions of the country, and who act accordingly."

Giolitti indeed had his moments of weakness. But what is

surprising is that, especially hated for the complete liberty he accorded the laboring classes, he was nevertheless attacked by the men of the Left who repeated accusations against him invented by their own adversaries.

Save for the most bitterly conservative classes—those that believed in Fascism—all Italians now admit that Giolitti's policy at the end of the nineteenth century and during the first thirteen years of the present century brought about a period of social peace and unusual economic prosperity. And yet, to read the newspapers of the period, one would believe that strike followed strike, that everything threatened to fall into ruins. As always, the policy of Giolitti was then very simple: convinced of the necessity of raising the economic condition of workers and peasants, he gave free rein to strikes; and the strikes, for all the momentary annoyance they caused, forced the proprietors to improve their system of production, which in turn conduced to a general enrichment of Italy.

As Giolitti declared to Parliament in 1911: "The results have proved that my policy, semi-revolutionary in appearance, was the only really conservative one."

On some fundamental ideas like these—and, in foreign policy, the safeguarding of European peace—Giolitti never changed his mind. These were, after all, the essential matters. In secondary matters he changed his opinion more often than his apologists would care to admit.

The tactical errors of the last years of his life were the result of personal resentment, for it is not true that men mellow as they reach old age. The apparent tolerance he observed toward Fascism during the first years of the adventure probably had no other origin than an unconscious rancor that he retained toward the Socialist leaders whom he had so often, and in vain, invited to participate with him in office. His most constant aspiration had been to create in Italy a great Labor Party which would subdue those great landed proprietors and industrialists who hoped to constitute a state within a state. I have already explained that it was too difficult then for the Socialist leaders to become ministers, but Giolitti did not sufficiently comprehend this. His antipathy for the *Popolari*—the new party of the Christian Democrats—had a very simple origin: Don Sturzo, their leader, did not belong to Parliament.

When on Fascism's coming to power I conspicuously re-signed from the Paris Embassy, Giolitti immediately wrote me: "I was sure you would resign, which is equivalent to say-ing that I approve your act. But your case is your case: as regards myself, I think I ought to give an appearance of hop-ing for the best. Who knows? Parliament may impart wisdom to Mussolini; at least he is a deputy, contrary to Sturzo." How little did he know Mussolini! And he held too great a grudge against Sturzo, with whom he had never got along.

Giolitti, this so-called dictator, was a great liberal statesman of the nineteenth century. He believed that all factions, all interests would end by finding an equilibrium in the heart of Parliament. If this deep faith in Parliament does not seem to agree with the legend that he was or wanted to be a dictator, it should not be forgotten that, after each of the many general elections he participated in, the new Chamber voted down his measures.

If Giolitti was a dictator, he was one like Cavour; he always succeeded in synthesizing in himself the consent of the major-ity. A great and honest servant of the State, he had no great faith in the absolute importance of programs, not by reason of cynicism or skepticism, but because he distrusted vast or pompous general ideas. He believed that politics was not peda-gogy—not even apostleship. He never made a secret of this, and never hid his meaning in grandiloquent phrases, and thereby he raised the level of politics in Italy where rhetoric is one of the worst dangers which parliamentarism has to fear.

XXII

THE TRIPLE ALLIANCE FROM ALGECIRAS
TO SERAJEVO

ALGECIRAS, AS WE HAVE SEEN,* WAS INDEED A SERIOUS CRISIS for the Triple Alliance in 1906. But powerful motives acted on all three of the allied nations to keep the alliance alive. France herself, despite appearances, desired it, and for a reason identical with that of Italy: that the destruction of the treaty would have unleashed so many suspicions of designs of territorial aggrandizement that war would have become inevitable. And Italy desired peace, were it only because she knew that time worked in her favor.

In the troubled history of the Triple Alliance between 1906 and 1915 Italy was the most loyal partner, while the silences, the hypocrisies, the frauds were all on the side of Vienna, and still more of Berlin, where it was thought that bad relations between Austria and Italy strengthened the Reich's position both at Vienna and at Rome.

But it would be exaggerating to believe that in Austria-Hungary they deliberately pursued a disloyal policy toward Italy. There was a sort of fatality in the Austrian policy, which sometimes saddened the most intelligent of the Austrians —a fatality due to two elements: first, the personality of the Emperor himself, judging European problems of the twentieth century as if he were dealing with a pre-French Revolutionary Europe; and, second, the different interpretations that from the very beginning were given at Vienna and Rome as to the very nature of the treaty and its most essential clauses.

* Chapter XV.

Studying these two elements, one will understand why the inevitable happened. Let us begin with the treaty and end with the Emperor, supreme arbiter in Austria, a semi-divine being, before whom the most powerful ministers were never anything more than minor employees.

Article II of the treaty imposed, from 1882, on the three governments the obligation of keeping among themselves an amicable attitude and of aiding each other in their difficulties. But, immediately following, another clause established that the support of each ally should be substantiated only "to the limit of its interests," which permitted Vienna and Berlin to refuse all support to the Italian Government every time it found itself in conflict with France over Italian interests in Tunisia or the Red Sea. "We have no interest there," came the invariable response from Vienna and Berlin, "and we have, on the contrary, powerful reasons for remaining on good terms with France."

On the other hand, the treaty obligated Italy to march beside her allies only in two cases of exclusively defensive war: if France should attack Germany; and if France and Russia together attacked Austria-Hungary and Germany. Any other case of war was excluded.

With regard to her colonial interests Italy had, therefore, to safeguard them by direct accords with France and Great Britain, which she did (as I have already mentioned) in 1902, informing her allies, who obviously approved, since afterward they showed themselves anxious to renew the Triple Alliance. But the difference of mentality between a democratic country like Italy and two autocratic regimes like the German and Austro-Hungarian never made it possible for these two to comprehend fully that for us the alliance no longer had any meaning if it ceased to be defensive. At Vienna and Berlin they always thought that, since Italy was caught in the machinery, she would follow at the last moment and carry out the plans made for her by the General Staffs of the Central Empires.

Another cause of misunderstanding, this being more direct and precise, was the formula of "compensations." On the second renewal of the treaty in 1887 the Italian Minister of Foreign Affairs, Count de Robilant, requested that the principle of a right of compensation for Italy be fixed, in the event that

Austria-Hungary should receive advantages as a result of a change in the *status quo* in the Balkans. For a long time Austria resisted the Italian demand. Robilant threatened not to renew the alliance; Bismarck then insisted that his colleague, Count Kalnoky, yield.

It is worth while reading the reasons which Bismarck brought forward to persuade Kalnoky. They shed a light on the worth of the campaign of calumny directed by the Central Empires against Italy when in 1915 she demanded the carrying out of that undertaking which had become Article VII of the treaty.

"A treaty" (so Bismarck wrote to Kalnoky on February 10, 1887) "will always have gaps, even when written in the most meticulous manner; one can always, if one wants it, escape its clearest stipulations. At this moment we need the assurance that Austria-Hungary will not be attacked by Italy in case she should go to war with Russia. That can only be obtained by the neutrality of Italy.* The addition that Count Robilant demands signifies nothing. It doesn't even pledge giving compensations, since their nature would depend, at the particular moment, on an understanding between Austria and Italy, and Austria can always postpone that understanding to infinity."

Kalnoky foresaw that in the event of Austro-Hungarian gains in the Balkans Italy would demand the Trentino, an absolutely Italian province which, in the hands of the Hapsburgs, pointed like a dagger toward Milan and Venice. And he had decided to refuse. Considering wars as quite normal events, the only compensation to which Kalnoky would have consented was one at the expense of France—Corsica, Nice, Savoy, Tunisia.

As to the Emperor, he required the most absolute intransigence from his ministers. He always represented the other element of absolute incomprehension between the two States. He considered it a sacred duty to leave the heritage of the Hapsburgs intact to his successor. And to this instinctive element he added in his mind a political consideration: the Empire was composed of a dozen different nationalities which— apart from the Hungarians and the Czechs, who were wholly within the monarchy—all had brothers in Germany, in Italy,

* These two sentences reveal the expectation of an offensive war against Russia, a thing Italy would never have consented to taking part in.

in Russia (the Poles), in Serbia, in Rumania; and the Emperor thought: "If I make one concession, where would I be able to stop?"

If he had been a man of any intellectual force he would have imagined a transformation of his Empire into a gigantic federation of free peoples. But such an idea—had he been able to comprehend it—would have seemed to him satanic.

Francis Joseph was one of the most narrow-minded leaders of the nineteenth and twentieth centuries. One needs only to reflect on an undeniable single fact in the life of Francis Joseph: during his seventy-year reign he had more ministers than any other sovereign; always, with perhaps one or two exceptions, he chose mediocrities and never failed to eliminate strong personalities. His first Minister in 1848 was Prince Schwarzenberg, the perfect type of the cavalry officer, but as the first Tisza said of his own son Stephen Tisza, "as bad a driver as he was good a rider."

As to ministries, Francis Joseph created a new one as soon as he had mounted the throne and—a revealing trait—it was the police that he chose to raise to the rank of a ministry. His innumerable letters and notes indicate to what a point he followed and encouraged this vile business. To police agents and spies he assigned the care of preserving order in his state. Denunciations prospered: drafting secret *berichten* (informations) became the favorite occupation of all the functionaries who sought rapid advancement and the disease spread even among members of the aristocracy. In the center of that mechanism the sovereign devoted many hours of his day to following with meticulous care these cases, these notes—often against his own ministers. Only spineless courtiers could want to remain in such an atmosphere; a man who was a man could not endure it.

Francis Joseph, through egotism and pettiness of spirit, was incapable of the supreme quality of a sovereign, that of suffering a great minister to hold and exercise power. In contrast to him, as already noted * William I of Prussia, a worthy man of mediocre intelligence was, notwithstanding, a great sovereign, for, despite the thousand little wounds to his pride, he continued to keep in power a man of Bismarck's stature. Victor

* Chapter X.

Emmanuel II acted likewise with Cavour. And yet he often suffered, and did not pretend otherwise, at seeing Italy give her confidence to this great liberal statesman.

This sole trait—reliance on denunciations—would explain the witticism that escaped the Empress Elizabeth when speaking of the Emperor one day, in the home of her parents in Bavaria: "Poor Franzy has the soul of a sergeant."

If one "idea" distinguished his reign, it was the transformation of unitary and autocratic Austria where everything was "K. K." (*Kaiserlich-Königlich*, i.e. Imperial-Royal), all in one, into a dualistic Austria-Hungary where everything became "K. u. K." (*Kaiserlich und Königlich*, i.e. Imperial *and* Royal). It was in 1867 that Francis Joseph finally tired of Magyar opposition, accepted the *Ausgleich* (Compromise) which was presented to him by the Hungarian Deak, and reinstalled the Kingdom of Hungary as a separate entity. He, the Emperor, became in Hungary the "King," respected because he had taken the oath to guard the "thousand-year-old" Constitution, and because he had been crowned with the sacred crown of Hungary in which, according to the Magyar common law (did not Bismarck say that all the Magyars are hussars and lawyers?) the authority of the King and laws of the nation are mystically fused.

The Magyars are marvelously endowed—I am thinking of the aristocracy—with the ability to spread about the world a deep impression of sincerity when they speak about their attachment to their laws and their liberty. Under cover of their millenary constitution they defend *their* rights over the Slav races which were subjected to the Hungarian crown, and also the liberty of imposing on these races, which they sincerely believe inferior, the benefits of Magyar authority.

When Francis Joseph accepted the *Ausgleich* of 1867 he finally obtained peace with the stubborn Magyars—whose patriotism would be admirable were it not conceived as a right to oppress their neighbors—but he paid his price with the liberty and the future of those Croats, faithful to their Kaiser, who in 1848 and 1849 had shed so much of their blood in the wars against the Italians. As crowned King of Hungary, he delivered them defenseless to the most violent Magyar oppression—just as happened elsewhere with regard to the Serbs of the Banat and the Rumanians of Transylvania.

The only ones who did not suffer inordinately from Hungarian oppression, against which there was no possible recourse where Vienna was supreme, were the Italians at Fiume, and this was merely because they were not numerous in the kingdom and it was thought good policy to influence them to hate the Slavs.

Again, Francis Joseph's error was not only moral, it was political; for he achieved the peace by betraying the very mission of his House. For centuries the Hapsburgs had a *raison d'être* in the fact that, governing from Vienna, they were the supreme and impartial arbiters of all subject races. With dualism Francis Joseph admitted that two equal and independent administrations, one of them German in Austria, the other Magyar in Hungary, formed two national hegemonies under which Italians, Czechs, Southern Slavs and Rumanians vegetated without political rights and without possibilities of normal development. This was the end of Austria, or, what amounts to the same thing, of Austria's reason for existing.

An enigma presents itself. How did this man who had no comprehension of the supreme duties of his mission, who avoided them with an intellectual cowardice that the lack of breadth of his mental faculties hardly excuses—for he always rejected the collaboration of those who might have been creative intelligences—how did this man succeed in enjoying for the entire length of a very long reign universal respect and good will?

The reasons, as is always the case, are multiple. One cause which, if not the main one, is not negligible, was the propaganda of the Roman Church, particularly that of the Jesuits who have always done their utmost to raise the prestige of a system based entirely on external manifestations of respect for the Catholic Church. It mattered little that so many of the finer spirits among the Austrian Catholics secretly complained that religion had become a lifeless formula, as in Imperial Orthodox Russia, and for the same reason, namely, that bishops and priests had become servants of the State, and were completely deprived of individual moral liberty.

In countries like England and the United States, which the

Catholic propaganda did not touch, what saved Francis Joseph was probably the dignified isolation in which the Emperor kept himself, his scorn of publicity and his dislike for all the vulgar play of limelight that came into fashion toward the end of his reign, with the last of the Hohenzollerns.

The most intelligent of Francis Joseph's ministers was Aerenthal. In 1910 and in 1911 I had a series of confidential conversations with him.* Being only a very young diplomat and able, consequently, to escape more easily the attention of the political world, and having quite a few friends and connections in Austria, I had been charged with telling the Austrian Minister some bitter truths which would have sounded too harsh coming from an ambassador. Convinced of the honorableness of our aims and of the reality of the facts, I talked to him without mincing words. We discussed everything: the failure to return our King's visit to Vienna, the naval armaments, the Italian university matter, the irritating policy of the Dual Monarchy toward Austrian subjects of Italian race. . . .

I was, indeed, pleased to see that Aerenthal, at first irritated, became interested and then sympathetic. As these facts have already faded out of historical record, and as what matters in diplomatic incidents is only the human element, I shall limit myself to quoting some remarks just as I wrote them in my notebook immediately after our conversations.

"How can I make you understand how disturbed we are over the complaints and cries of anguish [and I made it very clear to my interlocutor that I referred to the famous *grido di dolore* (cry of grief) of 1859] that come to us from the Italians of Austria? Italy has had a rebirth by virtue of the law of nationalities; how can you imagine, for an instant, that we could be indifferent to your efforts to denationalize the Italians?

"But if they could be happy and proud to be Italians and at the same time satisfied to be Austrian subjects, just as the Italians of the Canton of Ticino are proud of being Italians while remaining loyal Swiss, we would be delighted. Kill ir-

* With this aim I was sent to Budapest as Consul General, though I was a Counselor of the Embassy. At Budapest, furthermore, I kept in close contact with the Duke of Avarna, our Ambassador at Vienna, until the day when he said to me: "They won't understand you unless you are very stern; but, as you have to be so at your own risk, it would be better for me to know nothing about it. If you succeed I shall know it through San Giuliano" (Minister of Foreign Affairs).

redentism by doing justice to the grievances of the *Irredenti.*
It would be much better for you and for us; I believe in influences surer than those of territorial aggrandizement."

Aerenthal, who knew how much I shared his guiding thought
—friendship with Berlin but not vassalage, remained silent for
quite a while and then replied, slowly weighing each word:

"I believe you; and I believe not only in your sincerity but
in the objective truth of what you say. And yet, if I repeated
your words, admitting that I believed them, they would take
me for a madman here."

This was the severest judgment that could have been passed
on the Emperor and on the *Thronfolger* (heir to the throne),*
Archduke Francis Ferdinand.

Soon afterward I left for China. Three years more of illusions, mistakes and autocratic blindness followed. Then the
pretext for the catastrophe was discovered: the assassination
of the *Thronfolger* at Serajevo.

When the news came to Francis Joseph, on the evening of
the fatal July 28, 1914, that his nephew and heir had been
assassinated at Serajevo, the blind old man was silent for an
instant, then he murmured to himself, rather than to his aide-
de-camp, Count Paar, who described the scene: "God doesn't
allow defiances; a Superior Power has reestablished the order
I was no longer able to maintain."

These words reveal the deepest conviction of the Emperor,
his faith in the glory of his family, the maintenance of his
power, his right to reign over subject races without any control other than a "Superior Power." It is doubtful if in his
long life he had ever experienced a greater fright than the
horror he must have felt at the idea that his heir, Francis
Ferdinand, on his accession to the throne, might annul the
laws of succession of the Archdukes to the profit of his eldest
son by his morganatic marriage with Countess Sophie Chotek.
It was against this danger that, according to the Emperor, a
"Superior Power" had reestablished order.

To preserve the power of the Hapsburgs, and for that objective alone, Francis Joseph worked all his life. All his life he
believed that as head and heir of the Hapsburgs he had been

---

* "Heir to the throne" was the familiar nickname of Francis Ferdinand in
Austria.

invested with a superior right, and that his subjects were his property. It was almost more than the juridic concept of "divine right." The Empire over which he reigned was *his* Empire; the peoples who constituted it were *his* peoples.

Comparing such a firm and naive belief with the pompous utterances of a William II on his "divine right," simply proves that the Hohenzollern was not entirely sure of what he said. He spoke of his divine right too often and too loudly. Francis Joseph, on the other hand, was so certain of it that he never mentioned it; his exclamation on the death of Archduke Francis Ferdinand is the sole exception, and then he was only speaking to himself.

The only visible result of his complete belief in his right to absolute power was that, deprived of imagination, he was, notwithstanding, able all his life to make decisions which would have caused more intelligent men to tremble; for was he not the Emperor? He appeared strong, he was autocratic; he was never able to see the distant dangers that loomed up, the new deep-rooted forces that were working in the consciences of the peoples. When on his accession to the throne he suppressed a constitution the thing seemed dangerous to the old functionaries even though they regarded a constitution as only an idea of the "sects." They would have hesitated, even as in Prussia in the same epoch and for the same reason they hesitated and trembled. He did not hesitate. Braver? No; simply blinder; more unconscious, one might almost say. Just as one might also say that he dared and succeeded because he alone was imbued with the absolute conviction of his right to do what he did.

He is the last sovereign who sincerely believed in his legitimate right to govern peoples and to leave them as a heritage to his descendants. It is said that, in the evening of his long life, when the Great War had for months been drenching Europe with blood, he had a premonition that the Empire of the Hapsburgs was condemned to perish; a presentiment which must have added a touch of tragedy to the ordeals of his life.

I, for one, am not convinced of it. It was in his blood never to question the fate of his House; the only thing that might have caused him to doubt was neither wars nor defeats, but the fact that so many of his own Archdukes, members of his own family, no longer believed in the myth of the Dynasty.

But even those members, through fear or shame, hid their feelings on their rare visits with him at Schonbrunn.* The evening of his death he had to be taken from his desk almost by main force. "I have more to read, more to sign," he murmured like an automaton, when his aide-de-camp, General Margutti, finally decided to have him carried to a bed, the bed on which the last of the legitimists expired an hour later.

* One of them, Archduke Ludwig Salvator, author of travel books, friend of my father and occasionally a visitor in our house in the country, was a free spirit or, at any rate, he detested court life. I can still see him saying to my parents: "When I have to make my annual visit to the Emperor I tremble in anticipation; and yet I know there is really no reason for it."

XXIII

THE ORIGINS OF THE WAR

IN 1914 THE GERMANY OF WILLIAM II AND THE AUSTRIA-Hungary of the Hapsburgs were guilty of the same error as Hitler in 1939 and Mussolini in 1940: they despised their eventual adversaries too much. In 1939 Hitler believed, since they had allowed him to assassinate Czechoslovakia, that he could do the same to Poland; in 1940 Mussolini believed, like Pétain and Weygand, that Great Britain would be incapable of resisting after France's fall.

The former Ambassador of Austria-Hungary at London, Count Mensdorf, said to me one day after the monarchy he had loyally and skillfully served had come to its end: "Yes, you are right; they were mad, at Vienna and Budapest—Berchtold as mad as Tisza—to have unleashed the great war after Serajevo. But Berchtold, at least, and all the Austrians with him, always believed from the bottom of their hearts that they would end by letting Austria have her little war with Serbia; hadn't Europe swallowed without wincing all the acts of violence of the Central Empires? Fundamentally, we were tricked by the Entente; we were sure they had decided never to make war against us. . . ."

Mensdorf was not entirely wrong; and Hitler, in 1939, might have spoken almost the same words.

To judge the Austro-Hungarian responsibilities in 1914 one needs only to go back to the testimony of those who, down to the last minute, identified their interests with those of the Danubian monarchy: the Germans.

Here is what the German Ambassador at Vienna, Tschirschky, wrote to Chancellor Bethmann-Hollweg some months before the crime of Serajevo. It is part of a report which is still useful to reread, especially on account of its enrichment with marginal notes by Emperor William II.

After having studied the state of mind of the non-Slavic

political circles and of the military circles, the Ambassador remarked that a war against Serbia would be very popular in these circles if it could be utilized "for the solution of the Yugoslav problem, from the German point of view." (Of course, by the word "German" he meant the governing classes of German Austria, not his Reich.) The military and feudal circles felt themselves humiliated, remarked Tschirschky, by the fact that the Monarchy dared not frankly face the decisions that the situation imposed. He added: "These circles view with astonishment and grief the increasing strength of the Slavic wave; and all of them are anxiously wondering: 'What will happen to Austria?' The Germans are discouraged. One of their leaders told me recently in the House of Lords: 'It's the end of the Germans in Austria.' [A marginal note of William II: '*Kopf hoch!*'] In fact, they will lose all influence in the monarchy and I wonder if some day they are not going to be driven to secession. . . ."

And further on he writes: "A new Lombardo-Veneto has loomed up in the southeast of the monarchy, an *Irredenta* which can only look beyond the frontiers toward the new big and powerful Serb state. Official circles are no longer at all sure that the Slav regiments can be used against Serbia in case of war. . . . After the Serb victories in the Balkans the religious differences among the Yugoslavs no longer seem a serious obstacle to their national unity. . . .

"The idea of a united monarchy and the feeling of State solidarity are beginning to disappear. . . . The present internal conditions of the Austro-Hungarian monarchy are discouraging; as they are also from the point of view of their Germanic ally. Only superior wisdom and great energy on the part of the Central Governments could bring to the service of the State the centrifugal forces of the Slav peoples, thus continuing the policy of a great Power along side of the Germanic ally." *

It is evident that the last phrase of Tschirschky's dispatch contains a vague and prudent allusion to the projects that were attributed to the heir to the throne, Archduke Francis Ferdinand. Therefore, it had to do with very serious matters. What is the august German sovereign's marginal note here? "*Mit Blut und Eisen sind die Kerle noch zu kurieren.*" (One can

* *Die Grosse Politik des Europaischen Kabinette*, XXXIII, no. 12402.

still cure those fellows with blood and iron.) Such was the comprehension of the great ones of the earth in the years preceding the Great War.

That idea of the inevitability of "blood and iron" became more and more that of the Austro-Hungarian rulers.

Among a thousand proofs it was a mistake to forget the definitive words uttered by the Austrian Prime Minister, Count Sturgkh, at the Crown Council of July 7, 1914, where with his blind colleagues he caused the fatal ruin of his country: "A decisive act must be decided upon; a purely diplomatic victory will not suffice us. . . . If, for international reasons, we must first pass through a diplomatic phase, it should be well understood that it is being done with the firm determination to end it with war." *

This explains why the ultimatum to Serbia was drawn up in a way to make it inacceptable by even the most pacific sovereign State; why it was communicated to the Italian Government only at the last moment, when all discussion had become impossible; and why—a detail that the Austrophiles of France and England so easily forgot—the government of Vienna even went so far as to prescribe consultations with a jurist on whom they could depend to find an excuse for recourse to war, even in the inconceivable case of a complete acceptance on the part of Serbia of all the most humiliating conditions.

One man had the deplorable courage, at the time of the declaration of war against Serbia, to cry out in the plenary session of the Hungarian Parliament: "At last!"

He was Count Albert Apponyi who, as Hungarian Minister, had done so much before the war to render the lot of the Slavic subjects of the Crown of St. Stephen increasingly humiliating; and who, after the war, knew how to use his old age to become one of the most publicized orators of the League of Nations, where the naive Western democracies let the old wolf assume the role of the innocent lamb. His "At last!" expressed the feelings of all men of the Austrian and Hungarian governing classes—with, perhaps, a sole exception: the solitary inhabitant of Schonbrunn, Francis Joseph.

Apponyi's "At last!" did not even represent a cry of deliverance or despair; there might have been some nobility in

* *Diplomatische Aktenstucke,* 1st part, page 31.

that. It was the cry of the armed Colossus who, certain of the solidarity of a neighbor whom the entire world believed to be all-powerful, had found a pretext to annihilate a little bordering state, unarmed, penniless and, they hoped, friendless. At Vienna, as at Berlin, they believed that France, Great Britain, Italy—states of democratic form—were incapable of reacting. As for Russia, the leaders of Vienna were still savoring the humiliation of the scarcely disguised ultimatum by which they had forced her to keep silent after the Bosnian annexation. Not a single Austrian diplomat had been able to read the signs of destiny on the banks of the Neva. Only an Englishman, Ambassador Buchanan, had deciphered them. Of all the trash of diplomatic dispatches that issued from St. Petersburg at the time of the ultimatum inflicted on Izwolsky, a single utterance deserves remembrance; it was Sir George Buchanan who wrote his government: "The St. Petersburg Cabinet has yielded. It is so much the better for peace. But they are preparing for disaster in Vienna and Berlin if they think that Russia will ever suffer a second ordeal of this kind. The day, near or distant, when they again ignore Russia, no force in the world will prevent her from marching."

The assassination of Francis Ferdinand of Hapsburg and his wife at Serajevo on June 24, 1914, seemed to the camarilla of the Court of Vienna and to the feudal Hungarians a fortunate pretext sent by the gods.

That Serajevo was only a pretext is proved by the compilation of the memorial written in Vienna, actually several days before June 24, formally to request German assistance for an attack on Serbia. Twelve months earlier Vienna had already tried to obtain it, but on that occasion had also addressed Italy, which had rejected the idea of a war defined by Giolitti as "offensive." * This time, having decided to risk the *coup,* the Austrians addressed only Berlin, thereby violating both the letter and the spirit of Article VII of the Triple Alliance which obligated them in such a case to have a prior understanding with Italy. The famous memorial presented to the Emperor William after the death of Francis Joseph's heir, to assure Austria the support of her German ally, had been prepared and completely drafted previously, on the morrow of the

* See Chapter XLI.

German Kaiser's visit to Francis Ferdinand at the castle of Konopisht in mid-May, 1914. The assassination of Serajevo had no other result than to add to the already prepared document the following postscript:

"This memorial had already been completed when the terrible events of Serajevo supervened. One can scarcely realize the full import of this abominable assassination which has, nevertheless, if indeed that were still necessary, produced the irrefutable proof of the impossibility of putting an end to the antagonism between the Monarchy and Serbia, as well as the danger and intensity of the Pan-Serbian propaganda that recoils at nothing. . . . Under these conditions the necessity of breaking with an energetic hand the net in which her adversary wishes to suffocate her is imposed on the Monarchy."

The Bosnian crisis had been, as I have said, the dress rehearsal for that of 1914, with this difference, however, that in 1909 the Austrian statesmen dominated the events, whereas in 1914 Aerenthal's successors were but the victims of their passions and puppets of the events.

Aerenthal had had a view of the future, limited but clear; moreover, he was a man and—in a certain sense—a new man. Berchtold, his successor, was only the symbol of the old Austria whose real masters were the old narrow-minded bureaucrats, like Count Forgach, who one day said to one of his subordinates at the Ballplatz, Baron Szilassy, a Hungarian like himself: "I wish that in all the offices of the Ministry they would inscribe this maxim: *Serbia delenda est.*" (Serbia must be destroyed.)

I knew Forgach as a young diplomat at Constantinople and was aware of the hate he already had for anything Slavic, even before the ridiculous part he played before all Europe in the affair of the forgery of the Friedjung case. Minister in China from 1911, I never again saw Forgach, who became all-powerful at the Ballplatz. But from Pekin I returned and spent several weeks in Austria in 1912 and 1913. Duke Avarna, then Ambassador of Italy, Dumaine, Ambassador of France, Count Dudzeele, my wife's father and Minister of Belgium who, like myself, had known Forgach intimately at Constantinople, all insisted that the danger in Vienna was that, thanks to Forgach, the Ministry of Foreign Affairs, instead of acting as a counterweight to the preference of the military circles for war, excited them still more.

The memorandum which was to decide the European war could have issued only from a Ministry of Foreign Affairs directed by men of Forgach's stripe.

The fatal document started for Berlin on the evening of July 4. Count Hoyos, Berchtold's Chief of Cabinet, carried it. The next day, July 5, Emperor Francis Joseph gave a long audience to the Chief of Staff, Conrad, who left an exact report of the conversation:

"I expressed," wrote Conrad, "my opinion of the inevitability of war with Serbia."

"The Emperor: Yes, that's perfectly true, but how do you expect to make war if everyone attacks us, especially Russia?

"Conrad: Doesn't Germany shield us?

"The Emperor: Are we sure about Germany?

"Conrad: But we ought to know, Your Majesty, the situation we are in.

"The Emperor: A note left last night for Berlin; we asked for a point-blank reply.

"Conrad: And if the reply assures that Germany places herself beside us, shall we make war on Serbia?

"The Emperor: In that case, yes."

Francis Joseph would have been less preoccupied over the reply from Berlin had he known the caustic notations Wilhelm II had already inscribed on the margin of Tschirschky's dispatches.

The latter had telegraphed Bethmann-Hollweg from Vienna after Francis Ferdinand's assassination: "Even staid individuals express in my hearing the desire to settle their accounts with the Serbs. . . . I take advantage of each occasion to dissuade them, calmly but seriously, from any precipitate measure."

Beside the first sentence William II had written: "Now or never!"

And beside the second: "Who told him to say that? It is none of his business. It is up to Austria to decide what she wants to do. . . . Tschirschky must do me the pleasure of ceasing all these stupidities. We must be done with the Serbs and as soon as possible."

Three days after his meeting with Francis Joseph, on July 8, Conrad had a definitive conversation with Berchtold. The meticulous exactness with which Conrad reproduced it in his memoirs * is surprising; it is the language of a conspiracy, and he does not realize it.

"Berchtold: What will happen if Serbia lets matters slide until the mobilization, and then yields completely?

"Conrad: Then we invade Serbian territory.

"Berchtold: And if Serbia does nothing?

"Conrad: Then Serbia will remain occupied until all our war expenses have been paid.

"Berchtold: Shall we delay the ultimatum until after the harvest, and after the Serajevo inquest?

"Conrad: Better today than tomorrow; we have to exploit the situation. The moment our adversaries suspect anything they are going to prepare.

"Berchtold: We'll take care that the secret will be strictly kept and that nothing shall be known by anyone.

"Conrad: About what date should the ultimatum be sent?

"Berchtold: In a fortnight, July 22. It would be a good idea for you, as well as for the Minister of War, to go on leave for a while so as to dissipate any kind of anxiety."

Such was the atmosphere at Vienna when Francis Ferdinand's assassination seemed the most fortunate of opportunities, one which had been lacking in 1913, and one that at no price should be missed again. Apponyi's "At last!" was the avowal of the official world. Those who hesitated, like Tisza, did not do so from love of peace, but because they were not sure of being sufficiently aided by Germany. The moment William II's "Now or never" became known at Vienna and Budapest, there was not a Magyar nor an Austrian-German who was not for the war. At the time of the dramatic interview that took place on November 2, 1918, between the members of the *Deutschoesterreicher Staatsrat* and Emperor Charles, when the latter protested "not having wanted it" and a Socialist leader indicated approbation, the old Christian-

---

* Conrad's memoirs, *Aus Meiner Dienstzeit* (My Years of Service), has the advantage of sincerity where other writers, more anxious about public opinion, would have been tempted to gloss over the truth.

Socialist Dr. Mayer rose and, alone, had the dignity to declare:

"Let us be sincere, gentlemen. We all wanted the war: even the people wanted it. You need only recall the enthusiasm of the summer of 1914. . . ."

No one in the Austria of the Berchtolds and the Forgachs condescended to recall in the spring of 1914, when the war against Serbia was decided upon, what Aerenthal had marked in a dispatch of instructions he sent to Forgach in Belgrade on April 15, 1909:

"The question of our relations with Serbia represents only one part of the South Slav problem; that question can therefore be treated only in relation with the internal policies to be pursued as regards the Slav subjects of the Monarchy."

If one wants to find an excuse for people of Berchtold's stamp who brought ruin to the State they professed to serve, that excuse can only be found in the character of Francis Joseph. Hostile at first to the war, he rallied to it. Why? Because if war—a preventive war—was, without question, a graver and more dangerous adventure than an internal transformation of a federal character, it did not, nevertheless, touch the fundamental ideas of his reign: first, the supremacy of the Germans; second, the maintenance of the *Ausgleich* of 1867, with the supremacy shared by Germans and Magyars. Above all, war, atrocious though it always is, was for him only a mechanism which he had already seen in operation three or four times during his reign, managed on the one side by a War Office and on the other by a Foreign Office. Francis Joseph detested nothing so much as ideas and projects that went beyond the competence of the head of a Ministerial department, which would certainly have been the case had there been a radical recasting of the internal organization of the Monarchy. In short, Francis Joseph felt a kind of preventive jealousy of some unknown Metternich who would show himself capable of renovating the Empire. It is in this sense that this man, laborious and personally honest, this man, who all his life desired only to serve the State, can be considered a bad sovereign.

To comprehend the blindness of Imperial Austria as regards the Serbian problem one need only read the account of the trial of the Serajevo assassins. Reading it one realizes the enormous importance of this fact that was not realized in 1914: that the assassins of Francis Ferdinand and his wife were sons of Kmet—the Bosnian peasants subjected to the feudal semi-slavery that Austria made more unbearable than it had been under their old masters, the Turks.

At their trial one of the principal defendants, Gabrinovic, declared:

"We had no hate for Austria, but, though the occupation has already lasted thirty-three years, she has not improved the condition of agriculture nor solved the agrarian problem.

"These are the motives that determined us to make the attempt. Before we part I should like you also, Your Honors, to understand us and not consider us as ordinary criminals. We love our people, who labor under a heavy burden, who live in distress and misery, who have no schools and are deprived of all culture. The peasants comprise nine-tenths of our people. We had pity for their sad fate, we resented their sufferings."

And after him Princip, the other assassin, said:

"I see how our people are pining away from day to day. I am a peasant's son, so I know what happens in the villages. That is what decided me to avenge myself. I don't repent it."

Under the Turk, the Slav peasant was exploited by the great Moslem landowners; and peasant revolts were not rare under the Ottoman domination. But under the Austro-Hungarian regime, other exploiters, the great Hungarian landowners, were added. It was on the orders and in the interest of Magyar magnates that the Austro-Hungarian administration limited the cultivation of cereals in Bosnia and Herzegovina and even prevented the erection of mills. Did not the shareholders of Budapest flour mills have to be enriched?

Even what good the foreign masters did in Bosnia was, by a strange blindness, such as could only be turned against them. As a matter of fact, though Austrian economic policy in Bosnia-Herzegovina was supremely egoistic and still further augmented the peasants' misery, the educational activity was extensive and, up to a certain point, generous. But that was tantamount to the artificial creation of an intellectual class with the needs and hopes of all intellectual classes, while, at the same time, its access to public life was prevented and the country was exploited in a way hardly thought permissible in a Negro colony. It was as though they had sought to force the birth of these circles of discontent from which came the assassins of Serajevo.

In 1913 a gigantic trial had adjudged several dozens of students guilty of having "belonged to secret societies with hostile tendencies toward the State." And it was in such a country that they settled on the date of June 28 for the entrance in Serajevo of Archduke Francis Ferdinand, the date of the hundred and twenty-fifth anniversary of that battle of Blackbird Field which has a sacred place in Serbian history and folklore. That year the anniversary excited the Bosnian youth to fever heat, the reason being that it followed soon after the Serbian revenge on the Turks. Serbian writers have held that the Austrian Government expressly chose that day on which to humiliate still further the Serbian national sentiment. No; there is a simpler and even graver explanation: To their Austrian masters the Bosnians were only natives—and in what colony do the masters trouble about the susceptibilities of the natives?

It was merely that they did not think at all about the matter; that was the Austrian way. Just as, some years previously, during a visit in Vienna of the Chief of the General Staff of the Italian Army, a great official banquet was tendered him on the anniversary date of the Battle of Custoza when, in 1866, the Austrians had beaten the Italians.

In sum, Austria's mistake consisted in never having understood or respected the sentiments of the peoples she held under her arrogant tutelage. She neither understood nor respected them, because her ruling class was incapable of such feelings. And that was the cause of the death of Imperial Austria.

A legend more tenacious than history was formed in 1914 and afterward regarding Pope Pius X's attitude toward the Hapsburg aggression toward Serbia. This legend shows us Pius X praying and fighting against the outbreak of the war, horrified to see Christianity divided into two enemy camps, and dying of grief at the invasion of Belgium and all the horrors of war unchained. The truth is quite otherwise.

During the war of 1914–18 the religious question had only

a minor importance; both camps included Catholics, Protestants, Greek Orthodox members and Mohammedans. Catholic unity did not prevail any more than Mohammedan unity, which seemed so sure of its *jihad* (the Holy War proclaimed by the Sultan-Caliph, which neither Arab nor Hindu Moslem obeyed). The clergy of the different countries could all invoke Allah or the old God of Armies with opposite hopes.

One fact, however, during the tragic weeks of July and August, 1914, scandalized European opinion: that the war should have been provoked in the name of God by a powerful and decrepit sovereign, Francis Joseph, Emperor of Austria and Apostolic King of Hungary, the most Catholic of all the sovereigns and the most important of all Catholic sovereigns. When this Prince declared that he made war to chastise Serbia, millions of timorous souls imagined that the Pope would intervene to prevent the catastrophe. This hope gave birth to the legend. It was said at the time that Pius X, the moment he knew of the ultimatum to Serbia, had enjoined his Nuncio at Vienna to admonish the old Emperor and King in the name of the Almighty. Then, since the war happened just the same, it was explained that the Ballplatz diplomats and military men of the imperial entourage had prevented Pius X's messenger from talking with the Emperor. And here is the last act of the legend: The Pope having died suddenly on August 20, 1914, it was affirmed that the good Pius had succumbed to grief, having realized his impotence to avert the disaster.

It is time to establish the truth as to that legend, and here it is:

As soon as the danger of war became evident, Count Palffy, Austrian Chargé d'Affaires at the Vatican, several times informed Pius X's Secretary of State, Cardinal Merry del Val, of the intentions and the "duties" of the Dual Monarchy. The Cardinal's replies were deposited in the diplomatic correspondence of the Austro-Hungarian Embassy, correspondence that I have seen. They reveal that the Vatican saw with satisfaction, at least at the outset, an undertaking in which the crushing of Serbia would entail a diminution of the influence of Russia. The latter's prestige was detested by the Roman Church, which viewed it as the principal obstacle to a reconciliation of the Oriental churches with the See of Rome. In these conversations the Secretary of State spoke expressly in the name of the Pope who, he declared to the Austrian representative, deplored that Austria had not earlier inflicted on the Serbs the chastisement they deserved. It is sufficient to quote the following passage from a dispatch of Count Palffy to Count Berchtold on July 29:

"During the conversation I had two days ago with the Cardinal Secretary of State he spoke spontaneously of the great problems and questions now agitating Europe. It would be impossible to detect in His Eminence's words any spirit whatever of indulgence and conciliation. It is true he characterized the note to Serbia as very harsh, but he nevertheless approved it without any reservation and at the same time expressed, in an indirect way, the hope that the Monarchy would go to the limit. Certainly, added the Cardinal, it was too bad that Serbia had not been humiliated very much sooner, for then it might have been done without putting into play, as today, such immense possibilities. This declaration also corresponds to the Pope's way of thinking, for, in the course of recent years His Holiness has often expressed regret that Austro-Hungary has failed to 'chastise' her dangerous Danubian neighbor.

"One might wonder for what motive the Catholic Church evinces herself so bellicose at an epoch when she is governed by a chief who is truly a saint, imbued with veritably apostolic ideas. The answer is very simple. The Pope and the Curia see in Serbia the ravaging malady that little by little penetrated the Monarchy to the marrow, and which, in time, would end by disintegrating it.

"Despite all the other experiments attempted by the Curia in the course of the last decade, Austria-Hungary is and remains the Catholic State par excellence, the strongest rampart of the Faith which stands in our day for the Church of Christ. The fall of this rampart would signify for the Church the loss of its solidest prop; in the conflicts with the Orthodox Church she would see her most powerful champion struck down.

"Hence, just as for Austria-Hungary there is an immediate necessity of self-preservation to expel from its organism, even by force if need be, the dissolving malady, there is also for the Catholic Church an indirect necessity of doing or approving everything that would serve to attain that end.

"In this light, a harmony between the apostolic sentiment and the war spirit can easily be confirmed."

The widening of the conflict which from Austro-Serb became European did not do much to change the Pope's frame of mind. In his honest but narrow mind the march of the German army *nach Paris* assumed the form of a punishment that God had inflicted on the "eldest daughter of the Church" who had given him the worst worries of his pontificate.

We have seen that the proceeding of the Nuncio at Vienna is a legend. That Pius X died of grief is still another. I have it from his doctor, my colleague in the Italian Senate, that the malady of which the Pope died had for long months wasted the old man by slow degrees, and that the overwork of the last few weeks could, at most, but have hastened the end that he, Marchiafava, had already declared inevitable and due to occur very shortly.

XXIV

THE EIGHT MONTHS OF ITALIAN NEUTRALITY

WHEN THE FIRST WORLD WAR BROKE OUT I WAS IN CHINA as Minister of Italy. The Minister of Foreign Affairs, Marquis di San Giuliano, desired that the circular telegram that he addressed to the Ambassadors to solicit their views on the situation, should, by exception, be likewise sent to the young diplomat then at the head of the Pekin Legation, which was important in itself, but outside the scope of the terrible events. I dare state that the exception did honor to San Giuliano, proving he had not harbored rancor over the differences of opinion—sometimes very lively ones—which we had had in 1909 when I was Counselor of his Embassy in London, and again in 1910–11 at Rome, when he, having become Minister of Foreign Affairs, had asked me to remain with him as his Chief of Cabinet. San Giuliano was not only convinced that Germany was on the way to a formidable omnipotence—which was easy to verify—but also that France and England were no longer anything but two decadent nations.

When, in opposition, I stated my view that the Hohenzollern atmosphere was weakening the moral character of the Germans, and that history is made by men, he used to answer laughingly: "You talk like one of Croce's books."

At Rome, in the old Consulta—and this was what induced me to remain in it—I was perfectly in accord with his loyal intention to establish a reasonable understanding between Italian interests and those of Austria, without the necessity, humiliating for both countries, of always having to have recourse to Berlin to settle our differences.

I answered San Giuliano's telegram from Pekin:

"I only wish to think and judge from what I see here. German progress throughout the Far East was, from year to year, becoming more admirable. England would soon have been outstripped. Even from the diplomatic point of view Germany was on the point of conquering here the same primacy she exercised in Constantinople with Marschall. Despite that, and despite the great number of analogous situations throughout the world, the Imperial Government plays its entire game with the dice of war. This indicates that at Berlin brains are not on a par with German strength, or that they are possessed by a dangerous aspiration to world domination. In both cases our procedure is dictated. Neutrality, moreover, being for us both a right and an evident necessity, it remains to decide what form to give it. As for me, and unless you send different instructions, I shall intensify and develop our interests here, while not concealing my specially amicable relations with my colleagues of the Entente."

The "different instructions" naturally never came; but, some days later, just a brief letter from San Giuliano, written in his gout-tortured hand, in which he said:

"Dear Sforza, I am afraid you are right; and that the old and rickety carriage is surer than the marvelous auto. How I envy your Chinese serenity."

With this image San Giuliano, whose memory was amazingly retentive, evoked our old Hyde Park conversations when I must have used the comparison to conclude that in the marvelous German organization everything depended too much on the wisdom or folly of a single person.

Given a San Giuliano, there was nothing strange about the fact that when Austria sent her ultimatum to Belgrade, having left her Italian ally, down to the last moment, in the most complete ignorance, he should not have decided immediately to denounce an alliance whose most essential clauses the Vienna Cabinet had so openly violated.

But when San Giuliano commenced to meditate in September, 1914, the form that Italy's entrance into the war on the side of the Entente could take, his ideas were stamped with the imprint of a clarity of vision such as, I must admit, I had never been accustomed to perceive in him when we were together at London and Rome. He knew that death hovered over him, and he waited it stoically while he kept on working. When it came, on October 16, all that had gone into forming the dross of his intelligence—too great importance attached to contingencies, too much confidence in everyday artfulnesses—had vanished from his mind. Italy would have had everything to gain by keeping as a program the ideas he set down. To reduce them to their essence, they were:

To assure ourselves that the Entente, which inclined to consider Germany as the principal enemy, should not let themselves be induced to spare Austria, which was Italy's principal enemy (certain English hesitancies during the war proved how farsighted he had been);

To go to war with Rumania (and to this end he gave Baron Fasciotti, Italian Minister at Bucharest, instructions that were not confirmed by his successor, to the great harm of the entire Entente);

To carry the Italian frontier to the Alps, and as far as the Gulf of Fiume, where Dante had fixed * the limits of eastern Italy, and to annex some Dalmatian islands;

To establish a permanent entente, political and military, with the Serbian Government, to carry to the limit the war against Austria (which, on the one hand, would have eliminated all possibility of the survival of the Danubian monarchy, and, on the other, annexations in Dalmatia—and this despite the fact that Sazonow, for Russia had offered them to San Giuliano through Ambassador Carlotti as intermediary. A sidelight on San Giuliano: the too hasty overtures of the Russian Minister had offended rather than won him over).

For the post-bellum period, San Giuliano's ideas were no less farsighted. They can be summed up as follows:

A treaty of alliance between the victors, he wrote at the time in war terminology, in order "to guarantee the new map of Europe" (but even if he did not so state, it was plain that an alliance so vast would have functioned only in the interest of European reconstruction, and not at all *against* any particular country);

An accord to continue after the war, between Rome and Belgrade, which would guarantee a specific Italian influence in the Balkans.

* . . . *presso del Quarnaro,*
  Che Italia chiude e i suoi termini bagna.
                  Dante, *Inferno,* IX.
  (. . . near the Quarnaro, that shuts in Italy and bathes its borders.)

San Giuliano dead, Salandra, then Prime Minister, offered the portfolio of Foreign Affairs to Baron Sonnino, who accepted.

Of all the Italians in the public eye, Sonnino had been the only one, when the war broke out, to believe and say that Italy could or should intervene on the side of the Central Empires.

Giolitti, who, returning from a trip to London, was in Paris on August 1, went to the Italian Embassy and said to the Chargé d'Affaires, Prince Ruspoli, that "Italy by the treaty of the Triple Alliance had no obligation to enter the war, considering that Austria was attacking Serbia, whereas the treaty was purely defensive and prescribed Italian intervention beside her allies only in case they should be attacked."

These were the textual words that the Chargé d'Affaires naturally hastened to communicate to San Giuliano who, as soon as Giolitti had arrived at his Cavourian country house, wrote him: "Your opinion is the one I proposed to Salandra and the King; and it has been adopted."

Bissolati, the head of the reformed Socialists, wrote on August 2 to his friend Bonomi that he was "glad that a thesis of neutrality had triumphed," but that it was necessary "to prepare the spirit of the proletariat for war" against the militarist powers.

The editor of *Avanti*, Mussolini, screamed in his paper that the war was only an aspect of the struggle between capitalist governments, and that it was necessary to keep to neutrality, awaiting the dawn of the social revolution—which he guaranteed to his readers was imminent.

It was Sonnino alone, as I have said, who, during the first few days, felt that we ought to side with the Central Powers; he acknowledged it in a letter to the former Minister Bertolini, dated August 18, 1914; talking with Bertolini two weeks earlier, he had been still more categoric in his condemnation of neutrality. I had brought Bertolini with me to the conference of Spa as Second Italian Delegate. In our long evenings we often spoke of those days.

"How is it," I said to Bertolini, "that Sonnino, who was so ticklish over questions of national dignity, did not take into consideration the fact that, even putting aside the purely de-

fensive character of the treaty, Austria had violated it by preparing the ultimatum and the war without warning us?"

Bertolini then explained that if his friend's authoritarian
tendencies inclined him, without his realizing it, in favor of the
Central Empires, what decided him in those first days was the
naive and unavowed idea of countering the unanimous opinion of the country—the opinion common to the King, conservatives like Salandra, liberals like Giolitti, Socialists like
Bissolati. This was the result of Sonnino's essential trait of
character. The son of a Scotch Presbyterian mother and an
Italo-Egyptian-Jewish father, he was haunted by a puritan
and, seemingly, pharisaical mania to thank God that "he was
not as other men"—a mania which, if annoying in private life,
in public life threatens to be an obstacle to the comprehension
of affairs.

As a young diplomat before the war I often saw Sonnino in
his solitary house, near the Forum of Trajan; carved on the
oak shelves of his fine library I read each time his device:
Quod aliis licet non tibi (Things allowed to others are not permitted to you); and with my Italian lack of puritanism I was
each time astonished that this very worthy man did not realize
that such maxims have value only when they are *not* displayed
as a decoration.

But the reasons for Italian neutrality were so evident that
Sonnino recognized them immediately when, on San Giuliano's
death, he became Minister of Foreign Affairs.

We have already seen in Chapter XXII that Article VII of
the treaty of the Triple Alliance imposed on Austria-Hungary
and Italy—in case they should want to change the *status quo*
in the Balkans "with a temporary or permanent occupation"—
the obligation to "conclude in advance an agreement based on
the principle of a reciprocal compensation for each advantage,
territorial or other," that each one of the two Powers might
be able to obtain beyond their present position.

Even granting the first Jesuitical *distinguo* that Count
Berchtold formulated, namely, that the Austrian occupation
in Serbia was neither "permanent" nor "temporary" but only
"momentary," the fact remained that Austria made war to
create in the Balkans other "advantages," "territorial" or not;

that that fact obligated her to a "compensation"; and that she had violated the treaty by not proceeding to "a previous accord."

San Giuliano, rich in the bitter experience of his vain efforts to achieve an entente with Austria that was not merely formal —efforts in which I had collaborated in Rome with such good will—understood the uselessness of any discussion with a nation destined either to ruin or to become a still more direct danger for Italy, as well as for the independence of the Balkan peoples. The too logical-minded have reproached San Giuliano for not having denounced the treaty the day after its flagrant violation on the part of Austria. Such gestures may be very handsome individually; but one does not make them when the future of forty millions is at stake. However, we know San Giuliano's feelings as a dying man, and that they lacked neither breadth nor a sense of the future.

From the moment that he had the responsibility of power, Sonnino clung to Article VII of the treaty. Here was the legal proof of the Austrian wrong. As if he wanted to redeem his hesitations of the first days, in this Article VII he not only saw a legal title violated, but there came to him an awakening of the passion of his fathers for the letter of the law.

So once again the letter killed the spirit, which should have made him understand that a new chapter of history had begun, and that the Triple Alliance, violated as it had been by Austria, was only a wreck in a much vaster shipwreck. When Italy entered the war in May, 1915, Sonnino published a *Green Book* containing his negotiations with Austria. This man who, alone in Italy, had started by thinking that our country should cast its lot with that of the Central Powers, wrote in the dispatch which formally proclaimed the end of the Triple Alliance:

"Austria-Hungary, by neglecting the obligation flowing from the treaty, seriously disturbed the Balkan *status quo* and created a situation from which she alone could profit, to the detriment of interests of the greatest importance that her ally had so often affirmed and proclaimed.

"So flagrant a violation of the letter and spirit of the treaty not only justified the refusal of Italy to range herself beside her allies in a war provoked without her advice, but with the same stroke removed from the alliance its essential content and its reason for existing."

Italians and foreigners have reproached Sonnino for the lack of idealism and sentiment which seemed to have characterized the negotiations described in his *Green Book* as well as those with the cabinets of London, Paris and St. Petersburg, which ended in the treaty of April 26, 1915.

Far be it from me to contest this assertion. While still in China I read the *Green Book* in Pekin, and the sorrow I felt was even deeper than after our reverses of 1917. All our allies had had serious military checks; but none of them had had governments which had seemed to take pleasure in lowering the moral stature of their country. The phrase *sacro egoismo* with which they reproached Salandra was natural—its form apart—in the mouth of a statesman at the moment Salandra uttered it; for he had no other aim than to moderate, if not control, the admirable outburst of enthusiasm that then swept over Italy for a war of the democracies against militarism, and whose echo I heard in Bissolati's letters. I said "its form apart" because that phrase, *sacro egoismo,* in itself has no sense. Egoism can never be sacred, nor can the sacred ever be egoistic. But it often happens that senseless phrases become famous.

At the end of February, 1915, Sonnino decided to break off his discussions with Austria, discussions which, on both sides, always seemed like the petty bartering of neighbors disputing over fishing or road rights. On March 3 he ordered the Ambassador at London, Marquis Imperiale, to initiate secret negotiations with Sir Edward Grey for an accord between Italy and the Powers of the Entente.

In London Sonnino followed the procedures typical of a village lawyer. He irritated all his partners, which in itself was not of much importance, but he gave them a hundred occasions to assume a moral superiority apropos of the war aims, a superiority which proved to be only a bluff.

Sonnino's troubles were not those of a tortuous diplomatist but of an absolute lack of creative imagination. By rights he should have been a minister of Francis Joseph. Sonnino's mania was to hold fast to "the realities." But when one does not take idealism into account, or even sentiment, it is quite obvious that one has not the breadth of vision to embrace all the "realities."

The calmest study of his Treaty of London proves that he did not even glimpse the political necessities which the dying San Giuliano had so well understood.

While Giolitti foresaw that the war would last three years—Giolitti was the only one, with Kitchener, in the summer of 1914, to have that prevision—Sonnino believed that the war would be short. Proof of this rests in the fact that, being able then to demand anything of the Powers who were so anxious for our intervention, he limited the foreign loan to the derisory sum of fifty million pounds sterling.

San Giuliano was primarily preoccupied with the effective solidarity of the Allies in a war against Austria. Not in vain had he been Ambassador in London where he had observed the sympathies of Society for those Austrians and Hungarians who gave such wonderful hunting parties, and who were such fine horsemen (and however futile these reasons may appear, they were sometimes momentarily useful to Austria in relations with English officialdom, as they proved useful to little Otto von Hapsburg in Washington in 1943). Sonnino did not manage to secure for himself any assurance as to the conduct of the war, and, still less, any assurances for the future.

Having obtained by the Treaty of London a part of Dalmatia, he was obliged—contrary to what San Giuliano had thought—not only not to admit any accord with Serbia, but to consider her as a potential enemy. He thought he could parry the danger by exacting absolute secrecy for his Treaty of London which, naturally, as he should have foreseen, was known by the Serbs a fortnight after his signing of it.

XXV

THE WAR POPE: BENEDICT XV

POPE PIUS X DIED ON AUGUST 20, 1914, A WEEK BEFORE Austria decided to declare war against Great Britain; he had no other connections with the world conflict than those he had had during the period of the preparation of the Austro-Hungarian ultimatum to Serbia. These connections were described in Chapter XXIII with references to the government sources of the information.

It was felt at the Vatican that the end of the old Pope was near. However, there was no drama at the old man's death bed. Drama was reserved for the Conclave.

The majority of the Cardinals who were in Rome or could arrive on time were favorable to the Central Empires. The German and Austro-Hungarian Cardinals all gave the impression of obeying identical instructions to inspire in those about them a feeling of complete and immediate victory of the two Emperors. A German Cardinal kept repeating: *"Cito vincemus in bello"* (We shall win the war quickly). The Italians nicknamed him "Cito." Cito explained that in case Italy should emerge from her neutrality to attack the Central Empires her unity would again become a matter for discussion. Changing from wrathful to honeyed tones he added that in such case, the temporal power might well be restored. Cito never could understand why the Italian Cardinals, indifferent to the menaces to the Kingdom, were terrified when the restoration of the temporal power was promised them. Only the Spaniards, puppets of Merry del Val, considered with enthusiasm the hypothesis of a Rome again become papal.

At the Conclave the proud attitude of Cardinal Mercier alone opposed the Teutonic assurance.

Later, during the balloting, Cardinal Billot received the news that two of his nephews had died on the field of battle. Immediately Austro-Hungarian sympathies dwindled among the cardinals, subject, like all men in groups, to psychological movements independent of reason.

It was in this atmosphere full of contrasts that the cardinals chose as Pope, Cardinal Giacomo della Chiesa, Archbishop of Bologna. They had not thought of him at the start. He himself in all the earlier balloting had voted for his friend, Cardinal Ferrata, "the French candidate" as Poincaré wrote in his book *Au service de la France*, in that Louis XIV style of his that so often did a disservice to France.

The candidacy of della Chiesa did not appear until the fifteenth ballot, on the initiative of Cardinal Gasparri, who had been his associate in the Secretary of State's office. Not until the third turn did he obtain exactly the two-thirds of the votes required for his election. It was evening. The adversaries of the Archbishop of Bologna contested the election, asserting that it would not be regular unless it were proved that della Chiesa had not voted for himself. The expression of such a doubt, legitimate as it was insolent, excited a very lively debate in the Conclave. As it was late they decided that all the cardinals who had voted for della Chiesa should repeat their votes for him the next morning, if they wished, in the first balloting; they would then have proof that the two-thirds had been attained without the vote of the interested cardinal, who would abstain from voting. When della Chiesa, who had listened impassively to the discussion, retired to his cell he knew that he was already Pope, since he had not voted for himself.

Next morning, September 3, 1914, fate designated him as scrutinizer. Ever impassive, he had to verify that the necessary number of his peers had given their votes to his name. He read it thirty, forty times in a cold even voice. The balloting ended, he walked with firm step to his seat and there received the *adorazione* of the Cardinals. After which he retired to the sacristy where the three ritualistic white habits had been deposited; they had been prepared by the pontifical tailor in three different sizes; the smallest was still too ample and had to be fitted to him with pins. But when he appeared before Michelangelo's altar of Judgment the dignity of the head of the Church radiated from his puny figure. "As if he had been

Pope all his life," one of the cardinals who had elected him told me some years later.

The choice of the Conclave illustrated once again an unwritten law of the Roman Church: namely, that each pope must differ radically from his predecessor.

Pius X was immured in the scholastic formulas of the past, while della Chiesa hardly knew his way in theology; Pius X had no understanding of diplomatic negotiations, while della Chiesa was a career diplomat. Finally—since everything has some bearing—Pius X was a son of peasants, while Giacomo della Chiesa belonged to one of those Genoese families, so proud of their past, identified with the glories of the Genoan Republic.

Della Chiesa himself admitted that he knew nothing about theological questions. He had not had a seminary education, as he had not become a priest until he was twenty-six, after having taken his law degree at the University of Genoa. Consequently all his life he had an utter lack of unction, a direct and quick way of reasoning which struck me whenever I met him in the course of our diplomatic careers.

Ironic, reserved, distant, he was not made for facile friendships. His reserve was perhaps increased by the realization of his physical defect (he was slightly humpbacked, which, with his luminous eyes, suggested a resemblance to the portraits of Leopardi). Yet I have rarely known affections as deep as those which his cousin Giacomo Durazzo Pallavicino and his oldest friend Baron Monti had for him. The latter, a high Italian functionary, constantly served as intermediary between the Pope and myself in delicate negotiations. A unique exception, the Pope insisted that Monti continue to use the familiar Italian "tu" (thou) when they talked together, which, however, Monti never did unless they were alone.

The della Chiesas were relatively poor, while Durazzo Pallavicini was the wealthiest patrician of Genoa. When, after the University, young Giacomo wanted to enter the *Academia dei Nobili Ecclesiastici,* nursery of pontifical diplomats, his rich cousin Durazzo Pallavicino assumed the quite considerable expense involved. When the former student had become Pope a deputation of the Genoese aristocracy came to Rome to present him their felicitations. Among them was Durazzo who, seeing that the Pope was approaching him, bowed and stammered:

"Your Holiness. . . ."

The Pope answered: "You call me Holiness! Why, we are the two old cousins we always were." And addressing the kneeling deputation, he said: "Gentlemen, if I am Pope you have among you the one who made it possible; it is my cousin who paid for my studies."

This same fidelity to old friendships della Chiesa showed to Cardinal Rampolla. When the influence of the latter had vanished, della Chiesa had been the only one of the Vatican diplomats who, every evening, dared pass the portals of the Convent of Santa Marta where the former Secretary of State of Leo XIII, who had very nearly succeeded him, lived in solitude and abandonment. Della Chiesa's nomination to the Archbishopric of Bologna was one of those pontifical promotions intended to remove to a more distant field an element which seemed dangerous by reason of its fidelity to the vanquished. Furthermore, della Chiesa became Cardinal only after Rampolla's death; they did not want to have those two friends together in the Sacred College.

As long as he remained in Rome, as Undersecretary of State, until his exile to Bologna, della Chiesa tried, respectfully and prudently, to prevent the relations of France and the Vatican from degenerating to the point of disastrous rupture, the obvious termination, according to him, of Pius X's and Merry del Val's policy. He gained nothing by his efforts except to be no longer received by the Pope.

On the other hand, he took no position in the theological conflict unleashed by Vives y Tuto. He knew he was no theologian and kept silent. But he revealed the essence of his thought—and his good sense—when, having arrived at his archdiocese of Bologna, he systematically declined to manifest the least approbation for Bologna's Catholic press, which was violently attacking Christian democracy. In short, he abstained, which was a prudent way of revealing his opinion.

Having become Pope, he put an immediate stop to all the inquisitorial and persecutory fury which had raged at the Vatican, in the bishoprics and in Catholic journals. In his first encyclical he expressed his firm will to eliminate distinctions

and accusations among Catholics, reserving to the Supreme
Authority alone the surveillance of faith and the necessary
censures. An incident that happened to him personally, the
day after his ascension to the pontificate, perhaps contributed
—for men are only men, even though they be popes—to this
immediate disavowal of the habits encouraged by his predecessor. He found on his desk all the papers marked as reserved
for the Pope which had been piled together during Pius X's
last illness, and for the duration of the Conclave; among them
was a long letter to Pius X from Monsignor Pellizzari, Bishop
of Piacenza, near Bologna, which contained a formal denunciation of della Chiesa as "suspected of Modernism."

When the *Azione Cattolica,* the association that constituted
the Vatican's principal instrument in Italy, was reorganized,
Benedict XV personally ordered that the democrats persecuted
by Pius X should be represented, and that Sturzo, the future
leader of the Popular Party, should be among the directors.
Again, it was the personal sympathy of Benedict XV which
enabled Sturzo—notwithstanding the oppositions a strong personality always encounters—to become Secretary General of
the *Azione Cattolica* from 1915 to 1918 and, afterward,
chief of the Scholastic Secretariat. The Pope likewise consented
to Sturzo's realization of his idea of constituting the Federation of Italian Workers, known as the White Federation. All
these measures, each of which aimed at an ever more democratic orientation of Catholic forces, were finally, in November,
1918, crowned by the complete abolition of the *Non expedit,*
which allowed the Popular Party to make electoral campaigns
without encountering difficulty on the part of the ecclesiastical
authorities.

Germany and Austria had not considered the new Pope as
persona grata at the time of his election. At Vienna and Berlin
they regarded him a creature of Rampolla—and Rampolla
was the enemy. They did not pardon the Sicilian the veto,
thanks to which the old Emperor of Austria had deprived him
of the tiara at the Conclave of 1903; for one never forgives
a person for the harm one has done him. But in Paris and London, if not in Rome, they very soon concluded that the new
Pope was "Germanophile" because the Central Empires, short

of friends, had thought it wise to appear to be much more satisfied with Benedict XV than they really were.

The new democratic policy of Benedict XV seemed essentially contrary to the tendencies that had made Pius X convinced of the authoritarian empires' victory. Having no
understanding of the fecund conflict for liberty, Pius, in his
heart of hearts, would have preferred the victory of the Turk
himself to that of the "liberals" who had always inspired in
him so much mistrust and who, in France, had inflicted on
him so many sorrows; just as another Pius, fifteen years later,
would prefer the intellectual and moral insanities of Fascism
to what he called "the villainous fetishes of liberalism."

The fact that Benedict had completely disavowed the anti-
democratic policy of his predecessor was sufficient proof that
his judgment of the war was free of preconceived ideas. Actually, in the tragedy that bathed the world in blood he coldly
envisaged only the immediate interests of the Church. And
yet, even for him, there were great reasons for perplexity.
On the one side was England, Protestant, a beacon throughout
the world of that liberalism for which the Roman Church had
so little love; and beside England there was Orthodox Russia
which, even before the war, had given the Vatican so many
worries in the Balkans. On the other hand, the Pope had no
illusions as to the result of a German victory, which would
have swept out all that was left of Catholic prestige in Asia
Minor, and would, perhaps, have ruined the Catholic forces
in Austria itself. The Pope's thought soon crystallized into a
hope of peace without victory, including nevertheless, he
added, a restoration of Catholic Poland, the liberation of
Belgium, the elimination of all Russian influence from the
Balkans, and some territorial concessions of Austria to Italy.
Enunciated in a certain tone, each of his clauses might seem a
concession to the Entente. In reality—taken one by one—they
served only the precise interests of the Church of Rome, including the last, for Benedict wisely realized that only on the
good will of the Italian people did his chance of continuing to
live tranquilly in the Vatican depend.

His program and his hopes presented one inconvenience. In
proportion as the chances of victory for the Central Empires

dissipated, the White Peace that Benedict had wished for, from the first days of his pontificate, became the peace desired in Berlin and Vienna, the peace which the governments of the Entente opposed with all their might.

The most important act of his peace policy occurred on August 3, 1917; this was a note addressed "to the leaders of the belligerent nations."

The principles that he laid down, after having proclaimed that he had no particular plan and that he was not guided by the suggestions or interests of any of the belligerents, were:

Substitution of moral force for the law of material force;

Reduction of armaments to the limit permitted by the necessity of maintaining internal order in each country;

International arbitration;

Liberty of the seas;

Reciprocal renunciation of all war indemnities except in the case where a different arrangement should intervene;

Restitution of all the occupied territory (complete evacuation of Belgium with guarantee of her full political independence by the two belligerent parties, evacuation of the French territories, restitution of the German colonies);

Regulation of the territorial questions, such as those pending between Austria and Italy and between France and Germany, in a spirit of peace and with due regard to the desires of the populations;

Regulation in an identical spirit of the Armenian and Balkan questions, as well as the question of Poland.

It was then declared in Entente circles that the Pope had concluded accords with the new German Chancellor Michaelis through the intermediary of the Nuncio at Munich, Pacelli— the future Pius XII—as regards the "principles" of his Note. The Pope might have answered that if he had made soundings, he had not concluded accords. As a matter of fact, the response he later received from Berlin displeased him almost as much as the silence of the Entente.

The most important document that the Papal Note provoked was the response that President Wilson gave on August 27. The pontifical program, declared the American note, signified the pure and simple return to the pre-war status which, for the President, did not entail a just and durable peace.

The failure was, therefore, complete. This was a matter of surprise only in Austria, where they had placed some hope in the Vatican overtures.

But the least surprised of all was Benedict XV. He had long resisted the pressures of those who recommended putting to the service of peace the "high moral authority of the Holy See." With his habitual tone of sarcasm he used to reply:

"Authority? Strange that they should talk so much of it in the circles which have refused us all authority."

But when the Emperor Charles sent him in July, 1917, a "letter of filial obedience" in which he left "to his august authority" the decision of the sacrifices to which the Austro-Hungarian monarchy should consent to obtain peace quickly, Benedict had to do something. The soundings he attempted at Berlin were formulated in the Note. The author of it was the General of the Jesuits, Ledokowski. This detail (which was confirmed to me by Baron Monti) would tend to give authenticity to the rumors then current about the Vatican: namely, that the Pope hoped that the "regulation of the territorial questions between Austria and Italy with due regard to the desires of the populations" would be compensated by the devolution to the Austrian monarchy of the Polish crown. Ledokowski, imbued exclusively, as he was and as he wished to be, with the laws and principles of his Company, had nevertheless cherished in his heart an ardent Polish patriotism. The influence that Benedict had in the editing of the Note and in all that had reference to the overture was exclusively an influence of moderating simplicity; he did not want to pose as a *peacemaker* nor as arbiter.

If I could describe minutely the confidential negotiations which passed almost every week between Baron Monti, who communicated the Pope's desiderata, and me on so many affairs, great and small, it would be evident how very open and loyal, generous and yet practical was the spirit of Benedict XV. Nothing shocked him, nothing surprised him. In him were none of the prejudices which so often in the past had caused the Church to lose precious moments. While all diplomatic Europe kept on repeating, "This Lenin cannot last," the Pope asked me through Monti—but under the seal of secrecy— would I, if necessary, be able to facilitate the trip of some

Catholic priests to Russia. Seeing my surprise, Monti explained (and it was evident that he was repeating the very words of the Pope): "His Holiness thinks that even these crimes and this blood will one day be of service if it is going to be possible, when the wave of irreligion has passed, to attempt a Catholic evangelization in Russia. Orthodoxy no longer has any deep-rooted life; its end as the official religion offers possibilities which would never have existed so long as a Tsar, 'Protector of the Church,' continued to reign."

It was simple and it was true; but courage was required to express it at the Vatican in 1920. I promised my support in whatever form it might be able to take; and soon afterward, on the orders of the Pope, young priests began desperately studying Russian and the history of the Orthodox Church. A young Russian diplomat, Alexander Ezreinow, who had been converted to Catholicism, became a priest and was often consulted. He had a rapid ecclesiastical career. I cite this episode since it helps to explain why, even during the second World War, the Vatican hesitated, more than once, between waging an open war on "Communist Russia"—as it did during the civil war in Spain, under the influence of the Spanish episcopate—and contacts with the masters of the Kremlin.

The explanation of the thought and action expressing the character of Benedict XV consists, in my opinion, in the co-existence in him of two orders of ideas which are not, after all, contradictory save in appearance.

He thought as a Pope, therefore he must have thought that all possibilities are open to the Church, up to that universal domination that the misery of the times makes it dangerous to avow, but which was loudly proclaimed by the Gregorys and the Innocents. Never a word escaped him that might be interpreted as a renunciation of the supreme and distant aims of the Church. Thus, when exhausted Europe accepted the idea of Wilson and began to count on the League of Nations to save us from new disasters, Benedict—completely devoted as he was to the cause of peace—did not at all conceal his distrust of a League which claimed to be supreme, but in which no pope could have a part, for a pope can hardly admit of sitting an equal among equals. Consequently, in the Encyclical *Pacem Dei* of May 23, 1920, he completely ignored the Geneva institution, invoking, as if nothing like it yet existed, "the formation of a league of nations based on the Christian law."

But the inheritor of the distant medieval traditions of the Roman Church was at the same time a farsighted and modern man who had no illusions as to the importance of the moral forces he had at his disposal. He felt—and did not hide it from his intimates—that the Catholic influence was, in the complex game of war, very limited, and that it might excite more mistrust and hostility than respect: that conflicting interests far surpassed all moral prestige, as Wilson himself later had bitter proof.

This cool, clear view of the limits of his activity explains why Benedict never made any gestures that an imprudent man in his place would have been tempted to make; gestures which would have earned him the noisy popularity of the moment, but which would have left the Church still more divided.

The dying Benedict could justly say to himself that he was transmitting the unity of the Church intact to his successor, despite the duration and violence of the tempest. He succeeded in that task which was, in fine, his supreme duty, for he knew how, with humility, to fulfill the duties of his office. This humility was his grandeur and his wisdom.

Later we shall see that popes who desired to achieve ostentatious gestures and reverse the current of national life, as Pius XI did in 1929 with an organization that had illegally seized the power in Italy, usually had time, before they died, to regret bitterly their ephemeral successes.

XXVI

THE WAR: SONNINO, CADORNA, DIAZ, BADOGLIO

THE VERY DAY AFTER OUR ENTRANCE INTO THE WAR AGAINST Austria-Hungary the consequences of the Treaty of London * had no longer to be anticipated. The Italian Command understood it immediately, but not Sonnino, who for a long time— certainly down to early 1917—believed that the war would end with a relative defeat of the Hapsburg monarchy, not with its disruption. When, during my frequent visits to Rome, returning from Corfu and Macedonia, I showed him that I agreed with the beliefs of Bissolati and Salvemini, he said to me one day, irritably, "They are mad, they are idealists," the second attribution being for him more derogatory than the first.

General Cadorna, Commander in Chief of the Italian armies, had counted on the Serbian Army making a simultaneous offensive on Italy's entrance into the war, but the Serbs did not budge. Cadorna had not desired the annexation of the northern part of Dalmatia that Sonnino imposed; he had even counseled against it. Equally with his successor Diaz—who often repeated it to me in 1920 in Rome—Cadorna thought that in the event of a new war we would be obliged immediately to evacuate Dalmatia, but Sonnino, without taking account of Cadorna's advice, had included Dalmatia in the list of annexations. Naturally, the moment Italy entered the war the Serbs ceased all attacks against Austria and turned toward Albania. When, later, I discussed this period of the war with Pachich at Corfu, as well as with the highest Serbian military authorities, my remarks on their passivity were not contradicted. They were not very proud of this period, but they sought an excuse in a declaration that I had to admit, in my inner conscience, was not devoid of truth. "One of our trump cards," they said, "in fighting an enemy so much stronger than ourselves, consisted in the desertions we were provoking on

* Chapter XXV.

the Austrian front among the Croat, Dalmatian and Slovene regiments. Your Treaty of London, which took from the South Slavs half of Dalmatia, gave the Austrian Command a wonderful opportunity to give their Slav soldiers a popular war cry: 'The war against Italian imperialism.' "

Despite the evidence of the facts, Sonnino continued on his path. His moral character, which had all the qualities of its defects, included an absolute scorn for the phrases of the moment, above all for the propaganda which was then one of the favorite weapons. The awakening of nationalities in Austria had not been one of his studies before the war; and now he mistook this awakening for one of the clever dodges of that propaganda he despised. His most serious mistake consisted in never believing that Austria might disappear, as Bissolati and Salvemini had warned him in Italy, and I from Corfu and Macedonia.

Honest though he was, he did not escape the so common illusion of confounding the interests of his country with the concepts and forecasts he had formulated. Each year of the war was worth a century of experience, but he shut his eyes and remained faithful only to his Treaty of London, to the letter of the law.

On the eve of the great Austro-German offensive against Serbia (in the summer of 1915) the Italian High Command entered into an accord with the French to send a joint expedition to the Serbian front; it was to be commanded by an Italian general. In Paris, where they love royalty, they had thought of the Duke of Aosta. Cadorna anticipated gaining thereby an important advance on the Carso and perhaps the conquest of Trieste, as a result of the weakening of Austrian forces on the Italian front which had so difficult a terrain to cope with. But Sonnino opposed; he felt that a close Italo-Serb military collaboration would have led to the revision of his sacrosanct Treaty of London.

Later, when obliged to permit the sending of one division to the Macedonian front—a division which almost always had for neighbors the Serbs, with whom its members developed the most cordial relations—he continually warded off my pressing proposals to give more prominence to the exceptional services that our XXXVth Division was rendering to Serbia and the common cause. Our division, which had to defend a very wide front, had seen its effectives gradually increased to 70,000 men. The French army corps further east were often below that figure. "Let us call our division what it actually is, an army corps," I repeatedly told and wrote him. "You often complain of the Allies, but if we are the first to belittle the importance of our own effort, how can you expect others to do us justice?"

Nothing was done about it. So that this case, unique in the war, occurred: that we gave the Army of Macedonia the strength and blood of an army corps, but we ourselves, by calling it a division, prevented the extent of our collaboration from being acknowledged by all.

Later—especially when it became evident that the Entente would win the war with the participation of the United States, and that they would not be bound, when peace came, by any secret treaty—I pressed Sonnino, on several occasions, to have an understanding with the Serbian government of such a kind as would enable us to appear at the peace conference freer to defend our general interests without being prisoners of a quarrel on the Adriatic frontier.

This period was very painful for this essentially honest man. On the one hand, he did not want to see what was happening. He still hoped that the war would end, as he had forecast, with an Austria still quite strong and with the Yugoslav dreams dissipated. On the other hand, he could not help feeling that the forecast of the "idealists" might well become reality. In the summer of 1917 he accepted my proposal to bring Pachich to Rome with me and reach a compromise with him. So I came with Pachich who, in his cautious discussions, gave him to understand that he was ready to accept a very ample formula. Sonnino listened—and made no reply.

Pachich, who was as taciturn as Sonnino, only said to me: "I thought it would be like that," and he was not too disappointed, for, like Sonnino, he had at heart rather an aggrandized Serbia than an Austria destroyed.

I earnestly entreated Sonnino to recall me. But he, as earnestly, asked me to retain my post at Corfu.

"But what is the use, if you approve neither my words nor the policy that seems to me necessary over there?"

He answered, and I repeat his words textually: "You will continue to speak according to your conscience; I shall never contradict you. Even now I haven't done so. Only," and here he stopped a moment and then continued, as if a little ashamed, "I am like the peasants; it is on the market place, at the last minute, that I reduce my prices."

His wish that I continue in a way to neutralize his silence with my words was in no sense Machiavellianism, in the miserable meaning that modern hypocrisy has given the word. No one in the world was more incapable than Sonnino of such ideas and such maneuvers.

If, as was not the case, I had needed proof that his attitude had nothing to do with "Machiavellianism," but with a grievous moral tragedy that I respected even as I deplored the fatal consequences I foresaw for my country, I would have had that proof several months later when Wilson published his Fourteen Points. My duty was to reiterate my ideas once again to Sonnino. I fulfilled it in a long private letter from which I extract this sentence: ". . . and at the Peace Conference all will be able to do homage in words to Wilson's principles, while thinking only of safeguarding their material interests; we alone, enchained in a too antithetical formula, will risk being in disagreement with Wilson and everyone; and in a desperate conflict for the Treaty of London we shall risk compromising all our interests. European hypocrisy will gain face, as the Chinese say, by denouncing the Italian *sacro egoismo* which will risk being the least realistic of all the Allies' egoisms."

Some days later Sonnino replied, giving himself the sole luxury of failing to allude to my letter: "It must be admitted that the formulas of President Wilson may make the field of discussion more difficult; I ask you, therefore, to resume with Pachich the conversations you had with him before his last visit to Rome."

Pachich was not at Corfu at the time. Before he returned, three weeks later, Sonnino had written to annul his instructions and asked me "to await new ones," which never came.

My direct knowledge of the war was limited to Macedonia and Albania. Anyone who witnessed the jealousies among the Allied generals at Salonika knows that the victory of a coalition is infinitely more difficult than that of a unified power. One day at Salonika I wrote in the album of a French lady: "I have lost all respect for Napoleon since I have seen what it is to have to fight with a coalition,"—and that became almost a diplomatic incident.

If I have nothing direct and new to say about the bitter war waged by the Italian armies on the Alps and the Carso, I, however, knew well our two leading generals, Cadorna and Diaz.

Member of an old Piedmontese family which had always served the House of Savoy, Count Cadorna, General in Chief of the Italian Army from its entrance in the war to November, 1917, was a soldier by breeding, temperament and tradition.

In September, 1870, his father was in command of the Italian troops that took Rome; Cadorna, the son, a lieutenant of artillery, was at his side. He was then eighteen years old.

A normal career carried Cadorna to the rank of Chief of the General Staff in 1914, on the eve of the European war. He prepared and reorganized the Army for the great ordeal; and in May, 1915, when it entered the war against Austria-Hungary, he was its General in Chief, under the nominal supreme command of the King.

We have seen what diplomatic mistakes increased the difficulties of Cadorna's task, which was to conduct a war to the death against the Austrian monarchy and, at the same time, hold at a suspicious distance, without the least accord either strategic or political, all the other irreconcilable enemies of Austria, such as the Serbs and, in general, all the Slavs. Sonnino dared for a moment to insist that the task and problems imposed on Cadorna were simplified by this conception, when, as a matter of fact, all his difficulties were only increased by it.

Cadorna had written (before May 24, 1915): "This is not a localized war between Italy and Austria-Hungary; it is a general war, in which Russia and Serbia share with us the final objectives on enemy territory; the three armies must, therefore, act at the same time for the common purposes." And he added: "When the three armies shall have beaten Austria, Germany, reduced to her own strength alone, will immediately yield."

This was the very opposite of Sonnino's idea, *"la nostra guerra (our war)."* It was seeing clear; and it was not Cadorna's fault if Russia met a terrible reverse just on the eve of Italy's entrance into the war. But Cadorna was not without responsibility for his failure to insist to Sonnino that the Treaty of London should not run counter to his strategic conception of the conduct of the war. Sonnino insisted on including among the future annexations of Italy a part of Dalmatia, despite the contrary advice of the General Staff, which considered that Dalmatia, once conquered, would be indefensible. Cadorna should certainly have made him feel the danger that such annexations might provoke an abatement of the Serbian offensive will and, particularly, that these clauses might give the government of Vienna the means of persuading the Slav troops of the Monarchy that they were fighting against a would-be Italian imperialism. But Cadorna did not so impress him.

Military critics have accused Cadorna of having been too slow in his first operations when, war having been declared, Austria had not yet been able sufficiently to reinforce her positions on the Italian front. I do not agree with them, though it might well be that the first leap would have brought him nearer Trieste.

Cadorna could not be ignorant of the fact that a brilliant initial advance, even on Trieste, would not have decided the war; and that the war could only be won by the destruction of the Austrian forces, which would have transformed the World War into a siege of Germany. The ten battles he fought against the Austro-Hungarian Army attained their objective, which was to destroy the Austro-Hungarian force. Given the frightfully difficult theater of the Italian war—that stony Carso where each hill with its caverns constitutes a natural fortress— the ten battles could be only tactical victories; but the supreme objective was slowly attained, notwithstanding. No praise can do real justice to the army and the people who devoted themselves implacably to this bloody work without any apparent immediate result, but the lack of spectacular results often prevented full justice from being rendered to participants in this atrocious duel.

On its side, the Austro-Hungarian Army was no less heroic. It had had laid upon it the almost impossible task of holding chained in an exhausting siege-war the Italians and Serbs on the one hand, and the Russians and Rumanians on the other. Friends and enemies alike had elevated German military efficiency into a fetish, and people forgot that the value of the Austro-Hungarian effort might be judged by this fact: that it was thanks to that sustained effort and self-sacrifice that the German armies were able to develop freely and repeat for years that "maneuvers by interior lines," which was the essential secret of Germany's triumphs—until the day when the framework collapsed. The German and Austro-Hungarian armies covered themselves with military glory by destroying first the Serbs, then the Rumanians, then the Russians; they could even believe for a moment in October-November, 1917, that they had destroyed the Italian armies. But all these victories were only possible because Austro-Hungarians were being killed on the margin of the gigantic chessboard.

No one would ever have contested Cadorna's merit for this thankless work (and the more heroic for that!) of the slow destruction of the Austrian forces, had not the battle of Caporetto supervened.

If Caporetto weighs so much heavier on Cadorna's name than Charleroi on Joffre's, and the Chemin des Dames on others, it is because Cadorna sought to explain the rupture of the Italian front by moral causes, as Pétain and Weygand did in France in 1940. The truth is that the Caporetto breach in the dangerously long half-circle that formed the Italian front was due to military facts. There were in certain places in the Alps breaks in the continuity of the Italian line; and through one of these gaps the Germans and Austrians forced their way after a hurricane of artillery fire such as no front had up to that time experienced.

The moral causes that Cadorna invoked to excuse his defeat were, according to him, the pacifist propaganda directed by the Socialists on the one side, and on the other by Pope Benedict, with his message on the "useless massacre," which preceded Caporetto by three months. Worse still for his own moral renown, Cadorna, in one of his communiqués, tried to explain by this so-called crisis of the spirit of resistance of his troops the success of the Austro-Hungarian invasion. I read his blasphemous communiqué on October 29, 1917, while aboard an Italian torpedo boat on which, pursued by enemy submarines, I was crossing the Atlantic, having been called to Rome by Sonnino to confer with him; the German and Austrian wireless gave the world the news of their victory, and to stress the importance of it, gave the text of Cadorna's communiqué.

If the horror I felt at hearing a general exculpate himself by attacking his army did not change to fear for my country it was because I had known the man. I had appreciated his power of resistance, but I also knew that he was an autocrat, and that it was possible for him, in good faith, to believe that the fault and responsibility devolved on others—the "civilians" whom he had always mistrusted.

Actually, moral causes did exist which, though they played an altogether secondary part, contributed to the collapse of the Italian front in the same proportion that other moral causes contributed to the French defeat of the same year 1917. But these moral causes were only in small degree due to "defeatist" messages of the Pope and the campaign of some Socialist leaders who were then playing with the demagogic phrase, *"our* dead, *their* war"; the true moral causes, essential and direct, had but one name: Cadorna.

Cadorna, hard on others as he was on himself, was actually a Louis XIV general resurrected in the twentieth century. At the head of a professional army in which discipline was maintained by floggings, he would have done wonders in those masterly sieges that we still admire in the old battle pictures. He saw the war as a gigantic siege operation. Imbued with a kind of mystic sadism, he thought that it was a supreme honor for a regiment to resist indefinitely in a trench. The changes and reliefs customary with the English and the French were for him only democratic sentimentality. In the course of the campaign this mental inclination changed to brutality; and the real strength of character changed to an exaggeration of the majestic silence he found convenient in warding off the counsels and the control of civilians. The Italian middle classes—and the phenomenon was not only Italian—liked to think that an iron mask and an hermetic silence were sure signs of genius, and that brutality was energy.

But the millions of Italians at the front were sheltered from one thing only—news. Nothing was told them, yet they were paying with their blood to know. They were not an army as Cadorna conceived it, but a people in arms, and they felt themselves sequestered from the nation, without regular and periodic leaves to see their families, without sufficient food, the least insubordination paid for by decimations. (An inquest presided over by General Caneva later proved that in the decimations they shot soldiers who were absent the day the misdemeanor that occasioned the decimation had occurred, and that they had even shot volunteers who had come from the United States at their own expense to take part in the war.)

This psychological incomprehension of the moral necessities of modern war, in which the soldiers do not cease being citizens, was Cadorna's principal fault. Himself disposed to obey an iron rule, he did not understood that the great masses function under other laws.

Authoritarian, autocratic, he had, after the defeat of Caporetto, the merit of having continued with indestructible serenity to give orders for the formation of a new front on the Piave where the Italian armies halted their retreat, and started the battle anew. When Foch came to the new Italian front for a hasty visit, after a study of the maps he had a short dialogue with Cadorna:

"Artillery must be sent there. . . ."
Cadorna replied: "It has been done."
"The reserves must be massed there. . . ."
"It has been done."
After a long succession of "It has been done," Foch rose and said: "Why, everything has already been done!"

That was true; even truer than Cadorna imagined, for it was one of those modern miracles that he could not conceive. His "It has been done" depended, most assuredly, in good part on his orders; but his orders would have been of little avail had not this happened: that on the right bank of the Piave, sacred now in the memory of Italians, all the units, and even the troops still disbanded, had said to themselves, moved by a kind of mysterious order, that the enemy must not advance a step further on Italian soil, that here Italians must fight and die.

If Cadorna then understood or even dimly glimpsed that this admirable national unity sprang from a voluntary spiritual outburst while all his decimations had been in vain, it must have raised a doubt in his mind of the validity of his entire conception of life and men. An autocrat who begins to doubt is doomed.

With Cadorna, the myth of the "strong, silent man" disappeared from the Italian front, as it had twelve months earlier on the French front with Joffre. But if the French had had this good fortune a year earlier than the Italians, they also had had the bad fortune to replace Joffre with another myth—the myth of the "Great Captain," Nivelle. The consequence was paid in the sacrifice of a frightful number of Frenchmen.

After the ordeal of Caporetto, after the immediate reformation of the Italian line of resistance on the Piave, Cadorna was discarded and honorably relegated to Versailles as Italian representative on the new Inter-Allied Supreme Council. Likewise, for an essentially analogous reason—dogmatic infallibility, squandering of human lives, discontent of the troops—Joffre had first been pushed aside by a sham promotion to the new rank of "Generalissimo of the French Forces"; some weeks later, his discarding became definitive when they conferred on him the rank of Marshal.

In Rome, Orlando had replaced the decrepit Boselli as Prime Minister. Orlando's first task was to choose the man to whom the Italian army must be confided, at the moment that the retreat had been checked, when the troops were fighting heroically, but when the Austro-German offensive still continued its furious attempt to break the new line of resistance organized on the Piave.

Arriving in Rome from Corfu on the day after the defeat of Caporetto, I succeeded in getting away immediately to the front, where my three brothers were. I saw en route the sad stream of refugees fleeing before the enemy, as had happened in Belgium and France. But as soon as I saw the new front on the Piave I felt that Italy had won. Never had I seen men so stubbornly resolute. The enemy must not pass: that was the thought inscribed on every face. Italy was victorious in her apparent defeat.

When in November, 1918, immediately after the Armistice, I went to Constantinople with an Italian naval squadron as High Commissioner, I discovered that my sentiments of twelve months before had, even then, been shared by foreigners who had more shrewdly appreciated the situation than had been done at Berlin and Vienna, and perhaps in London and Paris. As everything was for sale in Constantinople when I arrived there, it was easy for me to obtain documents from the Sublime Porte. Those tragic and beautiful days returned to my memory while I read an Austro-German communication which, after having vaunted the success of Caporetto, ended by requesting a Turkish detachment to participate in the occupation—imminent, so they wrote—of Venice. Probably the Austro-Germans imagined that a Turkish flag floating over St. Mark's Square would help to crush Italian morale.

The response of the Grand Vizier, Talaat Pasha, was: "This is our greatest defeat since the Marne. If the Italians have succeeded in holding, after such a reverse, it is because they believe in the final victory; and that the Austro-German triumph, so great as it appears, is only a tactical success."

But even if this later seemed so to everyone, the responsible government in Rome in December, 1917, could not but consider the situation as grave. As a matter of fact, the enemy continued making furious attacks.

"The Italians," then declared Conrad, the Austrian General in Chief, "are like people who hang on to planks with the strength of despair; all one has to do is to cut off their fingers and they'll all fall."

At this moment General Diaz was chosen to succeed General Cadorna. He was the "Unknown General." Still relatively young, he was born in Naples in 1851. A career officer who had risen regularly through the grades, he was a good soldier, and had been wounded in the Tripolitan War, where he had fought as a colonel. Since June, 1917, he had commanded the XXIIId Army Corps, having at the head of this Corps directed a fortunate operation on the Selo, which was, nevertheless, only a secondary episode of a still larger action. Such was the man. A new man, therefore, uncompromised by antecedents, silent, without pretension to genius, he seemed to Orlando, when one of my friends suggested him, the opposite type to Cadorna. Orlando submitted his name to the King, who acquiesced. The nomination of Diaz was simply the result of the fatigue that the harsh personality of Cadorna had engendered everywhere.

But it was at once felt that if patient continuity in the resistance was demanded in Diaz, he should also have beside him some dashing spirits. Consequently Generals Badoglio and Giardino were chosen as Assistant Chiefs of the General Staff.

This was a new departure in Italy. The Neapolitan Diaz was to represent slow reflection and the Piedmontese Badoglio and Giardino the imagination and dash. Shortly afterward Giardino was sent to the Committee of Versailles. Badoglio remained alone with Diaz.

Although ten years younger than Diaz, Badoglio, having entered the war as a lieutenant-colonel, had become by 1917, through a series of rapid promotions on the field of battle, Commandant of an Army Corps. His Corps, the XVIIIth, covered precisely the zone where the Austro-Germans had opened their first breach on October 25, 1917, and through which all the invading troops had penetrated. It is one of the merits of Orlando that he had not regarded this as a reason for the elimination of Badoglio. I had Badoglio in 1920 as military collaborator in the negotiation of the Treaty of Rapallo, and in our conversations he never admitted having been guilty of serious mistakes; but if guilty he was, as others maintain, his moral equilibrium gained thereby, which was all to his advantage when he occupied his new post of supreme responsibility. The burning memory of past risks made him more modest and prudent; his natural ardor was given stamina by it. From November, 1917, to the final victory a year later, Diaz and Badoglio formed an inseparable team: for once, a refutation of the legend that a sole directing mind can alone mature victory.

Diaz and Badoglio began their combined command with two great advantages, notwithstanding the enormous losses of Caporetto. I have already indicated one: the spontaneous and ardent renewal of the spirit of resistance among all the Italian people, exactly the contrary of what had been hoped and foreseen in Berlin and Vienna. The other advantage was material: the shortness of the new line of the Piave permitted the Italian armies to organize in depth and to concentrate reserves in a manner to make them more easily maneuverable.

Diaz had taken command on November 8, 1917. The new enemy offensive against the line of the Piave and on the high Alpine plateau of Asiago began three days later. The attack lasted three weeks; its violence never abated; the Austrians knew that they must break the line that had been improvised before them if they wished to give a decisive value to their

October victory. The offensive continued to the end of December, 1917. Then only did the Austrians admit the truth—that they were not getting through; that they would not, as a result of their Caporetto victory, get through.

During those two months, on every day of which Italy's fate hung in the balance, Diaz, yesterday unknown, was the man for the situation. He knew that the Italians had determined to hold; he knew that there was no stroke of genius to attempt—that they must simply hold and die; and he personified this sentiment. He was able to radiate a contagious atmosphere of fatalistic optimism.

January, 1918, initiated four months of snow and storm that formed a priceless rampart. Behind this rampart Diaz improved his time. Not only did he, with Badoglio, reorganize the army and the defense technically, but—and this was his supreme merit—he was able to maintain among the combatants the fever of patriotic passion that the danger to the homeland had excited in November, 1917.

He did what Cadorna had never deigned to do, and he did it precisely because he did not set himself too high. He allowed all spiritual energies freedom to flow toward the combatants; he instituted in all the major units propaganda offices to explain to the soldiers the moral aims of the war. He made them realize why they were fortunate to fight, in order that their sons should not know war (which for Cadorna would have been rank blasphemy); he gave Wilson's new pronouncements the widest publicity; he allowed all the papers, of all shades of opinion, free circulation in the trenches.

In the organization of propaganda among the enemy, Diaz proved that he had understood the necessities of the war against Austria, as neither Sonnino nor Cadorna had ever understood them. Diaz admitted the good sense of the idea for which I had pleaded in vain from Corfu throughout the two preceding years: to organize a service of propaganda specially intended to show the sympathies of the Italian people for the cause of the oppressed nationalities in Austria and Hungary; and to employ for that purpose the Czech and Yugoslav prisoners and deserters. He encouraged the formation of Czechoslovakian units on our front; and he deplored the veto that Sonnino opposed to the formation of Yugoslav units. Diaz knew that I had been recommending this measure from Corfu to Sonnino, and he knew, too, that it would have provoked disruption among the Croat troops which were still fighting so well against us; and in a way which paid due regard to military discipline, he let me know that he hoped I would insist.

Orlando, then Prime Minister, collaborated in Diaz's new policy. Profiting by the awakening of enthusiasm for resistance, the Minister of the Treasury, Nitti, launched a loan called the Victory Loan which in a very short time rose to six billion lire.

In accord with Nitti, Diaz gave all the regimental commanders sums of money to help, without offending their dignity, families of officer and soldier combatants. Every combatant who was worried about the circumstances of his family could confidentially ask his commanding officer for assistance.

They gave each soldier and officer life insurance and also the promise of a bonus on the expiration of military service. In case of death they could count on a sum being given their families on the same day; survivors would be given a sum to help them resume their activities in civil life. They also established a fund for the combatants (*Opera Nazionale per i Combattenti*) with a capital of ten million lire.

The Italian is essentially a family man: these measures— which Cadorna would never have dreamed of—contributed tremendously to the maintenance of morale among the soldiers who knew that their wives and children were getting some consideration. (Abroad no one ever knew how much suffering there was among the wives and children of the soldiers during the war, especially in southern Italy.)

The good star of Diaz willed that, after the winter had passed, the Austrians decide to attack the Italian Army with all their strength (June, 1918).

In Italy, where they knew better than in Vienna how greatly Caporetto had tempered our troops, here and there one heard murmurs of impatience because we had not engaged soon enough in a decisive battle. Italy is the country where Fabius Maximus was criticized for his slowness, and where they called him *Cunctator* (the Delayer) because, after the defeat of the Romans on Lake Trasimene, he imposed prudence as the secret of the revenge against Hannibal. For Diaz, as for Fabius, the event would change the sobriquet into a title of glory.

The battle of the Piave (June 15–23, 1918) was the most formidable that the Austrians had fought in four years of warfare. All the forces of the Monarchy—sixty divisions—were for the first time concentrated against one sole objective, the destruction of the Italian Army, inferior in numbers by about ten divisions. With Italy destroyed, they thought in Berlin and Vienna that the Flanders front would quickly crumble under the combined weight of the two Central Empires; it would have been easy afterward to invade southern France, where there was not a man to defend the country.

The secret of the tactics Diaz and Badoglio adopted in the battle of the Piave was never to engage troops in the advance zone, but to reserve the effort of counterattack for the intermediate zone to which they allowed the enemy to advance. Good use of artillery did the rest. On their own admission the Austrians lost 200,000 men in the battle, 200 cannons, 2,000 machine guns. They lost something more important still: all hopes of being able to vanquish the Italian Army. The price the Italian Army paid for the victory of the Piave was 90,000 men. After that Diaz discarded every "adventurous" proposal. Like Foch, he judged that the definitive crisis of the European war would not come until the spring of 1919, and wanted to have armies in full force for that time. Foch and Diaz thought of armies, not of nations.

At the end of the summer of 1918, on the Macedonian front where I was stationed I reached the conviction—I had seen a great many Austrian deserters, even officers—that if the outer crust of the Emperor Charles's army was still hard, the Monarchy was, nevertheless, ripe for dissolution. I therefore urged a new offensive; and Sonnino, perhaps for the first time, was completely in agreement with me. Diaz objected that it was not worth while, at this time, to take risks; but once again, events got the better of the plans of the Command. The collapse of the Balkan front, that was at last perceived as imminent, determined the Italian offensive.

The battle began on October 24; the Austrian resistance on the Italian front was still so serious that in four days Italian losses mounted to 40,000 men. But this was the resistance of what in the Balkans I had called the "crust." Soon afterward the Austrian defeat was foreshadowed more clearly. They failed to resist the rapid advance of General Caviglia's army on their flanks. On the 30th their front on the Grappa crumbled. The defeat changed to a rout. November 4 was the end.

Caviglia, not without some right, attributed to himself the merit of the final success, as Badoglio had certainly been the principal artificer of the battle and victory of the Piave. And what of Diaz? If one were to say that Diaz was a prudent coordinator of the effort and decisions of his lieutenants and a skillful exploiter of favorable circumstances, one would have said enough to be truthful. But it would be too much to say that Diaz had no other role than that assigned by Thiers to the constitutional king who "reigns and does not govern."

Diaz as an historic problem should be differently viewed. Diaz was the *right man* in an extremely critical and psychologically complicated situation where certain mediocre qualities, which in other cases would have had a negative value, assumed a positive value in themselves and their results.

The entire period of his command furnishes a proof that in modern war a great problem of economy and social psychology is superimposed on the strategical problem. In November and December, 1917, on the Piave, in June, 1918, and in October, 1918, victory smiled on no leader endowed with a special and particular genius. Victory crowned the collective preparation and, also, the moral unanimity of all the Italian combatants, leaders and men in the ranks.

If there had been a merit in having conceived, or desired, or favored this military and moral coordination of the great human and social collectivity which was the Italian Army—and this merit certainly existed—it must be recognized as belonging to Diaz primarily, in his practical intelligence and his moral character exempt from jealousy and personal preoccupations.

If during the second World War the French had had a modest Diaz instead of their pompous generals, they might not, perhaps, have avoided the dangerous tardinesses of 1939, but they would not have had the jealousies and the conscious or unconscious treasons of 1940.

XXVII

THE PARIS CONFERENCE AND THE TREATIES OF 1919

WHEN THE PEACE NEGOTIATIONS STARTED AT PARIS IN December, 1918, Sonnino went there with the Treaty of London in his pocket, without any other diplomatic and psychological preparation than this "pound of flesh." Even on the Italian side he was morally alone; for his Prime Minister Orlando would have liked an attitude more comprehensive and useful to Italy's interests; but he never dared impose it on his Minister of Foreign Affairs. Sonnino's resignation—for Sonnino would have resigned rather than change—would have initiated a violent press campaign of the Nationalists, the future allies of Fascism, who were people incomparably skillful in the use of calumny, like their brothers of *l'Action Française* in Paris.

The inevitable happened; I say the inevitable, for, after a long war fought by a coalition, history has never recorded that a peace has been concluded according to plans conceived before the war in a wholly different atmosphere and equilibrium.

Sonnino through blindness and Orlando through weakness placed themselves beyond the scope of the permanent interests of Italy—which are always those of an organic entity of Europe—and outside the natural laws of political life. Sonnino, as he had done first at Vienna and subsequently in London at the beginning of 1915, pleaded his case like a lawyer, but when he wanted to be shrewd he was pathetic; as, for instance, when he gorged the Paris press with tens of millions of francs in exchange for articles favoring the Italian annexation of Dalmatia, but never in favor of things which would have been more to Italy's advantage, such as raw materials and colonies. One day Sonnino and Orlando, in a discussion with Clemenceau, quoted the French press as proof that France's opinion was on their side. The terrible old man answered not a word. He drew a piece of paper from a drawer and showed it to them: it was the list, amounting to some thirty million dollars, of subsidies that the Italian agents—the chief among them being the already notorious Aloisi—had paid to almost all the Paris dailies.

If the plans and methods of Sonnino were myopic and shabby, the conduct of the Allies toward Italy was on a par with them.

Wilson was wrong in attempting to preserve the integrity of his principles on the Italian sector, when he had yielded on so many others. He gave the impression in Italy of wanting to recover a lost virginity at our expense. But that does not lessen Sonnino's responsibility, for it was easy to foresee and had been foreseen that everything would turn out as it did.

The final mistake was the counterpart to the initial illusion— that of the short war. At Versailles, during the negotiations and afterward, it happened that the Italians who had been taxed with being idealists, with their heads in the clouds, were the only ones who had a clear vision of reality.

Salvemini, one of Bissolati's most faithful friends, on the eve of Sonnino's negotiations with London, based on his certainty of the war lasting only a few months, wrote in February, 1915:

"The war is not going to be a military parade; on the contrary, it is going to be a very serious task. Germany will want to carry it to our territory; she will almost certainly attempt one of those quick offensives, of which she has already proved she has the secret and the strength, obliging us to abandon the defense of Venice and the eastern frontier. We must be prepared for reverses, and, in any case, for long and great sacrifices."

Later Bissolati from the heart of the Carso, Salvemini from Florence,* and I from the Balkans, preached to Sonnino that under the solid crust of a formidable army (the Hungarians and the Croats were always among the best soldiers in the world) the Austrian Monarchy gave signs of mortal illness, and that understandings both for the war and the peace should be prepared with the peoples who would one day form the succession States of Austria. All was in vain. Sonnino always opposed the idea of the Czechoslovak legions, and not until it was

---

* Salvemini enlisted as a volunteer, like Bissolati, but sickness obliged him to leave the army after several months of service.

too late—and then despite him—were Czech units organized on our front. As for the proposed Yugoslav legions, which might have been so useful to break the morale of the Croat divisions who down to the last day, fought fiercely against us, he made it a question of a Cabinet issue: he went so far one day as to threaten Bissolati with resigning if he kept on insisting on his legions; and we never succeeded in overcoming his veto.

Sonnino had conceived the war as a short campaign which would end without the destruction of Austria, and he would never admit that fate had decreed that history would unroll along lines quite different from those he had foreseen when drafting his treaty.

In a skeptical Europe Mazzini alone had been able to read the future—sixty years before the event. He had prophesied that the bigoted anti-liberal Austria of the Hapsburgs would one day fall apart, and that the races subject to an hegemony which in his day was Teutonic, later becoming Germano-Magyar, would recover their independence. Italians faithful to the traditions of their country, from the Socialist Bissolati to the conservative Albertini, had exalted Italy's intervention as a sacrifice to make for a freer and juster Europe. The Italian soldiers who, on the Piave, won the first of the final victories for the Entente, fought for that ideal: people do not give their lives, as they did, for a *sacro egoismo*.

The finest victory crowned the sacrifice of half a million of our dead. Italy not only conquered along the Alps to the Quarnero, the most perfect geographical frontier existing in the world, but she also witnessed the disappearance of the great military power which, on her eastern frontier, had so often menaced her freedom of movement.

It is no exaggeration to say that no country achieved its war aims more perfectly than Italy. France, for example, in a Europe not really at peace, more than ever before had to fear the formidable German neighbor on her east, while Great Britain in the war of 1914–18 lost her old naval supremacy. Italy, by nothing more than the fact of Austria's disappearance as a great power, had at last gained her complete liberty of action and choice; she had seen the value of her international friendship double; she had acquired an influence in eastern

Europe that only the criminal follies of Fascism could destroy.

But the unfortunate Sonnino, in agreement, without wishing it, with all the elements which can only conceive victory as armed and grimacing at someone, believed in all good faith that Italy had lost the fruits of victory if she did not occupy Dalmatia, thus preventing the unification of the Yugoslav nation—whose existence as a State was, and remains for us, one of the solidest guarantees that the feudal and egoistic Hapsburg monarchy will never be resurrected, or that a menacing Germany will reach the Adriatic.

In the poisoned atmosphere of the Peace Conference, Sonnino was shocked in his honesty by the appetites and the egoisms his colleagues ill concealed under generous phrases. He was irritated that they spoke only of *his* egoism: his isolation increased, and, as a consequence, his powerlessness to negotiate. He felt himself alone, more and more alone with his Treaty of London that had turned into a diplomatic corpse.

Italy had gained the most complete victory, but she ought to have been told about it. Instead, she was only shown her isolated plenipotentiary, baffled, swindled—as when they profited by his momentary departure from Paris with Orlando to hand Greece the fatal gift of Smyrna. It was an act of spite, a move against Sonnino personally, not against Italy; and for that reason alone, if for no other, it was unworthy of statesmen. But that gift was a disservice to Greece and not to Italy.

Where justice was not done to Italy was when, profiting by the state of semi-rupture created by the imprudence of Orlando and Sonnino in leaving for Rome, it was decided at the Conference to distribute the mandates without assigning a single one to Italy. The mandates had been invented for the more or less evolved countries, which were to be "assisted" by one of the victorious powers. Italy's exclusion was a double mistake: first, because democratic Italy had shown in Eritrea, in Libya, in Somaliland, a colonizing capacity of the first order; second, because the confiding to Italy of a mandate of a German colony would have made it more difficult even for a traitor to Italy, like Mussolini, to come to an understanding with Hitler in the future. Even those who, like myself, have little faith in the duration and advantages of colonial empires, resented the stupid decision as a gratuitous affront to Italy.

But that was only an episode. What was more serious was that a press specializing in nationalistic mendacity succeeded in persuading a considerable part of the Italian middle classes that the ridiculous failure of Sonnino had been a tragic defeat for Italy.

What could have been more natural than the success of the slogan unfurled over Italy: "The victory has been mutilated."

For my part (and despite the outrages inflicted on me— always by "professional" patriots who imagine that nowhere, save among themselves, exists any authentic love of country) I am ready to admit the sincerity and respectability of these sentiments—except, it goes without saying, among the adventurers who carefully cultivated them so they could fish in troubled waters.

The conquest of Dalmatia, for instance, as conceived by Sonnino and his nationalists, was nothing but a manifestation of weakness or, at least, of distrust: a barbed-wire defense raised against neighbors much weaker than ourselves; whereas, convinced as I was of the reasons for Italian superiority, I wanted, after Sonnino's resignation, to open the doors of the Orient to Italian influence. But Dalmatia was filled with cities, monuments and relics of every kind of the old Italian glories. What was more natural than that a badly informed public opinion, ignorant of the fact that the immense majority of Dalmatians were Slavs who wanted to remain Slavic, should after the victory have bitterly resented the idea of not regaining these ancient Venetian possessions?

Strongly opposed as I was to a sterile anti-Slav policy which would have deprived us of all international liberty, for it would have riveted us to the protectorship of an Adriatic situation and made us heirs of the policy of repression of the Austria we had just destroyed, I must admit that I was more than once irritated during those years by the counsels of "a larger view" vouchsafed by foreigners who, without doubt, would have been annexationists—and against the true interests of their country —had they found themselves in a situation analogous to ours.

Adventurers and fishers in troubled waters apart, it is not really surprising that in the middle classes which are by definition better nourished with classical culture, the advantages and the nobility of a generous policy toward our neighbors, as extolled by Mazzini, should not have been immediately recognized; and that they felt, rather, a sense of irritation at the infantile exaggerations of the new-born Slav nationalism which was unable to understand that these glories and historical memories did not necessarily represent the danger of a foreign mortgage on their country; that, on the contrary, they might become the symbol of a fruitful understanding. All nationalisms have, at the same time, in a way that is contradictory only in appearance, two fixed ideas: the mania of greatness and the persecution mania.

Furthermore, during the war, it was thought in Italy, and sometimes not unreasonably, that among our allies there was a tendency not to do justice to our contribution to the war. The fact that Sonnino's policy, with its thesis of "our war" isolated from the general war, explained and excused certain of these attitudes, did not diminish the irritation of a people who, for the first time since its age-old divisions, had entered the bloodiest conflict of history as a unified nation.

Undeniable episodes increased this suspicious irritation. For example, at Caporetto the Italians had a terrible reverse, from which they quickly recovered and even extracted a renewal of moral strength. Nevertheless, the Italian authorities made desperate and lengthy efforts to discover the reasons for the reverse; whereas the Allies—who had had similar reverses—preserved a dignified silence about them. The Italians had the right to be proud of their moral courage in not concealing the truth. However, they found that everyone was talking about Caporetto, while no one seemed to think of Charleroi, Morhange, and the Chemin des Dames.

Likewise when, after Caporetto, the Italians alone established a new defensive line on the Piave and initiated an admirable resistance against the invaders, they did not relish that, abroad, credit should be given to the legend that the plan for the successful defense of the Piave had been drawn up by Foch, and that the arrival of Anglo-French reinforcements had contributed to it, both things being equally contrary to the facts.*

All this might have been no more than one of the unavoidable cases of friction between allies, such as existed among us all. But the discontent crystallized at the Peace Conference,

* Chapter XXVI.

where the lack of initiative and elasticity of the Italian negotiator left a free field for the egoism and incomprehension of the Allies.

Irritation and discontent were especially deep-rooted and sincere among the middle classes, who had given the Italian Army so many thousands of young officers, all dead on the field of battle. It was in this group that the Nationalist movement and, later, the Fascists, recruited an ardent youth who could not be expected to comprehend what their elders themselves had failed to comprehend: that an understanding with the new nationalities was the end, aim and guarantee of our victory. This ardent youth comprised the sincere and enthusiastic element of the movement, the element that suspected too late what lay hidden under the patriotic formulas of the adventure.

In Italy, in addition to Sonnino's fiasco, there was the Wilson failure, which was morally more important, for nowhere in Europe had the enthusiasm for Wilson been as sincere as it was in Italy.

Why did Wilson fail in Paris at the Peace Conference and in Italy?

Before answering this question I would like to say what, in my opinion, Wilson felt when he decided to go to Paris and to wage there, personally, his own fight. No man was ever inspired by higher motives: he went to fight not for himself, like Bonaparte, not even for his country like Cavour; but for the whole of the human race. Even his fight for democracy was bigger than he thought or said.

He used the word "democracy," but he used it in the same universal sense as Thomas Aquinas in his *Summa* spoke of "Christianity" and—eight centuries before the American president—invoked for the peace of the world the constitution of a *"societas nationum."* Thomas Aquinas, the Italian, did not think of Italy but of the world; just as Wilson, the American, thought only, or mainly, of the peace of the world, his former enemies included. Was he then not sufficiently conscious of the interests of America? On the contrary: he was so proud and conscious of the potential forces of his nation that he was possessed of the conviction that all America needed to become even greater, even richer, even happier, was a free world.

No European, no American has, in recent times, represented

higher ideals. In his spirit were revived the noblest souls of the two worlds: Shelley and Mazzini, Jefferson and Hugo. The whole of Europe—except, as Dante says, those who *mai non fur vidi* (who were never alive)—was enthusiastically behind him, after the defeat of the Central Empires in November, 1918. The spell did not last long, but it lasted long enough, at least in Great Britain and Italy, to have made it possible for an inexorable Wilson to win his victory.

Why, then, did Wilson fail?

An empirical answer might be: because he went to Paris and expected to negotiate the peace terms as an equal among men who feared and disliked him, like Clemenceau and Lloyd George; or who liked him, but were fearful of their own jingoes, like Orlando. If Wilson had sent to Paris a delegation of American plenipotentiaries—composed of Democrats and Republicans—and if he had remained, alone and inaccessible, in Washington, he might have imposed his will.

However, having decided to go to Paris, he should have made a choice between two courses: either never to have compromised on essential principles, or to recognize in all cases the old diplomatic method of compromise.

His undoing was that he began to compromise with Lloyd George and Clemenceau on a number of essential problems; he ended by compromising even with the Japanese on Shantung. Instead of remaining a prophet, he became a suitor after he had succeeded in forcing upon his reluctant "colleagues" the Covenant of the League of Nations. He thought—and it was his great mistake—that having created the remedy, the League of Nations, blunders and injustices might be corrected later. What he must have suffered through his long period of compromises is proved by the fact that, when he felt that he had gone too far, he tried to gain a new face, as the Chinese say, by resisting the Italian claims with respect to Fiume and Dalmatia.

My later action in public life in Italy proved how deeply I disapproved the annexation policy of my predecessor, Sonnino. In fact, as soon as it was possible for me to do so I agreed with the Yugoslavs about Dalmatia, though I successfully insisted on safeguarding the Italian character of the essentially Italian city of Fiume. When in 1939 Italy, Europe, the world

were faced by Hitler's decision to destroy our Western civilization, all the Italians realized—but too late—how right I was
when, until the last possibility of free speech had disappeared
from Fascist Italy, I continually reminded them that our safety
and prosperity needed a close entente with our Slavic neighbors. This *entente* was essential, as some day we might have
to oppose a new mad attempt of Germany at a *Drang nach
Osten*. It was this—and no more and no less than this—that
Wilson was thinking of when for the sake of Italy, from Paris,
he urged the Italians to make friends with their eastern neighbors. But I must admit that he did it in a clumsy way; the gods
had not given him psychological diplomacy as one of his outstanding gifts.

Apart from his methods, what was wrong with Wilson all
through the controversy over Fiume and Dalmatia was, as I
have already said, that he began too late to be uncompromising
with his Fourteen Points. How often did I hear, in those days,
wise far-seeing Italians say: "Wilson is right, Sonnino is a
fool; but so had Clemenceau been with many of his requests.
Why did not Wilson make a stand with the French? Why
only with us?"

Only later did I discover that those Italians were both right
and wrong: right in their remarks; wrong in their belief that
Wilson had resisted Sonnino for the reason that he was less
strong than Lloyd George or Clemenceau. Subsequent events
proved that Wilson had decided at last, but too late, to be firm
with everyone. The proof of my assertion may be found in the
second volume of Nicholas Murray Butler's *Across the Busy
Years,* which appeared in 1940.

In this volume, Butler tells a dramatic tale as to the fate
of the Treaty of Versailles. Invited by a group of Republican
senators, he had drafted, after a meeting with them in Washington, a statement of reservations to be included in the resolu-
tion of ratification. The senators agreed so heartily that Butler
left for California "feeling absolutely confident that the treaty
would be ratified and that the reconstitution of world order
under American leadership would shortly thereafter begin."
Kellogg, the future Secretary of State, was one of the senators
who had asked for Butler's draft. Having it in his pocket,
Kellogg could not resist showing it to his friend the French

Ambassador, Jusserand, who—as was his duty and his right—cabled it to Paris. When, a few days later, Jusserand learned from the Quai d'Orsay that the Entente governments would be wholly satisfied, he went to President Wilson and told him: "If you would consent to accept the proposed reservations, you could be certain that enough Republican votes would insure ratification." To which, Wilson in a stern voice replied: "I shall consent to nothing; the Senate must take its medicine."

Character is essential to make a statesman. But this was not character; it was the will to suicide. His resistance, as in the case of his long quarrel with Sonnino, in 1919, was a sort of blind, instinctive reaction against his long previous period of excessive concessions to Lloyd George and Clemenceau. It was a period on which he always remained sulkily silent, even with friends.

Wilson was an historian and a prophet; as such he lived in the past and in the future. He was too great to be a mere diplomat—as it would have been necessary for him to become when he decided to go to Paris and, not even a *primus inter pares* (first among equals), negotiate the most complex of treaties.

A Senator Lodge, a Colonel House, a General Bliss in Paris, in Wilson's place and backed by Wilson's uncompromising will from the White House, might have won for America and for the world the peace which Wilson, the prophet, had perceived in a moment of supreme inspiration, and which Wilson the diplomat undid.

XXVIII

ITALY AND THE NEAR EAST

SCHOOL HISTORIES OF ENGLAND, FRANCE AND ITALY WITH customary dogmatism taught the children during the troubled armistice of 1919–39 that Turkey was one of the countries defeated by the Entente.

The reality is somewhat different. For if the victorious nation is the one that gains all the advantages of a peace treaty, and the vanquished are those who have lost all the privileges they enjoyed in their enemy's country before the war, then in the war with the Entente, Turkey must be admitted the victor.

This Turkey was incarnate in Mustapha Kemal who later became Kemal Ataturk. In 1908, when I first met him, he was Chief of the General Staff of Mahmoud Chewket Pasha at the time of the latter's march on Constantinople where, at the head of his Army of Macedonia, he forced Abdul Hamid to grant a constitution to his subjects.

Mahmoud Chewket had been the instrument of the will of the Young Turks of Salonika, the city where the *coup* had been decided upon in a blaze of nationalistic feeling. Mustapha Kemal, then twenty-eight years old, was born in this motley port of the Aegean where the Turks were the more nationalist when they had, as happened often enough, Jewish blood in their veins. He quickly became one of the most eloquent and active propagandists of the new ideas among the officers, which was why Mahmoud chose him or was forced to choose him, despite his youth, as his Chief of Staff. Mahmoud did not belong to the central group of the "cells" of the Young Turks; by naming Kemal he gave a gage of fidelity to the movement.

Twelve years later, in 1920, the forty-year-old Mustapha was the chief, religiously obeyed, of all the Turkish military forces and, three years thereafter he became President of the Turkish Republic. A fine career, indeed, even in a revolutionary epoch.

But, however striking were the qualities of daring energy

and courageous prudence of the Turkish dictator, justice should be done to the true authors of Kemal's fortunes. Unassisted by the British post-war policy toward Turkey, Kemal and his friends never would have decided, first to depose and exile the Sultan Mehemed, and then to install themselves in Ankara to prepare the destruction of the Treaty of Sèvres, the most insensate of all the peace treaties. Truly Kemal should have prostrated himself before Number 10 Downing Street, where Lloyd George lived as Prime Minister, for there was the Mecca of his political fortunes.

If one wants to comprehend the relations of the Entente, including Italy, with Turkey after 1918, one must have a clear conception of the Entente's Ottoman policy from 1919 to 1922. The English statesmen then in power have given us their versions, notably Lloyd George and, before him, Winston Churchill—the latter in his book on the war and the peace negotiations, which is remarkable from many points of view. Since I do not have to justify to Lloyd George and Churchill, my political action of that period—events having proved how right I was in my Cassandra role—what I am about to tell will have at least the merit of being perfectly candid and objective.

The armistice between the Ottoman Empire and the Powers of the Entente, signed near the island of Mudros on October 30, 1918, aboard the British cruiser *Superb* by the delegates of the Sublime Porte and Admiral Calthorpe, had imposed on the Turks neither any serious stipulations requiring their disarmament and demobilization, nor punishment for their leaders, some of whom had been in the pay of the Austro-Germans and had been the most vehement advocates of an alliance with the Central Empires.

This proves, incidentally, that at that time the destruction of the Ottoman Empire, which was subsequently proclaimed as an essential necessity of the English policy, had not even been thought of. But this fact will surprise only rationalistic-minded folk of French or German mentality who have never been able to understand that the sudden about-faces so often attributed to "perfidious Albion" are due simply to the improvising empiricism so often at the root of the decisions of English policy.

Ten days after the Armistice, the British, French and Italian governments decided to confide their interests in Turkey to three High Commissioners. The Englishman was Admiral Calthorpe, signer of the Armistice; the Frenchman was Admiral Amet, who commanded the Republic's squadron in the Levant; and I was the Italian. From Corfu I traveled to Constantinople on board one of the vessels of an Italian naval squadron. As all Turkish authority had disintegrated, our task, pending decisions of the Paris Conference, was to govern. With our squadrons in the Bosporus and our troops in European Turkey, we were strong enough to impose our domination everywhere. The three High Commissioners met every week in one of the three Embassies, each time under the presidency of the master of the house. A Grand Vizier vegetated at the Sublime Porte, as did the Sultan at Dolma Bagché. No one paid any attention to either of them; for every kind of claim, for every request for reparations or protection, people hurried to one of the three Embassies as to the actual authority. Our work was accomplished without excessive nationalistic jealousies and our personal relations were always harmonious.

A single example among hundreds: I had decided to claim for Italy the Austrian Embassy at Pera which happened to be the former Palazzo Venezia that had passed into possession of the Austrians after the death of the Venetian Republic. Out of respect for his misfortune, I waited the departure of the Imperial Ambassador, Marquis Pallavicini. The following day I proceeded in person to the occupation at the head of a strong detachment of troops. When we hoisted the Italian flag on the façade from which the Austrians had long since removed a plaque of the old Lion of St. Mark, a corps of French troops in barracks a short distance away immediately and spontaneously came out to foregather with their Allied comrades and rendered the honors. I do not think that similar episodes, simple though they be, were very frequent in other sectors.

It is perhaps worth while adding that the Lion of St. Mark had been relegated to a corridor of the palace by the Austrians as a seditious emblem. I had it replaced on the façade, and Wilson's "experts" indited long reports to condemn my action, asserting that the Lion of St. Mark was my invention. Sonnino in Paris did not silence them, while at Constantinople everyone nodded approval.

Wishing to show the Turks that I came as a friend and not

as an invader, I had been the first to bring my High Commissioner's flag from the Admiral's flagship aboard which I had come, and had it raised above the Embassy where I was going to live. That same day the Italian troops drawn up in front of the Embassy saluted the raising of the flag painted with the arms of Spain which had covered the Italian shield on our façade during the long years of war, since Spain had taken charge of Italian interests in Turkey during the war. Our army band played the first notes of the Italian national anthem. A crowd of Greeks and Jews, Armenians and Turks gathered. They watched respectfully. No silent hatred, no rancor, even among the Turks! Everyone seemed to be thinking: Why did you not come sooner?

I soon discovered at Constantinople that the failure of the Dardanelles campaign was probably the military disaster of the Entente destined to have the most lasting and complex consequences. The highest Turkish authorities told me that just at the moment when they felt incapable of further resistance they saw, to their stupefaction, the initial indications of the British retreat by sea and by land. As often happens, the first authentic news of their victory came from their enemy —one more proof that a military victory is first and foremost a moral fact.

What struck me most on my arrival in Constantinople and on my first brief visit to old Broussa in Asia Minor was the relative abundance of foodstuffs. Since we, in Italy, had suffered so much during the war, we thought that the thousands of Italians who had remained in Constantinople would be dying of famine: I had brought a great supply of flour for them. They accepted it with polite thanks, but they preferred their Turkish flour—it was so much whiter and purer.

Verifying this abundance made us realize still more how dear had been the cost to the Entente of the Dardanelles defeat. But that was all in the past. What we must do now was to take account of the reality confronting us. And the reality was that Turkey was not dead—far from it. That an inept central government was giving the impression of a collapse is indubitably true, yet the real Turkey might find herself and recover; consequently it would be dangerous to draw the bonds too tight. Nothing could prevent us from remaining masters of Constantinople, but we risked finding ourselves in an empty house; and if the living forces of Turkey were to retire into Asia Minor, they would turn against us once they were beyond our range.

This situation and these forecasts I communicated from the outset to my government in Rome and to the Peace Conference at Paris. I had explicitly declared that I felt I could serve my country usefully only by working for an early and honorable peace which would assure us the greatest advantages, but which excluded all ideas of a partition of Turkey. Knowing of the projects formulated during the war for a division of the Ottoman territory into spheres of influence, and knowing that they still nursed such projects in Paris, I did not exact formal approval for my conception. It seemed sufficient to enunciate my program; I knew that, having the force of truth, it would finally impose itself. Far from being recalled, as I had implicitly proposed, Orlando and Sonnino did not in the least interfere with my political action. Their silence meant approbation, at least passive approbation. In his frank, blunt manner Sonnino let me know that if the course of events should show that I had deceived myself, I would be disavowed. To this I willingly consented.

The Sultan, weak and irresolute, much more preoccupied with his dynasty than with his country—the worst of crimes for a sovereign and one committed oftener than is generally believed—was, even physically, the typical last descendant of a doomed family. For his Grand Vizier he had chosen Damad Ferid Pasha who, as was indicated by his title of *Damad,* had married a sister of the sovereign, the Princess Alida. Ferid had studied at Oxford and was one of the most successful Oriental reproductions of the English gentleman. Actually, nothing and no one betrayed the least symptom of life or strength in the Turkish official spheres. Those in London who sought to persuade Lloyd George and Curzon that in the future they could do anything they wished in Turkey had every reason in the world to think they were right. The trouble was that none of these gentlemen, nor their emissaries or representatives in Turkey, had any contacts whatever with the few men who subsequently constituted the ruling class at Ankara, and whom I often met in the home of an Italian engineer and even, to the great scandal of my colleagues, at the Oriental Club. I knew that these men were not bluffing when they told me, quite dispassionately, that they could easily maintain their independence in Asia, whither they were already inclined to betake themselves.

Consequently, when on May 12, 1919, Admiral Calthorpe communicated to my French colleague and me that the Paris Conference had decided on the occupation of Smyrna by the Greeks, I was convinced that the affairs of the Entente were taking a wrong turn. But, as the orders were categoric, there was nothing to do but obey them. The debarkation was what it could not help being, what at a meeting of the High Commissioners I had formally declared it would be: an uncontested operation yet a bloody one, which would eventually inflict a mortal wound on those whose present action could possess the semblance of victory only to the "realists" who never see beyond appearances. Greece was doomed the very day that Athens went delirious with joy at the news that the blue and white flag flew on the ramparts of Smyrna, after what the Hellenic telegram called "an heroic battle."

On the arrival of the Greeks the Turkish troops retired to their barracks. They acted on orders of the Grand Vizier, who had sent emissaries to Smyrna recommending resignation and assuring them that the Greek occupation would be temporary. Furthermore, at that time there were in Smyrna none of those *fedaïs* (the sacrificed ones) who, later, appeared virtually everywhere in Anatolia, sworn to fight to the death for the Turkish nationalist cause. Who was it then that fired the first shot from the barracks that unleashed the massacre? My informants assured me that it was a Greek *agent provocateur*. If true, it certainly was not on instructions received from Athens. That sort of thing generally—and in all countries—is conceived by some military man, eager to have his easy "battle" and his still easier "victory." However that may be, if some hope had remained till then of a solution equally acceptable to both sides, all possibility of a compromise disappeared after the occupation of Smyrna. In policy, as in the moral domain, mistakes engender other mistakes.

Some time before, the Sublime Porte had believed it could ward off all danger by sending Mustapha Kemal far from

Constantinople. Consequently, he was entrusted with the command in Asia. Kemal had been the hero of the Turkish resistance at the Dardanelles: his popularity was universal. However, their desire to feel that he was far away from Stamboul prevented the Sultan and the Porte from realizing that in Asia he might become even more dangerous.

When the news of the occupation of Smyrna reached him, Kemal was near Samsun. He immediately convoked the people and roused them to fever heat by a speech which I have been told was one of the most moving ever delivered by that born orator. The Englishman in charge of the surveillance over that *vilayet* sent a telegram to Constantinople to suggest the immediate recall of the dangerous general. On the pressing proposal of our British colleagues, we invited the Sublime Porte to send him the order to return. In the style the Porte had inherited from Byzantium, Kemal was simply invited to come to Stamboul to discuss the general situation, and—more Byzantine still—his friends and future friends at once forewarned him, even from the precincts of the Sublime Porte itself, that the summons was on the way. Not having as yet decided to break with the capital, he was thus able to leave immediately on a pretended tour of inspection in the direction of Erzerum and so avoid having to disobey an order of the Sultan, since the official text of the order did not reach Samsun until after his departure.

Perhaps with a dose of political firmness the situation might yet have been saved. But I was the only one in Constantinople to declare to my government at Rome and to the "Four" at Paris that not only should they accept but should hasten a peace with Turkey—one that would satisfy both parties, and that an arrangement satisfactory to the Turks would henceforth constitute the only means left to us to guarantee the advantages that we might still be able to retain.

As for the Sublime Porte, every day it presented more and more of that spectacle of timid indecision which is symptomatic of all doomed regimes. However, one fine day the Grand Vizier had a stroke of genius, at least so he thought. Two weeks after the debarkation of the Greeks at Smyrna he asked me for a secret interview. I received him at the summer residence of the Italian Embassy at Therapia, on the upper Bosporus. After an avalanche of fine phrases on the popularity Italy had acquired by its chivalrous and generous attitude, Ferid went on to complain bitterly of the Powers that had permitted a country of former *rayahs* (subject peoples) to come and tyrannize over the grandsons of their masters.

"Don't they understand at Paris that this is the surest way to revive the danger of an anti-foreigner campaign? The day you find yourself face to face with the sanguinary but inevitable results of your policy you will again do what you have done for a century: you will accuse us. I tell you that if there comes a day of massacres the Great Powers will be responsible for it." And then, changing his tone as if impelled by emotion to the disclosure of a secret thought, he exclaimed: "Ah, everything would be quite different if a Great Power loved by the Turks had charge of the occupation of Smyrna and its vilayet. . . ."

He waited for an answer which did not come. I had, naturally, from the first ten minutes of conversation foreseen this advance, but as I did not rise to the bait poor Ferid was obliged to explain himself: why should not Italy organize a plebiscite of the Smyrna population which would unanimously choose an Italian military occupation instead of the Greek?

Performed by a rank amateur, this was the same old game that Abdul Hamid had played with incomparable mastery for thirty years: provoke jealousies among the Powers, envenom them when necessary, and thus maintain through their dissension Turkey's independence. But these methods operate successfully only as preventives. It was now too late. Furthermore, I doubted that such a project, even though crowned with success, would be useful to Italy. Italy, it seemed to me, ought to consider the whole of Turkey as a market for her industrial products; therefore, even if other moral reasons had not existed, Italy ought to oppose the scramble for Turkish territory which had been envisaged. As for Smyrna, it would not have been of any use to us as outlet for our surplus population, already populated as it was by a race still more prolific than our own. Held by force, not only would its occupation have presented a sterile and costly operation, but also the greatest obstacle to the future pacific penetration I had long hoped for. As for Turkish gratitude, it was only too clear that it would have evaporated a month after the departure of the Greek troops, and that they would have detested the new Italian occupation almost as much.

These thoughts flashed instantly to my mind, but it goes without saying that I did not impart them to the Grand Vizier. He thought my silence no more than diplomatic prudence. He left convinced that he had struck a masterly blow against inter-allied unity.

In the Orient everything becomes known; the news that is whispered in secret circulates faster than what is said openly in the Parliaments of the West. It did not take any time for Ferid's idea to reach the ears of Mustapha Kemal and his friends. A few days later one of them came to see me and told me respectfully, but without circumlocution, that his friends— meaning particularly Kemal—hoped that I would not favor the project of the Porte, as the new Turkey would consider it its duty to combat Italy in Asia as fiercely as she was prepared to combat the Greeks.

I could not but pay silent homage to the frankness of this declaration. It represented a new style in Oriental policy; very much, perhaps, like the hesitations of a diplomat when confronted by offers of territorial occupation.

My two colleagues at Constantinople, Admiral Calthorpe and Admiral Amet, were soon to comprehend—despite their military prejudices, which were as natural as they were worthy of consideration—that my views on the matter of the prompt peace were not so mistaken, after all. But to defend the measure openly was beyond the power of men who had scarcely recovered from the fever of war. However, more than once they must have thought that my status of incurable inferiority as a civilian was of some value when I made use of the liberty it gave me to tell my government and the "Four" at Paris the whole truth as it appeared to me.

In any case, all the prudent counsels of the British High Commissioner must have been neutralized by the reports that the officers of an *Intelligence Service* which had become more and more influential were sending to London. The style of these "specialists" in no way recalled the good old British traditions of tolerance and fair play. Western prestige suffered from the maladroitness of their methods in the atmosphere of political finesse which existed at Constantinople—for nothing is more mistaken than to suppose that strong-arm methods in the Orient are effective in everything.

For one who, in his first diplomatic post at Cairo, appreciated the supple action of the Cromers and the Wingates, and cherished a deep admiration for English traditions of liberty, it was sad to hear what my sarcastic friend Talaat Pasha, speaking of England, smilingly murmured one day:

"She is German without the German thoroughness."

Some of the masterpieces of the work of what was called in Constantinople the Inter-Allied Police, but which was actually a purely British police, deserve to be remembered.

We were told one morning that we had barely escaped a terrible plot against the Allies. Several of us remained skeptics, but not the British General, Commander in Chief of the Allied Forces, who took immediate action from the very moment his specialists informed him that a vast conspiracy was about to bring about a revolt, with the object of massacring all the leading *Rumi* (Europeans). He presented a list of the conspirators to the Turkish authorities, requiring their arrest; and, he warned them, if his request was not complied with he would himself take extreme measures. General Harington's list comprised twenty-eight names. Eleven of them were those of politicians who had already gone to Ankara and consequently were out of reach. The other seventeen were unknowns, whose names were not even sufficiently indicated. The arrest of those in Ankara was, of course, out of the question; and in a great metropolis like Constantinople how could one arrest men indicated simply as an Ali, a Fuad or an Ahmed?

The Turks were not in the least disturbed over so small a matter. They felicitated General Harington for having unmasked so terrible a danger, and promised to have the men who were still in Constantinople arrested. Nothing easier, they must have said to themselves, than to find at Stamboul and Galata some Alis and Ahmeds who weren't worth the rope to hang them. These they arrested and duly hanged. General Harington declared himself satisfied and ceased his threats. I later learned that the conspiracy had been invented by other Turks to frame their adversaries, and that they had counted on the credulity of the Intelligence Service. It was all comic opera, except for the poor devils who were hanged. The irreparable mistakes, those for which a government must sooner or later pay, soon followed. The policy of Mustapha Kemal and his friends at Ankara became unequivocally Xenophobic, including in its hatred both the French and the English. Only the Italians were not molested; this was the result of the peace policy I had pursued since the beginning of our occupation.

The English thought they could counter this policy by more rigorous measures. It was then that Kemal crossed his Rubicon. He raised armed bands; but his originality consisted in the methodical organization of a powerful army back of them. The stronger it became, the more the Turks turned toward him; even the bureaucrats of the Porte no longer concealed their sympathy for him. Henceforth, it was only a matter of time for the Turks. All understood what the solution would be. A single point remained in doubt: what decision would be reached by the Allies who, in April, 1920, at the Conference of San Remo, presided over by the Italian Prime Minister Nitti, had ended by all adopting the harsh terms of peace agreed on in London. In March, on the eve of San Remo, Lord Curzon stated: "Kemal's effective forces have been overestimated; Kemal is not the important factor some people declare him." The allusion was to me who, having just returned to Rome from Turkey to take the portfolio of Undersecretary of Foreign Affairs, continued to recommend a true peace with Turkey, the only point on which I was always in complete agreement with Nitti.*

We shall see the end of the adventure later. But here I had best give my impressions of that remarkable man, Kemal Ataturk, who never forgot, even during Fascism, that when, in 1919, British agents at one moment thought of deporting him to Malta, I gave him the assurance which he secretly came to request of me—that the Italian Embassy would not surrender him if he should ask for sanctuary. And since in Constantinople everything becomes known, even the most secret colloquies, that assurance sufficed to cause the abandonment of any idea of arresting and deporting him.

Much has been said of Kemal the reformer. But we are not

* See Chapter XXXI.

yet in a position to judge the result of this part of his work to which he devoted himself with an unbridled zeal for reforms that, to us Westerners, often appeared as useless as they were vexatious, since these measures of his not only cast aside, but often quite gratuitously ridiculed, all the Islamic traditions from which the Turkish people for centuries had drawn the best of their strength. Kemal's essential mistake in his work as an Occidental reformer was his determination to advance even faster than all the "enlightened" despots who had preceded him. All our new instruments of contact, from railways to war itself, impressed him as means for an imminent reconcilement between nations—a far too optimistic view of the situation.

But all the medley of Western reforms initiated by Kemal will some day be reckoned only as an episode and as a very secondary part of his activity. It is as organizer of the military reestablishment of his country and of its resistance, and as its leader in war that Kemal was one of the active forces of an historic movement. In such matters, where everything hung in the balance, he showed himself as prudent and calculating as he was foolhardy in questions such as that of fez versus hat. Urged by his friends, who might—and sometimes wanted to —become his judges, to strike rapid blows, he patiently took his time for long months, slowly increasing his war matériel. Only when he felt that all conditions favored him did he strike; but then, once he had launched his attacks, the inactivity with which his "friends" had reproached him yielded to a frenzy of movement and attack which did not cease until all the Greeks had been driven into the sea.

The rare gifts of balanced judgment of Kemal as military leader were once more revealed on the morrow of his triumph; when at Chanak, opposite the long peninsula of Gallipoli, he saw loom up the new danger of suddenly finding before his advance guard no longer fleeing Greeks but English, ready to stop his advance. Lloyd George had decided that the triumphal march of the Turks on Constantinople must be checked at the neutral zone of the Straits. This move, which might have caused a new war, had been decided by Lloyd George, despite the contrary advice of France and Italy and—what was more serious from the internal point of view of the British Empire —without consulting the Dominions.

Leader of an army that would have followed him anywhere without the slightest hesitation, Kemal eluded the terrible danger. With all possible speed he hastened toward the principal and easy objective, employing the cavalry protecting his flanks for a show of force and aggressiveness against the English at Chanak. But the cavalry officers had received the strictest orders not only to avoid conflict but to make friendly overtures. They met with unalterable good humor the coldest and most arrogant behavior. They put in operation all kinds of schemes for fraternization, even going so far as to ask the British for camp material and little favors that country neighbors ask each other. Never were the British forces at Chanak threatened; the menace was to Constantinople. However, in the absence of the other two Great Powers, Constantinople's defense was not, in principle, incumbent on Great Britain.

Another of the great military leaders of Young Turkey whom I knew very well was Enver Pasha. For some years he was one of the active spirits in Turkey, first during the initial phase of the Committee of Union and Progress, then during the war in Libya against Italy, and later during the Balkan war. Enver never lost courage, not even when the Balkan allies were at Tchatalja; but his moral and intellectual character was unpleasing on account of his boastfulness. He would have been quite incapable of conceiving or even comprehending that policy of audacity combined with long patience that Kemal imposed on himself in war—the policy which was the secret of his success.

Kemal reincarnated the old warrior spirit of the Osmanlis who menaced Europe under the walls of Vienna. However, in political action the task of the greatest of the Osmanlis was much simpler than that of their distant successor of the twentieth century. They were the victors who overran the lands of the vanquished and ignored them; and to victors everything is, or seems to be, easy.

The originality of Kemal's policy—and I have already said that I waive his Westernizing reforms as merely despot's play in the manner of Peter the Great—the originality of his policy consisted in this: that it was marked from the outset by two decisions which ran completely counter to what all dictators have done or are doing. The reason dictators are doomed to failure is that they are obliged to pursue a policy of appearances and prestige; they must supply glory to take the place of the liberty they have destroyed. Kemal alone had the moral courage to adopt and impose about him, from the start, a series of renunciations and, with still greater originality, to continue faithful to these renunciations even in the intoxication of military victories.

The Ottoman Empire with its Caliphate, and its threats of a *Jihad* (holy war) seemed to want to continue the pursuit of a world policy which long ago had become an anachronism. Mustapha Kemal was the first to understand that the new Turkey would find it advantageous to renounce all pretensions to influence beyond its own frontiers; and this idea he realized. Determined to remain master in Turkey, he boldly discarded all extra-national claims. From early in 1919, at Constantinople, I had proof that Kemal had already concluded that this was the only way to reestablish a really independent Turkey.

The chief of the powerful Mohammedan sect of the Senoussis, whose influence radiates from their religious center in the southern region of Cyrenaica, had fled to Broussa in Asia Minor when the war turned in favor of the Allies, and had lost all hope of seeing the Italians ejected from Africa. Convinced as I was, and as I am, that only a generous policy of local autonomy can assure the peace and prosperity of our two Mediterranean colonies, I did not hesitate to accept the overtures that the friends of Ahmed-el-Senoussi came to submit. In Eastern fashion, I had a series of interminable discussions with Ahmed-el-Senoussi and succeeded in convincing him of the desirability of an arrangement which would give him virtual autonomy in the interior on condition that he recognize loyally and formally Italy's sovereignty, and that he engage to favor our political and economic interests in the rest of Cyrenaica and in Tripolitania. On this basis Luigi Rossi, the Italian Minister of Colonies, subsequently concluded a convention which functioned very advantageously for us up to the day when the Fascist government denounced it under the illusion that Cyrenaica offered an easy field for military action with its appropriate issue of communiqués.

The desire for an understanding that my conversations had

evoked in the chief of the Senoussi might easily have been thwarted in Constantinople, where my relations with him had surely not remained a secret. As I had had warnings of intransigence on the part of Kemal's friends, I decided not to leave them in ignorance of the general trend of my policy. Kemal sent me the following message:

"The maintenance of Turkish domination over the Arabs was one of the causes of our downfall. We do not wish to have it even mentioned any longer. Let the Senoussis make such arrangements with you as they wish, and as you wish."

The frankness and courage of this response confirmed my conviction that we should soon witness a spiritual awakening in Turkey. Even much later, and when powerful, Kemal never changed his opinion on this point. This was a great and rare merit. He had understood that Imperial Turkey was a backward country, between Europe and Asia, and that, by becoming an exclusively Anatolian power, Republican Turkey could, in its turn, become a factor of progress destined, probably, to play a more and more active role with respect to Central Asia. These are the real political innovations that Kemal had the courage to plan and bring into effect. During his lifetime there was little talk about Kemal's political innovations. The eyes of the world—the world being what it is—were focused exclusively on his alphabetic changes and his doubtful sartorial reforms.

I believe that it has been worth while for me to stress the reasons why this dictator—the only one of his particular kind —achieved a real success, for he dared to do what no other dictator has ever done: he destroyed and threw away the empty and dangerous pretensions of national prestige bequeathed to him by the old regime.

XXIX

A NEW PARTY, THE *POPOLARI,* AND THEIR LEADER STURZO

On January 18, 1919, Italians in every city of Italy stopped to read on the bulletin boards—some with surprise, others with emotion, and all with deep interest—a huge notice printed on white paper that bore for heading the motto of our free Communes, the old word *Libertas.* This is what they read:

"*Ai Liberi e Forti* [To all free and strong men] who, in this grave hour, feel the high duty of cooperating without prejudice or preconceptions for the supreme ends of our fatherland, we appeal, that united they may uphold the ideals of justice and freedom. While the representatives of the victorious nations are met to prepare the basis of a just and lasting peace, the political parties of every country must contribute to strengthen these tendencies and principles which will serve to avert all peril of a fresh war, to give a stable order to the nations, to put into effect ideals of social justice and improve the social conditions of labor, to develop the spiritual and material energy of all countries, united in the solemn bonds of the League of Nations.

"And as it is not just to compromise the benefits of the victory won by immense sacrifices for the defense of the rights of peoples and for the highest ideals of civilization, it is the duty of all healthy democracies, all popular governments, without exception, to endeavor to bring about an equilibrium between the claims of national rights and those of international interests in the future peaceful progress of society.

"Therefore, we uphold the political and moral program, the heritage of Christian peoples, recorded in august words and today defended by Wilson, as a fundamental element in the future world order; and we reject the imperialism which creates dominating nations and fosters violent upheavals; therefore we demand that the League of Nations should recognize just national aspirations, hasten the coming of universal disarmament, abolish the secrecy of treaties, effect the freedom of the seas, uphold social legislation in international relations and religious liberty against all sectarian oppression, and that it should have the strength to apply sanctions and the means to protect the weaker peoples against the oppressive tendencies of the strong.

"To the better future of our Italy—secure within her frontiers and the surrounding seas—who, by the virtues of her sons in the sacrifices of the war has, with victory, fulfilled her unity and welded together her national consciousness, we dedicate all our activities.

"For a centralizing State, seeking to restrict all civic and individual activity, we would substitute, based on constitutional guarantees, a State truly popular in quality, recognizing the limits of its activity, giving consideration to the natural centers and organizations of the country—the family, the classes, the Communes—and respecting individual personality and encouraging private initiative. . . ."

After having declared the necessity of proportional representation, and so forth, the appeal continued:

"But these reforms would be vain and empty if we did not claim, as the soul of the new society, the true sense of liberty responding to the civil maturity of our people and the highest developments of its energies: religious liberty not only for the individual but also for the Church, for the unfolding of her spiritual mission in the world; liberty to teach without a state monopoly; liberty of class organization without government privileges or preference for any particular party; communal and local liberties in accordance with the glorious Italian traditions.

"This ideal does not seek to disorganize the State but is

essentially organic in the renewal of energies and activities which should find their coordination, valuation, defense and progressive development at the center, shaping themselves into vital nuclei able to check or modify forces of disintegration, agitation promoted in the name of a systematic class war and anarchical revolution, and draw from the heart of the people the elements of conservation and of progress, giving its value to authority as at once the force and exponent of the sovereignty of the people and of social collaboration."

The necessary and urgent reforms in the field of social welfare and assistance were mainly, according to the appeal, the reform of taxation, the solution of the Southern problem, the colonization of the *latifundia*,* and the fight against illiteracy.

The appeal, addressing "all men who know, in their love for their fatherland, how to combine a just sense of national right with a sane internationalism," ended as follows:

"We come forward in political life with our moral and social banner flying, drawing our inspiration from the sound principles of Christianity which consecrated the great civilizing mission of Italy—a mission that even today, in the new order of peoples, should shine out against the attempts of new imperialisms . . . in face of the Socialist demagogy which seeks the materialization of all idealism, in face of the old sectarian liberalisms which, based on the ideas of the old organized, centralized State, resist the new currents of emancipation."

Such was the charter of the new party, the *Partito Popolare Italiano*. Its creation was an historic event because—like the Socialist Party before it—the new party was based on these permanent Italian reasons that issued from the plans of the Risorgimento and the liberal parties that governed Italy from Cavour's day down to Giolitti.

Elsewhere,† I have mentioned the slow transformation of the relations between the liberal State and the Catholics in Italy. In 1916 another forward step had been taken by the nomination of a militant Catholic, Filippo Meda, as minister in the Coalition Cabinet headed by Paolo Boselli. Numerous

---

* *Latifundia:* the huge slave-worked estates of the Roman patricians under the Empire. In modern times the term is used to mean the great estates (often with absentee owners) worked by peasant labor.

† See Chapters XI, XIV and XXV, *passim*.

practicing Catholics had been ministers before Meda; but he had been nominated as their leader by other practicing Catholics, and his was the first case of this kind.

However, the essential event was the creation of the Popular Party, which was the expression of the will of several millions of finally awakened Italians. A young priest, Luigi Sturzo, who till then was known solely for his work in the administration of the Communes, knew how to interpret and crystallize the new tendencies without being in any way influenced by the Catholic hierarchy.

Emerging from the traditionalist atmosphere of a lower but ancient Sicilian nobility, Sturzo knew how to command and impose his will. He was a priest imbued with a deep idealism —one of those rare priests for whom the celebration of the mystery of the mass is, every morning, accompanied by an ever-new emotion—and convinced of the necessity of instilling in a Catholic world, which sometimes seemed petrified, the new blood of an audacious Christian Democracy; but, determined never to fall into the snares of Modernism, Sturzo left the hierarchy of the Church reassured by his unshaken religious orthodoxy. A man with the most diverse gifts, as several of his books—notably *Church and State,* a veritable *Summa*— have since revealed to the world, but hiding these gifts under a suspicious modesty which was not far removed from legitimate pride, he yet knew how to knit ardent friendships. He ignored hatreds, aided in this by his knowledge of the mistakes and the pettinesses of the former "clericals," the memory of whom sufficed to prevent his ever taking offense at anti-clerical opinions, rooted as they were in the ancient Italian Ghibellinism. As for that other coarse and abject form of anti-clericalism, made fashionable a little earlier by Podrecca and his *Asino,* and by one Mussolini, it was too far beneath him even to consider, as might be expected of any Italian having a sense of history.

In each line of the Appeal that I have reproduced in part one cannot but feel that it is the work of a single spirit, that of Sturzo, who wrote it after long meditations, which were more moral than political. What Sturzo wanted was a party which should become the national expression of the Catholic social movement that had already begun to establish itself in several Catholic associations, but he also wanted to give it a new vitality, which alone would be sufficient to destroy forever what remained of the old negative struggle of the Catholics against the Italian unitary State. Toward the Vatican, Sturzo acted during the weeks preceding the realization of his idea with a dignity and tact which were dictated by his Christian and Italian conscience. A few days after the Armistice, in November, 1918, he asked to be received by the Secretary of State, Cardinal Gasparri, and explained his plan. Gasparri, the only first-rate man the Church had had since Consalvi, saw at once that Sturzo was serving the Church, even with, and especially with, the affirmation of the independence of the new party. Sturzo made it quite clear that he did not wish to form a Church party like the German Center but—and thus he expressed it—a party *"fra Cattolici"* (among Catholics), and he asked if the Pope would suppress the *Non expedit.* Gasparri replied: "Admitting the hypothesis that the Pope consents, what will your policy toward the Church be?"

Sturzo replied: "No policy in opposition to it, obviously; but no special policy as a party. The Roman question is a national question." Gasparri was delighted with this reply, but he continued: "And what will your policy be? Sonnino's or Orlando's?" It was notorious that Gasparri despised Orlando for his weakness and detested Sonnino for his lack of intelligence and for what Gasparri called his "Protestant prejudices." Sturzo probably felt some Sicilian tenderness for Orlando, but he thought Sonnino's foreign policy most injurious to Italy and he said so frankly to Gasparri, adding: "It will be the duty of the first Congress of our party to determine its policy."

"And what will you do," interrupted Gasparri, "if the Congress orders you to collaborate with Turati and Treves?" *

"I would be disposed to collaborate with them; it would not frighten me."

"Bravo!" concluded the Cardinal. "It would be better to collaborate with Turati than with Sonnino. Very well, if you succeed, the merit will be yours; if you don't, the country will judge you. As you see, there is not the slightest reason for you

* The two leading members of the Socialist Party in the Chamber.

ever to speak of the Vatican. But don't talk about the Catholic Action either."

Thus occurred an historic discussion that did infinitely more for the good relations between the Church and the State than the pompous "conciliations" offered ten years later by Mussolini to Pius XI.

Sturzo never saw Gasparri again, as he never saw Benedict XV either before or after his meeting with Gasparri.

Sturzo did not even know then that the Pope, informed by his Secretary of State, asked with his customary sarcasm: "Has Don Sturzo fully understood that we love the Socialists much more than the old liberals like Sonnino?" *

At the first congress of the Party at Bologna in June, 1919, the *Popolari*—except for a group headed by Father Gemelli, since become a Fascist propagandist—were unanimous in declaring that they did not wish to speak in the name of all Italian Catholics, but only in the name of the party and on the democratic basis; that they did not wish to be the mouthpiece of the Church, since that was the function of the hierarchy, the Pope and the bishops. The Party even went so far as to declare that it was definitely not a "Church" party.

As anyone can see, it was quite incorrect to compare the new Party, as people did at first, to the German Center Party. Thanks to Sturzo's wishes, the Party did not call itself "a Catholic party." Sturzo, the priest, refused to make religion a basis of political division in a country that, in one way or another, is in great part Catholic; but Sturzo, the Italian and the innovator, also refused to indorse the long series of mistakes and blindnesses that comprised the Italian policy of the Church between 1815 and 1870.

Having witnessed, as an outsider, the birth of the Popular Party, and after having become acquainted with Sturzo and collaborated with *Popolari* ministers, who were as competent as they were honest, I often wondered why a group that responded to a profound historical reality and that had for

* All the details of this conversation with Gasparri were given to me by Sturzo himself and by my lamented friend and colleague in the Senate, Count Santucci, who accompanied him on his visit. Benedict XV's remark was confided to me by Baron Monti, Director General of the Ministry of Justice, who, as an intimate friend of the Pope from infancy—as I have already mentioned—was a devoted and constant secret ambassador from him to me.

leader one of the most intelligent and capable men in Italy did not prove equal to expectations. The answer came to me in Parliament, when observing from my bench of Undersecretary of State in 1919 this united and firm bloc which occupied the entire center of the great *aula* of Monttitorio. They were too numerous—there were more than a hundred of them. It was not only that the young Catholic democrats who had distinguished themselves in the public administration did not constitute their majority, but there was also a number of *arrivistes* and old clericals who, travestied into democrats by the needs of the hour, had joined the victors.

The King, whom at that time I used to see very often, one day asked me my impression of them. I answered: "If there were thirty or forty of them, Sire, they would constitute a formidable force and provide a precious lesson in moral sincerity; but numerous as they are. . . ." The King interrupted me: "Thirty or a hundred, the clericals are always too numerous." The King was anti-clerical, being Ghibelline by tradition, by temperament and, above all, perhaps from a desire to behave as an Italian which had become second nature. This he had perhaps inherited from his father King Humbert, who could not write *"Roma"* without adding each time *"Intangibile,"* by which he thought to gain popularity. Queen Elena, on the other hand, was virulently anti-clerical in a jocose, vulgar way.

The Popular Party's life was distinguished by three campaigns.

The first established the victory of "Popular Representation." The best of the *Popolari* had wanted to destroy once and for all the influence of local camarillas which, non-existent in the North, made political life in the South shabby and meaningless. The Socialists led the fight with the *Popolari;* that was natural, both parties representing the masses. Nitti, then Prime Minister, did nothing. The "Proportional" gave a more even tone to the political life of the South, but lessened the power of personality in the Chamber; just as in Germany and in Belgium the parliamentary struggle assumed an automatic character which is contrary to the very essence of a parliament.

Agrarian reform would have been a more certain and

definite achievement because, apparently practical and modest in its demands, it might have constituted an immense moral and economic advance. Sturzo had wanted for the peasants the right of preference in acquiring the lands worked by them, the improvement of the *latifundia,* and a serious step toward interior colonization. The *Popolari* Ministers of Agriculture, Mischeli, Mauri and Bertini collaborated intelligently with the party's agrarian projects.

The third campaign was for reform of education and the State's examinations. Croce was a supporter of it, and his entrance into the Giolitti Cabinet in 1920 was the signal for an accord between the Liberals and the *Popolari.* But parliamentary intrigues wrecked first the Croce project and then the Gentile laws, which were put aside in favor of a State monopoly that Italy had never even imagined as possible. The honor of the *Popolari* Party will always be that it was the first to have forcefully presented in Parliament two problems—agrarian reform and public education reform—which free Italy will have to solve among the first of her post-war problems.

Sturzo, who was the soul of his party, taken all in all, deserved highly of Italy. But why was he not as fortunate in his leadership as he proved himself forceful in the expounding of noble ideas?

What Sturzo lacked as a leader in a political world where Italian simplicity of mind was linked with what was possibly an excess of easygoingness was that, proud yet modest, he did not know how to become a "mixer." Or again, it may have been that he unconsciously felt that his black cassock was too great a novelty for those liberals in whose minds the affronts of the old Piedmontese bishops to good Christians like Santarosa or even Cavour had remained graven as symbolic proofs of impassable distances between lay politics and the cloth.

The youngest man in the government, I was perhaps the only one who had followed the birth and growth of the new party with passionate interest. This was not only because of the religious aspects of history, which have always seemed to me of profound value, but because, as a young law student at the University of Pisa, my professor of political economy had been Toniolo, the first theorist of a Christian Democracy in Italy. What a world of difference existed between him and Sturzo, the latter an ardent artist and philosopher, intensely faithful to the cause of suffering humanity and a man so independent in spirit that sometimes, despite his perfect Catholic orthodoxy, the ecclesiastical *imprimatur* on the first page of all his books amazes bigots ignorant of the deep respect Sturzo inspires in the Catholic hierarchy even though in general they bear no love for him.

Toniolo, on the other hand, was the Benjamin of the clerical world, like de Maistre in the Napoleonic period. Cold, methodical, devoid of imagination, Toniolo implanted in the student mind the thought that the supreme ideal of democracy was not ahead of us, but behind us—in the Middle Ages, with their corporations. When I met Sturzo I quickly divined his immense intellectual superiority to Toniolo. But how did it happen that our relations remained cool for so long a time? If on my part there was doubtless want of perception, there was on Sturzo's a surface timidity, masking a bitter pride for which he must have reproached himself as a sin, but which was natural to a man who felt himself superior to most of those poor "Excellencies."

When shared ordeals and the intimacies of exile created a strong bond of friendship between us, I one day repeated to Sturzo the remark I had made to the King on the Popular Party. Sturzo commented: "Do you know that the night of the elections, after thirty or forty telegrams announcing victories, and while these messages continued to pour in, I was overwhelmed? Two or three of my friends asked in surprise why I was so upset. I explained to them that too many followers imposed on us too many responsibilities, and too quickly."

Since there was certainly no lack of courage in this descendant of Norman knights, that utterance alone proved that the finely tempered mind of this new combatant was infinitely superior to the temper of the average politician who dreams only of getting his hands on some ministerial portfolio. It was a great pity for Italy, and perhaps for Europe, that Sturzo, surrounded by mediocrities and harassed by too many secondary problems, failed to manifest the statesmanlike qualities that potentially existed in him. If the Vatican had permitted him to become a member of Parliament instead of remaining in the shadows, he would have proved all his worth.

This is no "if" like the many "ifs" with which one can amuse oneself in changing the facts of history. In 1922 I felt, and Sturzo felt, that we must get rid of the ridiculous Facta Cabinet which served only to make way for the power of Fascism. Like so many others, I urged Giolitti to form a Government, but I alone was able to assure him that Sturzo would give him all his support under certain political conditions, all of which were acceptable to Giolitti. These conditions, I added, were those which would permit of Sturzo's entering the Cabinet with Giolitti as, for instance, Minister of Finance. Giolitti, who did not like Sturzo, was agreeably surprised, but he only remarked: "It's too bad he's not a deputy. That is the cause of so many equivocations. Can't he become one? But, *al peggio* [at worst], he might be appointed a senator; Calabiana * became one."

Giolitti, sometimes accused of being secretly a dictator, believed, as I said before, in Parliament. This unknown incident, at any rate, proves the falseness of the legend of a Sturzo veto against Giolitti in 1922, a veto which, had it existed, would have been one of the causes of the triumph of Fascism.

* Archbishop of Milan in the early years of the Kingdom of Italy.

XXX

THE NITTI CABINET

WHEN THEY RETURNED FROM PARIS,* ORLANDO AND SON-
nino had no other thought than to resign at the first opportunity. A pretext sufficed them. They were honest, and they
knew that they had lost all authority.

The Nitti Cabinet, hastily formed, succeeded them on June
22, 1919. Nitti, whom I knew only slightly, but who was well
aware of my constant opposition to Sonnino's fixed ideas, had
telegraphed me at Constantinople offering me the post of
Undersecretary of State for Foreign Affairs, and I had accepted. If I cite this not very important fact it is to make it
clear that, coming from China where I had been Minister from
1911 to 1915, and then from the war on the Oriental front,
and from Constantinople where I was High Commissioner
since the day of the Armistice, my eyes were as virginal as those
of Voltaire's Huron with regard to the Italian political scene.
Which gives me the right to believe that my judgment on the
Nitti period, the most discussed of the post-war periods, was
completely objective.

Nitti seems to have been attacked for the good he did. But
it was not realized that the numerous defeats in his domestic
policy (D'Annunzio's Fiume adventure was only internal politics) were due primarily to certain weak points in his personality.

To Nitti must be given the credit for the absolute honesty
and the lack of any government pressure prevailing in the
general elections of November, 1919. Conservatives were terrified at the result of these elections. With a total of 508 seats,
the *Popolari* had more than a hundred mandates, the Socialists
a hundred and fifty, while the rest went to different liberal
groups; it was therefore impossible to form a Cabinet without
either Socialists or *Popolari*. It was bad for old habits, but
good for the reality that exposed the aspirations and the dis-

* Chapter XXVII.

content of the Italian people. Discontent that votes, and that can assert itself, may very soon cease to be discontent.

Though a member of the Senate, according to the Italian custom I very often visited the Chamber of Deputies as a member of the Government. It soon became evident to me that the so-called "ungovernable" Chamber of Deputies was constantly improving, faced as it was by hard legislative work. The demagogic scenes of the first weeks had soon ceased, and had the Chamber continued its normal life it would have become very useful. The decision Giolitti took in the spring of 1921 to dissolve the Chamber was, in my opinion, the most grievous error of his last Cabinet. I was the only one in the Council of Ministers which decided on the dissolution to express a contrary opinion. The 1919 Parliament was free from any complicity and from all contact with Fascism, which cannot be said of the 1921 Chamber, as we shall see.

Another great service rendered by Nitti was to have opposed his veto to the Italian expedition to Georgia, preparations for which had been made during the last weeks of the Orlando-Sonnino Cabinet. Its origin was typical of the irresponsibility with which Lloyd George sometimes acted (since, when one is British Prime Minister, to speak is also to act). One day Orlando, while talking to him, complained of the Allies and of Sonnino, who had never given any thought to Italy's need of raw materials. Lloyd George answered: "You are right, but you can become richer than any of us. Georgia has oil—the Georgians hate the Bolsheviks; Italy has ancient traditions of commercial hegemony in the Black Sea. The Soviet regime will go from one revolution to another; when order is finally established you will be solidly installed in Georgia. . . ."

However, the Russian Communists need not see in this incident a new proof of the policy of encirclement that, without doubt, did exist against them on the part of Western conservatives. No, it was just typically Lloyd Georgian: a whim, an improvisation. But after it had passed through Orlando to generals faced by the prospect of unemployment, to industrialists and bankers who envisioned miraculous profits (and sure ones for them, even though in the long run the nation might have to foot the bill), the idea of the expedition to Georgia became the Promised Land. I realized it only too well in Constantinople at the beginning of 1919 when Sonnino had to let me into the secret of the "great plan," Colonel Gabba having arrived as advance guard to establish on the Bosporus the first foreign base of the expedition. I did not hesitate long before replying to Sonnino:

"It is true that I have received messages from several tribes and regions of Georgia and even from Azerbaijan expressing friendship for Italy; it is also true that distrust or hatred of the Moscow regime seems unanimous. It is therefore possible that an Italian military expedition and an Italian economic hegemony would be well regarded, at least at the outset; but in the long run it will not work. The Moscow regime will become modified and today's pro-Russians and anti-Russians in Georgia will again be united in agreement with each other against us. The European repercussions give me still greater anxiety; Italy's establishment in Georgia with British approval might some day be one of the causes for a Russo-German alliance against the Western world; and we would be the first victims of it in the Mediterranean and the Black Sea. I do not dare express an opinion on the vitality and the future of the Soviet regime, but I can assure you that it will never be overturned by the unfortunate White Russians whom we have saved by the thousands and whom we harbor now on Princes Island. These people are done for, devoid of courage, of ideals, of generosity; only rancors and hatreds remain alive in them."

As often happened, Sonnino made no reply. And the preparations for the expedition to Georgia continued.

It showed courage on the part of Nitti to break a whole system of interests, ambitions and hopes which had been created. He did it without hesitation the moment he came into power, and despite the fact that the economic organization of the adventure had been concentrated in the Banca di Sconto, which was reputed to have backed Nitti against Giolitti. (I say "reputed" since it was only a journalistic legend; Nitti was personally incorruptible, and he was as far above the Banca di Sconto as Giolitti, equally a man of crystalline personal honesty, was above the Banca Commerciale.)

Nitti was quickly repaid for this service he had rendered to

Italy and Europe by an anonymous but persistent campaign that some high military circles started against him. But since in Italy the military men obey, when one knows how to command them, the tragedy of the Nitti Cabinet was that this honest and intelligent man, competent as an economist and not devoid of general culture (more journalistic, it is true, than profound), did not know how to give orders. An eloquent and persuasive university professor, he was the victim of an illusion that is perhaps a professorial characteristic. When he had delivered a magnificent speech on the "necessity of producing more and consuming less" or on the supreme need of an organized Europe or other problems which he very clearly perceived, he thought he had done all that was necessary. But nothing ever happened, and for the very obvious reason that he simply preached sermons without making any decisions and without giving any orders; whereas a year later everyone obeyed Giolitti, despite his speaking and explaining much less.

The outstanding national and international incident of the Nitti period was the occupation of Fiume by D'Annunzio. It began a few days after the formation of the Cabinet, when Inter-Allied forces were occupying Fiume. At the beginning of July some French soldiers were wounded or killed in a scuffle; the Inter-Allied Commission determined on the reduction of the Italian contingent, whereas, had it been wise, it would have left only Italians in the Italian city of Fiume, save for increasing the number of British and French marines in the port. It was what I immediately suggested to Nitti that he should counsel Paris. He refused to do so, however, being convinced that the French would never listen to reason— which was the surest way to make them unreasonable. The atmosphere remained very strained; something was bound to happen; and Nitti kept on doing nothing.

On September 12 a group of officers and soldiers of the Sardinian Grenadiers, led by D'Annunzio, occupied Fiume; a mob of enthusiastic volunteers rushed to join them from all parts of Italy. Thus D'Annunzio became the master of Fiume, exploiting as a plagiarist of genius an idea that had originated exclusively in the minds of Major Rejna of the Grenadiers, and of the then very young Count Novello Papafava. They, however, soon wearied of the adventure, from the moment that it simply became a stage for the last drama in the life of the actor-poet.

If Nitti was obeyed so little during the entire Fiume affair it was partly due to the sincere emotion that possessed a great number of the Italian people; but still more to two weaknesses in Nitti's character. The Italians perceived these weaknesses with the same quickness of grasp which schoolboys show in understanding which of their masters will not punish them for kicking up a row. Nitti's chief weakness was that he was incapable of conveying the idea that his orders were backed by moral force. What was perhaps worse was that his lack of decision was interpreted by his enemies as "physical fear." On September 13, in his speech in the Chamber, Nitti attacked D'Annunzio's *coup* with an appeal "to the workers of Italy, to the workmen, to the peasants, to the anonymous masses in order that the great voice of the people may be a warning to all."

Either that declaration was simply literature or it was an invitation to the masses to act. Whatever was his intention, he should not have retracted the declaration three days later when he substituted for the appeal to the workers an appeal to the combatants. On September 25 he appealed to the elder statesmen under the form of a Crown Council. Giolitti alone offered a clear and simple suggestion: the occupation of Fiume by regular troops, and general elections. Nitti followed the advice with regard to general elections, but did not dare accept the first part of the suggestion, which was equally necessary.

The second moral weakness in Nitti's character requires a more delicate interpretation. He loved Italy with all his soul, but the Italy of his dreams was a goddess surrounded by statistics running vertically toward some North American material perfection, a goddess crowned by budgets of the seven fat cows. He ignored the secret forces of patriotism as well as the psychological imponderables. To eject D'Annunzio from Fiume required men who, even on the question of Italy's eastern frontiers, united in their hearts the desire for a generous understanding with our Yugoslav neighbors with the most ardent love of Italy, but with love for Italy's prestige as well—a Bissolati, for instance. During the war, Nitti had never believed in an Italian victory, but being an honest and loyal man, he did everything he could to make it possible. But imponderables such as Nitti's limitations make themselves felt, and the Italian people sensed them.

Nitti always treated our territorial problems from an exclusively economic point of view, as when he defined Libya *"uno scatolone di sabbia"* (a boxful of sand) ; yes, perhaps, but for this big boxful of sand thousands of Italians had joyfully died.

It is none the less true that, with regard to his strictly domestic policy, criticism of Nitti will some day be less severe. He did his best in a period in which all wills were at once violent and timid, the Communists thinking only of stabbing the Socialists in the back, the Socialists playing sorrily the role of Conservatives, the Conservatives proving themselves the worst enemies of their own interests, as nearly always happens, and the *Popolari* being too new at the game of major politics to count for much. Only two men seem to have seen clearly and to have known exactly what they wanted: Giolitti who, having retired to his old Piedmont, waited his hour; and the old Anarchist, Errico Malatesta, who in December, 1920, returned to Italy from a long exile.

Malatesta's intellectual roots were neither in Russia nor in Germany. As an adolescent he had taken part in the Benevento rising.* An Italian of Buonaroti's stamp, at sixty-seven he had lost nothing of his steely will; he wanted revolution, and was perhaps the only one who really did want it. Turning to the Socialists who talked of it but did not want it, and to the Communists who wanted it too perfect—which is a way of sabotaging it—he said: "If we let this favorable moment pass we shall later pay with tears of blood for the fear we have instilled in the bourgeoisie." Malatesta was the only one who foresaw Fascism.

In spite of numerous disorders, but with only a single revolutionary, the affair should not have proved too difficult. It required neither a genius nor a hero: only a little courage, which Giolitti never lacked. But still more needed was the renovating energy which Giolitti did not possess. If Nitti was in his utterances more progressive than Giolitti, in fact he was less so. In Giolitti there existed, actively or latently, throughout his life, the rancorous energy of the man who through a

* Chapter XIX.

long heritage of free citizenship feels how intolerable are the
haughty prejudices of nobles and the excessive egoism of
the rich. In Nitti, on the other hand, there was the man of
the Southern lower bourgeoisie, desirous of "doing good to the
people," yet, ready to ally himself with all the social forces
already in power. He would have been a priceless colleague for
Tanucci during the period of reform in the Kingdom of Naples;
but his eighteenth-century humanitarian paternalism succeeded
only in displeasing equally the conservatives and those who
aspired to more social justice in the world.

XXXI

THE GIOLITTI-SFORZA CABINET AND ITS FOREIGN POLICY

HAD NITTI HAD HALF THE ENERGY AND DEEP DEMOCRATIC conviction that animated Giolitti, the latter would probably never have returned to power. But after five months in office Nitti had already made manifest that his power of realization did not equal his good intentions. This explains the profound impression made by the electoral speech Giolitti delivered in his old and faithful electoral district of Dronero on October 12, 1919, on the eve of the general elections Nitti had decided upon. This speech was above all a terrible arraignment of the Italian ruling classes, which he pilloried as "presumptuous minorities, governments without intelligence, which have dragged the nation to war despite itself," and again as those who "have thrown Italy into war without any foresight, without precise agreements on political and colonial questions, without even supposing the existence of economic, financial, commercial and industrial necessities." After having drawn up a statement of what Italy had lost in human lives and wealth, Giolitti launched his governmental program: In the field of international relations, to do everything possible to avoid a new war; to appeal to all countries to join the League of Nations; to obtain the support of international labor; to abolish secret diplomacy; to reserve to parliaments the right of declaring war and concluding peace.

As regards the past, Giolitti proposed: "Immediate and serious" enquiries as to the responsibilities incurred; on the manner in which the powers of those in authority had been exercised; on the stipulations and the execution of the big contracts for supplies, "in order to let the country know how dozens of billions had been squandered." To meet the financial crisis he proposed the abolition of military expenses, a progressive tax upon the total of income and on inheritance, a supertax on great wealth, especially on war profits. He ended with a virulent attack upon the reactionary forces "which will no longer prevail, since the privileged classes of society that led humanity to destruction, can no longer alone rule the world whose destinies must henceforth pass into the hands of its peoples."

At first the speech was received with ferocious howls by the Nationalist press and a great part of the Conservative press. They nicknamed Giolitti the "Bolshevik of the Annunciation" —an allusion to the highest Italian decoration, the Order of the Annunziata, which had been awarded to him and which carried with it the nominal rank of "cousin of the King."

Nitti made the mistake of taking up a position hostile toward Giolitti's program and especially against the enquiry on the war which, he declared, "would inflame passions anew." A reaction supervened. Even those who had most ardently wanted the war were beginning to ask if the great ordeal would not have been infinitely better conducted by Giolitti. In his speech Giolitti had recalled, or, rather, revealed (for Soninno in his pettiness had not given him credit for it) the fact that he, Giolitti, had prevented war by his firm attitude when Austria-Hungary in 1913 communicated her intention of attacking Serbia, and that, at the beginning of the World War he had written San Giuliano, the Minister of Foreign Affairs: "The way in which Austria has provoked the conflagration is brutal and shows complete ignorance or a deliberate intention to unchain a European war. I may be mistaken, but my impression is that Austria, more than any other country, will pay for the damage."

These words, which he had never deigned to publish during the war when he was being attacked as Germanophile, proved that he had only been a friend of peace. In the same speech he explained his opposition to Italy's entrance into the war. According to the Treaty of London negotiated by Sonnino, England, Giolitti recalled, guaranteed to Italy loans so insufficient that a relatively poor country like ours had to raise within its own resources, and in a world at war, a minimum of fifty million pounds sterling per month. Giolitti was convinced that it would be a long war and judged that Italy had as many reasons as the United States to prolong a neutrality which would allow her to enter the furnace later, and consequently would

not compel her to consume in it all her resources. Giolitti did
not add in his speech that in the summer of 1914 he had foreseen that the war would last three years. "I was," he remarked
later, "like Kitchener, too optimistic."

When the first furies of the Nationalists had died down Giolitti once more became the man of the hour for all Italians, and
on the fall of the Nitti Cabinet in 1920 he came into power,
imposed on the Crown by the unanimous will of the nation. It
was a dangerous moment, for a great moral crisis was grafted
onto the economic crisis, the fatal legacy of the long war years.
There is always danger for a country when the two crises occur
together.

It was only too natural that Italy, poorer than the other victors, should have found the war a more exhausting ordeal, and
so intense had been the sufferings, so imprudently prodigal had
been the promises of a millennium to millions of soldiers that
nothing which happened could have been a cause for surprise—
except, perhaps a silent Oriental resignation on their part. The
inevitable result of the niggardly policy of Sonnino at the peace
negotiations had added to the difficulties of the situation in
spreading the impression that five hundred thousand Italians
had died in vain and that the victory had been "mutilated."

The revolutionary elements profited by it to mirror before
the eyes of a discontented and restless people the example of
Russia, as a myth and as an ideal. For the Italian combatants,
almost all of them peasants, to whom had been made a half-
promise that after the war each one of them would have his
parcel of ground, the Russian myth did not at all signify Communism, but the simple fact that the men who had really fought
the war had become the masters in Russia and that the estates
of the rich had been divided among the grandsons of serfs.

The shortsighted policy that aimed to surround Russia with
a *cordon sanitaire* did the rest. People thought: Ah! If they
are putting Russia in quarantine, it is because they are afraid
others will follow her example. And all of a sudden they ceased
giving much credence to reports on the Bolshevik horrors.

But here we have to do with a discontentment which was
more superficial than fundamental, a neurasthenic phase. Proof
of this exists in the general satisfaction the country felt on the

return of Giolitti to power, of the old Giolitti who never had any illusions on the advantages war would bring.

To deal with the economic situation, Giolitti at once imposed a system of new taxes which struck a hard blow at the wealthy while taking a lesser toll from small fortunes. He thus reaped a double advantage: a financial one, by producing a satisfactory budget (three years later when Fascism came into power Italian finance was again perfectly balanced, thanks to the measures Giolitti had taken); and also an evident moral advantage—the poor, to whom the Soviet gospel was being preached, saw that the rich were for once mercilessly smitten.

As for the foreign policy, Giolitti wanted to talk it over with me. Despite the gravity of the situation he had delayed for two days the formation of his Cabinet in order to give me time to return from London where I had gone to discuss the question of Inter-Allied debts with Lloyd George.

On my return to Rome we met immediately. Without mentioning the matter of his Cabinet, he began by asking my advice on the Fiume affair and on the entire Adriatic question. I replied that the Fiume affair, though there was in it a definite element of patriotic sentiments, was, in D'Annunzio's hands, only a pretext to attempt the conquest of Italy or, at the very least, to extract aesthetic sensations from it. "It is for you," I said, "as the new Minister of Interior, to think it over. In reality it is simply a case of internal Boulangism.

"On the other hand," I continued, "I am not at all in agreement with the self-styled prudent men and the self-styled practical men who think that, cost what it may, we should get rid of the Adriatic question. [Tittoni had been ready to accept the frontier a few kilometers from Trieste: Scialoia, to share Istria.] It is not a policy of liquidation which we must follow, but a constructive policy. We must assure for ourselves the best geographic and national frontier; but we must also in our own interests forget all about our proposed Dalmatian annexations, which would be only a bullet in the foot and deprive us of all diplomatic liberty in the future, for the entire policy of a great country like Italy would be confined to safeguarding detached possessions across the Adriatic. Above all, we ought to make Belgrade comprehend that the danger of a Hapsburg resurrection has not vanished, and that though such a resurrection would, it is true, diminish the value of the Italian victory, it would also constitute a mortal danger for the united Yugoslavs." I also told him that Italy should give the successor states of Austria-Hungary her support as a great Power, which would bring about for us a position of first importance in Central and Eastern Europe. I gave him the reasons and circumstances that made me sure that England and France would regard such a policy with equanimity, provided we explained it at London and Paris with frankness and dignity.

Giolitti remained pensive for a while and then remarked: "I confess I never have been so optimistic, but it is worth trying. Now, will you be the new Minister of Foreign Affairs? The Cabinet list has been ready for two days, but I waited your return to ask you to join me if we were in agreement."

"Parliament is a very stormy place," I objected, "and I am no orator—which I don't specially regret. But don't you think you would do better to find someone who is more endowed with what is needed to please the Chambers?"

In true Giolittian style he answered: "I have often heard you speak in the Chamber. When you have something to say you say it: then you sit down. For me that is true eloquence!"

I accepted.

The next day I left for the Inter-Allied Conference of Boulogne whose most important discussions were devoted to Greece. Venizelos was not at Boulogne; but his spirit was there, represented by Lloyd George. The Conference was nothing but a long controversy between the Prime Minister and myself. I had only two advantages over him, but they were sizable—I had studied the problem on the spot in Turkey where, even before the award of Smyrna to the Greeks, I had assured the demigods of the Conference of Paris that Turkey not only was not beaten but that her awakening would be formidable, and that as I was an enemy of all imperialist aims for Italy it could not be insinuated that I was anti-Greek if, in the interests of Greece herself, I were hostile to the dangerous Hellenic imperialist adventures. But at Boulogne in 1920 the influence of Venizelos was still tremendous.

Until then, diplomatically, he had had nothing but successes. By the Treaty of Neuilly, concluded with Bulgaria, and by the ephemeral Treaty of Sèvres with the Turks he could boast of having obtained Thrace, of having reached the Sea of Marmora and the Dardanelles, and of having acquired Smyrna and her rich hinterland for Greece. He had even signed an accord with the English and with Tittoni, the Italian Minister of Foreign Affairs, in the second part of the Peace Conference, on July 29, 1919, whereby the Italian Government engaged itself to transfer to Greece all the Dodecanese Islands with the exception of Rhodes, and even Rhodes, after a plebiscite, on the day that England ceded Cyprus to her. The same accord stated that Italy would lend her support to Greece for the annexation of southern Albania, and that in return Greece would, at the Peace Conference, support an Italian mandate over the Albanian State and that she would also recognize Italian sovereignty over Valona.

When, after becoming Minister of Foreign Affairs, I took cognizance of this convention that Tittoni had kept secret, I found it impossible to see in what way it could be useful to Italy and to a fruitful peace in the Mediterranean. Without sinning too greatly in pride, I thought, in the first place, it was not becoming for Italy to solicit the support of Greece and formally ratify that support in a diplomatic instrument. So much for the form. As to the substance, I considered, as did Giolitti, that there was a contradiction, after so many fine phrases on self-determination of peoples, in wanting the creation of a new and living Albanian State and simultaneously depriving it of one of its lungs, Valona. Moreover, I contemplated with great distrust the idea of a mandate over Albania. Albania, in my judgment, should enter the sphere of Italian influence, but certainly not by a juridic arrangement that would wound the dignity of the Albanian people. Relationships of this kind, to be beneficial, must exclude any appearance of inequality.

Believing as I did, I was determined to orient the Italian policy according to the ideas that Giolitti shared with me, and which were the only ones conformable with our permanent interests. I therefore denounced the Tittoni-Venizelos accord, which represented for us only a series of burdens without any corresponding advantages.

I notified my decision in a note to Venizelos in which I said that, taking advantage of the right given her by a clause of the said accord, Italy took back her full liberty of action on all the points envisioned in this document; but that the Italian Government remained animated with the most cordial desire for an understanding; that I was sure that the Hellenic government was animated by the same feeling in our regard; and that I counted on arriving at a new accord with Greece which would be as satisfactory as it was complete.

Each of my words responded to the reality of my sentiments. Hellenism is a vital force in the Near East; particularly at that time, when Greece possessed throughout Asia Minor those flourishing outposts which, three years later, victorious Turkey destroyed. And I was, as I am now, convinced that a nation rich in vitality like Italy should be in accord with all that has vital force in the Mediterranean community, and with the Greeks among the very first. After I had annulled the Tittoni-Venizelos accord on Rhodes, the British government accordingly revoked theirs on Cyprus.

But nothing more than the fact that accords of this kind could exist proves how real was the influence of Venizelos at the Conference. He was its siren; the Mussulmans must have thought that he had the *barraka,* the benediction of Allah which assures success.

Wilson himself, the unapproachable Wilson, was not insensible to the charms of the Hellenic statesman who knew how to display to the Scotch-American the wiles Homer attributes to Ulysses. Here is the story of his first encounter with Wilson —as Colonel House, then the most intimate friend of the American President, told it to me. After some minutes of generalities, Wilson, thinking thereby to put an end to the conversation in a courteous manner, said to the Prime Minister of Greece that he could count on his good will for the Hellenic national aspirations.

Venizelos answered: "I am grateful to you, Mr. President. However, what is important now is not little Greece: what is important is your sublime idea of the League of Nations. To work in the measure of my means for the realization of this great conception is my dearest wish. Consider, please, that I am a soldier under your orders for this noble task. . . ."

Wilson no longer thought of ending the conversation, and the colloquy continued for over an hour. Greece was not mentioned. But when Ulysses returned to his headquarters he must have thought: "I think we have obtained Smyrna."

Unfortunately for Greece, Smyrna was given her. The moment that Sonnino and Orlando quitted the Conference after their stormy discussions with Wilson as regards Fiume, Lloyd George, in agreement with the American President, called Venizelos, and under the pretext that the progress of Turkish nationalism in Asia Minor had become disquieting, asked him whether his government felt it had a force sufficient to debark at Smyrna in two or three days.

Venizelos was troubled by the briefness of the time; but he realized that the offer had only been made as a result of a broil with the Italians, which might only be temporary. Without hesitation he answered, "Yes!"

At Constantinople where, as I have already said, I was then High Commissioner, my English and French colleagues and I received orders to communicate to the Sublime Porte the decision concerning the Hellenic debarkation. It was a formal order. As far as I was concerned there was nothing to do but formally signify to my British colleague that it was a measure which would prove fatal both for the Entente and for Greece herself.

Even without Smyrna, the Treaty of Sèvres alone would have confirmed my most pessimistic presentiments. During the entire year of 1920, at each Inter-Allied Conference the military experts gathered in a room near ours and, under the presidency of Foch, each time declared that neither Great Britain, nor France, nor Italy had one division to add to the forces they already were maintaining in the Near East. Then Venizelos would step forward and under the admiring gaze of Lloyd George announce himself as prepared to undertake the entire affair. At the Boulogne Conference I declared: "Despite all appearances, I am the only man here who really cares about Greece. Remember that if one can die of starvation, one can also die of indigestion. . . ." As Venizelos had not come to Boulogne, Lloyd George objected that it was easy to "ridicule" the political and military decisions of a statesman who was not present to defend himself.

A month later we assembled for the long Conference of Spa. Venizelos attended and again renewed his offers. The Supreme

Council consisted of Lloyd George, Millerand and myself. Venizelos explained the reasons which convinced him of success. I was the only one to contradict him; I pointed out the danger that Greece would incur and I ended with this remark: "My only regret is that the attitude of Italy *may* be attributed to lack of sympathy for Greece, or even to a lack of trust in her, when, on the contrary, I am motivated by feelings of deep solicitude for her true interests. The only good peace is the one that is tolerable for both parties. By gaining too much, Greece risks losing everything. I am convinced [these were my closing words] that there is one man in this room who understands the profound sincerity of my words, and that man is Mr. Venizelos." I looked at him and saw that, patriot that he was, he had felt and understood that some day my warning might prove true. But the die had been cast.

Venizelos's fundamental mistake here, as before, was to have deceived himself on the extent of Great Britain's support.

Wilson—and I believe this is the only case in which personal resentment gained the mastery over his concepts—decided to give Smyrna to Greece to avenge himself on an Italy which had declined to rally to his point of view regarding Fiume. But it must be recognized that Wilson alone cannot be held responsible for so grave a mistake. A more active and enthusiastic advocate for the Greek cause was necessary, and the Greeks had him in Lloyd George. The reasons for the sudden philo-Hellenism of the British Prime Minister in 1919 and 1920 seemed so mysterious that diplomats and journalists cudgeled their brains and contrived the most extraordinary explanations. One of their discoveries had some vogue in Europe for a while. It was asserted that an Anglo-Greek banker, Zaharoff—a rather legendary figure—had succeeded in influencing the British decisions. However, it is one of those undeniable truths that the moment great problems are under consideration, the atmosphere of London is far above influences of this sort.

As often happens, the reality was much simpler. It was due partly to the sentimental heritage of the old liberal traditions which influenced Great Britain to favor the liberty of Oriental Christian races. Lloyd George was still a young man with easily moved emotions when England resounded to the Gladstonian apostrophes against "the unspeakable Turk." But, as happens often in England, a more practical issue combined with idealistic reasoning.

Just as Gladstone, sincere though he was in his Christian campaign against the Turks, was at the same time aiming at Queen Victoria and her Disraeli, Lloyd George also, under cover of homage to Wilson's Fourteen Points, believed he had found the means of continuing in the Orient the destruction of Mussulman forces and thus assuring with the fresh arms of the Greek Kingdom British domination in Egypt and the Arab world.

Venizelos had pleased Wilson with his talk about the League of Nations. And to Lloyd George he pictured the descendants of Themistocles and Epaminondas again in arms for the conquest of the Orient. During long months of diplomatic conferences I often wondered whether Lloyd George was not talking about a literary Greece which he had recently discovered and which he loved as one always does love one's own discoveries.

No one more than I admires the rare qualities of intuition and quick action of the former British Prime Minister. During the war he was always right in his quarrels with generals: as, for instance, when he wanted to break the enemy mass by a gigantic Anglo-Italian offensive against Austria, a concept that one of the noblest spirits, Bissolati—whose charm Lloyd George deeply felt—had suggested to him. But "West is West and East is East." And in the West Lloyd George had had to learn through personal experience. Furthermore, he, a civilian, distrusted the consensus of opinion of generals; and in the East what he believed to be the military truth had been depicted to him by another civilian, Venizelos.

Lloyd George believed that Venizelos would allow him to continue warring against the Turks with Greek forces without using a single Tommy; hence his praise and his gifts (of others' possessions). The mistake of the Hellenic leader lay in believing that eulogies and gifts meant that Greece would never lack British support and would thereby be assured the final victory. Lloyd George too wanted that victory over Turkey, but he had determined to pay for it with Greek blood only.

The masses in Greece, more prescient than their great man, felt how dangerous the situation was. The November, 1920, elections proved a resounding defeat for Venizelos' party. Even he himself was not reelected at Athens. Disillusioned, frustrated, realizing too late the risks of the program to which he had committed his country, he abandoned power and went into voluntary exile. King Constantine then returned.

Venizelos went to live on the Riviera. In response to the questioning of a French friend who asked him what he thought would happen, he predicted the victory of the Turks and the destruction of the Hellenic element in the Orient. I could not help remarking to this French enquirer, who happened also to be a friend of mine, when he reported this very sagacious opinion of Venizelos to me in Paris (where I was then ambassador), that here was a case of the usual and fruitless far-sightedness some politicians acquire only after they have lost the power they loved too much.

After the Turkish business, we had to deal with a far more important matter of negotiation: the settlement of the Italo-Yugoslav question which had become envenomed during Orlando's administration and which had not made any progress during Nitti's administration.

It was at the Inter-Allied Conference of Spa, in the summer of 1920, that for the first time I received the Yugoslav Minister of Foreign Affairs, Trumbich. With him, as with Millerand, Lloyd George and Curzon, I began to lay down the principles and create the atmosphere from which five months later the Treaty of Rapallo emerged.

When all Europe was convinced that the disorders natural to, or excusable by, post-war sufferings had only been a passing crisis and that under the experienced guidance of Giolitti the country had resumed its normal life, I convoked the Yugoslav plenipotentiaries at Rapallo to make a final settlement of the Adriatic question.

They arrived on the morrow of our national ceremony which had proved that, from the Alps to Sicily, the entire country was recovering from the post-war neurosis. On November 4, 1920, the flags of regiments cited for bravery on the field of battle had been brought to Rome to receive from the King *al valore* medals. In Rome, as in the cities where deputations of the regiments were beginning to return with their flags decorated by the hands of the King, the enthusiasm and reverence of the people for these symbols of heroism and suffering were profoundly moving. It was a good augury for the beginning of our diplomatic negotiations. But as I was not absolutely certain that the Yugoslavs would yield to all my demands (I knew that a Grand Council of the Crown held at Belgrade before the departure of the plenipotentiaries had excluded some of them) I had asked Giolitti to remain in Rome, although he was one of the plenipotentiaries for the treaty, together with Bonomi, the Minister of War, and myself. The moment success seemed assured I was to telegraph him to come.

For a long time the Yugoslavs resisted my demands. They found it hard to cede half a million Slavs; but, as I told them, it was not our fault if they were on our side of the Alps. One night the discussion reached a degree of dramatic tension rare in meetings of this kind. I reproached them for not showing in their civic duty the same courage they had given proof of during the war. "You know," I told them, "that the treaty I propose, together with the diplomatic entente I am offering, is acceptable to you; but you fear the chauvinists of Zagreb and Belgrade; you fear for your popularity. And what about myself? Do you think I don't know that I risk my own by tearing up the treaty that gives us Dalmatia? But I am ready to face unpopularity and hatred to serve my country. I have only this to say to you: when you return to Belgrade you will feel the pangs of remorse."

Turning abruptly, I left them. But by the visible emotion of my hearers I knew that they would not recoil from their duty any more than I would from mine.

Still, they demurred at yielding Zara, that ancient Dalmatian city so essentially Italian that I had decided to annex it, though from all sides in Italy I was advised not to insist too much. For instance, the editor of the *Popolo d'Italia,* Mussolini, to whom I had given a long interview at the Ministry of Foreign Affairs before my departure for Rapallo, had suggested "Zara independent, with an Italian diplomatic representative." Bonomi naturally supported me. Finally the Yugoslav Prime Minister, Vesnich, asked me to telegraph Giolitti to explain the reasons why the Yugoslav Government opposed the annexation of Zara to Italy. Giolitti replied that the negotiations must not be broken on account of Zara. His telegram reached me after the Yugoslavs had begun to yield. It was then that I did what I had the right to do, and what seemed my duty: I declared to the Yugoslavs that Giolitti, in his reply, absolutely supported my point of view. It was not only my love for Zara, that jewel of Italian art, that had determined me not to compromise; I feared that good Italo-Yugoslav relations—necessary, as I considered, for the expansion of Italy's political and economic influence toward the East—might be compromised or menaced if ever a young and ardent people like the South Slavs should, in an access of nationalist fever, try to de-Italianize Zara.

After I had won Zara, Giolitti arrived at Rapallo and thanked me for having corrected—he said it with a smile—the editorial obscurities of his telegram. The treaty was signed on November 12. It gave Italy an Alpine frontier as perfect as under the Roman Empire: all of Istria, the islands of Lussin and Cherso, Zara on the Dalmatian coast, privileges for the Italians of Dalmatia, the independence of Fiume, recognized as a free Italian city contiguous to territory of the Italian State —and Italian, therefore, practically speaking, but with that traditional autonomy of its long history more favorable to its economic life than a formal annexation.

It is appropriate to recall here that shortly before the Yugoslav plenipotentiaries' arrival in Italy I had sought to have repeated to them *ad abundantiam* that they should not come until convinced of the necessity of recognizing Italy's natural frontiers. The Italian industrialist, Volpi, who had to go to Belgrade on business and who had long known Prime Minister Vesnich, offered to be the bearer of my personal message. Volpi met with such opposition to the cession of the Alpine line to Mount Nevoso that he telegraphed me several times that I must be content with an intermediate line, and as neither objurgations nor the renewal of Serbian resistance had had the slightest influence on me, he again telegraphed that he had just found a formula conciliating the two opposing points of view: Italy should have the line of Nevoso but on lease from Yugoslavia for ninety-nine years, and that he was returning with what he called "a victory." Not thinking it was worth a discussion, I simply told him that one can arrange a lease on a business concession, but not on the frontiers of one's homeland.

This same Volpi, after Fascism's attainment of power, became Minister of Finance and one of the leading personages of a regime specializing in patriotic pride.

Morally, the Treaty of Rapallo represented the first peace freely consented to since the World War, and by that very fact created an atmosphere favorable to new fruitful *ententes*.

Twelve days later, in the Chamber, during the discussion on the treaty, and in my reply to the Nationalist Deputy, Federzoni, who had held that I could have asked for more, I declared:

"Would it have been wise to create with new hatreds a Chinese Wall where we want free and pacific outlets to the East? Signor Federzoni says that if we had better evaluated the international situation we would have asked for more. I say it is not so. We know that situation perfectly, but had it been a hundred times more favorable for us, I would have thought I was betraying the future destinies of Italy in asking for more. And you know very well, Signor Federzoni, that I have always held that opinion. . . . As for Fiume, of which the prosperity is not undermined by any clause, we have in our hands the means of assuring its future."

The last sentence contained an allusion: for fear that the general satisfaction shown by the country for the Peace of Rapallo would completely remove from the Nationalists the demagogic terrain for Adriatic agitation, the rumor was bruited about that a secret clause had assigned to the Yugoslavs the little port of Baross, opposite Sussak, and that Fiume ardently desired its annexation to the free city. With his habitual clarity Giolitti touched on this episode in his memoirs: "They made much ado," he wrote, "on the question of Port Baross, but we had to admit that Port Baross was outside the *Corpus Separatum* of Fiume, and it was on the basis of that traditional *Corpus Separatum* that we had diplomatic and historic grounds for wishing to make Fiume a free city. Port Baross, actually, belonged to the Croats who used it for their lumber trade. I had so notified the Parliamentary Commission of Foreign Affairs. But what all this amounted to was simply digressions."

As a matter of fact, the thorough researches I had had made in the Budapest archives had given us proof that Port Baross belonged to Croatia, and not to the *Corpus Separatum* of

Fiume. We could, therefore, easily have recognized it as Yugo-slav in the treaty, especially in view of the satisfaction with which public opinion accepted our transaction—as Mussolini himself admitted when he came into power.

Considering the pressure to which the Yugoslav plenipoten-tiaries had been subjected, we (Giolitti, Bonomi and I) thought it prudent to record immediately in a treaty what we had acquired, and not to linger in long technical discussions on the concrete realization of an idea that I had cherished from the start. I wanted to constitute for the port of Fiume, once the city had been recognized as Italian and independent, an Italo-Fiumo-Yugoslav consortium which would have represented the salvation of Fiume, since Yugoslavia would then have become interested in the life of the port. Ports like Trieste and Fiume cannot prosper unless they have the closest relations with their hinterlands. It was in order to oblige Yugoslavia to accept the idea of the consortium for the port that we refused to admit in the treaty that Port Baross was Yugoslav; we confined our-selves to stating in a letter to the Yugoslav Minister of For-eign Affairs that in our opinion this little bay should belong to Yugoslavia. Port Baross would thus become the contribution of the Yugoslav State to the projected consortium.

When an artificial agitation for Port Baross started, it would have been easy for me to rise and say:

"If our conception displeases you, you are free to do what seems to you right; our letter is only an engagement of the Cabinet now in power as it has not been ratified nor is it regis-tered at Geneva. It is an engagement deprived of all interna-tional value; a new Cabinet is free to have in that regard a different policy from ours, only thereby we stand to lose the consortium (the idea and the formula had already been accepted by the new Yugoslav Prime Minister, Pachich) and Fiume will go to ruin."

I observed once again on this occasion how in Giolitti the feeling of duty to the nation was on a par with the loyalty and most perfect delicacy of his relations with his colleagues. One day when the campaign against me was at its height because of the Port Baross affair, about which everyone was talking and, naturally, without having the least notion of what it was all about, I remarked to Giolitti how easily we might have explained to our adversaries that they needed only to come into power and they would not find themselves in the least bound by anything we had done as regards Port Baross, but that then they would either have to forswear their demagogy and save Fiume, or remain faithful to their fine phrases and destroy the commerce of Fiume. Giolitti merely replied:

"Yes, the reason that they are attacking you is that they know how indifferent you are to their attacks and that you will keep silent. But the day will come when they will be glad to pursue our policy, if only they can make people believe that they are bound by the engagements we made."

That is all he said. He wanted to leave me free to cut short the campaign if I wished, which I did not. Later I had the satisfaction of seeing governments which, like Fascism, continually vaunted their strength, modestly shielding themselves behind my engagements—engagements that had never existed. But their policy being deprived of all consistency, Fiume became one of its victims; became, in fact, a dead city.

As I have already noted, on Giolitti's attainment to power the legend of that masterless paradise that Russia was reported to have become exercised a certain fascination on the masses. I at once realized the danger and set about dissipating it. A few days after we came into office I declared in my first speech in the Chamber: "The policy of the barbed-wire fence around Russia has been morally very useful to the Soviets, furnishing them an alibi for the unspeakable suffering of the Russians. Bolshevism must live or die by itself, without any outside pressure."

A little earlier I had contributed to the cause of social peace what was in appearance a very modest contribution, but which later proved more useful than many anti-Bolshevik speeches. I had facilitated the departure of an Italian Socialist mission for Russia. These Socialist delegates were honest people, and on their return, several months later, when they declared that the Soviet world was a hell our workers believed them.

In September, 1920, the manifestations of feverish disquiet of a section of the Italian proletariat attained their peak. Using as a pretext the lock-out decreed by some industrialists in an ordinary economic controversy, the workmen of Piedmont and Lombardy proceeded to the occupation of factories according to the Russian revolutionary formula. The movement lasted a short time, then died a natural death. It died of the void created about it. Giolitti refused to leave his summer residence at Bardonecchia, in the Alps. From there he transacted government business. During the very early days of the occupation he received a delegation of industrialists; one of them, more infuriated than his colleagues, asked him to have the workmen occupying the factories bombarded. With his ever-courteous and ironic smile Giolitti responded: "And will you permit me to begin by bombarding *your* factories?" The proposal was declined.

A few days later it became apparent that the incident was about to end. The workmen had vainly attempted to enlist the engineers and office employees, who had all refused to join them. The workers felt powerless; the good old Italian common sense did the rest, and liberty triumphed without clamor or violence.

Giolitti faithfully describes this episode and the reasons that dictated his conduct in the following passage from his *Memoirs:*

"From the outset I had a firm and clear conviction that experience would teach the workers that they could not attain their objectives. As I saw it, the episode was repeating in a way and in different conditions the analogous incident of the general strike of 1904, which had roused such fear and then revealed itself so inept. I was absolutely convinced that our government's conduct ought to be like that of the government then in power. Accordingly, I let the experiment develop up to a certain point, in order to convince the workers that it was impossible for them to succeed and to prevent the agitators from blaming others for their failure."

Giolitti certainly had no need of my advice at that time. But as the legend of the Bolshevik dangers of 1920 became in some circles the principal reason for continuing to excuse the Fascist regime, as late as 1939 and even later, I wish to indicate— merely as the testimony of a witness—what I thought then. I was in Rome with the other Ministers; we assembled and affirmed our united agreement with any decision Giolitti would make. But I thought it my duty to write him:

"Strange as it may appear to you, will you allow me, as

Foreign Minister, to talk to you of what is happening in your neighborhood in Piedmont?

"It is generally believed that the fall of the Romanoffs dates from 1917; that is a fallacy; the fatal hour sounded for them in 1905 when, on the occasion of the strikes, the streets of St. Petersburg ran red with the blood of thousands of workers killed by Cossack charges. Should we act in the same way here we would create a legend and a religion. We shall appear to be acting as conservatives, and actually we shall have destroyed the liberal regime in Italy. I am sure that you are in agreement with me, but I declare to you that I should be acting against my conscience if I accepted responsibility for a different policy. If you do not answer I shall know that we are fundamentally in agreement."

Giolitti's silence proved to me that our views on the situation were identical. Benedetto Croce, our colleague of Public Instruction, shared them. Giolitti had been the first to succeed in detaching the great philosopher from his studies and inducing him to assume political responsibilities. By accepting the invitation to become our colleague, Croce had simply obeyed his sense of duty. Croce's advice, the impressions he made on me, during this period were a rare intellectual pleasure. It would not be possible to find a man in whom there blended more perfectly the lofty serenity of the thinker and the practical wisdom of the politician.

At the time of the occupation of the factories in Piedmont and Lombardy the Italian Socialist movement seemed, to all appearances, about to achieve complete success. More than two thousand Communes were in Socialist hands. Out of a total of 508 in the Chamber they had 156 deputies. But the miserable, even ridiculous end of this abortive occupation had sapped popular confidence in those Socialist leaders who were merely brawlers. Enthusiasm dwindled even for the most respected of the party chieftains. Had the traditional "torrents of blood" been spilled, the faith would unquestionably have flamed up. Finally, in January, 1921, at one of their Congresses the Socialist Party was divided by a schism into two violently hostile groups. That signified the end of any possibility of direct action.

It was what Giolitti expected. During the autumn of 1920

I had often heard him prophesy it. This certainty was one of the reasons for his apparent passiveness at the time of the occupation of the factories. Having avoided bloodshed he obtained this result: that several of the Socialist leaders, the most thoughtful, honest and enlightened among them, were led to initiate a fruitful contest against the violent excesses which broke out against their will.

The "timorous" spirits continued to be afraid; and fear has the characteristic of blinding its victims to necessary psychological changes. I am reminded, for example, of Sir George Buchanan who, before coming to Rome, had been a witness of the war and of the revolution in Russia; that excellent man saw symptoms of Bolshevism practically everywhere. One day I went to see Giolitti when Buchanan was visiting him. I chaffed Sir George, alluding laughingly to his fears, and Giolitti, who was then looking out of the window, said to him: "Look at those olive trees, Mr. Ambassador. You never saw any in Russia, did you? Well, you won't see Bolshevism in Italy any more than olive trees in Russia."

Sir George must have repeated these words in London, for some months later they were served up to me again by Lloyd George, then Prime Minister, as his own sentiments.

During 1921 the morale of the Italian masses and their economic condition made constant progress. In 1920 there had been 1,881 strikes in the country; in 1921 the figure fell to 1,045, with 720,000 strikers (most of the strikes lasted only a few days). These were almost the same figures as the 1915 statistics, the year of Italy's entrance into the war. In brief, the graph curve followed approximately the same course as in France and England, where they had had the same strike epidemic and disorders, but where they had not talked so much about them.

It was then that Fascism, revolutionary by birth, put itself more or less openly at the service of industrialists to break the workers' movement. Giolitti welcomed it as a counterweight to Socialism. But he was entirely convinced that Fascism could be kept within legal bounds by Parliament. And that is one of the reasons that determined him to call the general elections of 1921. When I maintained to Giolitti that from a past danger our industrialists—and he with them—were possibly forging a new one, of unknown consequences, he thought me pessimistic, and answered: "These Fascist candidacies are only fireworks; they'll make a great deal of noise, but will quickly burn out." Giolitti had an infallible eye for the men within his purview, and that was one of the reasons for his love of Parliament, but his perception of movements that were developing beyond his range of vision was not nearly so acute.

XXXII

THE INVENTOR OF FASCISM: D'ANNUNZIO

ITALIANS OF MY GENERATION WERE PROBABLY INITIATED IN the ideas which became successively D'Annunzian, Nationalist and Fascist, in early childhood, when everyone around them was discussing a Neapolitan deputy, Rocco de Zerbi, who had formulated the theory that Italy to strengthen herself needed a blood bath. De Zerbi, who, shortly afterward, implicated in some corrupt dealings, committed suicide, was doubtless the first Nationalist of free Italy.

His Nationalism consisted in desiring Italy to cease being Italy, with her sentiments and traditions (she was the only great European state that had abolished the death penalty), in order to become Germany, meaning, of course, the violent Bismarckian Germany.

The wretched Zerbi's crusade aroused no echo in Italy, just as there was none of the several scribblers who, later, began to appropriate the formulas of Charles Maurras and other French theorists of French Nationalism and apply them to a country like ours, whose historical origin is so completely different.

At that time the man who knew how to make the chords of patriotic love in the Italian heart vibrate with greatest intensity was Carducci, with his songs almost always inspired by the incomparable glories and disasters of our history. All the Italians of my age thrilled as adolescents at his evocations of our ancient Communal conflicts with the German emperors, at his rhetorical apostrophes aimed at the tepid and the skeptics. His sole thought, his sole love, was for Italy, which explains why he is little known beyond the Alps, despite his admirable poetic gifts. The poets of the generation preceding his, Leopardi and Manzoni, are universal poets; they were able to fuse in their verse the most ardent love of Italy with the eternal and universal sentiments of all poetry. They united Italy with the world, whereas Carducci tended to isolate her with his *Romanita*. But if Carducci was occasionally limited, he was never decadent; the love he bore for his country was too sacred.

The note of decadence was struck for the first time, in a form which became a national event, by a young poet who, coming to Rome from the Abruzzi, continued Carducci's exaltations but spiced them with a cruelty, sensuality and lust which ought to have made it plain to everyone that he was far from believing in the Rome of the honest and chaste Carducci.

Counterfeiting the formulas that Nietzsche was then offering a dumfounded Europe and, most often misunderstanding the German writer's deeper meaning, D'Annunzio began to preach to young Italians the gospel of a new life which had nothing Roman about it except the stage setting:

> *"Morire, o gioire!*
> *Gioire, o morire!"*
> (To die is to be happy! To be happy is to die!)

He combined the means to realize this aspiration in a quartette of master-emotions: will, sensuality, pride, instinct. Here we have a basic affirmation. But not with these four sentiments can one love one's country, for patriotism is conceivable only when it involves self-sacrifice for a higher cause; at most they can lead to Nationalism, which is not only the counterfeit and caricature of patriotism but, properly speaking, its very antithesis.

The patriotism of the Risorgimento Italians probably represented the noblest form of that passion. Mazzini, the prophet of the Italian awakening, went further still. He wrote: "I love my homeland because I love all homelands." At its very best, nationalism is the application of the Marxist principle of class conflict to national conflict: a theory of hatred and, what is worse, a stupid theory in this epoch when a nation's wealth and prosperity are indissolubly bound with the wealth and prosperity of its neighbors.

The Italian Nationalists, nurtured in the reading of Maurras, had not really found their man in D'Annunzio. With his aesthetic gifts as undeniable as his indifference to ideas, he was scarcely liable to let himself be bound by a theory, having been by turns a pagan with Carducci, a Russian with Dostoevski, a superman with Nietzsche, a free man with Whitman, a decadent with Maeterlinck and Barrès, and yet never having really plagiarized any one of them—simply because he was only a marvelous musical instrument seeking in the ideas of others merely the opportunity to clothe them in marvelous poetry.

For him the *Patria,* sacred for Leopardi and Manzoni, for Garibaldi and Mazzini, became, like other men's ideas, just the material for a musical rendering. One of his tragedies, *La Nave* (The Ship), was presented in Rome in 1908. One of its lines served as the *leit-motif*:

> *"Arma la prora e salpa verso il mondo."*
> (Arm the prow and set sail against the world.)

The verse meant nothing, or nothing more than a vague imperial appetite for conquest; but to a youth submissive to the domination of the poet's technical perfection it seemed almost a program, a program of grandeur and war.

G. A. Borgese, who has described the restlessness of the generation following D'Annunzio's in his grim and powerful novel, *Rubè,* also described in 1919 what D'Annunzianism meant for young people who, ignoring Carducci, read only D'Annunzio:

"His books depict . . . villas by the sea, horseback rides, modish clothes, drawing-room successes, notorious courtesans, luminous landscapes, descriptions of distant lands. Worse yet, they tell the adolescent that he is right in wanting to emancipate himself, in wanting '*abolir i divieti*' (to abolish inhibitions). . . . The D'Annunzian fantasy presents splendid tyrannies, endless voyages, thunderous conquests, rapes of the daughters of barbarian kings. . . ."

Then came the war; luckily, said the youth. It is true that as a man, D'Annunzio, no longer young, fought with courage and steadfastness. But that is beside the question; thousands of anonymous Italians who could, like himself, have remained in the chimney corner, did the same. It is in his imagination as a poet that he failed. And he was fated to fail. Prior to the Nationalists, D'Annunzio had exalted massacre and bloodshed, for it can hardly be denied that sadism is one of the forces of D'Annunzian poetics. And with the Nationalists, D'Annunzio had sung the "war fresh and joyous," just as he had copied it from the official theorists of the Germany of the last Hohenzollern. When tragedy supervened, with its horrors, but also with its sacrifices—sanguinary sacrifices, yet so grievously human—the sensuous poet's art became sterile, unable to apprehend the meaning of the drama. He dressed up his art in a noisy rhetoric, incapable of perceiving the very thing which in the brutality of war is yet its redemption—for example: the beauty of the resistance on the Piave, which began before General Headquarters had given the order, the flowering of an instinct that commanded the Italian soldiers after the retreat of Caporetto to die there if they did not wish to see the Prussians, the Austrians, the Hungarians invade the soil of their homeland.

It was admirable because it was human. But because it was human it remained incomprehensible to D'Annunzio.

The Fiume expedition was launched some months after the war. We have seen that it was conceived and prepared by others. D'Annunzio joined it only at the last moment.* But Fiume very soon became *his* affair—and something very different from what the Italians had imagined it would be, including those who had persuaded D'Annunzio to accompany them.

Fiume had become the symbol of victory for a great many Italians irritated by difficulties which they attributed to blindness of the Allies. From that point they quickly went to extremes: for them the loss of Fiume meant a jeopardized victory. We have already seen how this had come about. Sonnino who, though endowed with worthy qualities, had not an atom of the prophetic vision of Mazzini, had by his Treaty of London left Fiume to a Croatia which, he had never doubted, would become an integral part of a State reuniting all the South Slavs formerly subject to Austria-Hungary. Austria herself, he was thoroughly convinced, would be defeated, but only up to a certain point. He did not exclude the idea—so I gathered from my conversations with him—that the Croatia which he foresaw in the Treaty of London might preserve bonds, at least dynastic ones, with a Hapsburg monarchy emerging alive from the conflict. But the city of Fiume that

* Chapter **XXXI.**

Sonnino was leaving to the Croats was incontestably Italian. The question of Fiume was not therefore propounded for Italians in the same terms as the Dalmatian question, whereas, with regard to Dalmatia, there was from the outset a current of opinion counseling against annexation. Everyone was in agreement on an Italian Fiume, beginning with Bissolati, even though he had from the beginning of the war constituted himself the champion of a policy of friendship and understanding with the Slav nationalities.

D'Annunzio saw in Fiume only a means, an instrument; just as all his life he had adopted the most contradictory ideas from contemporary writers, seeking only material for his poetry. But, more than that, Fiume became his stage.

It is not at all surprising that the new generation whose intellectual development had been retarded by the war—as happened everywhere in Europe—should have been dazzled by the artificial brilliancy of a stage-setting which for them became an epic reality.

The elements comprising the little D'Annunzian world of Fiume were far from being homogeneous. First, there were the decadents who since before the war had recognized themselves in D'Annunzio: the men avid of pleasures, adventures and conquests. Besides these, coarser but more real, were the men who had risked their lives, won their officers' insignia in the war and found it hard to return to their humble, badly paid civilian tasks. (It may be recalled that several revolutions in ancient Rome were started by legionnaires returned from distant wars.) The last, but not the least, element comprised a great number of adolescents of the middle classes who for four long years had heard people talking about the war and who, at seventeen or eighteen, found a small but picturesque one within their own range.

All those elements quickly realized that it was all theatrical; D'Annunzio did not lack a certain quality of magnetic attraction for the masses, but the moment he attempted to exercise it on individuals his moral poverty at once became apparent, as it did in the numerous letters he sent me at Rome from Fiume. These missives, all in extraordinary handwriting in India ink, on sheets of paper as large as diplomas, with engraved letter-heads of a cobweb torn by a dagger, in turn promised me glory (immortalization in his odes) if I would aid him in his plans, or threatened me with a distant and veiled menace of violent death. Such wretched stuff sometimes made me even doubtful of his physical courage; for one attributes to others emotions he feels himself. And actually it was his letters—those of a writer-bravo of the Aretino type—that made me certain he would not for one second resist the cannons of the fleet when I persuaded Giolitti that the comedy of Fiume had lasted too long for Italy's honor.

A loyal follower of D'Annunzio and head of his publicity bureau, Pedrazzi, sketched in his Italian newspaper, on December 24, 1920, immediately after leaving Fiume, a fairly exact picture of the situation, though a trifle too flattering to the poet:

"To support D'Annunzio there are no longer any but valorous and decorated or mutilated young officers, of great heart and ardent faith, but men in whom the sense of a personal responsibility is lacking. . . . For them the warrior life has become a need, and surprise assaults a habit. To conclude the expedition meant to put an end to the delightful way of living enjoyed by rebels—somewhat laughable perhaps—still, a life of rebels, made up of songs, parades, voting assemblies, military festivities, a mixture of war and *opéra bouffe.*

"This atmosphere of generous and hare-brained juvenility has certainly unsettled D'Annunzio's mind and seduced him. Everyone shouts to him that he is a victor; but he thinks himself vanquished. Fiume is victorious and not he. His dream was vaster, too vast. Having come to Fiume to save the city, he has gradually become attached to the exercise of dictatorship, not through personal ambition but for the good he hoped to do. His vision, reaching further, passes the frontiers of the Adriatic. He dreams of noble crusades everywhere, wherever there are rebels in the world."

As everywhere and always, young men of pure and idealistic spirit were to be found in the adventure. But all of them became to a greater or less degree disillusioned with it; and, one after another, saddened as one is after a moral disillusionment, they quitted Fiume.

As for the Fiume population itself, it was profoundly Italian in the old municipal way, with passionate loves and hatreds.

At first it gave an enthusiastic reception to the man who had sworn to protect it against all danger of Slav domination. Nevertheless, when they realized in Fiume that the Italian and municipal interests of the city had been safeguarded by a formula (mine) which guaranteed its Italian character while making it independent, yet connected again with Italy, and with its economic future firmly based on a development of the port entrusted to an Italo-Yugoslav-Fiumean Commission, the application of my project was generally desired. However, everyone was now fettered by the dictatorial power that had been given to D'Annunzio by all parties when he first arrived.

And then occurred what later happened on a much greater scale in Italy with regard to Fascism: people talked two languages, one of them covert, but revealing that at last everyone understood who were the real protectors of Fiume; the other, a bombastic and pompous theatrical language, which continued to laud in a high-flown style what they cursed in their most intimate and secret conversations. The consequence was that Fiume, which, like Trieste,* could only prosper through a cordial understanding with the Slav hinterland, became the pathetic ruin it was under Fascism, with empty harbor and grass-grown docks. There was likewise a lowering of the moral strength of its inhabitants, obliged as they were, under the domination of gangs foreign to their mentality, not only to conceal their true feelings, but also to laud and adore idols which, after a brief period of exaltation, very soon became repugnant to them.

This was the dress rehearsal for what was to occur in a much vaster theater, the whole of Italy, for all the stage tricks D'Annunzio had displayed in Fiume were repeated in Italy. To begin with, the dialogue between the leader and the mob, and the clarion questions:

"For whom the future?
"For whom Italy?

* Some industrial circles of Trieste made the mistake at the time of D'Annunzio's adventures of believing that they should help every move that would destroy forever the possibility of any future competition by the port of Fiume. They did not perceive that the policy of understanding with the Slav world would have brought advantages to both ports. The policy of hatred that they favored, it is true, destroyed Fiume, but it also prevented Trieste's continuing economic progress.

"For whom the power and the glory?" To which the delirious mob shouted:

"For us!"

And with such stuff went all the grandiloquent utterances that induced foreigners to say that the Italians had lost their sense of the ridiculous; for foreigners were unable to realize that the Italian people were silent and that the cries were uttered only to cover their silence.

An Italian critic, Enrico Thovez, wrote a book proving that D'Annunzio had copied entire pages from foreign writers. The poetic imagination of D'Annunzio was so rich that doubtless the accusation did not trouble him in the least.

Yet D'Annunzio himself was the victim of the most gigantic plagiarism ever seen. For the whole Fascist conquest of Italy was simply a literal and enormously enlarged copy of the turbulent poem that the Fiume adventure had been for D'Annunzio.

D'Annunzio has been accused of cowardice for having quitted Fiume the moment Italian battleships, on my orders, fired salvos at his residence. No indeed, D'Annunzio was no coward. He would have stayed, he would even have loved to perish "buried under the ruins of Fiume" as he had threatened me in the past that he would do, had he felt that the citizens of Fiume were still with him. But he knew that they had reached the conclusion that my solution was a thousand times better for them than his speeches. Hence his loss of courage. On his departure from Fiume he was heard to mutter: "These people aren't worth dying for," another proof that he had only loved Fiume so long as Fiume consented to be his platform.

What was truly miserable was the lingering end of D'Annunzio in his gilded but enforced residence on Lake Garda. Mussolini's prisoner, yes, but lord of a princely domain, where he spent his last years whetting atrocious epigrams against the Duce and Fascism. However, he also gave out for press publication dithyrambic phrases for the regime whenever he was ordered to do so by the man in Rome who sent him his monthly allowance.

XXXIII

D'ANNUNZIO'S SUCCESSOR: MUSSOLINI

THOSE ITALIANS FOR WHOM FASCISM REPRESENTED A THEATrical denial of our finest moral traditions, and those who suffered in the prisons and the penal islands to which they were relegated have not for the most part paused to discriminate between what was good and what was bad in Fascism. In their eyes all that at any time was called Fascist is, and will remain, abominable. And yet the truth is that the origin of the movement that subsequently called itself Fascism was not devoid of a certain idealistic ardor for renovation. At one time it could even be hoped that such a movement might have some value in a country where the masses, save for those who had joined the Socialist Party, did not give a hundredth part of the interest and perspicacity they devoted to municipal affairs to the direction of the nation's political life—an inevitable result of historic centuries during which only the Communes were independent and Italian.

Millions of soldiers, returned to their firesides after four years of war, felt as never before the desire to become an active element in the national life. The establishment of the Popular Party gave the Catholic masses the framework and the leaders they needed. On the other hand, elements imbued with theories of sudden and turbulent revolt, overexcited by the war, joined the old Socialist Party, which was spineless enough to allow itself to be submerged by this new wave, not realizing its transitory nature. The newcomers stamped on the party a chaotic revolutionary character, giving it all the disadvantages of a revolutionary movement without having either its faith or strength. Others who became Fascists were men, equally unnerved, who could not resign themselves to denying or forgetting the sufferings and sacrifices of the war.

The Fascist program as it was drafted in 1919 was nothing but a collection of commonplaces and demagogic infantilism. Still, it would be unjust to judge by that indigestible gibberish the young combatants who at the start rallied to the *fasci*. The simple truth is that Italian youth was tired of the old formulas, and if chance had placed at its head someone who, even at the price of mistakes and illusions, had tried to open up a new, sincere and honest trail, the movement could have been useful, as all that is living and true always is. Salvemini, Lussu, Michele Torraca might have been, or might have eventually become, invaluable leaders. Unfortunately it was Mussolini who carried the day, and these young men who anxiously awaited a true and living watchword received from him, whom chance alone had made their leader, nothing more than the program which it is apropos to present here entire, the more so as it has now become unfindable, and official historians of the Fascist movement have taken good care not to reproduce it.

It constitutes, just as it is, the best portrayal I know of the intellectual and cultural value of its author, Benito Mussolini, less than four years before his coming to power. Here it is:

"1.—A Constituent National Assembly will proceed, as the Italian Section of the Constituent International Assembly of the peoples, to a radical transformation of the political and economic bases of the life of the community.

"2.—Proclamation of the Italian Republic. Decentralization of the executive power; autonomous administration of the regions and Communes entrusted to their respective legislative organization. Sovereignty of the people, exercised by universal suffrage of all citizens of the two sexes; the people retaining the initiative of referendum and veto.

"3.—Abolition of the Senate. Abolition of the political police. The Magistrature to be elected independently of the executive power.

"4.—Abolition of all titles of nobility and all orders of knighthood.

"5.—Abolition of obligatory military service.

"6.—Liberty of opinion and conscience, of religion, of assembly, of the press.

"7.—A system of education in the schools, common and professional, open to all.

"8.—The greatest attention to social hygiene.

"9.—Suppression of incorporated joint-stock companies, industrial or financial. Suppression of all speculation by banks and stock exchanges.

"10.—Control and taxation of private wealth. Confiscation of unproductive income.

"11.—Prohibition of work of children under the age of sixteen. An eight-hour work day.

"12.—Reorganization of production on a cooperative basis and direct participation of the workers in the profits.

"13.—Abolition of secret diplomacy.

"14.—An international policy based on the solidarity of the peoples and on their individual independence within the framework of a federation of States."

Ten months later, at the time of the occupation of the factories in Lombardy and Piedmont, Mussolini made a pronouncement in the same style. In a speech delivered September 20, 1920, at the Politeama Rossetti at Trieste he declared:

"I not only accept the unprecedented control of the factories, but their social-cooperative management as well. . . . I demand that the factories increase their production. If this is guaranteed to me by the workers, in place of the industrialists, I shall declare without hesitation that the former have the right to substitute themselves for the latter."

In the early days of the ephemeral occupation of the factories, he wrote in his newspaper above his own signature: "The workmen should not abandon their positions before having obtained guarantees."

Indeed, one must not exaggerate the proportion of sincerity existing in the declarations of a man consumed by the will to arrive and, consequently, ready to flatter and follow by turns the most turbulent movements. But with this reservation, his sincerity when he uttered and wrote these declarations is admissible. Whence the conclusion must be drawn that it was rather despite himself that the Fascist movement, which had begun with a revolutionary and syndicalist ferment, ceased to have that character.

The first authentic Fascists thought themselves disciples of Sorel. Remote from these, a different group had its origin in another bookish source, but in the latter case the connection was with Maurras, again a Frenchman, and these were the Nationalists. The two groups, while reciprocally despising each other, were united by the common basic ideology of violence; and above all by their identical need of making a way for themselves. The Fascist-Nationalist amalgam emerged from this combination with its double face of subversiveness and "conservative" reaction.

On their side, the great industrialists of Lombardy and the big landowners of Emilia and Tuscany, concerning themselves still less with formulas, had not awaited the fusion to try to enlist in their service Fascist organizations of the various regions. These organizations needed money; nothing pleased them more than to continue fighting. Bolshevism was pointed out to them as the common enemy. And as the name Bolshevism and the thing itself were equally detestable to the immense majority of Italians, it proved sufficient; the more so, since the program of 1919 had been forgotten by all the Fascists. It had been replaced by a theory of "dynamic action," a convenient one to excuse any and all about-faces.

Hence, even the Fascists in whom there remained a modicum of idealism changed, though hardly conscious of it, into private police in the pay of vested interests. What accentuated this metamorphosis was the fact that most of the industrialists knew very well that the Bolshevist danger no longer existed, and even that, despite the transitory disorders of the immediate post-war period, it never had existed. Mussolini himself had written in his newspaper, the *Popolo d'Italia,* in July, 1921: "To maintain that the Bolshevist danger still exists in Italy is equivalent to mistaking one's own fears for reality. Bolshevism has been destroyed."

Using the bugbear of Bolshevism, the industrialists were actually trying to destroy the Socialist spirit and even the socializing and reformative spirit which, thanks primarily to what amounted to a tacit cooperation between Giolitti and the moderate Socialists, had been gradually developing during the first twenty years of this century. Made fearful by the violences and excesses of the extreme elements of Socialism in 1919 and 1920, the industrialists had quite forgotten that it was thanks primarily to Giolitti's policy, semi-revolutionary in appearance but in fact conservative, that Italy had attained a prosperity and a well-being of which her tormented history affords few other examples.

Mussolini submitted to the metamorphosis (of Fascists become "company" policemen) rather than approved of it. Personally, he had tried to cash in on his Fascists in a diametrically opposite way: by a combination, which never came to pass, between all the moderate Socialists, the *Popolari* (Christian Democrats) and the Fascists, a combination from which a coalition government of the three groups would emerge. Later, he even protested against Fascism as "tyrannical, and subservient to private interests." But alas, as the Fates had decided, he belonged to the company of leaders who do not lead but follow.

When Fascism came into power, its leader still followed, but in my opinion he followed the day-by-day developments rather than a preconceived reactionary program which those who had financed Fascism were determined to impose. In the camp of the financiers, just as everywhere, there were far fewer carefully thought-out plans than the Socialists supposed. Dominating everything was a blind solicitude for immediate interests, even though that meant compromising interests that were permanent, vaster, and far more worthy of being defended.

If Fascism transformed itself from a regime of violence into a police government, it was due to the fact that the leaders of the new State sensed a spirit of general discontent, even among those who had financed their march. What later happened in Germany, where the Nazis were first paid and then feared by the industrialists, helps to make the phenomenon which had previously manifested itself in Italy easier to understand.

In this movement Mussolini was an essential focusing-point and at the same time largely responsible for the nature of these developments.

Some day, when time shall have allayed hatreds, it will perhaps be realized that the orgy of bloody brutality, which for years made a prison of Italy, and the insane war of 1940, both had their origin, in great part, in an almost unique case in history, that is, the pathetic disproportion between the legend artificially created about a man raised to the rank of a demigod and the actual capacities of this same man. By what I know personally about him, by his naive certainties as regards foreign affairs as he expressed them to me during our con-

versations in November, 1922, I am tempted to believe that
when Mussolini came to power, armed with the encyclopedic
knowledge (drawn from the dictionary) that every mediocre
journalist possesses, he was convinced he could easily solve all
the problems about which he had written a thousand times
with so much assurance in his facile articles. When he discovered the truth about the complexity of political phenomena,
and about himself, he had already become the wretched prisoner of the myth woven about him. Probably Cola di Rienzo
and Masaniello, who—leaving Mussolini's crimes out of the
comparison—were analogous phenomena of demagogic dictators born of the fantasy of an intoxicated populace, went
through identical crises of overt presumption and secret depression.

When the comedy turned into a tragedy, Fascism ceased to
be a power. Though the Fascists exercised authority with
flamboyant language their hearts were trembling. The Chinese, who have experienced everything, have a perfect ideo-
gram for that species of ruler: a man mounted on a tiger.

The transformation of the primitive Fascist regime into a
police government had its origin in that terror-haunted state
of mind; but even in their police government the Fascists ex-
hibited an utter lack of originality. There was hardly a single
Fascist law or "idea" which was not a copy—only worsened,
which is the forte of all imitators—of French legislation under
Napoleon III. Napoleon III retained the appearance of a
parliament while depriving it of all power; and so did Fascism.
In France the decree-law of May 25, 1852, created the omnipotence of the prefects, destroying the various local auton-
omies; Fascism did likewise. In 1855 French mayors were
appointed by the prefects; similarly Fascism appointed the
podestà to take the place of the *sindaci* elected by the people.
Napoleon III got rid of the Republican magistrates, and an
identical law enabled the Fascist government to expel the independent magistrates. Higher education, the power of the
press, one could almost say everything, was gagged in Italy by
decree-laws which were only bad copies, and worsened to an
extreme, of analogous provisions of the French Second Empire.

The psychology of the two regimes was identical in more

than one respect. The silence imposed on the nation was broken as frequently as possible by grand spectacles, by expositions, by commemorations aiming at exciting the public's imagination while keeping the critical spirit inactive. The affirmations were identical. "For a long time," declared Louis Napoleon in 1852, "society has been like a reversed pyramid standing on its point; I have replaced the pyramid on its base." Between 1923 and 1940 Mussolini repeated the same words a hundred times.

However, since nothing in history recurs in an identical way, there were also marked differences. The chief one was that the Second Empire, functioning under the shadow of a great name, in the midst of a material prosperity which was not a bluff, could trust in its police alone; whereas, under Fascism, recourse had constantly to be made to the reserves of the lawless element of social life which, for the first time, were in the service of a government, instead of constituting that turbid underworld always ready to join in rebellious movements, even the most idealistic ones.

Most pitiable of all those who have written about Mussolini are those who have cited the influence of Machiavelli, Nietzsche and Pareto (whose pupil Mussolini pretended to have been at Lausanne), or of Sorel. Mussolini never read them, for throughout his life he never read anything but newspaper articles.

The fact that Mussolini has hated the writer of these pages more than most of his adversaries is unquestionably due to the deep pity—authentic pity—I have always shown when speaking or writing about him. How often did I say, and in vain, to Poincaré and Austen Chamberlain and, later, also in vain, to the unfortunate Daladier in 1939, that foreign statesmen with their want of imagination and lack of courage would be the veritable authors of the war they were all fearing. During those years no one in France, in England or in the United States wanted to see clearly. And to think that poor Mussolini, at the very summit of his power, sent to me as his envoy one of my colleagues in the Italian Senate, a member of the Sicilian aristocracy, to offer me the assurance that my estates would not be confiscated if only while continuing to condemn Fascism, I would from time to time parenthetically remark in my books and articles: "But it cannot be denied that Mussolini has genius. . . ."

The following incident has, I think, its place here, though no glory is due me for not having taken it seriously. It happened after my resignation from the Embassy at Paris in November, 1922, when I had my final talk with Mussolini, then dictator in Rome. I had been declining, one after another, all his offers when he rose and said: "But don't you know that I can have you placed against a wall and shot?" It was ironically pleasing to see how the menacing Mussolini was taken aback by my rejoinder, as I smiled and said, "And afterwards?"

Alfred de Vigny would have understood. Vigny, who invented a poor weak pope, confronted by Napoleon, exclaiming: *"Commediante!"* (Comedian) and *"Tragediante!"* (Tragedian). And still more in the scene where the French poet made an officer of modest rank who had spoken with Talma's pupil say: "And yet I felt that here was a spurious and usurped force. I rebelled, I cried: 'He lies! His attitude, his voice, are only an actor's pantomine, a miserable parade of sovereignty whose vanity he must know. It is impossible that he believes in himself so sincerely! He prevents all of us from raising the veil, but he sees himself naked beneath it. And what does he see? A poor ignorant wretch, like all of us, and under all that disguise the weak human creature.' "

When one thinks of the obsequiousness of all the European statesmen in their dealings with this miserable Mussolini, thundering and parading, one should be able to find some excuse for those Italians who were confused by such homages.

And one can almost feel a sense of pity for the stupid and strutting *"Tragediante."*

THE BONOMI CABINET

THE CHAMBER, AS CONSTITUTED BY THE ELECTIONS OF APRIL, 1921, met on June 11 to hear the speech of the Crown. A general discussion lasting several days ensued, ending with a vote of confidence in the Giolitti Cabinet, giving it a 34-vote majority. The Socialists had reproached Giolitti for the blood shed by Fascist bands in all the cities of Italy, and the Fascists had complained of my foreign policy. Proof of the disingenuousness of their criticisms was made evident by the fact that they did not dare to attack my conception of a foreign policy which was at once European and Italian, confining themselves to assailing me with regard to episodes of no importance, such as the problem of Port Baross, the little town near Fiume. Giolitti, however, decided to resign, not because the majority was not considerable, but because he knew that some days later the *Popolari* would vote against the bill by which he intended to demand full powers for the reform of the bureaucracy; and there was no possible majority without the support of the Popular Party.

The King did not urge Giolitti to withdraw his resignation. Giolitti suggested as new Prime Minister either De Nicola, then President of the Chamber, or Bonomi, who had been our colleague in the Cabinet.

The King chose Bonomi, toward whom he had always felt well disposed—as far as he was capable of any feelings of this kind. What specially pleased the King about Bonomi was his simplicity, his desire for self-effacement, his efficiency devoid of all pretentiousness.

The history of the Bonomi Cabinet of June, 1921 to February, 1922 could only be the history of the conflict of Fascism with the social order and the authority of the State, with a government which always tried to do its duty but which was often badly served, and sometimes betrayed, by machinations within the administration.

The first months of the Bonomi administration comprised one of the periods when Mussolini's stock sank lowest among his friends. He was reproached for his favorable attitude toward the Treaty of Rapallo and his hostility toward D'Annunzio. He felt obliged to deliver a long speech to absolve himself. "In November, 1922," he declared, "it was unthinkable to consider a revolution to annul a treaty of peace—that of Rapallo—which, good or bad, had been accepted by ninety-nine out of a hundred Italians. . . . Nor could one bottle oneself up at Fiume, a peripheral point of the nation in an armed opposition to the treaty." To those who were reproaching him for not having unleashed a revolutionary movement to save Fiume, Mussolini replied:

"The Combat Fascists never promised to start a revolution in Italy in case of an attack against Fiume, especially after the disloyalty of Millo.* Personally I never wrote, or had D'Annunzio advised, that the revolution in Italy depended on my whim. Revolution is not a Jack-in-the-box whose spring can be released at pleasure. . . . History, a collection of past events, has little to teach mankind; but chronicle, that history which unrolls before our eyes, should be more profitable. Now, chronicle tells us that revolutions are made *with* the army, not *against* the army; *with* arms, not *without* arms; with organized groups, not with amorphous masses assembled in meetings. Revolutions succeed when the majority crowns them with a halo of sympathy; lacking this, they congeal and fail. In the tragedy of Fiume there was no defection of the Army and Navy. There was a sort of last-moment Fiumean revolutionary spirit which, however, never became clearly defined: it ranged from a few Anarchists to a few Nationalists. According to certain "emissaries" it would be feasible to combine the devil and holy water, the nation and the anti-nation, Misiano and Delcroix. I, who spurn every kind of Bolshevism, if I were forced to choose one, would take Moscow's and Lenin's, if only because its proportions are gigantic, barbarous, universal. . . . Therefore, an episode of civil war, like that of Fiume, could not have been liquidated by launching a vaster war at such a moment, and no one is capable of prolonging or artificially creating limited and over-extended historical conditions."

* Chapter XXXV.

There was nothing behind these utterances but an ardent desire to realize some personal profit, to insert himself among the candidates for a portfolio, whence arose the attempt at a "pacification pact," which of course Bonomi favored.

An incident at Sarzana on November 21, 1921, showed even to the blindest that Fascism was nothing but a gigantic bluff and that Bonomi could govern with more moral force than the Undersecretary of State Corradini, to whom Giolitti had, unfortunately, left the daily task of the repression of Fascism. At Sarzana, for the first time after months of tolerance, a Fascist "expedition" composed of five hundred armed riff-raff was annihilated by the calm resoluteness of a single captain of the Carabineers supported by only eight Carabineers and three soldiers. The five hundred Fascists—who had come from neighboring cities in trucks—occupied the gendarmerie of Sarzana and explained to the Captain that they were going to invest the city and liberate the ten Fascists arrested as the result of bloody outbreaks of violence in Lunigiana. While the Fascist leader—who was none other than Amerigo Dumini, three years later the assassin of Matteotti—parleyed with the Captain, the gang followed its customary tactics. It feigned impatience, shouted: *"Basta, basta, non più chiacchiere"* (Enough, enough, no more chattering) and pressed forward threateningly toward the Captain and his eleven men, who without hesitation fixed their bayonets. One of the Fascists then fired a revolver at them. At this point the Captain and his men, obedient only to the law, fired on the brawlers; two or three Fascists fell; the five hundred heroes, who had become accustomed to see force yield to them with a smile, lost their heads and fled. A Fascist "officer" wrote in his report of the incident: "The Sarzana affair is only a normal fact; it was bound to happen as soon as Fascism was faced by people determined to resist. . . . These squads, too accustomed to defeating an enemy who almost invariably fled or reacted feebly, could not, or did not know how to, hold their ground."

But that was not all. The population of Sarzana had been told by migratory field workers of Fascist columns firing at their train as it approached the city. As soon as the Fascist exploit became known, armed groups from the surrounding countryside, aided by exasperated peasants, hunted down the Fascists, who left half a score of their dead hanged on trees or drowned in swamps, as well as several dozen wounded. The police authorities again intervened, but this time to save the retreating Fascists from popular fury. At the time I was living on an estate belonging to my family not far from Sarzana, and everywhere I saw only delighted peasants wondering, asking, if at last *"la pace"*—peace—had been restored.

After the Sarzana incident Mussolini sent to Bonomi his most abject assurances that he wanted only order and conciliation. He was afraid.

The "Conciliation Pact" was signed August 2, 1921. Mussolini appeared to act in good faith, but the pact was violently attacked by Dino Grandi and his followers who were in the pay of the ferocious landowners of the Po Valley. Grandi had with him a majority of the *squadristi* (combat squads), and Mussolini, as usual, rallied without delay to the side of the strongest. Bonomi failed in his efforts to bring back a modicum of tranquillity to the country.

By their actions the Communists aided Fascism. Not that they were not fighting Fascism, but for them everything was Fascism: the State, democracy, the middle classes, even—and especially—the Socialists, who had remained liberal. The Socialists, in a sudden access of common sense and dignity, organized the *Arditi del Popolo,* the Sarzana incident having proved that only the fear of beatings would make the Fascist *squadristi* flee. The Communist Party forbade its members to join the *Arditi del Popolo,* an organization, it declared, that is "a maneuver of the bourgeoisie." Communism wanted the destruction of Fascism, but on a single condition, that Communism should remain the sole master. Nothing could better serve the Fascist cause.

Mussolini, seeing that the Communists prevented the union of anti-Fascist forces, that the Socialist leaders remained weak and divided, and—above all—that the violent element of Fascism alone had the confidence of the recruiters of *squadrismo,* suddenly decided to become the most violent of all. Having heard the rumor that Bonomi had decided to dissolve the combat squads by a decree, he had the heads of the party vote the following order:

"To all the Sections of the Party! To all the Combat Squads!

"It is rumored in the press that there will be an early offen-

sive of the Government against Fascism. . . . Sections of the
Party and Combat Squads form an indivisible whole. Dating
from December 15, 1921, all those inscribed in the Sections
will become part of the Combat Squads. . . . Dissolution of the
Combat Squads will thus become impossible, if the Government shall not have, previously, declared the National Fascist
Party as a whole unlawful."

The challenge had been given. The Fascist Party should
have been dissolved, since the entire party had joined the combat squads. But the Government dared not accept the challenge. At that period I often saw Bonomi in his modest
apartment in the Piazza della Libertà. Personally he was
ready to act, to take the risk. But he was head of a Coalition
Cabinet and had too few adherents. On February 16, 1922,
the Bonomi Cabinet was reversed in the Chambers: Socialists
and Fascists united their votes against Bonomi. Federzoni's
Nationalists staged demonstrations at Rome and Florence in
front of the headquarters of the Army Corps with cries of
"Long live the Dictatorship!"

Unfortunately the ministerial crisis, from which the Facta
Cabinet emerged, was the longest Italy had ever known since
1848.

The middle classes saw in all this a proof of the failure of
Parliament.

The satisfaction evinced by the Fascist leaders after a few
days of the Facta Government gave proof that the Bonomi
Government had always done its duty or had tried to do it. It
was only with the advent of Facta that "justice" began to function in a unique way. It is a matter of record that during the
early months of 1922 at Rome, Vercelli, Florence and a hundred other places in Italy all the Fascists accused of murder
and "personal violence" were acquitted and carried off in
triumph by their friends. In the rare cases in which justice,
ashamed, dared not render a verdict of acquittal, the accused
were granted provisional liberty to leave for another city where
they were safe from any pursuit.

With Facta, Fascism was already tacitly in power everywhere.

PART EIGHT: FASCISM

XXXV

THE FACTA CABINET

IT WAS NOT MERELY THAT FACTA, FROM THE VERY BEGINNING of his Government, was an agent in the service of Fascism—was a man of nothing. This sort of thing has since occurred more than once in parliamentary regimes: the President of the French Republic, Lebrun, was neither more nor less a traitor than Facta when, in 1940, he only opposed Pétain's maneuvers with futile tears, and sanctioned the defeat of France. On his entrance into the Inferno, Dante paused first before the flock of cowards *"che mai non fur vivi"* (who were never alive); but Virgil said: *"Non ragioniam di lor"* (Let's not talk of them) and led him on his way.

Were I to disobey the poet's orders it would be hard for me to find anything to say about the wretched little provincial lawyer who, quite dazed at becoming Prime Minister in February, 1922, passed from bewilderment to bewilderment to the end of October of the same year, when the "march on Rome" took place.

The Facta phenomenon is not unique in politics. Great premiers, reorganizing their followers, or preparing mutual understandings among them, have, in the interim, designated for outward manifestation of power some man as nearly as possible an utter nonentity. But probably no one had ever gone to such an extreme before—and what made it worse was that it should have happened in the turbulent post-war period.

I had been Facta's colleague in the same Cabinet when he was Minister of Finance; but the entire burden of financial

problems was borne by Giolitti and by Meda, the Minister of
the Treasury. Facta therefore had no opportunity to do well
or ill and, with a good bureaucracy helping him, was a good
rather than a bad official. I often saw him at the weekly audi-
ences of the ministers at the Quirinal and at Cabinet councils;
yet I have not the least recollection of even a phrase or of any
remark whatever of this ever-obliging little bourgeois who was
always smiling, always approving. The misfortune of being
chosen to preside over a provisional Ministry befell him by
reason of a parliamentary situation, which some thought would
soon be cleared up by the installation of a new Giolitti Ministry, while others thought the successor would be a Ministry of
All the Talents. Events demonstrated that that sort of game
is sometimes dangerous. Everyone knows what happened. The
Fascists, convinced of the incurable weakness of Facta, met in
congress at Naples. It was the occasion for the rallying of their
legions.

On October 24, 1922, their leader, Mussolini, left them,
going to distant Milan, where he was near the Swiss frontier.
It was safer! One never knows! On the 27th the Fascists intimated to Facta that he had better resign, which he did the
same evening. During the night of the 27th the "march on
Rome" was organized, Mussolini remaining at Milan. Meeting that same night, the resigning Ministry decided to resist,
not on Facta's motion but on that of three other Ministers, the
only resolute members of the entire Cabinet: Amendola, Alessio and Taddei. All the other ministers came over to their
opinion and it was decided to proclaim martial law. On the
morning of October 28 Facta submitted to the King the decree
proclaiming martial law, but returned to the Council, still in
session, with the decree unsigned. The ministers insisted on the
necessity of martial law and again dispatched Facta to the
King. Facta went, but returned a second time without the royal
signature. The news that martial law was not to be put into
effect spread like wildfire and, naturally, the number of Fascists immediately increased. In fact, Fascist numbers increased
so rapidly that on the evening of October 28 Mussolini, who
had not left Milan, was summoned to Rome to form a Ministry.

Did Facta, inconsistent as he was, hide some kind of idea

under his vacillating attitude? Not one historian of the epoch has given any thought to the Facta element, such a nullity was the man. But how often have men who are nullities done a vast amount of harm!

Sturzo, in his *Italy and Fascismo,* a book which in its honesty and serenity is more like the work of a philosopher-historian than the head of a political party, writes: "The position of the Facta Cabinet (in October, 1922) was not only insecure but had become untenable, and the Prime Minister was only awaiting the reopening of the Chamber to tender his resignation—at least so rumor said. . . . Facta secretly worked for the return of Giolitti, but his efforts bore no fruit."

Sturzo attributes the fact that the King had not signed the decree of martial law "to the fear that worse might happen, to the hope of a possible accord, to the weak and equivocal position of the Cabinet which, after having resigned, was deprived of all authority, to the counsel of certain army leaders."

Facta's responsibilities are far more serious. Not only did he not work for the return of Giolitti, but he did all in his power to prevent it. On that point I have the overwhelming testimony of Giolitti, of Taddei, Minister of the Interior with Facta, and others.

Facta, deputy of an electoral district bordering Giolitti's, had all his life been one of the faithful who silently followed the Piedmontese statesman. His only title was: friend of Giolitti. Nothing was more natural, consequently, than the general belief—shared by Sturzo in his book—that Facta "worked for the return of Giolitti."

When, subsequently, with the respect due his age, I expressed my astonishment to Giolitti that he had not thought it his duty in the autumn of 1922 to go to Rome and seize power, he replied to me: "I see clearly now, after what has happened, that I was wrong; but difficulties and obstacles and objections of all kinds that Facta sent me so that I should not budge from Cavour were infinite and inexhaustible; he even telegraphed me once, when I had decided to leave for Rome, that floods had made the trip dangerous." Giolitti added that he had not realized, until too late, that Facta had let himself be persuaded by secret proposals of the Fascists, who flashed before his eyes

the hope of remaining Prime Minister in a new Ministry composed of Mussolini and other Fascists. As a matter of fact
when, on October 28, one of the leaders of his majority advised him to withdraw his resignation, to be in a stronger position, he did nothing about it; and, in the position of having
resigned, he kept on negotiating with the Fascists. He thought
that by continuing in that status he was placing himself in a
better position for a portfolio. I asked Giolitti how a man who
ought to have been devoted to him had come to play such a
double game. Giolitti replied:

"He was not" (he spoke of the man as of the dead, in the
past tense), "he was not a bad man; but vanity had turned
the head of the persons of his entourage, and he yielded to the
entreaties he heard, day and night, to make his way without
me and against me. Poor man. . . ."

It was the vanity of Facta's wife that had turned the miserable man against his former chief. This *Madamina* saw in the
Italian tragedy only an opportunity to become herself the first
lady of Pinerolo and perhaps of all Piedmont, in place of
Giolitti's wife, who had always unconsciously crushed her with
her intellectual and moral superiority.

But, later on, I learned from Taddei that another feminine
influence had led Facta astray; one of those numerous titled
and "phony" titled adventuresses, who subsequently were all
on the Fascist payroll—assigned to deceive foreigners—had
shammed falling in love with the little provincial lawyer become Prime Minister; that the latter had fallen into the trap;
that the adventuress guided him in everything, and that she
had been instructed and paid by Mussolini to persuade Facta
that the head of Fascism appreciated him highly, and would
have need of his name and experience for the first Fascist
Cabinet which would inevitably be formed.

Taddei likewise confided to me that, fearful that such stupidity and irresponsible conduct might develop into treason, he
thought it his duty to go to the King and tell him about his
doubts; that the King burst into laughter at the idea of the
good Facta having become a Don Juan, but abruptly changed
the conversation and dismissed him, almost at once, with the
most marked coldness. The King's line of conduct and defense

was always the same: "I don't want to know, I don't *have* to know."

Facta's stupidity and levity became treason the night of October 28, 1922, on the two occasions when the Council of Ministers sent him to the King to have him sign the state of siege that the Cabinet had unanimously voted after listening to the argument of the three Ministers who remained conscientious with regard to their duty, Alessio, Amendola and Taddei. Both times Facta did submit the decree to the King, but both times adding all kinds of other considerations intended to induce the King not to sign—such considerations as the lack of authority of a resigned Cabinet (and that Facta himself had wished to remain in the status of a resigner); horror at the blood that would be shed; reasons for hoping that Mussolini would prove reasonable, and so on.

The King has been culpable of so many faults and criminal complicities that there is no reason to hide that—being what he was—the responsibility for the non-signature of the decree of a state of siege weighs more heavily on Facta than on him.

Being the kind of person I know him to be, I am convinced he would have signed if an energetic prime minister had instructed him that it was his duty, as constitutional king, to sign.

Queen Margherita, who had no love for her son (his physical defects wounded her vanity immeasurably), was not far from the truth when, talking with my wife one day, she exclaimed: "Victor believes and obeys only Elena and the Prime Minister in office, whoever he happens to be."

On an occasion analogous to that of October 28, 1922, I myself observed that the King dared not disobey a responsible Minister. D'Annunzio, master of Fiume, had obtained from Admiral Millo, stationed at Zara, a promise to bring his squadron to Fiume and recognize him as leader. A loyal and far-sighted officer, in whom I had full confidence, Colonel Cattaneo, flew from Zara to Rome to warn me that Millo had been persuaded by D'Annunzio who, Millo believed, was working for the Duke d'Aosta—D'Annunzio having so persuaded him. Cattaneo told me there was not a moment to lose.

I went immediately to the King, and in the vehicle that conveyed me to the Villa Savoia, a few kilometers from Rome, I wrote a brief letter that the King could copy in his own hand, reminding Millo of his soldier's oath of loyalty to him—no mention of anything else. The King hesitated, quibbled: "I'm willing to do anything you ask me, but if I am not listened to, if I am scoffed at, won't it be still worse?"

I objected that Fiume was the deed of an adventurer, but that the history of Italy had not yet been stained by *pronunciamientos.* . . . As he continued to dodge the issue, I rose and said: "Sire, if we are on the way to dishonor and disaster, which of us two will go before a High Court of Justice, you or I?" Recalled to his constitutional duty the King, pale with rage (which did not trouble me in the least), answered only: "Give it to me."

Docilely he copied it; and three hours later the letter was in the hands of Admiral Millo, who never again thought of failing in his duty. How could one doubt that Facta would have obtained a similar result had he wished it? The more so since, at that time, the King had a deep antipathy for Mussolini and for a kingly reason—a dynastic reason: the adventurer was flirting with the Duke d'Aosta, giving him hopes of the throne if. . . .

When, several days before the "march on Rome," the Government made the King feel that it would be best to abandon the tranquil refuge of his hunting lodge at Sant'Anna di Valdieri, in the Alps, and return to Rome, the King obeyed, as always. At the Termini station in the capital, where several ministers received him, as he stepped from the train he turned to the Minister of War, Soleri, and muttered in Piedmontese dialect: "If those fellows come to Rome, I'll take my wife and children and I'll go and settle in Savoy or Nice and live tranquilly."

Nice—Savoy—that meant abdication! It was the dream about which he had often in the past spoken to me as of a happy vision of calm days. Why did he stay on? Partly on account of the pressure of all the appeasers who assured him that Mussolini would very soon "normalize," once he had become Prime Minister. That word—normalization—was the illusion and hope of almost everyone, and continually utilized by Mussolini. Yet another and entirely different reason prevailed with the King: his hatred of his cousins, the Aostas, and his fear lest his departure should leave the way open to the throne for the Duke d'Aosta, whom he despised as the Bourbons in France must have despised the Orléans, ever ready to betray the elder branch of the family. The Duke d'Aosta—who as commanding officer of the IIId Army during the war had gained some popularity in Italy—had contracted a bad attack of thronitis: for two years he did not leave me a moment's peace, trying to persuade me to have him appointed King of Poland, King of Hungary. . . . When I mentioned it to the King he used to mutter: "If it were only *that*. . . ."

Guilty as he later became, it cannot be denied that the poor King was most unlucky in his own family: the Aostas, as false and treacherous as the Orléans (whose blood flowed in their veins) ; the Genoas, near-idiots and deformed; and, later, his own son, more Levantine than Italian; but, above all, on Fascism's attainment to power, the constant and crafty activities of the Queen in favor of the adventure.

Queen Elena in her childhood had seen the little nation, Montenegro, of which her father was sovereign, ruled in the most autocratic manner. Later, sent to St. Petersburg to learn her trade as a young princess, she lived on intimate terms with the group of ultra-reactionary grand dukes and their Montenegrin wives. Married to the Prince of Naples, the future King Victor Emmanuel, the simplicity and good-fellowship of Italian life always remained a closed book for her, as did the traditions and moral strength of some of the great Italian families. When the Fascists appeared—with their clamorous manifestations of respect, but also with their savagery—and when they began to suppress all liberties, she thought, poor woman, that life was at last becoming comprehensible to her. Were it possible to find an excuse for the violation of the most sacred oaths and the most elementary moral duties, the excuse for the King might be a wife who daily whispers: "Don't let it bother you—don't believe in those old Italian liberal fancies; and then, don't forget, they [the Fascisti] are strong; we'd better be friendly with them. . . ."

XXXVI

FASCISM IN POWER

THREE DAYS AFTER HE HAD BECOME PRIME MINISTER, MUS-
solini telegraphed all his *ras* : * "We must preserve discipline
and respect for others; in no case must we infringe on personal
liberties."

He repeated these same instructions several times on other
occasions during the first days of his regime. I am convinced
that he was sincere when he issued them, or that he was
motivated by the prudence required by his new role of statesman. It has too often been forgotten that when he seized the
power after the "march on Rome," he put only four Fascists
in his Cabinet. The ten other ministers, the most important
ones, were not Fascists.

A month later, on November 16, on the reopening of Parliament he had changed his tone: "Within these walls I could
make a bivouac for my men. I could constitute a government
composed exclusively of Fascists. . . ."

What had happened in the interim? The most natural
thing in the world. A fury of Fascist violence had broken out
anew all over the country. Drunk with an easy triumph believed complete, the leaders of Fascist gangs wanted all the
power everywhere. The municipal administrations, which were
all either liberal, or Catholic, or Socialist, were replaced by
Fascists; in the provinces the prefects soon became simply instruments in their hands. Mussolini favored that violence in
order to remain head of a party made up of violent extremists.
The fusion in a single party of the Fascists and the Nationalists, which was announced to the country on February 26,
1923, did the rest.

The Nationalists were few in numbers; they were still the
same little group which, under Federzoni's guidance and sub-
sidized by the metal magnates, had alone dared to declare, in

---

* The Italians called the Fascist heads of the various Italian provinces—men
like Grandi and Farinacci—*ras,* the title of the feudal Abyssinian chiefs.

August, 1914, that Italy ought to enter the war on Germany's and Austria-Hungary's side "because the Entente nations, inasmuch as they were democracies, were doomed to defeat." This small circle of Nationalists constituted a kind of literary club of writers without readers; they had borrowed their theories from classic authors of French and German nationality, a little from Treitschke, a great deal from Maurras. But such as they were, and despite the nebulousness and pretentiousness of their culture, they represented a precious asset for Mussolini, since they supplied him with a "doctrine," and with polemists and literary skill, even though second-rate.

Before the accord with the Nationalists, Mussolini had tried to achieve an understanding with the *Popolari* and the Socialists. In the course of the long talk we had together during the early days of November, 1922, after my resignation from the Paris Embassy—a conversation in the course of which, as noted before,* he attempted again to persuade me to go over to his side—he assured me that his program was and would remain a "democratic program."

Once the accord with the Nationalists had been concluded, however, Mussolini's desire to remain in power by the free consent of the citizens vanished. He fell into the easy way of violent suppression of his adversaries. And the formula which resulted, "the entire power to all the Fascists," made of them an army of occupation in a conquered country.

This was the end of the brief honeymoon of Italian public opinion and Fascism.

I do not know whether the existence of this honeymoon is admitted by anti-Fascist writers who have suffered bastinadoes, castor oil and Fascist prisons. But what I myself saw in the Senate and practically everywhere else forced me to admit that it did exist; there are few men who have had the general good wishes that followed Mussolini at the beginning of his power. And it is of slight importance if these were dictated more by resignation than enthusiasm; the fact remains that they did exist. Those who, like myself, at once declared an insuperable distrust of the adventure have not forgotten the beseechings of "prudence" with which for months they were pursued by their elders.

* Chapter XXXIV.

The conservatives expected of Mussolini a reinforcement of the principle of authority. The *Popolari* relied on their collaboration and their support in order to make use of a man whose strength, they felt, was more apparent than actual or, at least, to neutralize his action. The heads of industry and the great landowners who had supplied the funds for his "march" thought that they had found in him the ever-faithful vassal.

Many, even among those who had recently experienced Fascist violence, hoped that the chief would prove better than his partisans, that he would reduce the latter to obedience. But this general atmosphere of expectant good-will implied one condition—that Mussolini should be a leader who actually led, not one who followed.

A new electoral law (July, 1923) destroyed all possibility of a free atmosphere. Mussolini and his purveyors of formulas, the Nationalists, had understood too well that the brief trial of Fascism accorded by the Italian people had ended, and that free elections would deprive the Fascists of power.

In fact, the new electoral law—which a terrorized Chamber had passed with death in its soul, dominated by the basest of fears, the fear of "the worst"—stipulated: that of the 535 seats, 356 would be reserved to the candidates of the party which received the majority of the votes throughout the country, and that the remaining 33 per cent (179 seats) should be divided between the candidates of the minority parties proportionally to the number of votes they had received.

The elections took place on April 6, 1924. They were what could be expected in a period when the fear of Fascist menace had already, the year before, so far influenced the Chambers that they had voted an electoral law which sealed the death sentence of a free parliament.

Matteotti's assassination was the epilogue of this period.

On the evening of May 30, 1924, after having delivered in the Chamber a speech of absolute opposition—a speech which had disdained all the veils with which even the bravest began to conceal dangerous truths—Matteotti said to his friends with a smile:

"Now you can prepare my funeral oration."

Ten days later, on June 10—only the time needed to organize the plot—he was killed by five Fascists and his body hidden in a wood some leagues from Rome.

The tragedy of his death; the amnesty granted to the instigators of the murder; the scandal of the trial of the murderers, and their liberation two months after their having been found guilty—all that is unforgettable and is a part of Italy's history.

Then occurred one of those sudden and formidable changes of public opinion which, in a free country, would have at once swept away any government. But most of the leaders of the opposition, with only one or two exceptions, did not wish to hasten the crisis. They believed in, and hoped for, slower and less risky successes. The King, it goes without saying, was with them. A few days after Matteotti's assassination two men went to see the King, after consultation with Senator Albertini, who in the *Corriere della Sera* led a courageous campaign against Fascism with Amendola and me. They submitted to the King undeniable proofs that Mussolini had been the inspirer of the assassination. One of these two men was one of my dearest friends, the late Count Campello, who died while still young, and who, hunting frequently with the King, was considered one of his intimates. The King began to leaf through the documents Count Campello had presented to him; but as soon as he apprehended how terrible they were he stopped, grew pale, trembled, pushed the papers back toward his visitors, and rising to dismiss them, stammered: "I am not a judge; these things ought not to be told to me. . . ." He did not realize that at that precise moment, despite himself, he became an accomplice.

The Senate had the courage to discuss the assassination. Mussolini declared with unctuous phrases that he felt the deepest horror for the murder and swore that his own conversion to strictly legal ways was definitive. He had previously given pledges, or what seemed to be pledges, to the men anxious to avoid a conflict; he had yielded the portfolio of the Interior to a Nationalist in whom the King and the Pope thought they could have confidence; he consented that the Fascist militia should take oaths of fealty to the King, like the rest of the Army.

Three senators, Abbiate, Albertini and I, made speeches

insisting on the Government's responsibility for the assassination.

The definition of Fascism that I gave that day remained valid for the entire duration of the adventure:

"Fascism is a state of mind, explicable perhaps from certain points of view, but deprived of any positive system of thought; and, by that very fact, destined to be able to live exclusively in an atmosphere of uncontested prestige, or in an atmosphere of terror. Fascism will be able to fight many kinds of battles; but there is one battle it can never engage in and that is intellectual criticism."

It is this impossibility that explains everything: from murders to the suppression of the press; from the deportations to the condemnations of the Special Tribunals, and even to wars. For all Mussolini's military enterprises, from Corfu and Albania to Ethiopia and the war against France, Great Britain and the United States, were primarily inspired by the need to dazzle, to keep the Italian people in chains.

The speeches of the opposition senators were listened to in a deathly silence—save for mine, which they kept trying to interrupt—but were in vain. The Government received 225 votes in its favor; only eighteen senators voted with Abbiate, Albertini and me. But nothing would be more mistaken than to conclude from this vote of confidence that only twenty-one senators correctly estimated the situation. Their shouts during my entire speech proved that everyone felt the force of the dilemma I presented to Mussolini, seated opposite me: "Either you wanted the crime, and in that case . . . Or you did not want it, and your most intimate friends committed it in spite of you, and in that case . . . Either guilt or incapacity."

Moreover, a large proportion of the members of Parliament who voted for Mussolini hastened to say, privately, that their votes had been dictated only by the fear of terrible Fascist disorders.

From that day on, only in the embassies of the United States, France and Great Britain was there shown any sympathy for Mussolini. Two days after my speech I met at a dinner the French Ambassador, Barrère, who remarked to me: "Still, you have to concede that you only got eighteen votes." "Don't forget," I replied, "that only five voted against the

Second Empire which gave you Sedan. We are somewhat more numerous and we are risking more; but keep on, all of you, favoring Mussolini and you will see what happens to you some day."

Despite the majority vote that had pleased Barrère, and still more so the United States Ambassador, Mussolini was not sure of himself. He still felt weak, and for some considerable time he did not dare act against the press which, except for the newspapers in his pay, was unanimously hostile to him.

Newspaper man that he was, he felt that the press was his principal danger. On July 10, 1924, he had the King sign a decree giving the Prefects discretionary powers to confiscate any newspaper guilty of having published "false or tendentious news."

Despite the danger—and the real losses they soon had to suffer (confiscation is worse than censorship, for it entails losses of material, work and capital)—almost all the great dailies courageously maintained their open opposition. The public asked for and read no others. Confiscations and threats, legal and illegal, kept on being the order of the day, but the press remained steadfast.

On the reopening of Parliament the former prime ministers, Giolitti, Orlando and Salandra, joined their voices to the chorus of universal reprobation.

The irresistible pressure of public opinion manifested itself when it obliged Giunta, Vice President of the Chamber, and later Undersecretary of the Presidency of the Council, to resign the Vice Presidency under suspicion of having made a homicidal attempt against the deputy, Forni.

The most important newspaper in Rome in those days, the *Mondo,* edited by Alberto Cianca, who later shared my fight against Fascism in France and the United States, published on December 28, 1924, a formidable document in which Cesare Rossi, former chief of Mussolini's press bureau, formally accused him of being the true and principal instigator of the Fascist crimes.

Mussolini, who had for a long time remained undecided, then proceeded to a counter-offensive. He was impelled, some say, by the threats of his lieutenants; or perhaps he was convinced that he had, at last, to risk everything to gain all.

Whatever may be the case, the fact remains that on January 3, 1925, in the Chamber he crossed the Rubicon of fictitious legality and declared that all the crimes were "the result of a predetermined historical, political and moral climate" and that he assumed full responsibility for them. His speech ended with these words: "You may be certain that within forty-eight hours the situation will be completely clarified."

So it was. And the way the situation was clarified is typical of the methods of the Fascist era.

First, the speech was addressed to a Chamber exclusively composed of Fascists, the opposition having remained on the Aventine, where it had retired after Matteotti's murder; and, the moment the gauntlet had been thrown and his Ministerial responsibility for so much bloodshed admitted, Mussolini had nothing more pressing on his mind than prudently to close the Parliament, thereby preventing the opposition from returning to the Chamber and responding to his challenge.

He followed this move by immediately filling Rome and all the principal cities of Italy with gangs recruited from the nation's underworld; for—I should have stated what follows at the beginning of the chapter, so essential is it for a precise comprehension of the Fascist phenomenon—the Fascist movement, with its real or apparent reactionary tendencies, was the only one in history which enrolled under its banner all the disorderly elements of the country. I am well aware—as who is not?—that the purest and most idealistic revolutionary movements—American and French at the end of the eighteenth century, French in 1830, Italian in 1831, all Europe in 1848—included in their ranks, along with heroes and saints, not only malcontents like the Napoleonic officers on half-pay, but also all the social offal of the peoples who, having nothing to lose, are always ready to turn out, and for whom even the most righteous political causes constitute merely a fortunate pretext for immediate disorders.

After Mussolini's declaration of full responsibility in January, 1925, the violences continued, though under another form. The object was to terrorize even passive adversaries, so greatly did the Fascists fear an awakening of the nation's conscience.

It is a long list. First there was Amendola, the young conservative Deputy, who always had hoped that the King would intervene. He was one of the leaders of the Aventine conflict with Mussolini. He was assaulted in July, 1925, in Montecatini, an Italian watering place, and several months later died after indescribable physical sufferings.

Then came the October days of 1925 in Florence. Among the victims was the former Deputy Pilati; he had been severely wounded in the war; his last words to his wife were: "The Austrians at least left me alive; it took Italians to dispatch me."

Several attempted assaults upon Mussolini—real or pretended—provided the pretext for a more and more complete suppression of public liberties. A final "attempt" occurred at Bologna on October 31, 1926: this one was unquestionably made to order. Mussolini was passing by, in one of his parades, when someone fired a shot. A seventeen-year-old youth was immediately killed with a Fascist dagger as being responsible for the attempt. It was never known who had stabbed the boy, and the law never made any serious attempt to find out. Furthermore, an hour after the "attempt" a new offensive of violence was let loose in Italy against all the opposition; a state of war was imposed on the country and, five days later, a most comprehensive law was promulgated that finally gave legal form to the most stifling regime of oppression ever known. The Italians defined the attempt as "providential" in their behind-the-hand whisperings.

On November 25, 1926, the Special Tribunal for the Defense of the State was instituted. Within the control of this Tribunal fell all the "political" crimes: Fascist officers were appointed as judges and the procedure followed was that of a state of siege.

The day after the attempt at Bologna two incidents occurred in the dead of night, at exactly the same hour, which indicated that the violences were all committed on order. A seaside cottage at Forte dei Marmi, which I owned, was set afire; and at Naples, Benedetto Croce's library was pillaged. Everyone knew that Fascists would not have dared make these depredations on the property of two Senators without direct orders from Mussolini.

Later, in 1930 and 1931, men of distinction like Rossi, Bauer and Vinciguerra were condemned to twenty years' imprisonment. But besides these and many other almost equally well-known Italians, thousands of workmen and peasants were condemned to severe punishment: they called them "Communists," which was sufficient to deter the world from protesting. I feel impelled to recall here an anecdote, slight perhaps, but indicative of the ways of the period. My eldest brother Cesare was arrested for having had a mass said in his private chapel for the souls of Italians assassinated by Fascism. Since the entire region respected him for the nobility of his character, and as the Government did not want his arrest to be talked about, the judge went to the old fortress where he had been taken to interrogate him. My brother refused to answer questions: "Say only that I am happy to suffer with so many unfortunates about whom no one ever thinks." The judge expostulated: "But, Count, you know I have a family; tell me something." Then my brother, to satisfy him, said: "Well, say that I'm happy to be in prison in the same fortress in which my grandfather was imprisoned in 1849 by the Germans for having declared himself a partisan of the House of Savoy." The judge hesitated, then brightening, exclaimed: "Well! But that is against the King, not against Mussolini. I believe I can put it in the interrogation, don't you think so?"

Occurrences of this kind could be multiplied by thousands. They are the key to a moral fact never understood abroad: When Mussolini realized his mental incompetence (we have to grant him this merit) to head a great nation, he understood that he could only remain in power by resorting to bluffing, publicity and violence—and that violence within the country had to be the base of the edifice. Consequently he willed it; but Italian functionaries obeyed him only half-heartedly. Thus arose the legend that Fascism was less cruel than Nazism. So it was, but in despite of him; because it lacked the servile sadism of the German officials. But Mussolini, who had a flair for publicity, made use even of this fact, and when he found that he could not always obtain from his Italian functionaries the cruelty that served Hitler so well, he boasted to the world that his regime was not as sanguinary.

The same thing happened in the country's intellectual life. Lack of liberty caused a partial atrophy of the mental life. But, on the whole, Italian culture put up a better resistance than culture in Germany did. Take for example that imposing monumental work, the *Enciclopedia italiana:* published under Fascism, but compiled by Italian scholars who had been brought up in an atmosphere of liberty, its forty great folios are proof of the intellectual value and moral dignity of its authors; and the *Enciclopedia* does great honor to Italian culture. Only some articles on Fascism and others of evident clerical influence smell mustily of the days of slavery.

Under Fascism there were in Italy innumerable manifestations of mental and moral baseness; but, by going too far, they proved how much Fascism was the antithesis to Italy. So it was with the apologies of all the enemies of Italian liberty during the Risorgimento, from the Bourbons of Naples to Solaro della Margherita and as far as the old Neapolitan brigands who were represented as "heroic haters of foreigners, ever ready to answer the call of their kings."

And so it ever is: governing by terror debases equally the governors and the governed. When the masters live in fear, they inspire only fears. It is easy to imagine, even if one has not had the patriotic grief of witnessing them, the consequences of years of a public life based upon denouncers and spies. It must be faced that the Fascist methods that terrorized Italy for twenty years must inevitably have left some degrading traces.

Old Thucydides wrote: "The strength of the city is not in its ramparts, nor in its fleets, but in its men." Ramparts and fleets a dictator can create, but liberty alone makes men.

The Italian people have learned from their tortured history to recover quickly after falls into abysses. The economic ruin of Italy, the destruction of her international position, even the crime of the war against France, Great Britain and the United States may soon become memories of the past. But what counts is the moral life; and the preeminent problem of Italy, after Fascism, is whether in the blood of Italians there will still remain any of the clinging poison of the ever-changing Fascist mental conceptions, or whether the long masquerade—during which all theories in turn were adopted and rejected—will have proved a salutary example, like the drunken slave in Sparta.

XXXVII

THE FIGHT AGAINST FASCISM

IN JANUARY, 1931, AT AN INTERNATIONAL CONFERENCE OF "democratic parties of Christian inspiration" held in Paris, the delegate of the Italian *Popolari* Party (which had already been dissolved by Mussolini) severely criticized the weakness and the hesitations the German Center was then manifesting toward the Nazi Party. Despite the presence of Franz von Papen, who dazzled all the German members of the conference, the Italian delegate concluded with these words: "If you continue on this course you will end as in Italy." One of the German delegates, his vanity piqued, replied: "You forget, Dr. Ferrari, that we are not Italians."

My compatriot retorted smiling: "Oh, I don't forget that: it is just because you are Germans that it will be infinitely worse than in Italy."

Two years later events proved how right Ferrari was. Mussolini required six years to be sure that Italy was enchained; six minutes sufficed Hitler. And even after six years Mussolini and his men continued to be afraid. They were afraid, in spite of having the King in their service; afraid, in spite of a Special Tribunal that in a brief time issued sentences to a total of fifty thousand years of imprisonment at hard labor; afraid, even with all the newspapers in their hands. And they continued to be afraid when the English and French rulers feared them, and American diplomats admired them.

They never stopped being afraid, for a reason that did them honor; they were quite as brutal and corrupt as their Nazi colleagues, but they were a little less stupid. And for a reason that does honor to Italy: at once and everywhere and always adversaries rose up; and, whether they were killed or imprisoned, still others succeeded them. The list of Italians martyred by Fascism proves that political doctrines count for little in comparison with moral character, especially in a struggle rooted in moral repugnance, like that against Fascism. De Bosis was a Monarchist and Gramsci a Communist; Amendola was a Liberal and Schirru an Anarchist; Matteotti was a Socialist and Sozzi a Communist; Don Minzoni a Christian Democrat and Angeloni a Republican; Nello Rosselli was a Democrat, while his brother Carlo was a Socialist tinged with liberalism....

The name of the first martyr, Matteotti, soon became a universal symbol. His assassin, Mussolini, once again satiated his hatred of him when he encouraged—and perhaps compelled—the little mediocre Dollfuss to dissolve and annihilate the Austrian Social Democracy (in so doing Dollfuss passed the death sentence on Austria herself) and to destroy by cannon fire the majestic Matteotti Hof that the Austrian Socialists had erected in Vienna.

I lived with Matteotti in the intimacy of parliamentary sessions, where it is easy to judge a man. It would be impossible for anyone to have cared less about his own popularity, to ignore more completely than he did the gentle art of "making friends"; he did not allow even his comrades to violate his desire for solitude. But everyone felt his burning sense of duty, for which he was generally respected. Though an agnostic, he reminded one of our old Jansenists. His wife, sister of the famous baritone Titta Ruffo, was, on the other hand, an ardent Catholic; his love for her was a proof of his tolerant spirit in matters that had no connection with Fascist corruption and violence.

Matteotti seemed to lack the breadth of philosophic ideas and the intellectual attraction that emanated from another deputy, Amendola, who was also assassinated by Fascism, neither was he endowed with Lauro De Bosis' wealth of talents; but he was the confessor of his faith, and the purest of these martyrs.

Amendola died two years after Matteotti, in 1926, as a result of a Fascist attack led by that Carlo Scorza whom Mussolini, to terrorize the Italians, appointed Secretary General of the Fascist Party in May, 1943. Ten days before the assault Amendola had written: "Many lives must be sacrificed to lay the foundation of the Italy of tomorrow. We give what we are capable of giving, without counting the cost and without regrets." When he died he was only forty-three.

In the conflict without quarter against Fascism that Amendola led from the very first day, he made only one mistake: as long as he found it possible, he believed that the King's eyes would finally open; and that, when it had been proved to him that the Prime Minister was a murderer, the King would unquestionably dismiss him. When I used to say to him, "But that will be an additional reason to make the King fear him," he thought me too skeptical. But the moment he became convinced that the King was a voluntary accomplice he wrote in the newspaper *Il Mondo* an excoriating article on the "little nullity of a King." The paper was immediately seized, but Amendola showed me a copy and said: "It's the only one that matters, for I have a way of having it read to the King this evening."

Amendola has been accused of having been too conservative, yet, in the preface to the volume in which he collected our speeches at the Congress of the National Union, he wrote: "If you want Capitalism, you must run the risk of unions and class conflict; if you want fire, you can't avoid either smoke or light."

If Matteotti was the saint and Amendola the philosopher, Lauro De Bosis was the poet. With friends, in Rome, he had founded a movement with the object of bringing the King back to a sense of his duty. During his temporary absence in Switzerland his friends were arrested, one of them being Mario Vinciguerra, who was the author of books rich in original ideas on Italian and English literature, and one of the Italians of greatest integrity I have ever known. The other was Renzo Rendi, literary correspondent of the *New York Times;* both were condemned to fifteen years' imprisonment. Here was a case at once ironic and pathetic, for their crime, in a state officially a monarchy, was to have written and distributed circulars counseling anti-Fascists to remain loyal to the monarchy.

De Bosis had no other thought than to add his own to the sacrifice of his friends. He learned to fly—this young man who had written a poem on Icarus—and after having bought a tiny airplane flew it from Marseilles to Rome on October 3, 1931. Ruth Draper has thus narrated the last day of the twenty-nine-year-old poet:

"He reached Rome at 8 P.M. He remained about half an hour over the city, and eyewitnesses have described the flight as a feat of great skill and daring. He flew very low over the streets, and in places it seemed as if snow had fallen, so thickly were the leaflets strewn. He dropped them into the laps of spectators at an open-air cinema, and among the tables of cafés in the squares. One spectator recounted that the plane seemed to be mounting the Spanish Steps. There have been many rumors as to his fate, but no trace of the plane has ever been found. Whether he was shot down by pursuing planes or fell into the sea for lack of fuel will probably never be known." *

The daily anonymous sacrifices continued in Italy from year to year; but a new crime that shook the world occurred on June 9, 1937, when Carlo and Nello Rosselli were assassinated in a watering place in France by a gang of French Fascists in Mussolini's pay, who were at that time already preparing, in connivance with Marshal Pétain, the *coup d'état* that the latter accomplished after the defeat of France in June, 1940.

Nello Rosselli was a young historian who had conceived it his duty to remain in Italy and give his friends the impression that there too one could resist. He had been arrested several times, and having gone to France to spend several days of relaxation with his brother, he was assassinated, only because they happened to be together at the same time. It was his brother Carlo who had been condemned to death by Mussolini, the case against him being his indomitable energy and his intellectual and moral radiance.

Carlo had been one of Salvemini's students in Florence. There, with Salvemini and Ernesto Rossi, he had, in January, 1925, begun to publish the clandestine daily *Non Mollare* (Don't Give Up) which lasted until October, 1925, with a temporary break in June of that year when Salvemini was arrested and thrown into prison. Released some weeks later, Salvemini succeeded in escaping from Italy during the summer; but during the four succeeding years that Rosselli remained alive, either free or imprisoned in Italy, his old master still continued to be Carlo's faithful friend and adviser.

In 1926 Rosselli had succeeded in persuading Turati to flee from Italy. Having thought it his duty to return after the *coup,*

---

* Did he die through lack of sufficient fuel, or did Fascist planes shoot him down in Corsican territorial waters, the French Government remaining silent on the matter, not wishing to displease Mussolini? I have reasons for not excluding the latter hypothesis.

Rosselli was condemned in a trial held at Savona in 1927; but at the trial he transformed himself from the accused to the accuser and at once became one of the best-known figures in Italy. Deported to the Lipari Islands, he escaped in 1929 with other deportees, one of them being Emilio Lussu, who revealed himself in exile as one of Italy's most original writers. The escape, organized by Alberto Tarchiani, former editor in chief of the *Corriere della Sera,* was a masterpiece of audacity; it ranks with the most famous prison breaks in history.

Arrived in Paris, Rosselli immediately resumed the struggle, founding the *Giustizia e Libertà* group with Cianca, Lussu, Salvemini, Tarchiani and several other friends in Italy among whom Bauer, Rossi and, later, the then very young Garosci were among the most ardent. *Giustizia e Libertà* succeeded in infusing ardent life into several of the agitating groups in Italy. Bauer, Rossi and others paid for their heroic activity with long years of imprisonment; but their sufferings and firmness became the legend of the movement, which had always been characterized by its aspiration to find a formula conciliating the necessity of a social transformation with the maintenance of the philosophy of liberty.

Mussolini, who never concerned himself with ideas, would have continued to let the periodical *Giustizia e Libertà* and the other publications of the group appear in Paris. What determined him to have Rosselli assassinated was the action the latter undertook in Spain. After the Franco revolt against the Spanish government and the Nazi-Fascist intervention in Spain, numerous Italians rushed to volunteer in the weak armies of the republic. Rosselli immediately perceived that they ought to be united in a collective action; and with him action always followed the idea. The Italians of the Garibaldi Battalion fought heroically at Huesca, as they fought later with equal heroism under Pacciarzi's orders. The password given by Rosselli was: *"Oggi in Spagna, domani in Italia"* (Today in Spain, tomorrow in Italy).

That was too much for Mussolini's fears, and Rosselli was assassinated. Only a week after Carlo's death, Mussolini in his newspapers conceded the Fascist defeat of Guadalajara which free Italians had inflicted upon him. Salvemini wrote, "Having taken his revenge, he could admit his defeat."

Rosselli died at thirty-eight—a short life, but one marvelously rich in courage, ideas and moral will.

In a different sphere of action Guglielmo Ferrero, the world-renowned historian, was also a combatant who never yielded. The moment Fascism attained power in Italy, Ferrero threw himself into the struggle. He kept on fighting up to the day when all Italian liberties were suppressed: in 1925 he associated with Amendola and me in a project to launch a new democratic party in Rome, which could serve as a nucleus for every kind of resistance. This intensified the Fascist persecution of Ferrero. He managed to find refuge in Switzerland, where the University of Geneva honored itself by appointing him Professor of Modern History.

At Geneva, not only did he inspire admiration for Italian thought, but he maintained as well a center of welcome and understanding among all Italians in exile, for that was what his house in the upper part of the city became—the old Turrettini Palace built in the sixteenth century by other Italians who, like Ferrero, had preferred exile to the denial of their religious ideas. All the exiled, the persecuted, the people famished for Italy, knew for years that at the Ferreros' there was always a bed for them and a place at the table. For Ferrero, purified by grief, with his great kindness equaled only by the angelic kindness of his wife Gina, had learned this at Geneva, that it is not the giving that counts, but the manner of giving.

I often saw Ferrero at Geneva until his sudden death in August, 1940, and always admired his steadfast dignity. More than once I witnessed the same advances made by rich and highly placed Fascists as had formerly been tendered to Croce and me. They told Ferrero that the Duce "who admired him" would be glad to guarantee him the continued ownership of his Ulivello estate near Florence if only he consented—oh, not to cease, but only to soften, his attacks against Fascism. The day after each of these overtures Ferrero wrote a most vengeful article which the *Dépêche*—to which, like myself, he frequently contributed—was glad and proud to publish, that paper being the only newspaper in France with the courage to do so.

Simultaneously with Ferrero other writers and thinkers were obliged, after persecutions and prison, to leave Italy, continuing the struggle in the United States and Latin America. Among these were G. A. Borgese, who wrote his *Goliath,* dealing with Fascism, in English, and Max Ascoli, Lionello Venturi and many others not so well known.

I have spoken here only of men whom I knew and loved. But nothing would be more unjust than to forget the still more admirable group—the anonymous schoolmasters, small employees, small landowners, workmen, peasants—types Silone has immortalized—who throughout Italy have struggled, resisted and suffered. Nor should we forget that small but audacious group of young Communists who—especially after so many others were obliged in 1926 and 1927 to abandon open conflict in Italy—continued for years a secret and serried campaign against Fascism, sowing their path with anonymous martyrs.

One of them, Antonio Gramsci, was famous, or deserves to become so. It was Gramsci who not only organized the Turin workmen, but gave them a conscience; again it was Gramsci of whom the Fascist prosecutor said before the Special Tribunal of Rome in 1928: "We must prevent this brain from functioning for twenty years." The letters he wrote during his long years in prison reveal in this son of Sardinian peasants a powerful brain and an exceptional philosophic and literary maturity. He was a Marxian Communist. It would have been interesting to see whether or not—had he continued to live and live free— Gramsci would have repeated the evolution that detached from Communism such intelligences as Ignazio Silone, just as earlier it had detached an Antonio Labriola and a Croce. As Gramsci had a character of iron he could never have permitted to himself, while still in prison, any evolution that the popular mind might have interpreted as a weakening of his thought. His assassination—for it is averred that his death in prison was predetermined—constitutes one of Mussolini's crimes against the spirit.

XXXVIII

THE VATICAN AND FASCISM: PIUS XI
AND PIUS XII

A GREAT MANY AMERICANS OF THE TWO AMERICAS, MEMBERS
of the Roman Catholic faith, for years both admired and respected in Fascism the regime that ended the *dissidio* (separation) between the Church and the Italian State, substituting
for it an official "reconciliation." But these same Catholics,
after Fascism declared war against Great Britain, Canada and
the United States and after it had bound itself in an indissolu-
ble way with the most anti-Christian of movements, Nazism,
wondered whether in their admiration and sympathy for Fascism they had not become the victims of a masterpiece of propaganda as crafty as it was hypocritical.

When Pius XI became Pope in 1922, the reconciliation between the State and the Church was ripe in Italy; it would
have occurred under any democratic government. Here is what
a learned Irish Catholic, D. A. Binchy, wrote in this regard in
his *Church and State in Fascist Italy,** a book giving the impression that its author gradually reached the truth after long
sojourns in Italy, despite many anti-Italian prejudices brought
with him from his native Ireland.

"The relations of the Church with the State were improving; the old hostility between them had largely disappeared,
for even the Socialists had discarded their anti-clericalism, and
only the Fascists and Communists were now left to carry on the
Garibaldian tradition. Further, a powerful and growing party
of Catholics was there to watch over the interests of religion
in and outside Parliament. Among the ordinary people the war
caused a revival of spiritual values which was reflected in public
religious celebrations on a most imposing scale with which,
again, only Fascists and Communists attempted to interfere. A
mighty procession through the streets of Rome, which were
lined with 10,000 Italian troops, marked the culminating point

* Oxford University Press, 1941.

of the Sixteenth National Eucharistic Congress; and yet there are Catholic writers today who boldly affirm that such demonstrations were forbidden until Mussolini arrived to 'protect' religion. . . ."

The Sixteenth Eucharistic Congress took place in 1922; I did not see the spectacles that the Dublin University professor describes, for I was then the Ambassador of free Italy in France. But two years earlier, with my own eyes, I saw a spectacle still more moving, were it only because it unfolded from the Alps to Rome and not in one city alone. That was the transportation of the remains of the Unknown Soldier from the field of battle in the Alps to the capital. At all the stations where the train stopped, countless throngs of Italians came to kneel and pray. Improvised altars were built beside the railway; entire villages were emptied, all the inhabitants having gone with their priests to celebrate a requiem mass as the train passed. . . .

My wife, accompanied by a British statesman's wife who later sang impudent and imprudent praises of Mussolini, saw these scenes on the Lombard plain. The worthy lady who, while it was the fashion, became most enthusiastic for the man who in 1940 would attack an England he imagined to be dying, kept repeating to my wife: "But how dare they assert that present-day Italy lacks order and patriotism? Those who say it are criminals."

As for the solution of the "Roman question," it must not be forgotten that the basis of a conciliation had been laid in conversations between Prime Minister Orlando and Monsignor Ceretti (later Nuncio at Paris) in June, 1919. Some days later Orlando resigned, and Nitti succeeded him. I was then High Commissioner in Turkey; and as I have already mentioned, I received in Constantinople a telegram from Nitti offering me the post of Undersecretary of State for Foreign Affairs. I accepted, and on my arrival in Rome some days thereafter Nitti said to me: "Tittoni [the Minister of Foreign Affairs] is busy in Paris with the Peace Treaties; as for you and me, we must devote ourselves to two other essential problems—peace with the Yugoslavs and the official reconciliation with the Vatican."

The problem of our relations with our eastern neighbors,

the South Slavs, had probably been the principal cause for my choice as Undersecretary of State. Nitti knew how much I had been opposed to the unimaginative and ungenerous policy that Sonnino had pursued with respect to the peoples subject to the Hapsburgs. The new Prime Minister also knew that, rightly or wrongly, I was called "Wilsonian," and he hoped that I would be able to find a compromise. To tell the truth, he did not know that what I wanted was not a compromise but an understanding which would be creative of the collective strength I already felt was necessary in order to prevent the return offensive of a German policy of hegemony.

On the other hand, I knew nothing of the negotiations which Nitti had resumed with the Vatican from his first day in office, even before my arrival in Rome, although conversations I had had several months previously at Constantinople with Cardinal Bourne, Archbishop of Westminster, had prepared me to suppose that the problem was almost on the point of being considered. Having arrived at Constantinople on his way from Jerusalem, the Cardinal had been kind enough to visit me at the Italian Embassy and to thank me for the courtesy with which the Italian government agents had facilitated his sojourn in the Holy Land. Speaking of his pleasure at observing the excellent relations existing everywhere between Italian agents and the Franciscan missions, he told me that he saw in them the proof that the time was ripe for a conciliation. I could not but agree with him; and during a second conversation he returned to the subject and confided that the Pope was very favorable to the idea of an official conciliation.

In our first conversation Nitti had added that he had already had several secret exchanges of ideas with Cardinal Gasparri, Secretary of State of Benedict XV, and that the *entente* was certain, on the basis of the two following points: first, that the palaces and the gardens of the Vatican be recognized as a State theoretically independent, the object being to demonstrate in a material way the independence of the Holy See; second, that an Ambassador of Italy be accredited to the Vatican and a Papal Nuncio to the Quirinal.

Actually, Nitti had oversimplified the matter. My direct contacts informed me that Benedict XV, who desired an *entente* with Italy even more ardently than his successor did, thought he ought to ask a little more in one sense and much less in another than Pius XI was to ask in 1929. Benedict wanted more, because he thought it opportune to have the conciliation ratified by some sort of international guarantee (although, with the object of not wounding Italian susceptibilities, the word guarantee was never uttered—which proves that a final *entente* would have been easily reached). In another way he wanted much less, since, not only would he have been satisfied with an even more microscopic Vatican State, but he had never made the slightest allusion to a Concordat. For the well-being of religious life in Italy, Benedict counted not on treaties and concordats, as did his successor, but on the influence of the Popular Party which Don Sturzo had just founded and which had speedily brought to Parliament a hundred Christian Democrats. Furthermore, through the Pope's most intimate friend, Baron Monti, who, when I later became Minister of Foreign Affairs, was for a long time (as I have already mentioned) * his personal emissary to me, I knew the Pope's feelings. Monti had often repeated to me one of the Pope's favorite quotations in their intimate conversations: *"Historia Concordatorum, historia dolorum."* (The record of the Concordats is a record of sorrows.)

The conversations with Cardinal Gasparri were interrupted when Nitti was obliged to resign in June, 1920, and Giolitti, the Nestor of Italian statesmen, became Prime Minister for the fifth time, with myself as Minister of Foreign Affairs. Giolitti said to me: "The conversations have been very creditable on both sides, but the best thing for the State and the Church is to continue as in the past: two parallels that get on well together without ever coming into contact."

To tell the truth, for Giolitti it was both more and less than a question of principle—it was a matter of age. He was eighty years old; he had been Prime Minister longer than any other Italian since Cavour; how could he change his concepts?

After the conclusion of the Treaties of the Lateran of 1929, French political writers, and among them some of the best known, wrote (probably motivated more by patriotic fears than by an objective study of the situation) that Italy had "conquered what she has dreamed of for the last five

* Chapter XXV.

hundred years: Austria's position as the protectress of Catholicism in Central Europe and the Balkans." This kind of preoccupation is one more proof that, in some French traditional circles, ideas and judgments are still often based on superannuated notions. Italy—I mean free Italy—never dreamed of taking from Austria the Catholic supremacy in the Balkans. I have always believed that the reason the "Catholic" character of Austria's eastern policy failed to embarrass Austro-Hungarian diplomacy was that the Ballplatz and the Hofburg were no longer living entities; they were capable of utilizing only the instruments of the dead past. But Italy was and is for us a great living force for the future.

And what did we see in post-Versailles Europe? In Czechoslovakia, strongest of the new states created after the war, a "National" and anti-Roman Church current began to reveal itself even among her Catholic communities; to a lesser degree the same trend was observable in Croatia, where the *Obzor* in 1929 went so far as to proclaim: "The Vatican is our enemy." And one can easily surmise that that hostile sentiment has in no way diminished since the invasion of Slovenia and Croatia by the first Italian regime the Pope has blessed in Rome. As for Rumania and Bulgaria, Orthodox Church countries, every effort toward a union with the Roman Church has always been in vain.

Only in Hungary was the accord between the Vatican and the Fascist government favorably received, which proves my argument: that so long as the noble and brave Hungarian nation remains under the yoke of a group of aristocratic families who, under cover of a clamorous patriotism, think only of their *latifundia,* Hungary will remain, like the old Austria, a relic of the past.

It is interesting to examine the reasons that determined Pius XI to adopt a policy so radically at variance with the concept of his predecessor. I shall attempt this examination without giving consideration to any analogous quest for the Fascist reasons. The pontifical reasons constitute a factor of history; while those of a party, whose unique preoccupation was to remain in power, are merely in the field of day-by-day political reports.

The facts being more eloquent than any affirmations, it cannot be denied that, since the fall of the temporal power in 1870, the popes have enjoyed in Italy and throughout the whole world a moral prestige and an international liberty such as they had not previously known since the end of the seventeenth century.

Before 1870 the Church had been severely handicapped in Italy by the fact that she was identified with the Austrian and Bourbon regimes; just as, prior to 1789, she had seemed a lifeless thing in France, despite her great material possessions and her official position.

When, in the united and free Italy he had forged, Cavour laid down as the basis of his relations with the Church the famous formula, "A free Church in a free State," his idea had been that the Church herself would thereby gain in prestige and strength. With this thought he wrote: "As soon as the Church has tasted liberty she will feel rejuvenated by that healthy and invigorating regime." Marquis Visconti Venosta, who had married Cavour's niece, told me, in his old age, that more than once during his last illness Cavour murmured with the smile that hid the depths of his sovereign thought: "Who knows? Perhaps the Church will end by canonizing me. . . ."

Cavour's canonization seems hardly a near possibility. But his prophecy came true; it was only after the Church lost all her temporal power and was living under the regime of common liberty that she again became one of the world's moral forces.

Not only did the "prisoner" popes become the arbiters of more than one diplomatic controversy but, again, the Church was indebted to a liberal Italy, for her liberation from one of her worst humiliations, namely, the right of veto in the papal elections that some Powers still continued to exercise during the Conclave, despite all the formulas erected to safeguard the independence of the Cardinals. The Church had only succeeded in suppressing this right of veto during the final period of the "prisoner" popes. I should not be surprised if, with the Pope once again "free," some Ministers of Foreign Affairs were already thinking of elaborating some *ersatz* form of the veto of bygone times.

It must be conceded that certain elements of the Church

felt a joy they sincerely thought holy at the idea that the Cavourist Italy which they so heartily hated had at last been defeated with regard to its most essential principle. Did not the *Correspondent,* one of France's most important Catholic periodicals, declare in 1929 that the Lateran treaties had finally destroyed "the traditions of the Risorgimento, that gigantic Fiumean adventure"? Yet it must be admitted that it was not primarily the bait of a little territory that determined the Pope. The Concordat—which the Fascist regime alone had consented to, as Pius XI himself declared—was the principal reason.

But in the complex of politics no decision has its origin in a single root cause. Who says politics says life, and life is but the resultant of forces that are often in opposition.

We must therefore examine these causes, all of them. To begin with, we must have the courage to admit that the enormous indemnity paid by the Fascist government to the Holy See played a part in the latter's decision, but, of course, not in the vulgar sense of greed for money, but only because Italian money would enable the Roman Curia to maintain a greater independence with regard to certain pressures that Anglo-Saxon Catholics were increasingly applying. Since the war of 1914–18, the Holy See's budget received almost nothing from France, Germany and Austria. All the funds came from England and America; and with this money came respectful but increasingly firm insistences for some kind of proportional representation of the Catholic peoples.

During the war, Benedict XV had opposed with the most discouraging silence the offers that the Central Empires tendered him for the reconstitution of a little pontifical State; Erzberger, then head of the German Catholic Center, talked of a *Miniaturgebiet* (miniature territory). Erzberger's territorial clauses were analogous to those of the Lateran treaties of 1929; but Erzberger, an enemy, talked of 500 million lire to be spent by Italy, if Italy should be vanquished in the war. Ten years after the victory the Fascist regime paid 1,750 millions.

The Vatican's Italian personnel, which was accustomed to retain for itself the majority of Cardinal hats, which had for four centuries supplied all the popes,* and which occupies the great majority of Nunciatures, did not like the idea of being dispossessed. They thought, and still think in all good faith, that they are the best fitted to pilot the Church. But in order to resist the pressures from England, and above all from the United States, they had to have an independent financial basis. The one and three-quarter billion lire that the Italian taxpayers disbursed to the Pope have given the Curia greater strength to resist those naive people who maintain that the Church needs new blood.

Another of the lesser reasons could be found in the difficulty of not accepting constantly increasing offers from a regime that hoped to find in the "Conciliation" a sort of moral consecration of which it felt badly in need. Fascism being what it was, and the suddenness with which its head shifted from one extreme position to another being notorious, it is not indiscreet to suppose that at the Vatican they thought it dangerous to run the risk that the religious manifestations of the newcomers might suddenly change to acts of anti-clerical violence such as former liberal governments would never have even thought of.

But in my opinion the deep psychological reasons that determined the accord must be sought in the personality of Pius XI. Without these reasons the others would not have sufficed.

A distrust shared in common, a common hatred, constitute stronger bonds than those of common sympathies: and the Catholicism of Pius XI shared one hatred in common with the Fascist chiefs—the hatred of political liberty.

I have said the Catholicism of Pius XI, for it differed radically from that of his predecessor, Benedict, whose political concepts, as has been noted, were of a completely different order.

Benedict XV, who had been able to weigh the sad consequences for the Church of Pius X's medieval policy, trusting in the beneficent effects of liberty, had left to the Catholic laity the greatest possible autonomy in the social and political fields. Breaking with all Vatican traditions, he had the courage to

---

* The last non-Italian pope was the Netherlander Adrian VI, of Utrecht, elected 1522, died 1523. He succeeded Leo X and was followed by another Medici, Clement VII.

permit the creation in Italy of the Popular Party whose aim, under the guidance of Don Sturzo, was to associate the Church with a movement of social progress. Despite its mistakes—an excuse for which exists in the tumultuous haste of its formation and the post-war turbulence—the Popular Party might have become a really important element in Italy, where it represented permanent currents of thought, of sentiment and of interests. For the popes this party might have represented a true "conciliation"; for, in no wise compromising the Vatican and declaring itself independent of it, the party could have constituted a free defense of Christian thought.

But all this could not have been crystallized in protocols.

And the new Pope, like Pius X, was not only hostile to ideas of liberty, he was also a scholar whose mind had been formed in libraries and archives; he was ignorant of life's bitter struggle, and was convinced that a good treaty drafted in traditional form and foreseeing all cases, was more valuable than the uncertain equilibrium of parties—just as one of those fine catalogues, of which he was so fond, seemed to him of more value to a library than the most accurate familiarity with books. To those who warned him that dealing with faithless and lawless demagogues is always dangerous, he replied: "I know it, but at least they don't believe in the villainous fetish of liberalism." That was the bond between them.

Another fact must also be stated with regard to Pius XI: that in the general administration of the Church, even outside Italy, he was inspired with a single idea—the idea of resuming the policy of disciplinary unity inaugurated under Pius X, and of attaining what might be called the administrative unity of the Church.

Whence, throughout the world, the juridic centralization in the person of the Pope of all those questions that for centuries had been left to congregations and the bishops. Whence proceeded, in Italy, just as in every other country, the tendency to eliminate the democratic currents of the Catholic parties and to substitute for them the rigid framework of traditional sacerdotal forms. If in Italy Pius XI destroyed the Popular Party, in Germany he induced the Catholic Center at a given moment to renounce—in order to secure passage of a law favorable to the free schools—its alliance with the Socialists, substituting for it an alliance with the Nationalists and militarist Right. In Spain he fought the Christian Democratic movement in Catalonia, and especially its Republican character. In Belgium he imposed the *Union Catholique,* sacrificing to the conservative current the claims of the Flanders democrats. It is true that in France he condemned *L'Action Française,* which was conducting a campaign for the restoration of the Monarchy; but this condemnation was only an episode devoid of general importance, since the Pope never did issue the encyclical that had been announced and which would have refuted the nationalist doctrines of *L'Action Française,* and proclaimed in their place a Catholic law of ,international morality.

The encyclical, which never appeared, had been prepared by Church scholars. Pius XI must have yielded to the pressure of the Fascist government with which he had made his most important treaty, a government which would have seen in the encyclical a condemnation of its policy of nationalist hatreds.

This attitude of distrust of liberty, and that desire to centralize in the power of the Pope all the forces of the Catholic laity wherever they existed, compelled Pius XI to demand that the personal power of the pontiff should be more emphasized, that the figure of the Pope should be still more apotheosized, that the submission to the moral law dictated by the Church should henceforth be confounded in a sort of pontifical cult. One may rest assured that no miserable personal vanity was mixed in it: it was just the inevitable consequence of Pius XI's policy, which was to force a belief in a unity of sentiments among those who had wished to suppress in the heart of the Church the fecund free battles for unity of ideas.

In Italy even the blindest must have ended by recognizing what had happened. The vital force of the religious organizations was destroyed, the Popular Party dissolved, and Sturzo, who had devoted his life to restoring the citizenship of religious thought in Italian political life, exiled. The Pope, after having acquired the belief in his own omnipotence, found himself alone when the leaders of Fascism faced him with this dilemma: either submit, or—open war. Had he trusted liberty he could have chosen the open conflict. Alone, he had to accept compromise after compromise, one humiliation after another.

On the morrow of the signing of the Lateran Treaty, Pius XI, filled with the joy of his personal success, had uttered words that later, in his honesty, he regretted—as, for example, when he declared that he had met on the other side "a man sent by Providence," a man who, like himself, did not believe in the "villainous fetishes of liberalism." Yet many are the foreign Catholics who, after long sojourns in Rome, have honestly avowed their surprise at having found that most of the leaders of liberal Italy were practicing Catholics in Catholic families, whereas not one of the Fascist leaders was either Christian or Catholic. For example, D. A. Binchy, whom I quoted before, stated: "Indeed I think that far more ecclesiastics have been imprisoned during the ten years of 'reconciliation' than during the entire period of *dissidio*."

It is related in Rome that when Cardinal Gasparri was returning to the Vatican with his secretary, after having signed the new Vatican-Fascist treaties in the Lateran Palace, his vehicle had to stop in a narrow street where two men, surrounded by curious spectators, were fighting with their fists. The Cardinal remarked to his secretary: "I wonder how long it has been since they signed a Concordat. . . ."

Many Italian Catholics had similar misgivings when they learned, a few days later, that the Secretary General of the Fascist Party, the most powerful man after Mussolini, had declared in a speech in a threatening tone: "Let it be known that the State, which we must all adore on bended knee, will never suffer either limitations or diminution, and that it will remain the absolute master of all persons everywhere."

But it was Mussolini himself who threw the camp of those who had tried to keep their illusions into utter dismay when, in a speech delivered in Parliament on May 13, 1929, he declared in an ironic and scornful tone: first, that the Christian Church would have remained a paltry sect, like so many others, had it not established itself in Rome; second, that the State, which remained "Fascist, exclusively Fascist, essentially Fascist," would leave nothing but a desert behind it if ever Catholic action should dare to combat it.

The day after the speech Pius XI, in a letter to Cardinal Gasparri, characterized Mussolini's references to the Church as "heretical, and worse than heretical."

It is interesting to note that even Catholic scholars like Binchy * have reached the conclusion, and have declared that if, contrary to Benedict XV, Pius XI believed he should give thought to a Concordat it was because, for the first time, the Church found herself faced in Italy by "a pagan pantheistic State."

What is not generally known is that during the last months of his life Pius XI often declared to old intimate friends that his deepest grief was to have signed—thinking he was doing good—treaties with "people without faith and without God," like Hitler and Mussolini. On this point I have irrefutable documentary evidence which, unfortunately, cannot be published at present.

During his very last days Pius XI stated, speaking to the Sisters of the Cenacolo at Milan that Mussolini's laws against the Jews were "a case of veritable apostasy." One of the most disturbing phenomena of the present era is that the harshest words against Fascism have never been widely disseminated by newspapers and reviews supposedly Catholic, even when those words emanated from the Pope.

Pius XI was not a man possessed of the extensive scope of political knowledge of his predecessor, Benedict, but he had two qualities rarely found among sovereigns: moral courage and intellectual integrity. And he proved it, but too late, when, in the evening of his life, his eyes were opened and he apprehended that Fascism was not at all what, in his terror of "the

* I have quoted Dr. Binchy as I believe his book to be of first order. His documentation could not be better. Only in the cases where the author relies on oral traditions does one realize how difficult it is to understand certain Italian conceptions which to us seem so simple, but which, it seems, are not simple for foreigners. Dr. Binchy says, for example, that the conduct of the princely Roman families, the Caetani, the Boncompagni, the Sforza-Cesarini, and others, was abject at the time of Rome's occupation in 1870, "since they hastened to seek favors from the new Government." I hope I don't show myself guilty of the clan spirit (after all, our two branches separated in the fifteenth century) in observing that the Sforzas of Rome, as well as the Caetani, were declared adversaries of the temporal power long before 1870, which did not prevent them from remaining very good Catholics. Perhaps it is this, and nothing but this, which is puzzling to one coming from countries like Ireland, where anti-Italian tradition has been so strong.

Reds," he had imagined it; and that, on the contrary, Fascism and Nazism were, to say the least, as dangerous for Christian civilization as Russian Sovietism. And as soon as he saw the truth he spoke out, not caring that in so doing he, the Pope, had to retract some of his former statements. Speaking to a group of Catholics in the summer of 1939, he said: "Late, too late in my life, have I discovered that the dangers to the Faith do not come only from one side; they come from the opposite side as well; henceforth I shall devote what remains of my life to helping my sons partake of my discovery." *

It was, apart from any other consideration, an admirable act of humility. And Pius XI kept his word. One may even say that he died in the effort to enable Catholics to "partake of his discovery." The last two days of his life were devoted to writing a speech which he wanted to deliver to all the Italian bishops, a speech intended to tell them that the dangers were equally serious from both sides—the Nazi-Fascist and the Communist. On his deathbed his last words to his doctor were: "Let me have another day; I have such an important duty to fulfill."

The Conclave which followed Pius XI's death, the first Conclave of the "Conciliation," was also the first to be held publicly. It is true that Prince Chigi, Marshal of the Conclave, had sealed all the doors of the Conclave with the traditional seal of his arms, but everyone had forgotten a new and devilish device, the radio. And through it Fascist propaganda daily inundated the Cardinals' cells.

According to an unwritten law of the Conclave, after having appointed a *"papa politico"* a *"papa santo"* should have been appointed; and his name was in every Cardinal's mouth: Della Costa, Archbishop of Florence, who had always openly expressed his horror of Fascism. That would have been a disaster for Mussolini, who parried the danger with a shrewd bit of trickery. He had his propaganda, his radio and newspapers declare that Della Costa, "a prelate of incomparable goodness," would be most acceptable to Fascism as Pope, and the Cardinals were caught in the snare. In the ensuing confusion

---

* I quote from memory, but sure of the exact meaning, from the text which appeared in the *Osservatore Romano* and to which not enough attention was paid; another proof of the wide and cowardly conspiracy in favor of Fascism.

they rallied round the name of Pacelli, Pius XI's Secretary of State. It was thought that the pontificate of the deceased Pope would thus be continued. It was not realized that latterly Pius XI had changed his ideas in an almost miraculous way; but not so Pacelli. Pius XI was as passionate and impulsive as his successor was prudent and wily. When Pacelli took the same name as his predecessor and became Pius XII he must have been thinking more of the Pope of too many Concordats than of the grand old man ready to fight and voice condemnation, whose soul had awakened in the last months of his life.

Pius XII had no more ardent desire than to have Italy remain out of the war. If Mussolini hurled the nation into it in 1940, it only proves that the Vatican's political influence in Italy is greatly exaggerated by foreigners, especially by Americans.

Pius XII's chief merits during the war were mainly negative, but yet real; he constantly refused to endorse the assertion that the war of the Axis was a crusade against Bolshevism. And this was no slight merit, considering that the pressures, especially from Mussolini and Franco, were untiring and often menacing.

He erred mainly in appearances, as when too often he received German or Italian soldiers going to fight or returning from battle; this provided an opportunity for the Nazi-Fascist propaganda to transfer to the war in general the benedictions uttered only to individuals. During the first World War Benedict XV never received either an Italian, French or British soldier.

Benedict was unquestionably prudent, but he was undeniably more free; and in the Vatican he was sure of the respect of democratic Italy. Whereas Fascism weighed heavily on the Roman Curia, not only with its potential violence, but also with the vexatious bond of the Lateran Treaties. An alliance with crime always exacts a penalty.

XXXIX

THE FOREIGN POLICY AND THE WARS OF FASCISM

IN HIS MAIDEN SPEECH AS PRIME MINISTER, ON MAY 16, 1922, Mussolini declared that his foreign policy would be based on the principle of "Nothing for nothing."

During the long conversation he had with me a few days before at the Consulta, after my resignation from the Paris Embassy, he tried this formula on me, and was visibly taken aback when I replied smiling: "It is magnificent realism; but don't you think, Mussolini, that your realism would be even more dangerous if wrapped up with some idealism? Don't forget that Sonnino's Treaty of London was the most perfect and stupidest 'nothing for nothing' of our diplomatic history."

Mussolini would have liked me to continue my explanations. But he could not very well solicit them from me: had he not become "infallible"? And then, only six minutes had elapsed since he had reminded me that he could have me shot if he so wished. . . .

Our conversation fell on the relations between France and Italy, on Tunisia, where he recognized—the single sensible application of his "nothing for nothing"—that we could admit without mental reservation France's hegemony in Tunisia on condition that the many Italians there should continue to enjoy the position guaranteed them by our treaties.

The first Mussolinian application of the "nothing for nothing" occurred some weeks later at Paris during the Inter-Allied Conference for War Debts and Reparations in January, 1923. After so many tragedies and crimes inflicted on Europe, people have forgotten what this Conference was, what it might have been and what it could have contributed to the world's advantage, and the harm Mussolini did there—less from satanic desire to envenom Europe and prepare reasons for war, though there was something of that in it too, than through sheer naive journalistic stupidity.

When the British Prime Minister, Bonar Law, went to Paris in January, 1923, to present his project for the liquidation of war debts and reparations to an Inter-Allied Conference in which Poincaré represented France, and Mussolini, then in power, represented Italy, his doctors had counseled against the trip; they went so far as to warn him that it might prove fatal. To which Bonar Law replied: "That's not a good enough reason."

But if Bonar Law had no want of moral strength, persuasive vigor was lacking, the buoyant spirit that alone could have dissipated French hesitations and Fascist incomprehension.

Bonar Law offered France and Italy precious concessions: British solidarity against Germany as to reparations and war debts. For Italy, especially, the Bonar Law plan was of a sort that we could hardly have bettered ourselves: it signified practically the annulment of our debt to England. Mussolini's refusal can only be explained by the vague desire of a newcomer to power who hopes to make an impression with brilliant exploits, pushing his ingenuousness to the point of believing in the possibility of forming a continental bloc against England. In fact, that is what he himself admitted in interviews at that time.

The Bonar Law plan would have liquidated our war debts to England and would perhaps have prevented the occupation of the Ruhr—which was a disaster from all points of view, since it ended with an act of weakness as regards Germany and because it gave the death blow to the unfortunate Weimar Republic.

Mussolini sided with Poincaré against Bonar Law without the least "nothing for nothing," either moral or material, in favor of Italy. What hopes could Poincaré have held out to the novice adventurer? In the evening of his life I often asked Poincaré; but he never answered save with vague platitudes on Franco-Italian friendship.

Mussolini explained his reasons still less. But that is the privilege of dictators which they share with doctors, who bury their mistakes. The only thing Mussolini stated in an interview was that Germany "was in a condition to pay, and consequently she should be forced to do it"; he even spoke of "German bank-cellars gorged with gold."

Three months after this defeat in Paris Bonar Law sought in the tranquillity of Aix-les-Bain a relaxation of his physical sufferings. As I was a guest at a neighboring château he asked me to come and see him. He wanted to ask me for an explanation of what had remained a mystery to him : why had his plan, so useful to France and so generous as regards Italy, been rejected amid sarcasms?

I was frank in telling him what I thought had been his psychological mistakes; either he or his people had lacked strength of persuasion. I pointed out to him that his principal error had been to ignore Mussolini, Mussolini the actor, thirsting for publicity. "You should," I said, "have procured for Mussolini a dramatic success to dazzle the Italians; that is what counts for him, not Italy." I also added that he should have appealed to Mussolini against Poincaré. He listened to me with the sad smile I knew so well and, taking his famous sham pipe from his mouth (the only pipe he was then allowed to "smoke"), he said: "I understand; if Mussolini is the comedian you tell me he is, Lloyd George should have been in my place."

In his last years Bonar Law never concealed the depth of his moral disapproval for Lloyd George.

At the time that Mussolini was aiding Poincaré's advance into the Ruhr he was secretly offering arms to the Weimar Republic to resist France. It was adventurism of the vulgarest type raised to the rank of foreign policy of a great Power. This was the epoch when Mussolini was, on the one hand, at the mercy of equivocal characters ever ready to suggest to him "grandiose plans" (since he had at his disposal millions in secret funds) and, on the other hand, was restrained by the good sense of the permanent Secretary General of the Ministry of Foreign Affairs, Contarini, whom I had appointed to that post, who shared my views as regards foreign policy, but who had the soul of a rabbit under a proud Sicilian physiognomy. Contarini was of service only in arranging things rather poorly after they had begun to go awry. Mussolini felt too greatly in need of claptrap and "successes" not to prefer the advice of adventurers to that of Contarini.

A magnificent occasion for Mussolini occurred—or was created—on August 23, 1923. A group of individuals, whose names were never known, attacked the automobile of the Ital-

ian General Tellini who, near Janina in Greek territory, was in
process of determining the frontiers of Albania; the General,
four Italians of his staff and an Albanian interpreter were
killed. Less than twenty-four hours later—a diplomatic speed
record—Mussolini sent an ultimatum to Athens in which he
declared Greece responsible for the assassination committed on
her territory, and exacted the following reparations: an ultra-
speedy investigation made with the assistance of Italian authorities; capital punishment of the culprits "within five days";
a humiliating ceremony of "expiation" in the course of which
at Piraeus the Greek flag was to be lowered before the Italian
flag; and payment of fifty million lire. Athens replied on August 30, declaring herself disposed to negotiate, but protesting
against the tone and tenor of the Italian note. On August 31
the Italian fleet, which had been held ready since before
August 27, appeared before Corfu, shelled the old disarmed
castle which served as a shelter for refugees from Asia Minor
and debarked troops which occupied the island. Mussolini
declared that he would maintain the occupation until his demands had obtained full satisfaction.

D'Annunzio, who had managed the Fiume exploit in 1919,
was sulking. The Fascists were expecting miracles; Mussolini
thought his Corfu would be a still greater Fiume, but this time
it had to be a definitive conquest which would dissipate the
memory of D'Annunzio, who still frightened him. It was to
be a conquest that would annihilate the opposition.

But suddenly, on September 12, Mussolini announced that
he would evacuate Corfu on September 27 without insisting on
the prior execution of the ultimatum. On the day announced,
the Italian fleet left the island and brought back to Italy a
considerable stock of postage stamps that they had not had
time to put in circulation and which carried this surcharge:
Corfu: Occupazione Italiana. In the roadstead of Piraeus
there was an exchange of salutes, not between the Italian and
Greek fleets, but between the Interallied and Greek fleets. The
culprits, whose capital punishment was to have taken place
"within five days" according to the Mussolinian ultimatum,
remained unknown. On only one point did the Duce obtain
satisfaction: he received the indemnity of fifty million lire,

from which he allotted a generous share to the victims of the bombardment. The cost of the enterprise to the Italian treasury had been eighty millions.

What had happened? A poorly disguised ultimatum from the British Government had obliged Mussolini to capitulate.

Why General Tellini and his staff were assassinated was never known. The crime could profit neither the Greeks nor the Albanians; and not a few people in Italy ended by believing in the hypothesis that Mussolini himself had organized the massacre which gave him the opportunity for a brilliant exploit.

"How was it," they began to whisper, "that the squadron was so exceptionally ready to put to sea immediately? And how could it be possible that for such an unpredictable incident a meticulous ultimatum should have been ready in a few hours?"

Personally, I think it was too dangerous a game, even for the man who ten months later had Matteotti assassinated, and who in 1926, two hours after the Zaniboni "assault" at Bologna, issued a series of decrees suppressing all that remained of Italian liberties. But if I recall these rumors, the first of which was whispered to me by functionaries of the Ministry of Foreign Affairs, it is to show in what kind of esteem the man whom the American and French press were beginning to exalt was held in the highest and best-informed Italian circles.

In the meantime, what became of Dalmatia; that "martyr" Dalmatia, which had been one of the themes of Fascist propaganda against me? It was no longer being discussed; it had not been discussed for years. In January, 1924, an Italo-Yugoslav treaty of amity confirmed and pretended to develop the Treaty of Rapallo that I had concluded in November, 1920. Recalling that the new treaty "was hailed by the Fascist press as a stupendous invention of Mussolini's genius," Salvemini remarks in a valuable little book: "The truth is that Nationalists and Fascists, with Mussolini at their head, in 1920–21 had branded Count Sforza a 'traitor' for having negotiated the Treaty of Rapallo in which Dalmatia was given to Yugoslavia, and that in January, 1924, Mussolini did nothing more than continue Sforza's policy by coming to a new compromise over the problem of Fiume." *

A little later, in May, 1924, Mussolini established an accord with the British Government over the question of Djubaland, which Great Britain had promised Italy since 1920; and Mussolini did what his predecessors had refused to do: he consented that part of this territory already ceded to Italy—the Doiran Triangle—be yielded to England.

It was not this, however, that created the long intimacy which began that year between Mussolini and the British Foreign Office. The basis for that long understanding was Sir Austen Chamberlain's visit to Rome in December, 1924, when, after Matteotti's assassination, Mussolini's fall seemed imminent to everyone in Italy. Mussolini offered the gratuitous help of Italy against Turkey, with whom the British Cabinet was then in very strained relations; and in return received tokens of personal cordiality from respectable English people. At the time I wrote letters from Rome to Sir Austen putting him on guard against "complicities for which some day England will pay dear." He did not answer then; but ten years later, in London, he confessed to me that he had never for a moment been proud of his Italian expedition—which seemed to me a very unsatisfactory explanation of his action, all the more so as Lady Chamberlain, who had accompanied him, disguised herself as a Fascist propagandist—which was as stupid at it was indiscreet.

There now began a decade of Mussolinian recantations, half of which would have been sufficient to make any other government ridiculous: *for* the League of Nations and *against* the League of Nations; *for* disarmament and *against* disarmament; *for* Germany and *against* Germany; *for* France and *against* France. . . . Yet the world's orchestra continued to play up to Mussolini until his attack on Ethiopia, which, some years before, had been received as a member of the League of Nations on the proposal of Mussolini himself. The moral indignation of British public opinion obliged the cabinets of London and Paris—where Laval was considered a veritable crony of Mussolini—to apply the sanctions provided by the Covenant.

* Salvemini, *Italian Fascism*, London, 1938, pp. 67, 68.

But how were they applied? The Committee on the Sanctions spent five weeks deciding what sort of sanctions might be most effective. After a month of deep study, it decided that no embargo should be put on coal, iron, steel or cotton, all essential raw materials for war; and no embargo was put on oil, which would have instantly stopped the war. But behold, an embargo was put on camels, mules and donkeys. The embargo also included aluminum, a material which Italy produces in such large quantities that she exports it. In London and Paris they evidently thought that this was statesmanship. The only sanctions adopted with the idea that they might become effective were those that boycotted Italian exports. The British Government had counted on a longer resistance of the Ethiopian armies and Eden declared in the House of Commons on June 18, 1936:

"We have to admit that the purpose for which sanctions were imposed has not been realized. It is not necessary to give a detailed account of the reasons for that fact: they are many. One of them was a miscalculation by military opinion in most countries that the conflict would last very much longer than it has in fact done, and that in consequence the sanctions, which everyone knew could not operate at once, would produce their effect and assist thereby to obtain a settlement."

The war came to a sudden end in the spring of 1936 with the occupation of Addis Ababa, Ethiopia's capital, by Marshal Badoglio, who had previously insisted on the departure from the Army of all Fascist politicians, like Ciano.

Mistakes and crimes in foreign policy always provoke new mistakes and new crimes. Mussolini's success in Ethiopia made possible his intervention in Spain. The Spanish civil war and the complicities of the London and Paris governments with Franco constituted one of the principal reasons for the European intellectual and moral debasement from which issued the treason perpetrated by France against her ally, Czechoslovakia, at Munich in 1938; just as from Munich stemmed Hitler's aggression against Poland, the European war, and finally, on June 10, 1940, Mussolini's entrance in the war against France, already in her agony, and against Great Britain.

In spite of so many important events that have taken place

since Germany began the second World War in September, 1939, a curious fact to keep in mind remains: that history affords no parallel for the phenomenon of a gigantic war, like the totalitarian conflict of 1939, being preceded by a long period during which that war was being fought, and even bitterly fought—as in Spain—while the Powers, with eyes shut tight, confined themselves to repeating: "There is no war." This period of the "undeclared war" was one of the most shameful psychological moments of Europe, which gives it its continuing interest for our study today. Why did it last so long, why was it an undeclared war, and why was it fated to end with mortal danger for the democratic Powers?

During this period which ended with the Munich fraud, the world, surprised and bewildered, beheld two great Powers, Great Britain and France, humiliated and flouted everywhere, in every field and sector of Europe and Africa. And those two great Powers, instead of taking a stand and showing their enemies that they had force and will, continued for years proclaiming through their presses and the public speeches of their leaders: "It isn't serious; Mussolini is really our friend; no, no indeed, it isn't at all as dreadful as they say."

It began in Manchuria; it continued with the war in Ethiopia and the war in Spain. In the nineteenth century similar offenses would have more than sufficed for a proud England to say: "We must draw a line to our tolerance and our patience." Yet, if one takes the speeches of all the statesmen in office in France and in England during this period, one finds only pious phrases showing, or attempting to show, that, after all, the offenses of Nazism and Fascism to Great Britain and France were not too bitter or too humiliating. It appeared at times that the French and British had become suddenly Christians in the sense of the first century of the Christian era, that they believed themselves obliged to love and respect those who offended them. . . .

The sad truth is that everyone in Europe was guilty of slackness; and of lack of the moral courage to face reality. Everyone was guilty, the Right as well as the Left—the Tories, the Socialists and the Communists. Everyone had his part in the responsibility for the tragedy which reached its climax in September, 1939. But the main guilt in this situation of falsehood, of false prudence, of hypocrisy, of lies, in brave nations like France and England, is the guilt of the French Conservatives and the British Tories. This class in England who for so long subscribed to the famous American slogan of several generations ago, "my country, right or wrong," became meek to such a point as to be heard saying: "We are surely wrong, and Hitler may be right, and Mussolini may be right too." It was the duty of the members of the traditional aristocracies in England, Italy and France—who have always boasted of their patriotism while enjoying so many privileges—to serve their countries even more faithfully and loyally than the workmen and little people who enjoy so few privileges.

The reason the upper classes were unconscious traitors to their duty was due to a lack of generosity and, even more, to a lack of intelligence; they let themselves be hypnotized by the so-called Bolshevik danger. Hitler's subtle propaganda convinced them that he was the defender of the principle of private property and Christian civilization. Consequently the men in power in London and in Paris, possessed by the fear of Russian Bolshevism, thought it wise to accept any compromise with Hitler.

When I recall the numerous diplomats and statesmen with whom I have been in contact during all these years I find it impossible to be guided by political antipathies or sympathies. In England, Tories like Baldwin and Chamberlain and Socialists like MacDonald were equally guilty. In France, Tories like Reynaud were just as guilty as Léon Blum, head of the Socialist government. The simple truth is that we were confronted by a collapse of the leading classes of the two nations, and it would be extremely unwise to lay the exclusive blame on any one party. Those men of the Left—MacDonald in Britain and Léon Blum in France—remind me of a witticism current in Germany when Brüning, the Catholic leader—later an exile in Boston—was Chancellor: "What is the resemblance between Brüning and a violin? Both are held with the left but played with the right."

The same was true of Léon Blum. When a general election gave a sweeping majority to the Left, some technical details in French constitutional law prevented Blum from assuming immediate power. For four weeks he was the "Dauphin" beside the dying King—the previous Cabinet. It was during this interim that he asked me to have a talk with him. It took place in his modest apartment in the old Paris, near Notre Dame, which the newspapers of the Right had already started to describe as the sumptuous residence of a rich Jew.

When I called on Blum the Fascist military activities in Spain had already begun. I at once said to him: "When in 1932 I went to Madrid I warned Azaña that if he did not help us to get rid of Fascism, Fascism would end by killing the Spanish Republic. He agreed with me, and yet did nothing. Now it is your turn. If you don't pick up the gauntlet, the French too will be lost. I am very well aware that you are an honest man and that you hate the Socialists who promise all things to the crowds, and never keep any of their promises. I know too that your aim is social reforms in France, which is very much in need of some of them, being as she is, rather behind the times in social laws. But, Monsieur Blum, you must realize that all Europe is confronted by a terrific danger. From Italian sources I have learned the truth of the Spanish invasion. The primary aim of the Spanish war, which is promoted by Nazis and Fascists, is to encircle France. On the day they win in Spain, France will have lost; she will no longer be a first-class power, but just a second-rate country surrounded by enemies. You can't save France now with social reforms. What you must strive for is a complete reordering of the international situation. They haven't sufficient pluck in Italy and Germany to say openly that they are sending troops to Spain. On the contrary, they deny that they are sending them. Nazi and Fascist dictators are ever the most accomplished liars, but we know that they are sending troops to Spain, and it is up to you to challenge them. If you don't, you are lost."

Blum, a brave man, as he proved at the Riom trial, responded: "Yes, you may be right; but I am thinking of the many Socialists who, after attaining power, have completely forgotten their promises to the working classes. The world must see one Socialist who, when in power, does the very things he promised he would do."

"But," I objected, "the dangers which are confronting you are infinitely more serious. France is in mortal danger. Don't you believe it is your first duty to try to save her?"

"Yes, you are right," he answered, "but put yourself in my place. I am a Socialist; if I do anything that risks bringing France into the war it will be said that I did it for no other reason than to defend the Reds in Spain, and I fear that half of France would not follow me."

"In that case," I replied, "you should decline the office of Prime Minister."

Shortly after my conversation with Blum I was invited to London to make a private speech to the House of Commons. We had a very long discussion, and some Unionist members— that is, members of the Right, the old Tories—told me afterward, "We quite understand your fears, and perhaps you are right, but still there is this Red danger, you know. We loathe Fascism, even in Italy, but if we have to choose between Fascism and the danger of Bolshevism, we are going to choose Fascism." The representatives of the British upper classes were so biased by their social fears, figments of their imagination, that they could not see the reality.

The Duchess of Atholl, one of the richest women in Scotland, told the English, in a long campaign, of her conviction that the Soviet danger in Spain was a slogan invented by the Fascists; that Spain was in danger of becoming a German protectorate, which would be a mortal danger for France and, consequently, a mortal danger for England. The Duchess, who represented in the House of Commons one of the most conservative constituencies in Scotland, lost her seat at the next general election.

The slogan of the Bolshevist danger has been Mussolini's chief invention. Just as his chief discovery, long before Hitler, was that a lie is a lie if you repeat it one, three, four or ten times, but if you are brazen enough to repeat the same lie two thousand times, it becomes gospel truth for the whole world. That is what happened as regards Spain. They kept on reiterating that Spain was in danger of becoming Bolshevistic and, more is the pity, the world believed them. I happen to know Spain rather well, and if there is a nation in the world which is constitutionally anti-Communistic, that is Spain.

Bolshevism is a most distasteful thing to the Spaniards, not by reason of their traditional conservatism, but because Bolshevism implies a government of inexhaustible and suffocating rules; and Spaniards, being the most individualistic of all peoples, hate rules and order.

What decided Hitler, and subsequently Mussolini, to risk the second World War was the contempt they acquired for France and Great Britain during the Spanish war, and especially during the most ludicrous episode of the Spanish adventure, when the Non-Intervention Committee was functioning in London. This Non-Intervention Committee was established despite the protests of many honest people in Europe who said: "It is impossible to go on with Hitler and Mussolini. They deny that they are sending troops to Spain, yet we are continually hearing of battles even between Italians sent by Fascists and Italian volunteers fighting for the Spanish Republic." It was to satisfy public opinion that the French and British cabinets had created the Non-Intervention Committee, which soon became the greatest European humiliation in the diplomatic debacle that preceded Munich.

It may prove interesting to show how the Committee operated.

One morning at a meeting of the Non-Intervention Committee at the Foreign Office in London the Italian Ambassador, Grandi, said solemnly: "I give you the formal assurance on the part of the Fascist government in Rome that Italy has decided not to send any troops to Spain." Lord So-and-so, Chairman of the Committee, complimented the Italian Ambassador, and took cognizance of this beautiful declaration which assured peace to Europe. Two days later the Italian newspapers arrived in London and everyone read of a speech by Mussolini in which he declared: "I am proud that the heroic Italian legionnaires in Spain are shedding their blood in order to create again a new Roman Empire. . . ." With this knowledge a Liberal member of the House of Commons asked, "How is it that the Fascists gave the most complete guarantee to the Non-Intervention Committee that there would be no Italian troops in Spain, and two days later we read a speech of Mussolini complimenting the Italians who shed their blood in order to make Fascism in Spain?"

The timid, terrorized answer of the British Government was: "The Chairman of the Non-Intervention Committee has suddenly become ill: we really don't know what to answer until he recovers."

As a consequence of hundreds of incidents of this kind, Hitler and Mussolini emerged from the war in Spain convinced, and not unreasonably, that everything would be permitted them, that France and Great Britain would swallow any kind of humiliation from the two despots, and that the patience of public opinion in the two countries was limitless.

When the war came, those in France and England who had been responsible for the Munich capitulation, all of them, at once, through a kind of common instinct took this position: "Yes, we did sacrifice our honor, but it was an heroic necessity. In September, 1938, we were not ready, while now . . ."

It was a lie. The twelve months of breathing time were much more useful to Hitler than to the French or British. The German war factories, whose output was already in full force, produced from September, 1938, to August, 1939, many of the innumerable tanks and planes that later frightened Holland, Belgium and France into defeat and capitulation. During the same period the British factories were painfully slow in starting their organization. The French factories were, if anything, worse than the English as to speed. Moreover, the destruction of Czechoslovakia gave the Germans more than a thousand Czech tanks, fifteen hundred Czech planes, the entire war material for forty Czech divisions and, more valuable than all that, the Skoda munitions factory, one of the finest in the world.

But the Franco-British diplomatic blindness of that period was even more dangerous than their technical slackness. Hitler and Mussolini worked upon French credulity in a most effective way. The Führer continued to menace England and spare France; while the Duce tried to appear rather friendly to Chamberlain's England, but assailed France in the vulgarest ways. The classical phrase *sorella latina* (Latin sister), which in the past was sometimes used in speaking of France, was now invariably printed in Italy *sorella latrina*. Hitler's emissaries kept repeating to everyone in France that the Führer did not want Alsace, while at the same time Mussolini was demanding Nice, Tunisia and Corsica. Once I ventured to tell Daladier that the two men were in complete agreement in the casting of their double roles, both having but one aim, and that aim to cheat the French. Daladier's pseudo-Napoleonic face became pale with rage, and, had he dared, he would have called me an *agent provocateur* and asked me to leave France at once.

Daladier was always afraid of not appearing sufficiently "realistic." In those times, "realistic" was the appellation claimed by all the appeasers who were ready to serve Hitler and Mussolini. A few days after my conversation with Daladier, the French Minister of the Interior, Albert Sarrault, made some prudent allusions at a Cabinet meeting to the danger of the flatteries that the Paris press was bestowing on the Fascist regime. Another minister, de Monzie, belonging to the appeaser group, quickly interrupted: "I did not know that it was possible for Count Sforza to make his influence felt in the Council of Ministers. . . ." (An allusion to the fact that I was writing an editorial twice a month for *La Dépêche,* whose able and courageous editor was Albert Sarrault's elder brother, Maurice.)

And, for fear of appearing "anti-Fascist," the most ludicrous and abject decisions were taken on that day to continue flattering Mussolini, giving the vulgar dictator an excuse to despise France and to keep up the deception of French public opinion with the legend of "Fascist friendship."

What poor Daladier was, what the feelings of the French ruling class were, during the first months of the war with Germany—with an Italy which they should have known was dangerous on their flank—can not be better shown than by the Finland incident.

The Soviet Government in November, 1939, decided to invade Finland, persuaded that the Finns would not dare resist. But the Finns did resist, organizing on their Mannerheim Line an heroic defense which won the world's admiration. Though the admiration was natural, the political facts remained unchanged: the Finnish war represented only a new episode in the historic struggle between Russia and Germany for hegemony in the Baltic Sea. Immediate military necessity and possible future diplomatic developments should have warned France and Great Britain not to divert any of their forces from the main theater of the war. But the contrary happened, in France much more than in England. Only a few days were required for all the appeasers who molded upper-class public opinion to become furious clamorers for war—but against Russia.

Charles Maurras, the royalist leader hated and despised by the royal pretender, Count de Paris, wrote on February 9, 1940, in the weekly *Je suis partout:* "Are we going to help the Finns? If we don't, we shall pay for it very dearly, because nothing will survive, nothing, nothing. Everything is now at stake in Finland. The destiny of Europe and of our planet hangs on this diamond chain, this golden nail. To decide what we must do we need not even think of honor, of generosity; a little common sense should be enough. Frenchmen, do you want to live? Even more, do you want not to die? Then, go and help Finland."

If I select this out of a thousand such articles of that period, it is because Maurras' rhetorical outbursts appeared in *Je suis partout,* a weekly read then by many young French army and naval officers. A few days before the German invasion of Poland *Je suis partout* had declared in one of its editorials that the most dangerous enemies of France were not Hitler and the Nazis but "three men, Churchill, Sforza and Beneš."

Daladier did not know much, but he was surely aware that he had not even enough tanks and artillery for the French front. He also knew that the British military leaders were against an expedition to Finland. But "big business," which had been flattering Daladier—adopting him, so to speak—was for war with Russia (with a vague foolish hope that Hitler might become an ally of France in this "holy war." Daladier's Egerian nymph, the Marquise de Crussol * and her friends were for war with Russia, their patriotic reason being that it was the fashionable thing, and Daladier—poor deluded man that he was—gave way. He announced one day in the Chamber of Deputies in a speech, half flamboyant, half trembling, that fifty thousand men were ready to sail to Finland. Only fifty

---

* This lady represented the spirit of big business more than the aristocracy. Daughter of the sardine-industry king, it was said of her in "good society": "C'est une sardine qui s'est crue sole" (She is a sardine who thinks herself a sole).

In France the aristocracy erred through stupidity; big business through rapacity.

thousand men, and Mannerheim had told him that three hundred thousand were necessary. Furthermore, Norway and Sweden, afraid of Germany, had refused passage for the troops. At the last moment the British Government asked Finland if an Allied expedition of such a size was required. The Finnish government did not even deign to answer and proceeded to sign a hasty peace with Moscow.

It was the same conspiracy—an unconscious conspiracy— against France that impelled Weygand when he was head of the *Armée d'Orient* in Syria, to besiege Daladier and Gamelin with urgent reports and plans aiming at a war to be waged from Syria against Russia, in the direction of Baku and its oil fields. Oil was the "realistic" pretext; but the real aim was a "holy war" against Communism, a war in which it would have been easy to destroy all the gains that Labor had won in France.

Since 1920 I have known Weygand well, and he always gave me the impression of being an able, clear-minded man, although more in his place as a chief of staff than as a commander-in-chief. What spoiled Weygand was his inability to resist the suffocating atmosphere of the French Academy, of which he had become a member and thus had the entrée to the Paris reactionary salons.

I have to remark here, parenthetically, that Weygand was not always a blind instrument of the reactionary prejudices of Parisian high society. So long as he saw clearly, so long as he was not blinded by the reactionary influences around him, acting even through his wife, a member of the lesser provincial nobility—a connection of which he was rather proud—Weygand, himself a man of obscure birth, had proved quite firm. Long before the Spanish war I had had secret conversations with him in Paris where he already occupied the singular and theoretical position of eventual chief of allied war operations. As at that time there were no "Allies," no mention was made of his office which, moreover, comprised only four or five officers occupying a few rooms in the Hôtel des Invalides, which could be reached through a little side entrance on the Boulevard des Invalides. I explicitly stated to him that Mussolini had started on a path that, despite him, would eventually lead him to a war with France; that this would involve the ruin of France and Italy, and that it had to be forestalled. Weygand promised me his most zealous support if I should succeed in having orders given him. I am convinced that he was then sincere. But in 1939 he had changed; if not to the same degree as Pétain—in whom treason was active and pre-conceived—Weygand had yielded to the mentality described by the slogan which raged like wildfire in Paris some years earlier: "Better Hitler than Blum."

Henri de Kerillis, the only deputy of the Right who clearly foresaw the danger and, alone, warned the electors and his colleagues of the Chamber, whom he never succeeded in convincing, repeated to me, shortly before the war, an anecdote proving what the once loyal Weygand had become. Meeting de Kerillis at the Cercle Interallié in Paris, Weygand took out of his pocket a small volume and, handing it to him, asked if he had read it. "It contains," he said, "some admirable ideas." The little book was *Gerbes de forces* (Sheaves of Strength) by the pro-Nazi French writer Chateaubriant, a fanatical and blind justification of Nazism in every field. De Kerillis, who loves France beyond everything, was dumfounded. "But, General," he answered, "it is a shameful book, it is Hitlerian propaganda." Weygand did not even deign to reply; he left de Kerillis without a word. This French general had come, step by step, to dislike and perhaps to hate a France which was a republic.

On June 18, 1940, the day of my very narrow escape from Nazified France, Weygand made a remark to an old friend of mine at Bordeaux, who repeated it to me a few hours later, just as I was leaving Bordeaux and France. "This collapse," Weygand had said, "is sent by God; it will help the French to understand what happens to them when they forget the Church." In the interests of truth I must add that my friend, an honest Catholic of the Montalembert type, was horrified. "These Frenchmen," he said, "who threaten to become the masters of tomorrow, will destroy religion in France, just as the Spanish generals and bishops and dukes are destroying it in Spain."

But let us not take religious phrases of old generals too

seriously, and especially when they are members of the French Academy. They may like to show that they had read de Maistre—or Maurras.

The political state of mind of Weygand and his kind can be better illustrated by the following incident which took place in Tours, when the city was for a brief time the capital of collapsing France. I have the story in an identical form from two Ministers who were present.

At a Cabinet meeting Weygand said: "According to authentic information which has reached me, the Communist deputy, Thorez, has arrived in Paris, preceding the Germans, and with his friends has proclaimed a provisional government."

Mandel, the Minister of the Interior, interrupted him: "You are mistaken, General; a few moments ago I had a telephone conversation with the *Préfet de Police* and he told me nothing of the kind."

But Weygand insisted, saying sharply: "I am quite sure of the authenticity of my information. I have it from several sources and all reliable."

Mandel did not answer but went to a telephone in the same room and asked for Paris and the *Préfet de Police,* Langeron.

"Is it true," all the Ministers heard him asking, "that Thorez is in Paris and that a provisional government has been formed?"

Langeron having answered that nothing of the kind existed, Mandel asked him to repeat his statement to General Weygand, to whom he handed the receiver with only this glacial remark:

"I wonder, General, what you would do to an officer telling you lies of such dimensions."

What had been, and what really was, the Communist danger? There is no doubt that after his treaty with Hitler, Stalin had favored "Red" sabotage in the French munition factories. But some outstanding French industrialists confided to me that the most efficient sabotage during the eight months from September, 1939, to May, 1940, was the work of some of the most powerful French businessmen who, like Weygand, had read and admired Chateaubriant's *Gerbes de forces.* Hitler, more crafty than the Communists, had discovered that in order to paralyze war production it was better to have in his service a few technicians and industrialists than millions of "organized masses."

Certain that the war was near and that, after a period of false neutrality, Mussolini would not resist the opportunity of entering it—so greatly did he despise England and France—I decided, after having received the unconditional adherence of some of the most representative and respected men of Italy, to get in touch with the French Government with the object of saving the peace and saving Italy. I went to Paris from my place on the Riviera, where I constantly saw my friends from Italy, and, on August 27, 1939, I met, not in their Ministerial offices but in two private houses, two of the important Cabinet Ministers whose duty it was to make decisions. A witness who took an exact note of my words was present at one of the two identical conversations.* I told the two Ministers: "The war is a matter of days. England and France have given me the impression that they are going into this war as if it were an unpleasant and boring job, but with no great anxiety as to the outcome. That is a terrible mistake. This war is not going to be won without imagination, audacity, creative power. If to dodge all risk and take the line of least resistance is all you do, you'll lose your fight before it begins. Please believe me; Mussolini, it is true, is not very intelligent, but he is the craftiest of actors and he is going to play a terrible trick on you. He'll lie down just long enough. He'll let you hope, through Lagardelle, and through de Monzie, that he'll keep his neutrality. He will even make you pay for it. The best help he can give Germany is to furnish her with fresh supplies and protect her southern flank. He'll declare war against you just a fortnight before Hitler's victory is assured so as to have a share in the loot. If you want to save France and perhaps peace, you must send to Mussolini, and immediately, the following declaration: 'We give you forty-eight hours to reach a decision; with us or against us.' You must, at the same time, explain to the

* Jules Romains, *Seven Mysteries of Europe*, New York, Knopf, 1941, pp. 58-61. In his narrative Romains emphasizes especially my interest in the safety of France, as if I had not been an Italian prompted chiefly by his duty—as an Italian—to the honor and supreme interest of his country. But it is not always easy for the French to comprehend what a "foreigner" thinks. Is it possible that history has made the French too "insular," while it has made the Italians (in spite of the shameful Fascist episode) more internationally minded than any other people in Europe?

Italian nation that it is not your fault if you are obliged to take precautions against a regime which has publicly proclaimed that it wants to take French territories; you must declare to Italy that you consider a war between our two nations a crime, but that it is Mussolini, not you, who thinks of war. If Mussolini tries to evade the issue by a promise of neutrality, you must answer that you have always had faith in any previous Italian government, but that due to Fascism having so frequently violated its word, you feel obliged to ask the permission to occupy two or three cities in Piedmont. . . . Within a week Mussolini will be overthrown and Italy will go to war against Germany, if Hitler has dared to go on with his plans. But if you flatter Mussolini as de Monzie and two or three other Ministers tell you to do, you are lost, you and France."

I was conscious that I made a deep impression. That is why I continued: "But, for the love of God, don't consult the General Staff. Instead, give them orders. Do you want to know what happened when, in Italy, I decided to crush D'Annunzio's ludicrous regime in Fiume? As long as I consulted the generals, all was impossible; but when I told them: 'If in four days D'Annunzio is not ousted from Fiume, you will find yourselves on the retired list,' everything became possible. Almost all generals, your generals—they are all the same. The only thing to ask them is: 'How will you carry out this operation when we give you the orders for it?' "

Alas, the generals were consulted. And because of the hesitations of two Ministers the last chance to save the peace and to save France disappeared.

These two men were lacking in courage, that is, in moral courage, the rarest of all courages. But there was also an unconscious misunderstanding between them and me. They liked and admired Italy, but only in words. They had never felt as deeply as I have always felt that a loyal and active *entente* between my beloved Italy and their beloved France was essential to the prosperity and strength of our two countries and to the growing union of Europe. Unfortunately, it seems to be more difficult for Frenchmen, even for the most progressive, to think internationally than it is for the Italians, even those most loyally devoted to their own country, as in my own case.

Two months after the invasion of Poland I had a long conversation with Eduard Beneš in Paris on October 12, 1939,* at the Hotel Crillon. Beneš talked, as he always did with me, with the frankness of an old friendship and a constant mutuality of interest. In the conflict against Fascism which as an Italian, as a European and as a friend of peace, I had led for fifteen years, I had met many statesmen prodigal with enthusiastic phrases, but only one who had been always ready to act, only one who had understood, without false hesitations, the supreme danger, and that was Eduard Beneš. If, during the long Fascist period, there had been one man with even one quarter of Beneš' vision and strength of will in power in London or Paris, the Fascist bluff would have collapsed and peace would have been saved. But in London and Paris Beneš then seemed like a living specter of remorse; and, since no one likes to feel remorse, he was called a troublemaker.

Beneš disclosed everything about France's attitude during the Munich crisis. To give me an idea of the incredible levity of most of the French ministers, not only as regards the French people, misled and deceived by their press and their leaders, but also as regards the nations faithfully allied to France, Beneš repeated literally, from his photographic memory, the numerous appeals he made in 1938 to the conscience of the French government through the French Minister at Prague. "France should tell us in time," so Beneš a hundred times cautioned the French plenipotentiary, "what her attitude will be when the crisis comes. She owes it to us, in order that we may be able to take our measures and decide on our tactics toward the Reich."

Instead of being responsive to these appeals, as loyal as they were tragic, the French Minister answered the day after each conversation only with distrustful remarks based on foolish rumors of German secret proposals to Czechoslovakia. Beneš added: "If you were horrified at the fact that six weeks, three weeks, before the treason Daladier and Bonnet reiterated to me that they would remain faithful to our treaty, can you

* In a little book containing three lectures of mine at an American university in 1941 the date of our conversation was given inaccurately, due to the fact that the publication was based on a stenographic text with the errors inevitable in that kind of reproduction. I call attention to the error as it is essential for the comprehension of Beneš' thought to have the exact date.

imagine how I felt, what I feared, and in what an impossible position I was placed by these people who were even more stupid than they were cowardly . . ."

Beneš was the only one in Paris who, at that time, shared without an instant's hesitation my absolute certainty that the conduct of the French leaders would hasten Mussolini's entrance into the war. "Yes," Beneš agreed, "he'll have to make war, he is condemned to it whatever happens. . . . But who realizes it here? The French leaders are not organizing war but disaster; just as they never have understood Mussolini, today they haven't the least comprehension of Hitler."

What would Beneš have done *if* official France had had the courage and the dignity to talk to him frankly and in time? Beneš had three times refused to agree to Hitler's terms, even when they seemed on their face acceptable. He knew too well what the Nazi terms were worth. Despite the fact that "ifs" are the most futile kind of game, I did ask Beneš what he would have done *if*. His answer was: "It's hard to say; but at least France's conduct would have been honorable and we would have had time to prepare ourselves better. But there is one thing I can say with certitude, had we been notified of a definitive change made by France in her Central European policy, and had Czechoslovakia been obliged to change her course radically, I should not have remained at the helm. As I see it, Czechoslovakia can exist only as an example of democracy in the world. As for me, I would not have countenanced treason to democracy. And I proved it by my resignation a few days after Munich. And this I can also positively say: I never would have accepted as an actual possibility a compromise of my people with Nazism and Hitler, or with any other dictator or dictatorship whatever. Even alone, even invaded, we would have shown the world with what constancy and—if necessary —with what tireless resilience we would have resisted our enemies, as we did during the first World War."

In Hitler's and Mussolini's hatred of Czechoslovakia there was in the Führer's mind more than greed for territory, and in the Duce's more than a desire for international convulsions. The main reason for the hatred of the two despots was that the country of Masaryk and of Beneš had become the soundest and healthiest democracy in the old world—a democracy which had succeeded in curbing Bolshevism without curtailing freedom. This was Prague's crime, more than the fact that she had created a strong army next door to Germany and had developed Czech industry and Czech agriculture in a way that was an example to the Germans themselves. The Czechs were gaining markets everywhere, even at the expense of Italy in the Balkans and Latin America, and at Germany's expense in the United States.

One of the most incomprehensible instances of the suicidal blindness of Western political leaders in Europe during the undeclared war from 1935 to 1939 was the fact of their not having realized that Czechoslovakia, far from being in sympathy with Russian Bolshevism, was diametrically opposed to pro-Russian totalitarian tendencies.

Czechoslovakia was born in 1919 of two forces: one, the tenacious national will of the Czech people through centuries of German oppression; the other, the personality of Masaryk. America might well be proud of that part of Masaryk's intellectual development which took place during the years he spent in the United States. I know of no other European public man of the twentieth century who has at once been so completely national and international. Here are a few of the thoughts he constantly reiterated in his books and speeches, thoughts that ripened in his mind after his residence in the United States. To these ideas he remained ever faithful during his long presidency in Prague.

"Our love for our compatriots should show itself by social laws. . . ."

"Our Czech ideal is a people without beggars. . . ."

"I will know nothing of an idealism which forgets bread. . . ."

"One should not idolize one's own people. I willingly concede the superiority of other peoples, and this does not decrease the love I bear for mine. . . ."

"Whenever a Czech is called, a man should answer. . . ."

One of Fascism's few sincere acts was its constant manifestation of hatred toward Czechoslovakia. There were no deceits or recantations in that regard, as so often occurred in Fascism's attitude toward France and Great Britain.

Almost as sincere was Mussolini's attitude during the period of neutrality—or non-belligerency, as he defined it—toward France from September, 1939 to June 10, 1940. In a speech on September 23, 1939, Mussolini not only declared that his policy would continue to correspond to the "existing political accords and pacts" (those with the Reich), but he spoke of "the liquidation of Poland" as of an irrevocable fact, despite the time-honored relations of friendship between Poland and Italy, relations which seemed to have been preserved even under the Fascist regime, were it only because of the latter's sympathy for the regime of the "colonels." The reaction of the entire French press was almost unanimous in declaring, "Mussolini is obliged to speak that way, but we are sure that his great Latin heart . . ." etcetera.

At the end of May, 1940, some of the most eminent Italians asked me to join with them in summoning the King, in a last appeal, not to sign a declaration of war against France and England. We told him that this final offense would never be forgiven by the Italian people.

On June 4 a strange visit convinced me that Italy was going to founder in the abyss. Two Italian generals (one of whom has since died in Greece) came to see me early one morning, dressed in hunting costume, in my country place near Toulon; they told me it was war, that I ought to leave immediately as the "hazards" would endanger my life. One of them even added: "This war is a crime, but we are soldiers; we must obey. And yet we cannot remain impassive witnesses of individual attempts at assassination."

A few hours later I left for Paris, where I had long interviews with Paul Reynaud, the French Prime Minister, and his Undersecretary, Paul Baudoin. This time they could not help but agree with me, but it was too late, and nothing could any longer be done about it.

It was hard to recognize Reynaud, not only on account of the defeat that already marked him, a defeat that already overshadowed every face and gripped every heart, but because in his case there was an obvious inner collapse which had destroyed his sense of duty. Historians and novelists have always liked to exaggerate the role of women; but the transformation of the audacious, active and intelligent Reynaud into a sly tatter of humanity admits of no other possible explanation than—a woman. We spent an hour together, and the first twenty minutes were quite normal; after that it became nauseating. Every five minutes the ringing of his private telephone bell summoned him and a frantic feminine voice urged him to have done with me; I could not hear the words but I heard the voice, and Reynaud's frightened look and his lavish excuses told me all. It was his mistress, Countess Hélène de Portes, surveying from afar the meeting of her Paul with one of the rare partisans of resistance who had been able to see him.

All political conversation became impossible. He finally asked me to arrange with Paul Baudoin a policy for the Italians living in France. This man with whom I had just been talking had already become the head, or at least the responsible executive, of the defeatist party.

Leaving Reynaud, I went to see Baudoin, whom I reminded of the action I had taken since the spring of 1940 with regard to the 900,000 Italians living in France, and of my articles in the *Dépêche de Toulouse,* aimed as much at them as at the French, in which I foretold Mussolini's intervention, and in which I repeated dozens of times to the French: "We must keep on ardently hoping that the irreparable will not happen between two great peoples destined to mutual understanding, whatever may be the dangerous mistakes and the unhealthy dreams of demagogues. Above all, whatever happens, one must not confuse a people with its regime. To make that distinction will give ultimate proof of a nation's political and moral maturity." *

Baudoin accepted all my proposals. And on a corner of his desk I wrote the following proclamation to the Italian people:

"Italians! The Fascist regime, by forcing you to fight against a free Europe, betrays all your vital interests. Even a victory of the totalitarian dictatorships would betoken the enslavement and degradation of Italy. The Government of the French Republic has never attempted the slightest propaganda in Italy. And even today it does not appeal either to Latin fellowship or to the bonds that a million Italians prospering fraternally in France know are so real and strong. But France spontaneously wishes at this time to give you the most solemn

* *Dépêche de Toulouse,* April 23, 1940.

proof of her true sentiments, sentiments that the servile Fascist press has for years hidden from you and falsified. France declares on her honor, before the world, that the day of the Allied victory, and whatever may be the fate of the conflict with respect to Italy, not an inch of her territory, either at home or overseas, not a penny of indemnity, not the smallest economic or moral sacrifice will be taken or asked from a free Italian people!

"Italians of Italy and the entire world! This is what France promises you today when she is attacked by your Government; and she will keep her promise, because victory of the Allies is certain, as is your liberation."

Baudoin approved immediately, and gave the order in my presence that the proclamation should be posted in all the departments inhabited by Italians as soon as Mussolini should enter the war. The proclamation was widely broadcast over the radio after June 10, 1940.

I also wrote a proclamation for the Italians living in France. They did not wait until June 10 to give these proclamations the widest circulation, and the results were surprising. In three days fifty thousand Italians in the south of France alone, in Provence, Languedoc, Dauphiné and Savoy enlisted to fight for France, stipulating only two conditions, suggested by me, which were: that they should fight under the Italian flag, and fight against the Germans, not against the Italians.

The catastrophe supervened. General Hunzinger, sent by Pétain to Rome to negotiate the armistice, blandly offered the Italian generals the list of the fifty thousand "traitors." As the Italians pretended not to understand, he was so insistent that one of the generals answered him, despite the dangerous presence of high Fascist officials: "Offer us what we ask of you, not what we want to ignore."

The reason that the Italian officers in Rome were amazed at such baseness was that they knew nothing about the eager will to treason of the French generals who, on June 16, ranged themselves about Marshal Pétain and the Cabinet that succeeded Reynaud and in which Baudoin was promoted Minister of Foreign Affairs, with Weygand for Defense and Darlan for the Navy. The next day, June 17, Pétain decided to ask for the armistice.

Since Bordeaux was being rather heavily bombed at that time, for no other reason than to shake French morale, I had stopped at Royan, a few miles to the north, with my family and a group of Italian friends. However, I went every day to Bordeaux to urge those of the French Ministers who were my friends not to capitulate but to continue the struggle from North Africa.

On the morning of the 17th, Pétain announced to the French over the radio that he had assumed the Government, that France could no longer fight, and he added: "It is with a heavy heart that I say we must cease the fight. I have applied to our opponent to ask him if he is ready to sign with us, as between soldiers after the fight and in honor, terms to put an end to hostilities."

At Bordeaux the same morning I saw successively Campinchi, the Minister of the Navy of the preceding Cabinet, Jeanneney, President of the Senate, Herriot, President of the Chamber, and Mandel. This is what I told them: "If from Algiers or Rabat you cry out that you are France, if de Gaulle reiterates from London that this is a battle lost, but not a lost war, Pétain will collapse." All agreed with me and several of them wanted to act, but the request for an armistice formulated that day by Pétain and the abject relief of so many professional "patriots" broke all resistance.

At three o'clock I went to lunch at the Chapon Fin. All fashionable France seemed to be there, and the news had circulated from mouth to mouth. Admiral Darlan, surrounded at his table by young naval officers, commented on it with optimistic assurance; Pietri, later Pétain's Ambassador to Franco, stopped at my table to voice his grief as a Frenchman from Corsica, therefore "of Italian descent"; the Marchioness de —— and Countess de ——, hatred in their eyes, said to me: "Well, anyway, it wasn't you anti-Fascists who succeeded. . . ." Farther away from where I sat Mandel was lunching with a courageous woman friend when a gendarmerie officer came to arrest him by order of Pétain. I witnessed the lamentable scene and admired the stoical indifference of Clemenceau's pupil, but I was the only one to observe it. All the bearers of the "great names of France," all the politicians, who crowded the big room, were quick to bury their noses in

their plates. The atmosphere of Fascist cowardice was beginning to pervade France. When I got up I shook hands with
Sir Ronald Campbell, the British Ambassador, who whispered
to me: "Have you observed that only at our two tables was
there an atmosphere of grief?" All the others believed in a
good peace "as between soldiers," as Pétain had said—a good
peace which would deliver France from that "dirty Republic."

Several hours later when I again saw Herriot he urged me
to leave France, saying: "You have no idea to what an extent
all is lost."

Then I countered: "Why don't you leave too? One can keep
on fighting anywhere." He replied:

"I am the Mayor of Lyon. . . ."

I promised to leave, and he embraced me.

That evening with my family and a friend, Tarchiani, I
embarked at Verdon aboard a little Dutch tramp we discovered by chance en route from Cape Town. Four days later,
having survived three bombardments, we arrived at Falmouth.
The next day, after orders received from Downing Street
commanding Falmouth's amazed police officials to treat the
group of ragged and starving Italians with every mark of
consideration, we reached London.

There I found a populace naively sure of winning. It was
only the leaders who thought all was lost; but, as Churchill
told me, they were "determined to show the world how the
English die."

It was that decision which in the long run gave them the
victory, for the spirit is what counts.

XL

INTERNAL ITALIAN PROBLEMS

THE ITALIAN COLLECTIVE PSYCHOLOGY WAS NOT FORMED, AS
in France, around a royal court and a centralized civilization,
nor as in England, around an elastic but unshakable pyramid
of social relationships. There is only one country in the world
where the historical and moral formation of the people is
analogous to ours, and that is China. This proceeds from the
antiquity and variety of historical roots existing in both lands,
where the perfection of the past spreads like a dark shadow
over the originality of the living. Both are countries where
sculptors' chisels and painters' brushes are often more skilful
than profoundly revealing; where religious traditions and
religious indifference neutralize each other in daily life; where
the peasants are toilers equally stubborn and equally patient,
too patient sometimes; where a millenarian history has made
all men a little skeptical.

But skepticism failed to save China, after centuries of slumber, from a revolution which began in 1911 and still continues.
Will it be the same for Italy, despite the safety valve of Italian popular distrust of prophets and innovators? That may
indeed happen after too many grievous ordeals, after too
many proofs of incompetence and egoism of the so-called
ruling classes.

One must first understand just what that much-discussed
Italian skepticism, about which foreigners have such decided
opinions, really is: a skepticism that sympathizers call ripe

tolerance, while for the malevolent it can only be a proof of the abasement of the moral conscience.

If a specifically Italian skepticism does exist, it has two faces and two extremes, like everything Italian and, perhaps, like everything human.

Among the poor devils struggling for a difficult material living it is mainly a matter of mental laziness when faced by problems less immediate than those of their hunger: their poor and humble philosophy is the *non te ne incarica* (don't burden yourself with it) of the Neapolitan masses. If the phenomenon is more current in Italy than elsewhere it springs from the fact that, besides the severest daily hardships, there is an undeniable psychological cause, though foreigners can hardly grasp it: skepticism and opportunism are exaggerated because people are ashamed of them. Is it vanity or is it pride? How often, when one succeeds in perceiving this double sense, the most skeptical remarks betray the bitterness of the quatrain, cynical only in appearance, of a little-known poet of the fourteenth century, Bindo Bonichi:

> *Un modo c'è a viver fra la genti*
> *Ed in ogni altro to ti perdi i passi:*
> *Cessa da' magri ed accostati a' grassi,*
> *Odi e ascolta e di tutto consenti.*

(There is one way to live among people—follow any other and you'll lose your way: Shun the lean ones and court the fat; give ear, listen, and to all say Amen.)

The skeptical remarks so frequently on the lips of even the finest spirits have often seemed to me only the result of a bitter knowledge of history and of life—a knowledge and bitterness that it is not surprising to find particularly keen among the intellectual élite of a nation whose history has been a series of often atrocious ordeals, all the more as this élite has always wanted to react with that typically Italian emphasis which seems to pervade everything, like a poisonous and luxuriant plant in such crises of intellectual and moral abasement as Fascism.

Among all the Italians whom, as a young man, I most esteemed or loved, a superficial observer would have noted a spirit of skepticism which, in reality, was no more than a mask hiding a proud dignity. It is this same dignity that explains the rarity of memoirs written by Italian public men in comparison with those of France and England: an uncomfortable feeling of the mediocrity of the work achieved in comparison with what had once been dreamed.

This skeptical spirit in its most purified form can be discerned in Manzoni's *Promessi sposi,* the most Italian book of the nineteenth century. When foreigners sing the praises of this book—Goethe was the first to do so in a monologue with his Eckermann—their eulogies sound false to our ears, our feelings about it being so much more intense. Is it the foreigners who are wrong? Perhaps not; it may be only one more proof of the difficulty of feeling as Italians feel. Manzoni concerns himself exclusively with souls, and deliberately ignores political systems, religious systems. Every page reveals a scorn, but implicit rather than expressed, for political events, whether it be the war of Montferrat—*"Quella bella guerra"* (That beautiful war)—or the tumults at Milan under the Spanish regime.

The legend of Italian skepticism popularized, especially in the international political world, a quality or, as others think, a defect, of the Italians: their talent for *combinazione* (finding ways of agreeing). I have participated in a good many of the post-war Supreme Councils and in other international conferences. All my colleagues, like myself, kept searching for *combinazioni,* for they are the very essence of a normal political and social life. The civil greatness of England asserted itself only when that Italian art had been nationalized and *combinazione* became compromise.

Why, then, is *combinazione* a matter for criticism when the Italians and, still more, when the French attempt it, while compromise is served up to us as a supreme proof of English wisdom? The answer is a simple one: because it is an English principle never to speak of moral principles, nor of programs with inviolable ideals. Consequently their worst compromises do not shock us.

In Italy, and still more in France, they love to build scaffoldings of general formulas; but as life is much more exacting than formulas, both countries have to end by having an understanding with their adversaries. And that would be all to the good if only so much fuss had not previously been made over the insurmountable antithesis of the two programs.

One day when I had negotiated a treaty of fundamental importance with our Slav neighbors, the Nationalists asked me in the Committee on Foreign Affairs what had been my guiding principle. I answered with a quip which contained, however, more than a bit of truth: "I wanted the malcontents to be equally divided between the two nations as I believe that is the only way to make a durable treaty."

The reply was so Italian that for an instant—oh, for just an instant!—it did not seem to displease even my adversaries.

It may be that despair, or the desire for vengeance, or the appearance among the masses of leaders bringing them a message at the same time national and international will provoke among the Italian people a wave of hope and action that will sweep away the remains of the old despondent skepticism. But the essential need is a general movement of renovation similar to that which happened in France in 1789 when the Vicomte de Noailles on the famous night of August 4 proposed the abolition of the privileges of the nobility, and clergy, "the odious remains of feudalism."

That general movement of renovation has never taken place in Italy.

It was the common people of San Masaniello who, in the seventeenth century, rose against the Spaniards in Naples; and in the eighteenth century it was the working class people of Balilla who broke out in revolt against the Germans in Genoa, while the bourgeois and the nobles did not budge. On the contrary, it was the bourgeoisie and the aristocracy who during the Risorgimento in the nineteenth century rose against the *Tedeschi* (Germans) and against the Bourbons, while the masses remained inert and sometimes even, as in Tuscany, rose against the innovators.

However, a sudden general union of all Italians in one of those miraculous awakenings, such as occurred in France in 1789, is no longer an impossible dream.

The great leaders of industry have so basely compromised themselves (save for a few honorable exceptions) in their servility toward Fascism that morally they no longer count

for anything: Italy will regard them only as among the defeated and the guilty. From another aspect the long torment
of Fascism will have proved to everyone, even to those who
think themselves conservatives, that the most valuable treasure to preserve is liberty. In my opinion it is tremendously significant that in the second year of the war initiated by Mussolini against the United Nations, Benedetto Croce should have
written in a book published in Italy: "To affirm, as has been
done, the indispensable union of moral and economic powers
is equivalent to proclaiming, not the submission of the former
to the latter, but on the contrary, the hegemony of the moral
forces over the economic. . . . The economic forces must not
determine the moral forces, as happens, for example, when
relationships are established between liberty—which is moral
life—and certain economic systems, or between liberalism and
Manchestrian free competition." *

If it be true, as Gramsci wrote in prison, that "Croce is the
lay pope of Italian thought," it will be realized that it would
be fruitless to seek elsewhere as authoritative a declaration on
the utter unimportance of the sham economic "liberty" as compared with plain, unqualified liberty.

From another aspect—whatever the Marxist theorists may
have said about it—it is undeniable that the masses feel national patriotism infinitely more than some Socialist leaders
suspect. During my sojourns in America in the second period
of the Fascist tryranny, at every step the realization was forced
on me how completely false was the legend of the emigrant
who had left our shores shaking his fist at stepmother Italy. If
those who gave currency to this legend had studied economic
laws with fewer preconceptions and less superficially, they
would have realized that, in an over-populated country like
ours, without natural riches, and in which the effort to reestablish unity had for a long time prevented the accumulation
of any capital, it was extremely easy to explain why wages
were lower than in America, and more uncertain than in
France or Switzerland.

The simple truth is that the emigrant had neither a good
nor a bad comprehension of economic laws, and perhaps did
not even wonder why the wages he earned in America were

* B. Croce, *Il carattere della filosofia moderna,* Bari, 1941; page 241.

higher than those he had had to accept in Italy. Consequently, almost invariably sad but resigned, he abandoned the land of his birth only because he realized that in so doing he was bettering his lot and that of his family, the family he often left behind. But if, abroad, the emigrant's psychology underwent a change, this always was evident in a patriotic sense. At home he had sometimes heard it said that the proletarians, that is, the poor of the whole world, are brothers, and that their common enemies are the rich of any country or caste. Yet here, in America, in contradiction to this, his new working companions insulted and derided him, and only because he was poor, ragged, and an Italian; he was taunted with the weakness, real or imagined, of his country, and told that Italy was of little account in the world.

But, as we all know, petty moral persecutions, scorn openly expressed of one entire category of people toward another, are the surest ways of initiating a feeling of fellowship among the members of the persecuted groups; and they serve above all to reinforce in them the innate pride of the human soul. So it was that beyond the confines of Italy sentiment for the homeland was strengthened among our emigrants, and it was abroad that they felt most keenly the need of a strong, rich and respected Italy. If the many emigrants who returned to Italy taught their friends and relatives that one should arrive in America well dressed and with new valises, they induced them as well to understand the necessity of showing the world that we, too, knew how to make our country more prosperous. The psychology of the poorer classes sometimes undergoes slow and silent transformations that escape the not always very perceptive scrutiny of the ruling classes.

It is undeniable that, if the propaganda against Fascism in the United States and South America had slim results during the first years of the adventure, it was because too many anti-Fascist orators were unable to convince the masses that they loved the Italian homeland and desired its true glory with infinitely greater sincerity than the Fascist adventurers, who had Italy too much on their lips to have her in their hearts.

It must not be forgotten in free Italy that if the Italian people want fundamental agrarian and economic reforms, they also want these reforms to make Italy stronger and more united. And so it will be, if Italy's leaders prove worthy of the Italian people. During the French Revolution the Normandy peasants, like those of Provence, went joyfully to battle for a France that had made them landowners. The French peasants owed everything to the Revolution, which, incidentally, explains why even a century and a half later they retain a deep-seated distrust of the nobles and the Church, those old-time holders of too many fields and forests. In Italy the peasants gained nothing by the destruction of the old thrones in 1859 and 1860. True, in certain regions, as Tuscany and Venetia, their condition was better than in the France of the *ancien régime,* but it certainly did not hold true for the valley of the Po, for Latium, the South, Sicily and Sardinia, where only the Socialist propaganda succeeded, though with the greatest difficulty, in gaining for the people a little more well-being and dignity.

Free Italy's main problem will be to convince the Italian peasants that the State is not a *camorra* managed by the white-collar and necktie gentry, no matter whether they be Catholics, liberals or extremists. Even when the Italian peasant seems dejected, as in Basilicata, where everything is hostile to him— the *galantuomini* (gentry) as well as the climate—he is one of the easiest human beings to win over. It will not be at all difficult to induce him to adopt and approve an ethical conception of agrarian Socialism which will save him from a Marxist or pseudo-Marxist bureaucracy. Mediocrities can lead workers' revolts, but never peasant risings; a Francis of Assisi with eyes turned a little more toward the world we live in, and not always toward *"frate sole"* (Brother Sun) will more easily transform the minds and warm the hearts of our millions of peasants than a hundred Lenins.

Italy's chief problem is agrarian—a problem which is at once moral and economic. Those who would solve it by imitating outside methods will not succeed; and those who think that a stroke of the pen will suffice to have all the great estates suppressed will not be believed by the peasants. The peasants will believe only those sincere enough to show them that the problem is complex, that it has to do, primarily, with a gigantic transformation of the Italian soil, and a real transformation, not a comedy like the Pontine swamps that Mussolini sub-

sidized merely to impress American tourists. Our peasants will
believe if they feel that the agrarian reform represents for the
new leaders the most urgent and sacred of duties, even though
its difficulty and complexity are admitted. All the other problems are secondary.

Of infinitely less importance is the institutional problem:
whether to continue the monarchy or establish a republic.

Although it is true that the historical formation of southern
Italy is monarchist, such is not the case with respect to north
and central Italy, including Rome. In the Middle Ages the
unity of the Faith gave the Italian masses a power and vitality
which were no longer in evidence when the institution of the
principato (principality) became general. Milan's cathedral,
an incomparable jewel with its thousand spires seeming to waft
a marble forest heavenward, was the masterpiece of the anonymous Lombard people. The Viscontis and the Sforzas never
could have built it; those powerful houses could only give to
the Lombard soil the massive towers of the *Sforzesco* castle.
So it was throughout all Italy, where our cathedrals, at Genoa
as at Lucca, at Venice as at Florence and Orvieto, were the
expression of the soul of a free people. And so it was with
regard to the most wonderful adventure of the Middle Ages,
the Crusades. No prince could have organized them. The
Fourth Crusade—almost exclusively Italian—was the political
masterpiece of the Republic of Venice, but aided by the adventurous spirit of a free generation.

Art, culture, the individualistic spirit were living forces in
the hearts of the people as long as they were not regimented
by sovereigns. In this sense Mazzini interpreted the deeper
thought of the Italians.

It must be admitted that the same Italians were not displeased with the solution that Cavour's practical genius and
the stupidity of the former sovereigns evolved in 1860. Anti-
monarchic distrust was aroused in the most perspicacious and
independent minds in Italy only when it was observed that in
the social broils of 1893 in Sicily and Lunigiana, and in the
Milanese disorders of 1898, all the machinery of the monarchy
operated exclusively in favor of the privileged classes. The
same thing held true a quarter of a century later with regard
to the Fascist *coup d'état*. In 1940 the crime of the totalitarian

war, accepted and ratified by the King, made the cup run over. It may be that a fraction of the Italians is still for the Monarchy, but after so many shameful acts and treasons this could be so only for reasons of expediency. The others, aside from moral and ideal reasons, would maintain that proof has been given of the identification of the problem of social progress with the necessity of an institutional transformation of the Italian State.

But the problems examined several times in this book, of the relations of the Government and the Italian people with the Catholic Church is more weighty. The anti-Fascist writers and polemicists who found refuge abroad during the Fascist regime, from Salvemini to the most youthful among them, have been unanimous in affirming their repugnance to any anti-Catholic conflict. The old anti-clericalism of the epoch of Pedrecca's *Asino,* a journal Mussolini admired in his youthful days, stirs only their disgust or irony. The Lateran Treaties of 1929 risked wakening a less vulgar form of anti-clericalism; but even the most Ghibelline element of Italian thought did not react in unison. If all liberal and democratic Italy was unanimous against the Concordat, this unanimity did not exist with regard to the treaty establishing the Vatican State. Yet even those who disapproved it—and there were many— thought that if this diplomatic formula were to end old prejudices that harmed us abroad we might as well accept it. For centuries Italy has had the Republic of San Marino; she might just as well have two San Marinos.

This attitude is so much the more fortunate, considering that with the suppression of the Monarchy nothing could be more hurtful to Italy's moral unity than to have it appear that the republicans are, *ipso facto,* anti-clericals, while the conservatives are Catholics.

As for the relations between the Italian State and the Church, satisfactory *de facto* solutions will very easily be achieved, with a modicum of good will on both sides, even after the suppression of the Concordat, whose disadvantage for the Church Pius XI, one of its authors, during the last months of his life had ended by admitting.

But let us not forget that the relations between free Italy and the Vatican will depend on a movement of Christian

Democracy in Italy and throughout the world. The centralization of the Church, begun after the Council of Trent, strengthened the organs of the Curia but weakened the radiation of Catholic power throughout the world. Christian Democracy can become one of the supreme forces of Italian life only when it realizes that, aside from questions of dogma, the powers resident in the Vatican are only those of a gerontocratic administration which must receive from its peripheries the vivifying gusts of a moral springtide.

Perhaps that too will come to pass; and if it does it will be of great benefit to Italy and the world. In such case even the infamies and crimes of Fascism will have proved of service: for Fascism's gross paganism will have brought comprehension of the necessity of returning to the most sacred springs of the dignity of the spirit, just as the loss of political liberty will have induced an understanding that all the disadvantages of a free life are preferable to a nation's abdication to a single man or to a gang.

As long ago as the beginning of the sixteenth century, when the old Italian liberties were in their death throes, Machiavelli replied to the timid ones who lamented the disorders liberty entails:

"I maintain that those who blame the quarrels of the Senate and the people of Rome condemn that which was the very origin of liberty, and that they were probably more impressed by the cries and noise which these disturbances occasioned in the public places, than by the good effects which they produced; and that they do not consider that in every republic there are two parties, that of the nobles, and that of the people; and all the laws that are favorable to liberty result from the opposition of these parties to each other. Nor can we regard a republic as disorderly where so many virtues were seen to shine. For good examples are the result of good education, and good education is due to good laws; and good laws in their turn spring from those very agitations which have been so inconsiderately condemned by many. For whoever will carefully examine the result of these agitations will find that they have neither caused exiles nor any violence prejudicial to the general good, and will be convinced that they have given rise to laws that were to the advantage of public liberty. And if it be said that these are strange means—to hear constantly the cries of the people furious against the Senate, and of a Senate declaiming against the people, to see the populace rush tumultuously through the streets, close their houses, and even leave the city of Rome—I reply, that all these things can alarm only those who read of them, and that every free state ought to afford the people the opportunity of giving vent, so to speak, to their ambition—above all, those republics which on important occasions have to avail themselves of this very people."

XLI

ITALY AND THE WORLD

WHY WAS THERE IN EUROPE, IMMEDIATELY AFTER THE VERsailles Treaty, so long a period of hesitation before it was realized that waiting was dangerous, and that in order to reconstruct Europe something more than pious wishes was needed?

In Italy the situation seemed to have been understood better than elsewhere. In the address I delivered in 1922 when presenting my credentials as Ambassador to the President of the French Republic, I insisted strongly on the necessity of organizing Europe. President Millerand replied that, like myself, he considered it necessary to work for the organization of peace "throughout the world," which, I thought at the moment, was going rather too far.

The hesitations stemmed from the very nature of the treaty. Recognizing its nature, one can approximate the judgment future generations will some day pass upon this document. The Treaty of Versailles could be compared—and the comparison constitutes its definition—to a bronze statue that two gangs of workmen are casting together, but with each gang working on its side and each throwing into the furnace different kinds of ore. On one point only were the two worker gangs in agreement: to speed the job. The contradictions and antitheses of the treaty explain a good part of the post-war hesitations, even among those not quite so blind. That, at least, is my memory of the Supreme Councils of 1920, 1921 and 1922 where I was far from being alone in resigning myself to errors which I knew were errors, and in declaring that these errors were unavoidable.

A peace wholly Wilsonian, or one entirely Westphalian, would have produced more immediate, and consequently more beneficial, reactions.

But, after all, we should not be too surprised at the long duration of the crisis of which our generation is at the same

time the guilty one and the victim. The war of 1914–18 and
the long and troubled armistice that lasted to 1939 was the
beginning of a revolution. The second World War is still
more a revolution, and revolutions are long.

England's lasted half a century. France's—the greatest adventure of the eighteenth and nineteenth centuries—commenced in 1789; after the two Bonapartist adventures our
fathers thought it ended victoriously in 1877 when the electors
crushed the intentions of MacMahon, but such was not the
case. The war of 1939 and France's defeat of 1940 revealed a
world of people who would gladly have accepted a German
victory if it signified the death of the Republic and the return
of an old regime dear to the hearts of the old defeated generals, from Pétain to Weygand.

As for Italy: her political transformation, undertaken by the
men of the Risorgimento and continued by their liberal in-
heritors down to Giolitti, constituted without doubt a gigantic
work; but there was neither time nor courage for undertaking,
after the political transformation which had monopolized all
minds, the social reforms that were quite as urgent. The Fascist adventure was the ransom Italy paid for not having given
earlier consideration to the redemption of the agrarian and
industrial lower-class workers.

If the political and social transformation of countries which
have been forming complete historic entities for centuries are
so slow, why should it be thought strange that Europe is taking
so long to know herself and, after erring, again to find her
way?

As for the grossest mistakes of the Treaty of Versailles,
it has been often said that they were the effect of the spirit of
vengeance, of hatred, of fear, that the phariseeism of the moment called justice. To a degree, yes, but even more than to
the voluntary error of politicians lacking imagination, these
mistakes were due to an historic factor, of which almost everyone was more or less the victim at the end of 1918. This is
the factor: in 1814 and 1815 in Vienna and London they had
for a long time grown accustomed to the idea that Napoleon's
victories were only ephemeral. Long before 1859 Cavour had
foreseen the downfall of Imperial Austria. Contrarily, in
November, 1918, from Flanders to the Piave the victory

occurred as an unforeseen event—and for the masses, at least, it was psychologically unexpected.

When in the summer of 1918 the German forces in France began to retreat almost everywhere, the Paris dailies extolled, and very properly so, the ardor of the French offensive, as well as the English and Italian ones; but they were very careful not to make too evident the fact that the German military organization was exhausted, that it was compelled to evacuate all France. The disillusions of 1915 and 1916 had been too bitter a lesson; people were distrustful of too definite anticipations. It must even be acknowledged, for that explains everything, that the Reichstag discussions in the authoritarian Germany of 1918 got closer to the truth of the situation than was the case in our Parliaments. At Berlin the men who as late as 1916 and 1917 had shown a semi-servile, semi-infantile credulity with regard to the mendacities of their General Staff —Stresemann, for instance—were having their revenge, opening their eyes and speaking freely, showing once again that defeat is a harsher but much simpler mistress than victory.

The suddenness of the Allied victory, of a victory that then seemed so complete, helped to warp minds unprepared for it. At Paris, especially, they forgot that neighbors are never completely out of the game: that after Rossbach came Jena; after Jena, Sedan; after Sedan, the Marne; and after the Marne, the Maginot Line. . . .

In Italy it was approximately the same as in France from the point of view of psychological preparation for a clear-eyed exploitation of the victory. If in France Foch was still preparing in October, 1918, for a winter campaign (he often admitted it in his conversations with me), the same held true for Diaz on the Italian front. The battle of the Piave, the first of the great decisive victories of the Allies in 1918, was the finest manifestation of the collective will of an entire nation which had recovered possession of herself after a major reverse and, alone, before the arrival of any Allied contingents, had organized a resistance that finally crushed any possibility of an Austro-Hungarian offensive. But it was on the opposite side of the trenches rather than in Italy that it was perceived how decisive those last days were. And in fact they accelerated the movement for national independence of the Slav populations

of the Hapsburg monarchy. Had the Italian rulers then realized that, thanks to the Piave victory, the disintegration of
the Hapsburg monarchy was finally about to take place, it
would have been very much easier at that time to conclude
agreements with the Slav neighbors.

But for Italy at least, if not for Germany, a country politically less mature, the long shame of the Fascist masquerade
will have rendered a service to the intellectual probity of the
country. The cure will prove to have been more complete in
Italy than in the countries that were only half Fascisized, like
some mental zones in France and Spain, like Hungary, like
Rumania, like Poland.

The day when nationalist follies shall have subsided, we
shall witness, not a return of the unqualified patriotism of the
1848 kind—a patriotism which was of the purest in Michelet
and Hugo as well as in Manzoni and Leopardi—but a sudden
maturing of the fraternity of Europe, the symptoms of which
are today scarcely visible. This may seem to be simply a dream,
but it really has nothing to do with dreams.

It is perhaps as well to recall at this point that Imperial
Austria has become an historical memory less than a century
after Metternich—the master of Europe from 1815 to 1848—
had said of Italy that she was merely a "geographical expression."

During the entire Middle Ages the Italian communes did
nothing but wage war with one another, and even the prophetic
genius of Dante could not detach itself from the municipal
passions of his times. His apostrophes against Siena or against
Pisa are charged with more venom than the *Gott strafe England* of 1914–18. When one hates a well-known neighbor
whose language one speaks, the hatred is keenest of all.

The concept of the State's absolute sovereignty was born
of monarchic absolutism—kept under control at first by what
remained of moribund feudalism and, on its demise, by the
liberal currents of the nineteenth century. But subsequently
there was a resurgence of the concept and it became more
dangerous in the patriotic absolutism of democracies than under the kings, and still more dangerous in the deification of
the nation preached by dictatorships. But why should we doubt
that intoxicated nationalisms will some day end in the same

way that religious hatreds have ended, even though at one time it appeared as if they never *could* end, and that Protestants and Catholics would continue with sadistic joy to assault each other's minorities to the end of time.

The *real-politikers* forget that for long historic periods all right-thinking people believed that slavery was a law of natural necessity. And yet not only has slavery been suppressed, but more was accomplished toward its total suppression in the half-century succeeding the American War of Secession, since 1865, than during the ten preceding centuries. It is an historical fact that there are epochs when some apparently unsolvable problems, once having been clearly stated, end by being solved.

And we ourselves, we who have journeyed to the halfway milestone of the *cammin di nostra vita* (the pathway of our life), have we not seen with our own eyes, in so brief a time, a major social transformation in the disappearance of the duel? When I tell my children that once, as a young man, I fought a duel, they listen to me amazed, as if I were telling stories of the Crusades.

Why should there be any rational difficulty in admitting that war, as a juridic institution, may also disappear?

Does this mean that the great historic revolution is in sight? Certainly not. But the European working classes, influenced by reason, if not by love, have already understood the change that is to come. Those who do not want to understand it are the groups that continue to consider as criminal any surrender of even the minutest part of our national sovereignties in favor of vaster and more complex interests and organisms than any of our individual States. This became clearly apparent in 1935 and in 1936 during the first attempt at application of the sanctions which—as has been observed *—were applied to half-heartedly by the British and French statesmen, overanxious not to ruin definitively their dear Mussolini.

But two world wars in the course of the same generation have taught the masses, if not all their leaders. The organization of Europe, with its consequent elimination of European war, when it is once really understood by all European nations will progress relatively faster than happened in the case of other transformations, such as religious toleration, which was

* Chapter XL.

achieved only after centuries of wars of religion. We are at the crossroads: tomorrow's Europe will be what we make it—for us, or against us.

If this reorganization of Europe is done with the consciousness that it is the expiation for two wars, we shall be able to pass on to those who come after us the light-giving torches of intellectual and moral treasures which comprise the most genuine heritage of our national traditions.

But if we act with regard to the European ideal as did the blind shepherds of the Holy Alliance with respect to national ideals, it will imply that, once again, the "conservatives" will have proved themselves the most valuable allies of destruction.

The supreme mission of those spirits whose task it will be to forge the history of the free world after the second universal war must be to fill the gaps left in this work by the nineteenth century.

The work of that century was titanic; and the writers of Fascism and Nazism, when they tried to neutralize it by covering with beggarly sarcasms the "stupid" nineteenth century, knew what they were about.

The errors and the gaps of a century that began with the violent liberating outbursts of the French Revolution and continued with the epic of the Italian Risorgimento have seemed more serious to us because they coincided with unpredictable material developments that emphasized their incidental ill effects.

So it happened that liberty was finally recognized as the supreme ideal of life, as the sole condition of the progress of human society. Yet, it appears that liberty, when applied to all the economic activities of a world that is facing the risk of becoming more and more mechanized, has permitted the birth, and later, the egoistic arrogance of a new tyranny—the tyranny of wealth—even more hateful and more despicable than the old dynastic and aristocratic tyrannies which sometimes learned wisdom from history. Whence the necessity of curbing, or destroying if possible, the new financial oligarchies that obtrude and flourish even in those nations that think themselves democracies.

The other danger, which it will be our task to face and to defeat, is that of the excessive liberty of national states with relation to a superior international law to which all nations should yield.

After their conflict with the tyrants, the peoples of the nineteenth century gave their support to the principle of nationality. In the course of this book we have seen that in Italy men fought and died throughout the centuries for an ideal that was both national and universal. But this did not occur everywhere. The pure goddess—Nation, free Nation—little by little became transformed into a hideous idol—Nationalism. The name itself came into use in France during the anti-Dreyfus agitation at the close of the nineteenth century, and at once became identified with the most vulgar form of racialism, anti-Semitism—that Socialism of imbeciles—and with monarchic absolutism. Since then the monster, Nationalism, has done its fell work, with two world wars and thirty millions of dead.

The evil can be restrained only by a new conception of international relationships based on a Declaration of Interdependence of Nations, which will be for human society what the Declaration of Independence was for the American colonies at the end of the eighteenth century.

The American Declaration of Independence proclaims that "whenever any Form of Government becomes destructive of these ends [life, liberty and the pursuit of happiness], it is the Right of the People to alter or to abolish it, and to institute new Government, laying its foundation on such principles and organizing its powers in such Form, as to them shall seem most likely to effect their Safety and Happiness."

The voice of the fathers of American liberty was raised only in the interests of the people of the United States because at that time the world was not yet bound together by the achievements of applied science; and because, protected by the ocean, Americans wished first to assure themselves of being masters in their own home. Indeed, the only possible problem of the period was that of national liberties. France and Italy, who followed America on the path of liberty, likewise had the same aspiration.

Now, only a few hours' flight separate Rome and Paris from New York and Chicago; and now the two greatest oceans are already shrinking to the dimensions of lakes. Whence the urgent need of filling the second gap in the great liberation fresco begun, but left unfinished by the nineteenth century.

Tomorrow's task will consist in protecting all the independent nations, for each is a treasure house of art and thought whose disappearance would leave Europe and the world duller and infinitely less rich.

But the new law of Interdependence of Nations must also be proclaimed—the law that will leave them free to regulate their domestic affairs as they wish, but which will oblige them, under pain of necessary sanctions, to abandon the bloodiest of the old sovereign rights, that of waging war. The whole social, moral and economic progress of the world depends on this reform.

Fortunately, as I have partially outlined in this book—this splendid ideal is riper in the minds of men than the pseudo-realists imagine.

XLII

L'ENVOI

HERE I AM AT THE END OF THIS BOOK, WHICH IS UNEVEN because, here and there perhaps, it is too subjective. However, it has the merit of sincerity.

The moral abasement of France under Napoleon toward the close of his adventure has thus been described by Châteaubriand in his brochure *De Bonaparte et des Bourbons:*

"The whole of France became the empire of mendacity: newspapers, pamphlets, speeches, prose and poetry, all disguised the truth. If it rained they insisted the sun was shining; if the tyrant walked among silent workers, it was said that he advanced amid the acclamations of the crowd. The sole object is the Prince: morality consists in devotion to his caprices; to praise him is one's duty. Above all, one must exclaim with admiration when he has blundered or committed a crime. . . . No book could appear which did not include a eulogy of Bonaparte, like a tax-stamp of slavery. . . . The crimes of our republican Revolution were the work of passions which always left something unbroken; there was disorder in society but not absolute destruction; morality was wounded, but it was not annihilated. . . . But how can one cure the wounds made by a government that has established despotism as a principle—a government that, while speaking only of morality and religion, consistently destroyed morality and religion by its institutions and its scorn; . . . one that mistook the stupor of slavery for the peace of a well-organized society? . . . The most terrible revolutions are preferable to such a State."

In Italy, under Fascism, the abasement was still more cruel and more destructive, for a long enjoyment of liberty, after a century of fighting for it, had elevated men's minds.

When the Fascist terror supervened, the timorous accepted it with resigned silence; and by a progressive degradation they reached the point of public manifestations of enthusiasm for the men and ideas that still horrified them. But the work of moral shame did not stop there. It finally reached the point in Italy—and still more in Germany, and in the France of Vichy —at which those who lacked the strength to revolt, in the long run ended by trying to forget their afflictions and to persuade themselves that their condition was not, after all, so abject. That was the first step. The second step quickly followed: not only did they cease complaining even among their most intimate friends—for that involved recognition of their abasement —but they contended, in order to deceive themselves, that the situation had its good sides.

The mendacities of the victims thus confirmed the publicized lies of Fascism, whose chief psychological discovery was this: that a lie remains a lie if not sufficiently reiterated, but that it becomes gospel truth if one thunders it a thousand times with increasing assurance.

Wherefore, it has become necessary to dissipate anew, in this book, those legends that had already been reduced to nothing by others. Have we not all encountered, even toward the end of the second World War, a continued belief in Fascist fabrications by people who would be ashamed to be taken for Fascists?

The mendacities of Fascism, implicit or explicit, constituted an abasement of Italy—Italy, that country which Fascists described to the world as unworthy of liberty. What wonder then that other countries should have been unmoved by Italy's condition?

One special form of cowardice or, at least, of moral laziness is particularly widespread, since it often appears in free countries: the tendency to concede, with a pretense of philosophic thinking, that "the world is moving toward" this, that, or the other thing.

No one questions that the world is always moving toward new forms and new transformations: economic transformations, religious transformations, technical transformations; and there is no harm in trying to foresee, for example, whether the economic future will be Communistic or one of free competition. Where moral cowardice begins is in the acceptance of any one of these prophecies in order to spare oneself any effort of will or thought, in a hypocritical admission that one is obeying a "historic necessity," thereby escaping the moral necessity that conscience imposes on us.

This book will not have been entirely useless if it shall have made the reader feel, through the study of two centuries of Italian life, that what counts for a nation's progress is the courage of truth, respect for human personality and—to sum up all—the cult of liberty.

What counts is not to know toward what the *world* is going, but to know toward what *each one* of us is going. In a world passing through a less fateful crisis than ours, Mazzini said to the Italians: "You will not create better conditions unless you yourselves become better. Let each of you always do his duty, civic and moral, and Italy will be better."

Convinced that an international solidarity is the most urgent of conquests—since even the most sacred claims of social justice can only be satisfied in a world at peace—I am equally convinced that this international solidarity must be attained, not through the repudiation of homelands, but through a purification of one's love for one's homeland.

The first condition for this purification is the most absolute and constant respect for the truth or, at least, for what we deem in conscience to be the truth. That has been my sole guide in the writing of this book.

With nations, as with our individual souls, falsehood degrades love.

FINIS

APPENDIXES

I

CHRONOLOGICAL HISTORY

1713—Treaty of Utrecht ends War of the Spanish Succession. Duke of Savoy becomes King of Sicily.

1714—Turco-Venetian War.

1717—Spanish forces occupy Sardinia.

1718—Spaniards occupy Sicily.

1720—Austria exchanges Sardinia for Sicily, the House of Savoy becoming kings of Sardinia with Savoy and Piedmont.

1734—Carlos of Parma captures Naples.

1735—Carlos retains Naples and Sicily, but has to surrender Parma.

1743—British squadron imposes neutrality on Carlos at Naples.

1759—Ferdinand VI dies; Carlos of Naples succeeds him as Carlos III. His younger son, Ferdinand, succeeds at Naples.

1768—France acquires Corsica from Genoa.

1773—Pope Clement XIV suppresses Jesuit Order.

1795—Bonaparte appointed to Italian command.

1796—Bonaparte in Italy: Piedmont retires, Lombardy given to French, Bonaparte occupies Ferrara and Livorno. Austrians shut up in Mantua.

1797—Bonaparte defeats Austrians decisively at Rivoli, forces Treaty of Tolentino on Pope. Italian conquests merge Cispadane and Transpadane Republic into Cisalpine Republic.

1798—Coalition of Austria, Russia and Naples against the French. French take Naples, occupy Tuscany and Piedmont. Ferdinand secures himself in Sicily.

1799—French checked in North Italy, but Russians under Suvarov retreat through the Alps.

1800—Bonaparte crosses the St. Bernard and reconquers North Italy by victory at Marengo.

1802—The Cisalpine becomes the Italian Republic, with Bonaparte acting as its president; he concludes concordat with Pope, and is declared consul for life.

1805—Italian Republic makes Napoleon king.

1814—Vienna Congress reinstates Sardinia, gives Venice to Austria.

1821—Revolution in Piedmont suppressed with Austrian help; Victor Emmanuel abdicates, and Charles Felix succeeds him.

1831—Risings in Papal States; Austrians occupy Bologna, to support Papacy.

1832—French troops occupy Ancona as a check on Austria in Italy.

1846—Pius IX elected Pope, begins reforms.

1848—Revolt in Sicily, then in Naples; Ferdinand concedes a constitution. Revolts in Lombardy and Venetia. Radetzky's victory at Custozza results in Italian armistice. Murder of Rossi and flight of Pius IX. Roman and Florentine Republics proclaimed.

1849—Renewal of war in Italy. Charles Albert, defeated at Novara, abdicates, is succeeded by Victor Emmanuel. Peace follows, with Austrian troops remaining in Piedmont. Savage suppression of Sicilian revolt.

1852—Cavour minister in Piedmont.

1858—The Plombieres Interview (Cavour and Napoleon).

1859—Italian war of liberation; Napoleon intervenes; battles of Magenta and Solferino; Peace of Villafranca; cession of Savoy and Nice to France; incorporation of North Italian states in a "Kingdom of North Italy" by plebiscite.

1860—Garibaldi's Sicilian expedition; invasion of mainland; he enters Naples as dictator; meets Victor Emmanuel, "King of Italy"; siege of Gaeta.

1861—United Kingdom of Italy proclaimed (excluding Rome and Venetia) after fall of Gaeta. Cavour dies.

1862—Garibaldi, attempting to capture Rome, is defeated by royal troops at Aspromonte.

1865—Italy joins Bismarck's Austria in "Seven Weeks' War" against Russia; Italians defeated at Custozza; armistice at Nikolsburg; Austria cedes Venetia to Italy. Garibaldi, attacking Rome, is defeated at Mentana.

1869—Decree of Papal Infallibility.

1870—Rome, occupied by Royalists, becomes Italian capital; Pope becomes "prisoner of the Vatican."

1882—Italy joins in Triple Alliance with Germany and Austria.

1911—Italy demands protectorate of Tripoli; Turco-Italian War. Italy annexes Tripoli.

1915—Italy declares war on Austria.

1917—Germans shatter Italian center at Caporetto; retreat of Italians, pursued by Austrians, ends at the Piave.

1918—Failure of last Austrian offensive at the Piave leads to rout of Austrians on the Italian front.

1919—D'Annunzio seizes Fiume. Peace treaty of St. Germain-en-Laye with Austria.

1920—Treaty of Rapallo (Italy and Yugoslavia) to settle Fiume question.

1922—Mussolini sets up Fascist Ministry.

1924—Adriatic Treaty between Italy and Yugoslavia.

1929—Vatican treaty with Italy restores temporal sovereignty to the Papacy.

1935—Italo-Ethiopian crisis.

1936—Italians take Addis Ababa. Madrid complains to League of Nations that Italian troops aid Franco.

1938—England signs treaty with Italy recognizing conquest and annexation of Ethiopia.

1940—Italy joins Axis partner, Germany, in second World War by attacking France.

1942—Italy loses African empire to British and American troops.

1943—Italy surrenders; Mussolini flees; Allies conquer Sicily, invade mainland.

II

CHRONOLOGICAL TABLES

I

SOVEREIGNS OR HEADS OF STATES
IN ITALY DURING THE NINETEENTH AND TWENTIETH CENTURIES

Italy

Napoleon, king, 1805–1814.
Victor Emmanuel II, of Savoy, king, 1861–1878.
Humbert I, of Savoy, king, 1878–1900.
Victor Emmanuel III, of Savoy, king, 1900–

Sardinia

Charles Emmanuel IV, of Savoy, king, 1796–1802.
Victor Emmanuel 1st, of Savoy, king, 1802–1821.
Charles Felix, of Savoy, king, 1821–1824.
Charles Albert, of Savoy, king, 1824–1849.
Victor Emmanuel II, of Savoy, king, 1849–1861, king of Italy until 1878.

Lombardo-Veneto

Francis 1st, emperor (of Austria) 1815–1835.
Ferdinand, emperor (of Austria) 1835–1848.
Francis Joseph, emperor (of Austria) 1848–1859.

Veneto

Francis Joseph, emperor (of Austria) 1859–1866.

Venice

Daniele Manin, Head of the Provisional Government, 1848–1849.

Parma and Piacenza

Ferdinand, of Bourbon, duke, 1765–1802.

Maria Luisa, of Hapsburg, duchess, 1815–1847.
Carlo II, of Bourbon, duke, 1847–1849.*
Carlo III, of Bourbon, duke, 1849–1854.
Roberto, of Bourbon, duke, 1854–1859.

Modena

Francis IV, of Hapsburg-Este, duke, 1814–1846.
Francis V, of Hapsburg-Este, duke, 1846–1859.

Provinces of Parma and Modena

Luigi Carlo Farini, dictator, 1859–1860.

Massa e Carrara

Maria Beatrice, d'Este, duchess, 1790–1829.

Lucca

Felice Baciocchi, prince, 1805–1814.
Maria Luisa, of Bourbon, duchess, 1815–1824.
Carlo Lodovico, of Bourbon, duke, 1824–1847.*

Tuscany

Ludovico, of Bourbon, king, 1801–1803.
Carlo Lodovico, of Bourbon, king, 1803–1807.*
Elisa Baciocchi, grand-duchess, 1807–1814.
Ferdinand III, of Hapsburg-Lorraine, grand-duke, 1814–1824.
Leopoldo II, of Hapsburg-Lorraine, grand-duke, 1824–1859.

Pontifical States

Pius VII, pope (Chiaramonti), 1800–1823.
Leo XII, pope (Della Genga), 1823–1829.
Pius VIII, pope (Castiglioni), 1829–1830.
Gregory XVI, pope (Cappellari), 1830–1846.
Pius IX, pope (Mastai-Ferretti), 1846–1870.

---

* Carlo Lodovico, born in Parma 1799, duke of Lucca and later on duke of Parma, under the name of Carlo II, is the same as the child-king in Tuscany.

Roman Republic

Carlo Armellini
Mattia Montecchi ⎫ Comitato Esecutivo, 1849.
Aurelio Saliceti ⎭

Giuseppe Mazzini
Carlo Armellini ⎫ Triumvirs, 1849.
Aurelio Saffi ⎭

Two Sicilies

Ferdinand I, of Bourbon, 1760–1825.
Francis I, of Bourbon, king, 1825–1830.
Ferdinand II, of Bourbon, king, 1830–1859.
Francis II, of Bourbon, king, 1859–1860.

II

POPES,

AFTER THE END OF THE TEMPORAL POWER

Pius IX (Mastai-Ferretti), 1870–1878.
Leo XIII (Pecci), 1878–1903.
Pius X (Sarto), 1903–1914.
Benedict XV (della Chiesa), 1914–1922.
Pius XI (Ratti), 1922–1939.
Pius XII (Pacelli), 1939–

III

CHRONOLOGICAL DATA OF NINETEENTH AND TWENTIETH CENTURY ITALIANS QUOTED IN THIS BOOK

ALBERTINI, LUIGI.—B. 1872. Publisher and editor of *Corriere della Sera*. Ousted by violence from both offices by the Fascist government, 1925. D. 1942.

ALFIERI, COUNT VITTORIO.—B. 1749. His most famous tragedies written before 1786; his *Vita*, 1790. D. 1803.

AMENDOLA, GIOVANNI.—B. 1886. Organizes with Beneš, Borgese and others the Italo-Yugoslav Congress of Rome, 1918. Minister of Colonies, 1922. Fights Fascism in Parliament, 1922–26. Gravely wounded by the Fascists. D. 1926.

AOSTA, EMMANUEL PHILIBERT OF SAVOY-AOSTA, DUKE OF—B. 1869. Commander of the IIId army during the 1st World War, 1915–18. D. 1931.

ARESE, COUNT FRANCESCO.—B. 1805. Senator, 1854. D. 1881.

ARIMONDI, GIUSEPPE.—B. 1846. Serves in the Eritrea and Ethiopia campaigns, 1887–96. Resisting to the last in the battle of Adua. D. 1896.

ARMELLINI, CARLO.—B. 1777. Minister of Interior in Rome, 1848. Advocates a united democratic Italy in the Roman Assembly, December 23, 1848. Triumvir of the Roman Republic, 1849. D. 1863.

ASCOLI, MAX.—B. 1898. Imprisoned by the Fascists, 1928, escapes to the United States, 1931. U. S. citizen, 1935. Dean of Graduate Faculty, New School of Social Research, 1934–41. Chief Consultant Co-ordinator Latin-American Affairs, 1941.

AVARNA, DUKE GIUSEPPE.—B. 1843. Ambassador to Vienna during the Bosnia crisis (1908–09) and during the first months of the 1914–15 war. D. 1916.

AZEGLIO, MASSIMO D'.—B. 1798. Author of *Gli Ultimi casi di Romagna*, 1846; of *Proposta di un programma per l'opinione nazionale italiana*, 1847. Wounded at the battle of Monte Berico, 1848. Prime Minister, 1849–52. Governor of Milan, 1859. D. 1866.

BADOGLIO, PIETRO.—B. 1871. Assistant-Chief of General Staff, 1917–18. Military adviser of Count Sforza for the Treaty of Rapallo, 1920. Ambassador to Brazil, 1924–25. Commander of the campaign against Ethiopia, 1936. Prime Minister after Mussolini's fall, 1943.

BELLI, GIUSEPPE GIOACCHINO.—B. 1791. Writes his two thousand *Sonetti* between 1820 and 1849. D. 1863.

BENEDICT XV (GIACOMO DELLA CHIESA).—B. 1854. LL.D., 1875. Priest, 1878. Archbishop of Bologna, 1907. Cardinal, June 1914. Pope, Sept. 3, 1914. Makes his "Appeal to Peace," Aug., 1917. D. 1851.

BERCHET, GIOVANNI.—B. 1783. Exile in London, 1821, where writes his most famous poems. Returns to Italy, 1848. D. 1851.

BISSOLATI, LEONIDA.—B. 1857. Editor of the *Avanti,* 1896. Deputy, 1897. Volunteer in the Alpini during the war, gravely wounded, 1915. Cabinet Minister, 1916–18. D. 1920.

BLANC, BARON ALBERTO.—B. 1835. Minister for Foreign Affairs, 1893–96. D. 1904.

BOITO, ARRIGO.—B. 1842. His opera *Mefistofele,* 1875. D. 1918.

BONGHI, RUGGERO.—B. 1826. Minister of Public Instruction, 1874–76. D. 1895.

BONOMI, IVANOE.—B. 1873. Minister of Public Works, of War, of Treasury, 1916–21. Prime Minister, June, 1921–Feb., 1922. Author of *Dal Socialismo al Fascismo,* 1924; of *Bissolati e il movimento socialista,* 1929.

BORGESE, GIUSEPPE ANTONIO.—B. 1882. Author of *Storia della Critica romantica,* 1905; of *Rubé,* 1921. Organizes with Amendola and others the Italo-Yugoslav Congress, 1918. Voluntary exile to the U. S., 1931. Professor of Italian Literature, University of Chicago, 1936. American citizen, 1938. Author of *Goliath,* 1937, of *Common Cause,* 1943.

BOSELLI, PAOLO.—B. 1838. Deputy from 1870 to 1882. Prime Minister, 1916–17. Senator, 1921. D. 1932.

BROFFERIO, ANGELO.—B. 1802. Arrested as one of the "Knights of Freedom," 1831. Fights the monarchical idea in Piedmont, 1848–49. D. 1866.

CADORNA, CARLO.—B. 1809. Cabinet Minister, 1848–49. Ambassador to London, 1869–75. D. 1891.

CADORNA, LUIGI.—B. 1850. Chief of Staff of the Army, 1914. Commander-in-Chief of the Italian armies during World War I until Nov. 8, 1917. Author of *La Guerra alla fronte italiana,* 1921. D. 1928.

CARDUCCI, GIOSUE.—B. 1835. Professor of Italian Literature, University of Bologna, 1860–1903. Senator, 1890. D. 1907.

CATTANEO, CARLO.—B. 1801. Editor of *Il Politecnico,* 1939–44. Head of the War Council in Milan, 1849. Exile to Switzerland, 1849. D. 1869.

CAVALLOTTI, FELICE.—B. 1842. After a playwright career enters Parliament, 1873, where remains until his death, in a duel, 1898.

CAVIGLIA, ENRICO.—B. 1862. Commander in chief of the VIIIth army, 1918.

CAVOUR, CAMILLO BENSO, COUNT DI.—B. 1810. Enters army, 1826, resigns, 1831. Editor of *Il Risorgimento,* 1847. Deputy, 1848–61. Minister of Agriculture, 1850. Prime Minister, 1852–59 and 1860–61. D. 1861.

CHARLES ALBERT.—B. 1798. Regent of the Kingdom, 1821. King of Sardinia, 1831–49. Abdicates after the battle of Novara, March 23, 1849. D. in Oporto, Portugal, Aug. 28, 1849.

CHARLES FELIX.—B. 1765. King of Sardinia, 1824–31. D. April 27, 1831.

CIANCA, ALBERT.—B. 1884. Editor of *Il Mondo,* 1921. Leaves Italy, 1926. Co-founder with Rosselli of *Giustizia e Libertà,* 1929.

CICERUACCHIO (ANGELO BRUNETTI).—B. 1800. Shot by the Austrians after the fall of the Roman Republic, 1849.

CONFALONIERI, COUNT FEDERICO.—B. 1785. Arrested by the Austrians, 1821, condemned to death 1823, commuted to life imprisonment, but freed 1837. D. 1846.

CONSALVI, ERCOLE.—B. 1757. Cardinal, 1800. Secretary of State, 1800–06 and again after Napoleon's fall until 1823. D. 1824.

CONTARINI, SALVATORE.—B. 1869. Secretary General of the Ministry of Foreign Affairs, 1920. Senator, 1921.

CRISPI, FRANCESCO.—B. 1818. Exiled to Piedmont after the Sicilian revolution, 1849; to Malta, 1853; to London, 1855. Assistant-Chief of Staff of the "Thousand," 1860, organizes the civil administration in Sicily under Garibaldi's dictatorship. Deputy, 1861. Minister of Interior, 1877–78 and 1887. Prime Minister, 1887–91 and 1893–96. D. 1901.

CROCE, BENEDETTO.—B. 1886. Author of *Estética,* 1902. Starts publication of the review *Critica,* 1903. Author of *Hegel,* 1907; of *Logica,* 1910; of *Filosofia di G. B. Vico,* 1912; of *Teoria e Storia della Storiografia,* 1917 and of many other famous works, philosophical, literary, historical. Minister of Public Instruction, 1920–21.

D'ANCONA, ALESSANDRO.—B. 1835. Professor of Italian Literature, University of Pisa, 1860–1900. D. 1914.

D'ANNUNZIO, GABRIELE.—B. 1863. Author of *Canto Nuovo,* 1882; of *L'Innocente,* 1892; of *Il Trionfo della Morte,* 1894; of *La Fiaccola sotto il moggio,* 1905; and of many other novels, plays, verses. Volunteer in the war, 1915–18. Goes to Fiume, Sept., 1919; ousted from Fiume, Dec., 1920. D. 1938.

DE AMICIS, EDMONDO.—B. 1846. D. 1908.

DE BOSIS, LAURO.—B. 1901. His drama, *Icaro,* 1937, receives in Amsterdam the Olympic Prize for Poetry, 1928. Organizes the *Alleanza Nazionale,* 1930. Flight over Rome and disappearance—Oct. 3, 1931.

DEGOLA, EUSTACHIO.—B. 1761. D. 1826.

DE ZERBI, ROCCO.—B. 1843. Deputy, 1874–93. Commits suicide, 1893.

DIAZ, ARMANDO.—B. 1861. Chief of General Staff, 1917–18. War Minister under Mussolini, 1922–24. D. 1928.

DI GIACOMO, SALVATORE.—B. 1860. Besides his perfect lyrics in Neapolitan dialect, author of *Storia del teatro San Carlino,* 1891, and of *La Prostituzione in Napoli,* 1899. D. 1934.

FACTA, LUIGI.—B. 1861. Minister of Finances, 1911–13 and 1920–21. Prime Minister from Feb. 26, 1922, to advent of Fascism. Senator, 1924. D. 1930.

FEDERZONI, LUIGI.—B. 1878. Minister of Colonies, 1922–24; of Interior, 1924–26; of Colonies, 1926–28.

FERRARI, FRANCESCO LUIGI.—B. 1891. Influential member of the Popular Party since 1919. Obliged to leave Italy, 1926. Author of *Le Régime Fasciste Italien,* 1928; of *Pensieri sulla Monarchia,* 1930. D. 1933.

FERRERO, GINA.—B. 1872. Author of *Vantaggi della degenerazione,* 1903; of *Anima della donna,* 1918; of *La donna nella vita,* 1920; of *La rançon du machinisme,* 1930; and of other books, among which the life of her father, the criminologist Cesare Lombroso, and various volumes on her son, the young poet Leo Ferrero, died in 1933.

FERRERO, GUGLIELMO.—B. 1871. Author of *Europa giovane,* 1897; of *Grandezza e decadenza di Roma,* 1902–04; of *La Guerra europea,* 1916; of *Memorie e Confessioni di un sovrano deposto,* 1920; of *La Tragedia della pace,* 1923; of *Da Fiume a Roma,* 1924; of *La democrazia in Italia,* 1925; of *Le Donne dei Cesari,* 1925; of *Discours aux Sourds,* 1925; of *Entre le present et l'avenir,* 1926; of *La rovina della civiltà antica,* 1926; etc. Takes a leading part, with Amendola, Sforza and others, to the last important struggle for freedom in Italy, the Congress of the Associazione democratica, 1926. Voluntary exile from Italy, becomes professor of modern history, University of Geneva, 1930. Author of *Bonaparte en Italie,* 1936; of *Le Congrès de Vienne,* 1936; of *Pouvoir,* 1940. For his political and scientific thought see also *Colloqui con Guglielmo Ferrero* by Bogdan Raditsa, a Croat author who married his daughter Nina, in 1935. D. 1942.

FERRI, ENRICO.—B. 1856. Editor of *Avanti,* 1900–05. Professor of Criminal Law, Universities of Bologna, Siena, Pisa, Rome, 1884–1929. Senator, 1929. D. 1929.

FOGAZZARO, ANTONIO.—B. 1842. Author of *Vauolda,* 1876; of *Malombra,* 1881; of *Daniele Cortis,* 1884; of *Piccolo Mondo antico,* 1895. Senator, 1896. D. 1911.

FORTUNATO, GIUSTINO.—B. 1848. Author of *Dieci anni di vita politica,* 1891; of *Il Mezzogiorno e lo Stato italiano,* 1911; of *Questione meridionale e riforma tributaria,* 1920. D. 1932.

FOSCOLO, UGO.—B. 1778. Author of *I Sepolcri,* 1807. Exile to London, 1816. D. 1827.

FRANCHETTI, LEOPOLDO.—B. 1847. Editor of *Rassegna settimanale,* 1876. Author of *La Sicilia nel 1876,* 1877. Deputy, 1882–1909. Senator, 1909. D. 1917.

FUCINI, RENATO.—B. 1843. His book of Poesie appears in 1872; his *Veglie di Neri,* 1884. D. 1921.

GARIBALDI, GIUSEPPE.—B. 1807. Exile to Marseille, 1834. After participating in wars to preserve the independence of Uruguay returns to Italy and defends Rome against the French, 1849. Commander of the *Cacciatori delle Alpi* in the war of 1859. Leader of the expedition of the "Thousand" in Sicily, 1860. Commander of an army of volunteers in the war of 1866; and of an Italian corps in the Franco-Prussian war of 1870. D. 1882.

GARIBALDI, RICCIOTTI.—B. 1847. D. 1924.

GASPARRI, PIETRO.—B. 1852. Cardinal, 1907. Secretary of State, 1914–31. D. 1934.

GENTILE, GIOVANNI.—B. 1875. Author of *Pedagogia,* 1913–14; of *Sistema di Logica,* 1917; of *Origini della Filosofia contemporanea,* 1917–23; etc.

GIACOSA, GIUSEPPE.—B. 1847. Author of *La partita a scacchi,* 1873; of *Tristi Amori,* 1887; of *Come le foglie,* 1900; etc. D. 1906.

GIARDINO, GAETANO.—B. 1864. Commander of the army of the Grappa, 1918. Military Governor of Fiume, 1923. D. 1935.

GIOBERTI, VINCENZO.—B. 1801. Author of *Del Primato morale e civile degli Italiani,* 1842–43; of *Il Gesuita moderno,* 1846–47; of *Del Rinnovamento civile d'Italia,* 1851; etc. D. 1852.

GIOLITTI, GIOVANNI.—B. 1842. Deputy, 1882–1928. Prime Minister five times from 1892 to 1921. D. 1928.

GIORGINI, GIAMBATTISTA.—B. 1818. Senator, 1872. D. 1906.

GRAMSCI, ANTONIO.—B. 1891. Editor of *L'Ordine Nuovo,* Deputy, condemned to twenty years of jail by the Fascist Special Tribunal, 1926. D. 1937.

GRANDI, DINO.—B. 1895. One of the leaders of the "March on Rome," Oct., 1922. Minister for Foreign Affairs, 1929–32. Later on Ambassador to London and other Fascist employs until 1943.

GREGORY XVI (MAURO CAPPELLARI).—B. 1765. Cardinal, 1826. Pope, 1831–46. D. 1846.

GUERRAZZI, FRANCESCO DOMENICO.—B. 1804. Dictator in Florence, 1849. Exile to Corsica, 1853. D. 1873.

HELEN, QUEEN.—B. 1873. Marries Victor Emmanuel of Savoy, prince of Naples, 1896. Queen of Italy, 1900.

IMPERIALI, MARQUIS GUGLIELMO.—B. 1858. Ambassador to London, 1910–20. Senator, 1913.

LABRIOLA, ANTONIO.—B. 1843. Professor at the University of Rome, 1873. D. 1904.

LAMARMORA, ALFONSO.—B. 1804. Commander of the expedition to Crimea, 1855. Prime Minister, 1860. D. 1878.

LANZA, GIOVANNI.—B. 1810. Prime Minister, 1869–73. D. 1882.

LEO XIII (GIOACCHINO PECCI).—B. 1810. Cardinal, 1857. Pope, 1878–1903. D. 1903.

LEOPARDI, GIACOMO.—B. 1798. His first canzoni published in 1819. D. 1837.

LOMBROSO, CESARE.—B. 1835. Author of *Genio e Follia,* 1864; of *L'Uomo delinquente,* 1876. D. 1909.

LORIA, ACHILLE.—B. 1857. Professor at the Universities of Siena, Padua, Turin, 1881–1932. D. 1938.

LUSSU, EMILIO.—B. 1890. Deputy 1919–26. Co-founder with Rosselli of the political movement *Giustizia e Libertà,* 1929, after his escape, with Rosselli, from the Lipari islands. Author of *La Catena,* 1929; of *Marcia su Roma e dintorni,* 1933; of *Un anno sull'Altipiano,* 1938. One of the founders of the Action Party, 1943.

MAMELI, GOFFREDO.—B. 1827. Writes the hymn *Fratelli d'Italia,* now called *Inno di Mameli,* 1847. D. of wounds at siege of Rome, 1849.

MANCINI, PASQUALE STANISLAO.—B. 1817. Minister for Foreign Affairs, 1881–85. D. 1888.

MANIN, DANIELE.—B. 1804. Head of the Republic of Venice, 1848–49. Exile to France, 1849. D. 1857.

MANZONI, ALESSANDRO.—B. 1785. His *Inni sacri* appear 1815; the *Promessi sposi,* 1825–26. D. 1873.

MARCHIAFAVA, ETTORE.—B. 1847. Professor of Anatomy, University of Rome, 1872–1922. Senator, 1913. D. 1935.

MARGHERITA, QUEEN.—B. 1851. Queen, 1878–1900. D. 1926.

MARONCELLI, PIERO.—B. 1795. Arrested by the Austrian police, 1820, condemned to death, 1822, sentence commuted to twenty years' imprisonment. Freed 1830, exile in Paris and New York. D. 1846.

MASCAGNI, PIETRO.—B. 1863. His *Cavalleria rusticana,* 1890.

MATTEOTTI, GIACOMO.—B. 1885. Deputy, 1919–24. Murdered by the Fascists, June 10, 1924.

MAZZINI, GIUSEPPE.—B. 1805. Arrested, 1830. Exile, 1831. Founds the *Giovine Italia,* 1832. Arrives in Rome and becomes head of the Roman Republic, 1849. Exile again, 1849–72. D. 1872.

MEDA, FILIPPO.—B. 1869. Deputy, 1909–24. Minister of Finances, 1917–18, of Treasury, 1920–21. D. 1939.

MILLO, ENRICO.—B. 1865. Senator, 1913. Minister of the Navy, 1913–14. Governor of Dalmatia, 1918–21. D. 1930.

MUSSOLINI, BENITO.—B. 1883. Editor of *Lotta di Classe* and of *Avanti,* 1912. Editor of *Il Popolo d'Italia,* 1914. Starts the Fasci, 1919. Prime Minister, 1922–43.

NIGRA, COUNT COSTANTINO.—B. 1828. Minister to Paris, 1860–76, later Ambassador to St. Petersburg and Vienna. D. 1907.

NITTI, FRANCESCO.—B. 1868. Prime Minister, 1919–20. Exile in Switzerland and later in France after advent of Fascism.

ORIANI, ALFREDO.—B. 1852. Author of *La lotta politica in Italia,* 1882. D. 1909.

ORLANDO, VITTORIO EMMANUELE.—B. 1860. Deputy, 1897–1925. Prime Minister, 1917–19.

OROBONI, ANTONIO FORTUNATO.—B. 1791. D. in the Austrian prison of the Spielberg, 1823.

PACCIARDI, RANDOLFO.—B. 1899. War volunteer, 1915–18, three medals *al valore*. Founds the association *Italia libera,* 1925. Exile from Italy, 1926. Commander of the Garibaldi brigade in Spain, 1936.

PARETO, VILFREDO.—B. 1848. Author of *Sociologia generale,* 1916. D. 1923.

PASCARELLA, CESARE.—B. 1858. Author of *Villa Gloria,* 1885, etc. D. 1940.

PISACANE, CARLO.—B. 1819. D. in Sapri, Calabria, shot by the Bourbonians, 1857.

PIUS VII (GREGORIO CHIARAMONTI).—B. 1742. Cardinal, 1785. Pope, 1800–1823. D. 1823.

PIUS VIII (FRANCESCO CASTIGLIONI).—B. 1761. Cardinal, 1816. Pope, 1829–30. D. 1830.

PIUS IX (GIOVANNI M. MASTAI).—B. 1792. Cardinal 1840. Pope, 1846–78. D. 1878.

PIUS X (GIUSEPPE SARTO).—B. 1835. Cardinal, 1893. Pope, 1903–14. D. 1914.

PIUS XI (ACHILLE RATTI).—B. 1857. Apostolic Nuncio to Poland, 1919–21. Archbishop of Milan, 1921. Pope, 1922–39. D. 1939.

PIUS XII (EUGENIO PACELLI).—B. 1876. Cardinal, 1929. Pope, 1939.

PORTA, CARLO.—B. 1776. D. 1821.

RAMPOLLA DEL TINDARO, MARIANO.—B. 1843. Cardinal, 1887. Secretary of State, 1887–1903. D. 1913.

RATTAZZI, URBANO.—B. 1808. Prime Minister, 1862 and 1867. D. 1873.

RICASOLI, BARON BETTINO.—B. 1809. Dictator in Tuscany, 1859–60. Prime Minister 1861–62 and 1866. D. 1880.

ROBILANT, CARLO FELICE NICOLIS, COUNT DI.—B. 1826. Minister for Foreign Affairs, 1885–87. D. 1888.

ROSMINI, ANTONIO.—B. 1797. Author of *Delle cinque piaghe della Santa Chiesa,* 1848; of *Psicologia,* 1846–50; of *Introduzione alla filosofia,* 1850; of *Origine delle idee,* 1851. Other works appeared after his death, in 1855.

Rosselli, Carlo.—B. 1899. Officer of the Alpini, at 17 years of age, during the war, 1917. Editor of *Non mollare,* first underground anti-fascist paper, 1925. Professor of Political Economy, University of Genoa, 1926. Editor of *Il Quarto Stato,* 1926. Marries Miss Marion Cave, then teaching at University of Florence, 1926. Organizes expatriation of Turati, elderly Socialist leader, by motor-boat to Corsica, 1926; arrested on return, tried at Savona, Sept., 1927, and condemned to 10 months' imprisonment. After term expired, sent to penal island of Lipari; escapes, with Lussu and others, 1929, and immediately founds movement *Giustizia e Libertà.* Commands first Italian corps fighting for Spanish Republic, 1936, is wounded at battle of Monte Pelato. While at Bagnoles de l'Orne, France, to cure a phlebitis contracted in Spain, murdered by six members of the Cagoulards, under orders of Mussolini, 1937.

Rosselli, Nello.—B. 1900. Author of *Mazzini e Bakunin,* 1927, and other historical works. Condemned to five years' banishment, 1927. Murdered with his brother Carlo, 1937.

Salandra, Antonio.—B. 1853. Prime Minister, 1914–16. D. 1931.

Salvemini, Gaetano.—B. 1873. Deputy, 1919. Arrested, 1925, deprived of citizenship, exile in France, England, United States. Author of *The Fascist Dictatorship,* 1927; of *Mussolini diplomate,* 1932; of *Under the Axe of Fascism,* 1936; of *Italian Fascism,* 1938; of *Carlo e Nello Rosselli,* 1938; and of other works written before Fascism on Mazzini, on the French Revolution, etc.

San Giuliano, Antonino Paternò Castello, Marquis of.—B. 1852. Minister for Foreign Affairs, 1905–06 and 1910–14. Ambassador to London, 1906–09; to Paris, 1909–10. D. 1914.

Scalviti, Giovita.—B. 1791. Exile to Switzerland and to London, 1821. D. 1843.

Scialoia, Vittorio.—B. 1856. Minister for Foreign Affairs, 1919–20. Many times Italian Delegate to the League of Nations. D. 1933.

Sella, Quintino.—B. 1827. Many times Cabinet Minister between 1862 and 1876. Author of important studies on geology. D. 1884.

Sforza, Count Carlo.—B. 1873. Minister to China, 1911–15; to Serbia and Macedonia, 1915–18. High Commissioner to Turkey, 1918–19. Senator, 1919. Under-Secretary of State, 1919–20. Secretary of State, 1920–21. Ambassador to France, 1922, resigns on arrival in power of Fascism, Oct., 1922, and starts opposition in Senate until 1927, when any opposition became impossible. Acclaimed leader of opposition against Fascism by the Pan-American Italian Conference of Montevideo, 1942. One of the leaders of Action Party, 1943. Author of *L'Enigme chinoise,* 1928; of *Makers of Modern Europe,* 1931; of *European Dictatorships,* 1932; of *Les Frères ennemis,* 1933; of *Europe and Europeans,* 1937; of *Pachich and the Union of the Yugoslavs,* 1939; of *The Real Italians,* 1941, etc.

SILONE, IGNAZIO.—B. 1900. Author of *Fontamara,* 1934; of *Bread and Wine,* 1936; of *The School for Dictators,* 1938; of *The Seed under the Snow,* 1942; etc. Exile to Switzerland.

SOLARO DELLA MARGHERITA, COUNT CLEMENTE.—B. 1792. Minister for Foreign Affairs of King Charles Albert, 1835–47. D. 1869.

SONNINO, SIDNEY.—B. 1847. Prime Minister, 1906 and 1909–10. Minister for Foreign Affairs, 1915–19. D. 1924.

SPAVENTA, SILVIO.—B. 1822. Founds secret society *Unità italiana,* 1848. Condemned to death, 1852, but commuted to imprisonment until 1859. Minister of Public Works, 1873–76. D. 1893.

STURZO, LUIGI.—B. 1871. Priest, 1894. For fifteen years Mayor of Caltagirone, Sicily; for twenty years Vice-President of the Association of the Italian Communes. Founder and Secretary of the Popular Party, 1919–26. Author of *Sintesi sociali,* 1906; of *Dall'idea al fatto,* 1919; of *Riforma statale e indirizzi politici,* 1923; of *Popolarismo e Fascismo,* 1924; of *Pensiero antifascista,* 1925; of *La libertà in Italia,* 1925; of *Italy and Fascism,* 1927; of *The International Community and the Right of War,* 1930; of *Il Ciclo della Creazione,* 1932; of *Essai de Sociologie,* 1935; of *Politics and Morality,* 1938; of *Church and State,* 1939; of *Les Guerres modernes et la Pensée catholique,* 1942; of *The True Life: Sociology of the Supernatural,* 1943. Obliged after suppression of the Popular Party to leave Italy, goes first to London and later to United States.

TARCHIANI, ALBERTO.—B. 1885; sub-editor of *Corriere della Sera,* 1919. Leaves Italy, 1925. Co-founder, with Rosselli, of movement *Giustizia e Libertà,* 1929. Goes with Count Sforza to United States, 1940.

TITTONI, TOMMASO.—B. 1855. Minister for Foreign Affairs, 1903–05, 1906–10 and 1919–20. D. 1931.

TONIOLO, GIUSEPPE.—B. 1845. Professor of political economy, University of Modena and, later, Pisa, 1878–1918. D. 1918.

TORNIELLI, COUNT GIUSEPPE.—B. 1836. Senator, 1879. Later, Ambassador to Madrid, London, Paris, where he dies in 1908.

TREVES, CLAUDIO.—B. 1879. Socialist leader from 1919 to 1922. Exile to France after Fascism. D. 1933.

TRILUSSA (CARLO ALBERTO SALUSTRI).—B. 1873. Author of *Quaranta sonetti romaneschi,* 1895; of *Altri Sonetti,* 1898; of *Favole romanesche,* 1900; etc.

TURATI, FILIPPO.—B. 1857. Founds *Critica sociale,* 1891. Deputy, 1896–1924. Exile to France, 1926. D. 1932.

VENTURI, LIONELLO.—B. 1885. Professor of History of Art, University of Turin, 1915. Refuses oath to Fascism, 1931, and since then exile in France and United States.

VERGA, GIOVANNI.—B. 1840. Author of *I Malavoglia,* 1881; of *Mastro don Gesualdo,* 1889; and other minor works. D. 1922.

VICTOR EMMANUEL I.—B. 1759. King of Sardinia, 1802–21. D. 1824.

VICTOR EMMANUEL II.—B. 1820. King of Sardinia, 1849–61, of Italy, 1861–78. D. 1878.

VICTOR EMMANUEL III.—B. 1869. King of Italy, 1900–   .

VISCONTI VENOSTA, MARQUIS EMILIO.—B. 1829. Minister for Foreign Affairs, 1863–64, 1866–76 and 1896–1901. D. 1914.

VOLPI, GIUSEPPE.—B. 1877. Governor of Tripolitania, 1921–25. Minister of Finances with Mussolini, 1925.

INDEX

171